TRAVELING BLACK

TRAVELING BLACK

A STORY OF
RACE AND RESISTANCE

MIA BAY

THE BELKNAP PRESS OF
HARVARD UNIVERSITY PRESS
Cambridge, Massachusetts
London, England

First Harvard University Press paperback edition, 2023
Second printing

Library of Congress Cataloging-in-Publication Data
Names: Bay, Mia, author.
Title: Traveling Black : a story of race and resistance / Mia Bay.
Description: Cambridge, Massachusetts : The Belknap Press of Harvard
    University Press, 2021. | Includes bibliographical references and index.
Identifiers: LCCN 2020039186 | ISBN 9780674979963 (cloth) |
    ISBN 9780674278622 (pbk.)
Subjects: LCSH: African Americans—Segregation—History. |
    African Americans—Travel—History. | Segregation in transportation—
    United States—History.
Classification: LCC E185.61 .B288 2021 | DDC 305.896/073– dc23
LC record available at https://lccn.loc.gov/2020039186

To my mother, Juanita Bay, whose travel stories, love of Black history, and fierce critical intelligence guided my path

CONTENTS

Introduction   1

1 The Road to *Plessy*   18
How Travel Segregation Took Shape

2 Traveling by Train   63
The Jim Crow Car

3 Traveling by Car   107
Race on the Road in the Automotive Age

4 Traveling by Bus   151
From the Jim Crow Car to the Back of the Bus

5 Traveling by Plane   192
Segregation in the Age of Aviation

6 Traveling for Civil Rights   230
The Long Fight to Outlaw Transportation Segregation

7 Traveling for Freedom   268
The Desegregation of American Transportation

Epilogue   306
#BlackTravelMatters

Notes   323
Acknowledgments   373
Illustration Credits   375
Index   377

Introduction

IN 1922 JOSEPH K. BOWLER TOLD A REPORTER FOR THE *CHICAGO Defender* that he never ventured to the South without a "Jim Crow traveling kit." Designed to allow Bowler, a minister who lived in Massachusetts, to travel through segregated states in relative comfort, the kit included "a pair of soiled overalls purchased from an auto mechanic, a miniature gasoline stove and a small table top the size of a scrub board." The contents of Bowler's kit vividly illustrate some of the indignities and discomforts that Black travelers could expect to encounter in the "colored" railroad cars of his era. He wore the overalls, he explained, to avoid the expense of "soiling" good clothes in the "dirty Jim Crow coaches." They protected him from the tobacco juice that white conductors and news vendors often spat on the seats, and were especially useful in "parts of the Mississippi [where] the white farmers use the Jim Crow coaches as luggage cars in which to transport chickens and hogs." The stove and table top allowed him to prepare and eat meals. They were key components of his kit, given that "the dining car is a closed corporation as far as our people are concerned." "White people below the Mason Dixon line maintain that we are animals, virtually camels, and can go without food or water for several days," noted the intrepid traveler, who both carried and cooked all the food he consumed on his journey. If he had not, he explained, he would have had to "sneak into the back of some depot like a little poodle and ask for some food," or "risk being shot to death by invading a dining car to secure my meals."[1]

Many Black travelers shared Bowler's concerns—whether or not they chose to wear dirty overalls and carry stoves. African Americans loathed segregated streetcars and railway compartments more than virtually any other form of segregation. In the research for his detailed account of race relations in the American South, *Following the Color Line: An Account of Negro Citizenship in the American Democracy* (1908), journalist Ray Stannard Baker found that "no other point of contact is so much and so bitterly discussed among Negroes as the Jim Crow car."[2] A third of a century later, Swedish sociologist Gunnar Myrdal, in his monumental study *The American Dilemma* (1944), made the same point: "It is a common observation that the Jim Crow Car is resented more bitterly among Negroes than most other forms of segregation."[3]

By the 1940s African Americans did not have to travel by train. They had new options to choose from, but they found all of them problematic. The intercity bus lines that first began operating in the late 1920s offered an affordable alternative to traveling by rail, but during their early years of operation many bus companies refused to serve Black passengers. Even after the courts forced them to, they did so "only grudgingly and in the most uncomfortable seats."[4] "If you think riding a Jim Crow car out of the South is no fun," wrote one Black traveler in 1943, "you should try bumping along on the back wheel of a bus, with the odors of the motor keeping you restless."[5]

Cars initially seemed to offer those who could afford them an escape from the humiliations of Jim Crow travel. But while Black motorists could choose their own seats in their own cars, they could not expect to be treated with respect once they stepped outside their vehicles. "It used to be that black people only took a trip [if] some body died or was dying," remembered *Chicago Tribune* columnist Jeannye Thornton in 1972. Driving usually involved a "nonstop trip," because hotels and motels that accepted Black guests were almost impossible to find. Even rest stops were hard to locate: "Bathrooms were always at the next service in the next town 50 miles down the road and when you finally got there, they were always separate and filthy." African American travelers ended up driving "all night [and] sometimes traveling to a big city before even considering stopping to stretch." Not only were roadside accommodations unappealing, driving through the South could be dangerous. "Who knows what could happen to a black family with northern license plates traveling some lonely road?"[6]

Even travel by air was far from free of discrimination. Flying itself was never subject to southern segregation laws, but in the early days of air travel some airlines refused to carry Black passengers, and others assigned them to segregated seats. And when they escaped segregation in the air, Black flyers often encountered it on the ground. Southern airports had segregated waiting rooms, restaurants, and restrooms, and the taxis and ground transportation services that carried passengers to and from airports were divided by race.

American identity has long been defined by mobility and the freedom of the open road, but African Americans have never fully shared in that freedom. Travel segregation began on the stagecoaches and steamships of the Northeast—the nation's earliest common carriers—and moved from there to railroads, train stations, restaurants, roadside rest stops, and gas station restrooms, all of which were eventually segregated by law in the South. As new modes of transportation and accommodations developed, new forms of segregation followed.

In *Traveling Black*, I explore the intertwined history of travel segregation and Black struggles for freedom of movement in America from the antebellum era to the present day. The chapters are organized around the successive forms of long-distance transportation adopted by Americans, and they follow the experiences of generations of African American travelers as they encountered and resisted segregation and discrimination on stagecoaches, steamships, and railways, and in cars, buses, and planes. They document a sustained fight for mobility that falls largely outside the organizational history of the civil rights movement. The final chapters highlight the successes of that fight—recording the struggles that led to the overthrow of Jim Crow transportation—and close with a discussion of inequities in modern transportation. In studying how segregated transportation worked, and how and why its eradication became so central to the African American freedom struggle, this book examines Black mobility as an enduring focal point of struggles over equality and difference.

The history of travel is a critical but often overlooked aspect of the Black experience in America. Historians, like anthropologists, tend to study their subjects in ways that privilege "relations of dwelling over relations of travel"— to borrow James Clifford's phrase.[7] This may be particularly true in the field of African American history, where we often study the members of a group with an almost unparalleled record of displacement and migration as "Black southerners" or "Black northerners" or residents of specific communities.

Although such approaches are vital to understanding Black people's deep roots
in particular places, they do not always capture the significance of movement
in African American life. Repeatedly displaced during slavery, Black southerners kept moving long after emancipation, in a series of migrations that took
them from their regions' plantations and farms to its cities and towns, and
beyond. The Great Migration of more than six million southern Blacks to the
North and West between 1916 and 1970 only accelerated this process, adding
a new chapter to what Ira Berlin has called Black America's "contrapuntal narrative" of "movement and place."[8]

Within this narrative, few African Americans ever escaped travel restrictions entirely. We associate Jim Crow cars and buses with the South, but travel
segregation was never neatly confined to one region of the country. An arti-
fact of emancipation, it took shape alongside the abolition of slavery, arriving
first in the northern states that abolished slavery in the wake of the
American Revolution. These densely populated states were home to many
of the nation's earliest common carriers, most of which went into business at a time when white northerners were reluctant to interact with
their formerly enslaved Black counterparts on equal terms, especially
within the close confines of stagecoaches, steamboats, and railway cars.
Antebellum-era white northerners often insisted that African Americans
ride on the roofs of stagecoaches, on the outside decks of steamboats, and in
the railroads' dirtiest and most dangerous coaches—which came to be known
as Jim Crow cars.

These segregated spaces were never as entrenched in the North as they later
became in the South, where Jim Crow cars began to be mandated by law
starting in the 1880s. Indeed, that same decade saw some northern states pass
legislation designed to protect Black civil rights. But racial discrimination in
transportation followed Black travelers up and down the railroad lines that
took so many of them out of the Mississippi Delta, the Virginia Piedmont,
and other regions across the South during the Great Migration.

Some of the segregation that followed African Americans north was closely
linked to the South's Jim Crow system. Prior to the 1950s, many conductors
on southbound trains began herding Blacks into the Jim Crow car as far north
as Chicago and New York and as far west as Los Angeles. "A Negro car is set
aside for the convenience of passengers traveling south of Washington, so they
will not have to change," explained agents for the Pennsylvania Railroad,
which routinely assigned all of its southbound Black passengers to this car

until 1949. That year a lawsuit brought by ministers who were assigned to the Jim Crow car in Chicago finally forced the Pennsylvania Railroad to abandon this practice.[9] But in California the Jim Crow seating of Dixie-bound Black passengers persisted even after that. As late as the mid-1950s, African Americans who secured tickets on the Southern Pacific's streamliner from Los Angeles to New Orleans would find themselves "all together in car 22 . . . at the front of the train just behind the engine."[10] Such forms of segregation were even more ubiquitous in border cities such as Cincinnati and Washington, D.C., which were for many years what one journalist termed "Big Change Terminals." Gateways to the South, these were stations where railway officials forced all southbound Black passengers who were not already seated at the front of the train to, as one reporter put it, "dutifully tote their shoe boxes filled with fried chicken, pigs feet, cake and cornbread, blankets and squealing kids into the Jim Crow Car."[11] African Americans who traveled by bus likewise had to move to the back of the bus in Washington, D.C., and other border cities—although some bus lines, like the railroad lines, seated Blacks in the back as far north as Chicago and New York, "to 'save Negroes the embarrassment' of having to change to a rear seat in Washington."[12]

White northerners also practiced forms of travel segregation and exclusion that were in no way dictated by southern customs. White-only hotels and rooming houses were common in virtually every region of the country right up until the 1960s, when they were finally outlawed by the Civil Rights Act of 1964 and the US Supreme Court case *Heart of Atlanta Motel, Inc. v. United States* (1964). "It is understood that the southern states from Maryland to Texas are the colored vacationist's No-Man's-Land, but it is not so generally understood (except by Negroes) that the same thing is true of the rest of the country," explained the African American writer George Schuyler to his white readers in 1943. This point had been driven home to Schuyler in the spring of 1943, when he and his wife had sent out a letter seeking vacation accommodations for a "colored family of three" to 105 northeastern vacation spots, all of which placed regular advertisements for guests in the Sunday section of a greater metropolitan newspaper.[13] They received only one positive response. The Anchor Inn in the Poconos was happy to accommodate the Schuyler family. Seventy-four of the businesses did not even bother to reply to the inquiry; most of the others claimed to be "sold out" or "booked to capacity, from now until Labor Day." The few that were willing to explain why they could not accommodate the Schuylers clearly spoke for the rest. "We have never had colored guests at the Oakledge Manor," a Vermont hotelier explained, "and fear that our other guests might make you feel 'left out' of our activities and entertainments."[14]

Finding food on the road was likewise a national problem. While more welcoming than hotels, northern restaurants practiced overt and covert forms of segregation and exclusion that varied from place to place. In Ohio, which passed a civil rights law banning discrimination in public accommodations in 1884 but never enforced it, some restaurant owners served only whites and even placed signs advertising that fact in their windows. In New York, which had stronger antidiscrimination laws, Black customers were rarely refused service, but their patronage was discouraged in other ways. Often seated only after a lengthy wait, Black diners were routinely ushered to tables in "undesirable locations . . . near kitchens, bathrooms, swinging doors" and other out-of-the-way spots and were subject to rude service.[15] Such practices were common enough to make the writer and frequent traveler Langston Hughes wonder "where and how America expects Negro travelers to eat." Having been, by a "conservative estimate," refused service in restaurants in at least a hundred cities, he had no answer. "Many communities have no Negro operated restaurants. And even where there are colored restaurants, how is a complete stranger supposed to know where the Negro places are located? Colored travelers do not usually have time to walk all over town looking for a place to eat."[16]

Hughes's lament highlights one of the defining difficulties of traveling Black, which was simply that Black travelers could never be sure where they were welcome. Localized rather than uniform, and far from obvious, the nation's patchwork of segregationist laws and practices took shape unevenly over time. As C. D. Halliburton pointed out in the *Philadelphia Tribune*, they varied so much that they inevitably put any Black person "in unfamiliar surroundings in the most uncomfortable state of uncertainty, embarrassment and insecurity."[17] This problem was most acute in the North and West, where there were no segregation signs and few Black restaurants or hotels. Blacks had little choice but to try white establishments, but, as Black editor P. L. Prattis complained, "you could never know where insult and embarrassment are waiting for you."[18]

Segregationist practices were inconsistent even in the South. Jim Crow laws were largely similar across the region, and "white" and "colored" signs divided many facilities by race. But there, as Prattis noted, Black travelers navigated a landscape made mystifying by any number of "contrary and con-

Sign in the window of a restaurant in Lancaster, Ohio, 1938.

fusing customs." Although accustomed to segregation, Albon Lewis Holsey, an Atlanta native and Tuskegee Institute staffer, described a 1925 trip spent "Zig-Zagging through Dixie" as a "veritable night mare." Not only did he encounter "the general discomforts of racial discriminations," he was confounded by how frequently they varied from place to place.

On arriving in Memphis, Tennessee, where he had to transfer from one railroad station to another, he found that the city's redcap porters and Yellow Cab drivers did not serve Black travelers. But when he reached Little Rock, Arkansas, just four hours away, he had no such difficulties: a redcap grabbed his bags and "whistled for a Yellow Cab." In Tulsa he once again secured a cab, but only after some covert arrangements. The "white Taxi cabs" that served the station, he was told, "won't haul colored passengers in the day, but at night, when no one is looking they will." Lucky enough to have arrived in the evening, he could get a ride, but he would have to meet his driver "in the shadows behind the station." Holsey's attempt to book a Pullman sleeping car for an interstate trip out of Dallas presented other, more alarming, complications. "The railroads," an agent for one of the trunk lines informed him, "are willing to sell the space to any passenger who is able to pay for it, but it is dangerous for colored people to ride in Pullman cars in Texas. In the first place, the Texas Law has never been interpreted to mean that the [Pullman] Drawing Room is a separate accommodation"—so traveling in one might be illegal—"and in the next place, you can never tell what may happen."[19]

A complex pastiche of law and custom created racial rules that were too inconsistent to be easily followed—or endured. Tennessee-born journalist Carl Rowan, who resettled in Minnesota after serving in the navy during World War II, revisited the land of his youth in 1951 only to be immediately reminded that to be Black in the South was to face "a life of doubt, of uncertainty as to what the reception will be, even from one building to another." Some airports had segregated waiting rooms and restrooms; some did not. He had no trouble renting a car, but he was plagued by "doubt as to which filling-station would allow me to buy gasoline and also to use the toilet. Doubt as to which restaurant would sell me food, even to take out." Indeed, Rowan even wavered on whether he should keep the car he rented, and eventually decided to return it and travel by train and bus. "I did not know whether I would be stopped by policemen if I drove about town in the car," he explained. "I knew that small-town policemen often become suspicious of a strange Negro in a new car."[20]

The doubts faced by Black travelers were not just about protocol. They were also about safety. As Rowan's experience reminds us, traveling Black could involve greater dangers than simply being refused service. African American drivers have always attracted undue attention from the police, so traffic stops were one great fear. But travel of all kinds held danger. In the South especially, African Americans who breached segregation's codes, knowingly or unknowingly, could be subject to violence. As some of the travel experiences featured in this book will show, taking the wrong seat got many travelers beaten, and some killed.

THE UNAVOIDABLE INDIGNITIES
OF TRAVELING BLACK

Unpredictable and dangerous, travel discrimination was a nightmare because it was virtually impossible to avoid—especially in the South. Black southerners could and did shield themselves from some of segregation's slights by

keeping to themselves. Indeed, the accommodationist philosophy promoted
by Booker T. Washington, one of the region's most famous African American
leaders, encouraged Blacks to accept Jim Crow and seek economic empowerment by creating and patronizing Black businesses—some of which catered
to Black travelers. However, even Washington conceded that this approach
had its limitations. African American travelers could sometimes find Black
hotels, livery services, and other travel amenities, but such businesses were
not universally available, and few major common carriers were Black-owned.
"We have no railroad cars and no steamboats, and we have to use yours,"
explained the Black lawyer and politician George Henry White to his former
colleagues at a congressional hearing in 1902, in the course of an unsuccessful
attempt to secure congressional legislation outlawing segregation on American railroads.[21]

Although privileged in other ways, elite Blacks were often even more familiar with travel discrimination than their poorer counterparts. Affluent
enough to be early adopters of new travel technology, they began riding railroads, buses, and planes, and buying cars well before the Black masses could
easily afford to do so, and were sometimes all the more unwelcome as a result. The use of prestigious modes of transportation by affluent African Americans could be galling to whites, who resented sharing all but the rudest
public accommodations with Blacks on equal terms. "White people have a dis-
tinct aversion to 'associating' with black people or meeting them in any relation that implies a social equality, even in public conveyances or places," an
editorialist for the New York Times explained in 1894. "It is not that white
people object to the presence of negroes. They only insist that negroes shall
be kept in their place. A negress in an unoccupied passenger [seat] on a parlor
car would be looked sourly on by her white fellow passengers, even if they
did not enter protests against her presence, whereas the same negress visibly
employed as the nurse of white children, would be innocuous and welcome."[22]
One southern politician made the same point more bluntly in explaining his
support for the passage of separate cars laws. The target of such laws, he
maintained, was not "good old farm hands and respectable Negroes," but
rather "that insolent class of Negroes who desired to force themselves into
first class coaches."[23]

In the end, no class of Negroes could fully escape traveling Black: it was a
formative part of life for wealthy Blacks, poor Blacks, and everyone in between.
Race leaders such as Booker T. Washington, Mary Church Terrell, Ida B. Wells,

W. E. B. Du Bois, Pauli Murray, Thurgood Marshall, Bayard Rustin, and Martin Luther King Jr. all traveled many miles to speak to a national audience. Other inveterate travelers whose journeys crisscross this book include Jack Johnson, a boxer who was an early car connoisseur; Jackie Robinson and countless other Black baseball players who preceded him in the Negro leagues; and musicians such as Duke Ellington, Ella Fitzgerald, and the blues singer Leadbelly, whose "Jim Crow Blues" featured the chorus "you gonna find some Jim Crow, everyplace you go."[24] This book includes many of their travel stories.

But *Traveling Black* also tracks the quotidian experiences of ordinary Black travelers. Among them were vacationers who, like the Schuyler family, simply sought a place to get away. As W. E. B. Du Bois noted in 1917, "ever recurring race-discrimination" discouraged easy getaways, especially among African Americans of modest means. Unlike Du Bois, who could afford to travel from his home in New York to elite Black vacation spots such as Idlewild in Michigan, they often had to "stay near home."[25] However, even those who ventured farther could not escape Jim Crow humiliations. Ron Reaves, who grew up in Oklahoma in the 1950s, is a case in point. His father was a janitor who worked three jobs in order to be able to afford a car, which he used to take his family to the beaches of California or to Chicago in the summer. They had no brushes with discrimination at hotels or restaurants as they drove west because both were luxuries that they could not afford. Instead, they drove nonstop for twelve hundred miles. But the segregated landscape through which they traveled still made a lasting impression on Reaves, who remembered seeing "plenty of 'no colored' signs at Phillips gas stations and the like" and experiencing the sting of discrimination still more directly at some of the service stations where the family was able to stop. Although permitted to buy gas, they "had to pee out back and drink water from a dirty dingy ladle that was set up next to nice porcelain water fountains."[26]

Whether or not they took vacations, few Black Americans could avoid encountering travel discrimination at some point in their lives. Many, if not most, of the travelers featured in this book braved Jim Crow cars and other forms of discrimination for practical reasons: they traveled to find employment, to attend school, to report for—or return home from—military service, to visit relatives, to tend to the sick and bury the dead. Members of an increasingly mobile society, African Americans could no more stay off the nation's roads and railways than could any other Americans, which made traveling Black an issue that cut across class lines.

Opposition to travel segregation was deep, persistent, and wide-ranging. Not surprisingly, the early Black activists who founded and led civil rights organizations such as the National Equal Rights League, the National Afro-American Council, the Niagara Movement, and the NAACP routinely denounced the segregation of Blacks on common carriers as one of the great evils faced by the race. This segregation was also denounced by leaders who were less oriented toward civil rights—such as Booker T. Washington, whose program of Black accommodation did not extend to embracing the Jim Crow car. Even Marcus Garvey's Universal Negro Improvement Association (UNIA) condemned Jim Crow travel. Committed to ideals of racial purity, the UNIA was a Black separatist movement not usually associated with the protests against segregation. But opposition to the mistreatment of Black travelers figures prominently in its statement of principles. Crafted at a 1920 meeting that brought together twenty-five thousand of the organization's delegates, the UNIA's "Declaration of the Rights of the Negro Peoples of the World" opens with complaints about Blacks being barred from "public hotels and inns of the world" and "jim crowed . . . on the public conveyances and common carriers in the southern portion of the United States."[27]

Opposition to segregation on common carriers crossed the Black political lines because such segregation always involved more than racial separation. Black separatists, such as Garvey's followers, might have embraced Jim Crow transportation had Blacks ever been supplied with facilities equal to those used by whites. But almost all Jim Crow cars, and other facilities set aside for Black people, were both inferior and deeply uncomfortable. At issue were questions of economic justice and human dignity. The physical discomforts of Jim Crow travel made travel segregation odious even for Black leaders who did not oppose segregation per se. Garveyites objected to paying "the same fare charged for first-class accommodations" to ride on trains where "[our] families are often humiliated and insulted by drunken white men who habitually pass through the jim-crow cars going to the smoking car." Not surprisingly, Booker T. Washington had similar objections. "What embitters colored people in regard to railroad travel is not separation . . . but the inadequacy of accommodations," he wrote in his 1913 article "Is the Negro Having a Fair Chance?" Black travelers never got "equal accommodations for the same money." Ending such discrimination was a "matter of justice and fair play" rather than "social equality," Washington maintained. The railroads ought to "give one man as much for his money as another man."[28] A complex character, Washington lent covert support to legal challenges to Jim Crow, but neither his criticism of the railroads, nor the court cases he funded, did anything to mitigate the unequal conditions and economic exploitation endured by Black travelers.

Instead, economic inequities not only persisted but spread to new forms of transportation. With the advent of intercity buses, Black southerners had to pay full fare to sit in the vehicles' worst seats, and could not even count on being able to sit down. Southern custom dictated that seating white passengers took priority over seating Black passengers, so on overcrowded buses the latter had to travel standing up—or wait for the next bus. African Americans who traveled by car got another kind of raw deal at Jim Crow service stations, where paying for gas did not secure them access to these establishments' restrooms, snack bars, or water fountains. When commercial airlines debuted in the 1930s, Black flyers were similarly shortchanged. Although subject to relatively minimal discrimination while in the air, they could rarely make use of the airline's meal vouchers at southern whites-only airport restaurants, and should their plane be grounded in the South, they would be "sent to some colored person's house for lodging while the white passengers are put in the best hotel in town."[29] This book captures these experiences, as well as the long history of Black protest they inspired.

GENDER, JIM CROW, AND CIVIL RIGHTS

Traveling Black tells a story that is both old and new. Travel and transportation are central to the study of the segregation era, which is generally bookmarked on one end by *Plessy v. Ferguson* (1896)—a railroad case in which the US Supreme Court gave sanction to de jure segregation—and on the other end by the Montgomery Bus Boycott and other protests designed to end segregation in transportation. Yet *Plessy* is better remembered today for establishing the doctrine of "separate but equal" than it is for sanctioning Jim Crow cars. The Montgomery Bus Boycott and the Freedom Rides are almost never discussed as the culmination of a long and sustained history of Black protest against segregated transportation. Most studies of segregation are centered largely on the South and are more grounded in the history of particular communities than in the experiences of Black people in motion. Once one of the most resented forms of segregation, travel segregation is now one of the most forgotten. And yet it is no accident that so many flashpoints of the civil rights movement took place on buses.

The obscurity of travel segregation is highlighted by the recent rediscovery of the *Green Book*, a guidebook once used by African Americans to find hotels, restaurants, and other accommodations that served Black travelers. This publication is now familiar to at least some modern-day Americans thanks to its cameo in the Hollywood film *The Green Book* (2018)—a Black and white road movie that borrows the book's title without seriously engaging with its content. But despite the fact that it was published more or less annually between 1936 and 1967, until the last decade or so *The Negro Motorist Green Book* was known only to those old enough to remember using it. First rediscovered by African American writer Calvin Ramsey, who published a children's book about Black travelers on the road called *Ruth and the Green Book* (2010), it is only now beginning to make its way into the history books.[30]

But while the *Green Book* is finally being archived and studied, it is still considered largely in isolation. Few of the scholars, writers, and filmmakers who are looking at it seem to be aware that the *Green Book* was only the best-known and longest-running of several travel guides that appeared during the segregation era, and that its antecedents can be dated back to a railroad guide that the abolitionist newspaper *The Liberator* published in the early 1840s.[31] *The Liberator*'s "Travellers' Directory" listed the railroad timetables coupled with notes on whether each railroad welcomed Black passengers. The Boston and Lowell Railroad's summer schedule appeared under an entry that stated *"Humanity respected,"* while the Eastern Railroad's timetable was prefaced by the heading: *"An odious distinction on account of color, and bullying propensity to carry it out."*[32]

As the instructions in the *Liberator*'s directory underscore, the difficulties faced by Black travelers extended over many generations and represent a problem in Black life that attention to the *Green Book* alone cannot begin to address. In this book I discuss the challenges of "driving while Black," but I also emphasize that the difficulties encountered by African American drivers were nothing new.

Traveling Black reconstructs the history of a moving color line that dates back to the pre–Civil War era of stagecoaches and steamships. A phenomenon that first emerged in a time when most Black persons were not free, it was shaped not only by the regional racial politics of the antebellum era but also by the intersection of gender ideology and the technological advances that moved Americans out of stagecoaches and steamships and into trains, planes, automobiles, and buses. Prior to the early nineteenth century, the vast majority of Americans traveled either on foot or on horseback. The very wealthy sometimes rode in private carriages, but most travelers had to brave the elements, as well as America's public roads.[33] The development of common carriers in the 1830s changed the space of travel, moving it indoors and creating new kinds of sheltered mobile spaces that were at once private and public, and more accessible to women.

Stagecoaches, steamships, and railroad parlor cars not only enabled people to get from one place to another faster than ever before, they also transformed travelers into passengers and allowed them to travel in relative comfort and seclusion. They also fostered the development of hotels, waiting rooms, restaurants, and other public accommodations designed to make travelers feel at home. But this new travel landscape favored some passengers over others.

Travel spaces such as railroad cars and steamship cabins were contested sites of social contact from the outset because they brought together diverse classes of Americans while also drawing "private" women into "public" spaces. Because these spaces were compact and often crowded, they raised questions about what constituted "respectable contact among strangers." Some early travelers recoiled at the idea of sharing close quarters with "the rich and the poor, the educated and the ignorant, the polite and vulgar." "Talk of ladies on a steamboat or in a railroad car! There are none," huffed Pennsylvania state senator Samuel Breck in a travel diary written in 1835. "I never feel like a gentleman there and I cannot perceive a semblance of gentility in any one who makes part of the traveling mob."[34]

These "modern improvement[s] in traveling" proved irresistible to most travelers, who made the best of new mobile spaces in which they found themselves by embracing railroad cars, steamship cabins, and other travel accommodations as potentially homelike spaces. To travel by train, according to nineteenth-century enthusiasts, was to enter a "flying drawing-room" or "a home adrift."[35] These public perceptions of travel as a quasi-domestic activity were marketing gold for the carriers. Stagecoaches, the least comfortable of nineteenth-century conveyances, were embellished with decorative moldings, curtains, and upholstered seats; railroad cars and steamships offered expansive homelike amenities such as parlor cars or cabins—many of which were set aside for women. Designed with middle-class gender ideals in mind, all these spaces promoted what railroad historian Amy Richter has called an "ideal of public domesticity." Rooted in "a shared fantasy that sought to bring order, comfort, and familiarity to sites of rapid social and cultural change," this ideal "attempted to bring the cultural associations and behaviors of home life to bear upon social interactions between strangers."[36]

A product of the Victorian era, ideals of public domesticity helped make railroad cars and steamship cabins safe spaces for white women. But the white home at the center of these ideals was rarely welcoming to Black travelers. As Barbara Welke and other legal scholars have shown, gender and race played a central role in the rise of both de facto and de jure segregation of southern railroads. Prior to the 1880s, racial segregation on trains was informal and inconsistent; when it occurred, it usually involved conductors refusing to let Black travelers ride in what was then known as the "ladies' car." A product of the domestic ideals that led steamboats, railroads. and other carriers to set aside separate spaces for women, ladies' cars were special coaches for the exclusive use of women and their travel companions These nonsmoking cars had upholstered seats, women's bathrooms, and other amenities that were absent in more traditional gentlemen's cars, which were known as smokers. Gender dictated even the arrangement of these cars. Typical nineteenth-century trains were made up of a baggage car, a smoking car, and a ladies' car, which was invariably at the end of the train, where its occupants would not be exposed to the soot and sparks cast off by the train's locomotive. They were also at least somewhat safer in the case of a crash.

But as emancipation opened up the possibility of travel by rail to an ever-growing number of Black passengers, gender proved to be an increasingly problematic proxy for race. Middle-class Black women, and sometimes Black couples, sought access to the ladies' car, and when they were refused access, they sued, achieving enough success in the courts to make the railroads hesitant to segregate by race. These victories did not last. By the end of the nineteenth century, ladies' cars were becoming less common. Determined to keep all Black people in their place, southern states had begun to pass "separate car laws," which divided passengers by race rather than gender. Designed to give segregation a more secure legal footing. these laws required virtually no change in the actual facilities offered to Black and white passengers. They simply relegated all Blacks, male and female, to the smoker. These new arrangements were sanctioned by the Supreme Court in *Plessy v. Ferguson* (1896), an unsuccessful challenge to Louisiana's Separate Car Act that made all legal challenges to segregated transportation more difficult. *Plessy* ruled that the Fourteenth Amendment's equal protection clause did not prohibit state legislatures from requiring separate public facilities for Blacks and whites, so long as these facilities were equal and not just separate. The decision gave judicial sanction to a wide variety of Jim Crow practices.

As the history of Black resistance to segregated transportation underscores, *Plessy* was not the last word on the subject. The *Plessy* decision upheld a Louisiana law mandating separate but equal accommodations for Blacks and whites on *intrastate* railroads; it did not provide decisive support for segregation on *interstate* trains, or require railroads that traveled through several states to honor out-of-state segregation laws. It also posed no legal obstacle to suits challenging the equality of segregated accommodations. Accordingly, both before and after *Plessy*, African American travelers navigated an interlinked national railway system in which the boundaries and character of separate but equal accommodations were not clearly defined. Black passengers in the South often traveled Jim Crow even when traveling interstate, but they were not always required to do so. Segregationist practices were never entirely consistent from state to state.[37] Nor were they legally unassailable.

On the contrary, state segregation practices left room for Black men and women to mount continuing challenges to Jim Crow, generating an endless series of largely forgotten court cases, petitions to state railroad commissions, legislative maneuvers, protests, publicity campaigns, and appeals to Congress. Black travelers also filed complaints with the Interstate Commerce Commission (ICC), a federal agency established in 1887 to regulate carriers that provide transportation between the states. The legislation that established the ICC included a nondiscrimination clause prohibiting carriers from "imposing unreasonable prejudice or disadvantage" on any of their customers. This clause went largely unenforced before the 1960s but would eventually play an important role in the desegregation of interstate transportation and in the larger civil rights struggle.

A cross-class issue, Black resistance to segregated transportation was both broad and diffuse. For civil rights organizations such as the NAACP, travel often took a backseat to the issues of education and lynching, but individual travelers pursued these cases even without organizational support and kept pressing Black leaders for help with test cases and other protests. The story of travel segregation adds strong evidence to scholarly arguments that the civil rights movement has a history that begins long before the famous protests of the 1950s and 1960s.[38] Indeed, Black resistance to segregation could be described as a constant civil rights movement.

In *Traveling Black*, I tell the story of that movement from its beginnings through the early 1960s, when a new generation of civil rights leaders finally forced the federal government to take decisive action to end segregation on interstate buses and trains and to bar Jim Crow roadside accommodations. I recount that momentous victory, and also note its limits. I have written this book at a time when Black drivers face rampant racial profiling, which sometimes turns lethal, and intercity public transportation has declined to the point that most of the bus lines and railroads African Americans fought so hard to desegregate no longer exist. I close the book with an exploration of how and why African Americans are still traveling Black.

1

The Road to *Plessy*

How Travel Segregation Took Shape

"I REMEMBER DISTINCTLY THE FIRST TIME IT DAWNED UPON ME with irresistible, crushing force that there was something radically, painfully wrong with the color of my face," wrote Mary Church Terrell, a prominent leader of the National Association of Colored Women's Clubs, in an unpublished essay written sometime during the first few years of the twentieth century.[1] Her revelation dated back to the years immediately following the Civil War, when she was "not more than five years old." It took shape around an encounter she had while traveling by train with her father, the wealthy Memphis businessman Robert Church.[2]

Mollie Church, as she was then known, was seated by herself in what she remembered as the "best car" on the train—her father having stepped out into the adjacent smoking car to speak with an acquaintance. As she waited for him to return, she was suddenly confronted by a conductor who challenged her presence in that car. Although Tennessee would not pass laws mandating racial segregation on trains until the early 1880s, African Americans were not always welcome in the comfortable passenger coaches where Robert Church had seated his daughter. Known as ladies' cars, these were first-class, nonsmoking coaches designed to accommodate women and their traveling companions. Their occupants were typically white women and their families, so the five-year-old Terrell struck the conductor as being out of place. "Whose little nigger is this?" he asked the other passengers in the car after unsuccessfully demanding answers from "the frightened little girl." He wanted to know "who I was and what I was doing in that car," Terrell remembered, "instead of sitting in the smoker, 'where I belonged.'"[3]

Terrell was rescued by the return of her father—a hot-tempered man who threatened to shoot the conductor if he did not let his daughter retain her seat. But she had nonetheless been introduced to the race problem by way of a confrontation that she experienced as an assault on both her gender and her race. Unsure what she had done to merit the conductor's disapproval, Terrell later asked her mother about the incident. "I asked her why the conductor had wanted to take me out of a nice clean coach and put me in one that my father said was dirty. I assured her that I had been careful to do everything she told me to do. For instance, my hands were clean and so was my face. I hadn't mussed my hair; it was brushed back and perfectly smooth. . . . I hadn't soiled my dress a single bit. . . . I was sitting up 'straight and proper.' In short, I assured my mother I was 'behaving like a little lady,' as she had told me to."[4]

Terrell's story records a particular moment in the South's journey to Jim Crow, reminding us that the path from slavery to segregation was not seamless, especially on the South's railroads. Jim Crow cars and segregated travel accommodations first took shape in the antebellum North, which was home to many of the nation's earliest common carriers: that is, transportation systems and services, like steamships and carriages, where individuals bought passage to travel alongside strangers. Whites displayed little interest in segregating social spaces so long as most Blacks were slaves. But with the gradual abolition of slavery in the North in the early nineteenth century, the enclosed social spaces on the common carriers that first began connecting American cities and towns around the same time inspired white racial anxieties. These were assuaged by the creation of many of the nation's first segregationist regulations and statutes. Such divisions received little attention in the South until after the Civil War, when nearly three million ex-slaves became free to travel by choice for the first time. With emancipation, however, the regulation and segregation of Black mobility became a persistent preoccupation among white southerners.

Racial segregation on boats, stagecoaches, and trains was initially a matter of regional custom, carrier regulations, and the preferences of individual customers or carrier operators. Never systematic, such segregation emerged in fits and starts amid a transportation revolution that saw Americans using first boats and wagons, and then railroads, to move goods and people around the country more rapidly than ever before. American society was becoming ever more mobile, just as two successive waves of emancipation transformed the social fabric of American life.

Middle-class Black travelers, such as little Mary Church and her father, were prominent and disturbing symbols of African American freedom and mobility and therefore became the primary target of early travel segregation regulations in both the North and the South. More able than other Blacks to afford to travel on trains, stagecoaches, and steamships, they were threatening because they were clearly not servants (Black servants and slaves were usually permitted to travel with their owners). They entered the coaches and cabins of common carriers as fare-paying customers, claiming accommodations that were generally thought to be the exclusive preserve of well-to-do whites. Black access to first-class travel accommodations often raised questions of gender as well as race and class. Steamships, canal boats, and other vessels traditionally set aside special ladies' cabins for women, who could also expect to find a berth inside stagecoaches, and by the 1840s some railroads had begun reserving their most comfortable cars for female travelers, making the first-class car a ladies' car.

These divisions worked well enough so long as all Black women who traveled first-class could be assumed to be enslaved maids, but the gradual abolition of slavery in the northern states troubled such divisions. "In the North the white no longer distinctly perceives the barrier which separates him from the degraded race," French visitor Alexis de Tocqueville observed after touring the United States during the early 1830s. And as a result, he wrote, "he shuns the negro with the more pertinacity, since he fears lest they should someday be confounded together."[5]

Such sentiments were still stronger in the post–Civil War South, where the terms on which Blacks would travel would be hotly contested. Travel segregation laws had not been necessary before the Civil War. They might well have been adopted immediately thereafter, but for the influence of Reconstruction. During this era of radical Republican rule, white southern lawmakers found themselves constrained by the combined influence of congressional supervision and the power exercised by Black politicians and voters—who supported federal and state-level protection for Black civil rights. Southern whites did not welcome sharing space with Black travelers, but their attempts to banish all Blacks to Negro cars and other segregated accommodations were not always successful—as we see in Robert Church's successful opposition to the conductor who wanted to move his daughter to the smoking car.

With the collapse of Reconstruction in 1877 and the restoration of white rule shortly thereafter, such laws became a possibility. Travel was a key site for the emergence and codification of southern racial segregation, which began in the 1880s with the creation of laws requiring all railroad companies to furnish separate coaches for the transportation of white and Black passengers. These laws received Supreme Court sanction in *Plessy v. Ferguson* (1896), a railroad case that held that separate facilities for Blacks and whites were constitutional so long as they were equal. The landmark decision provided enduring constitutional support for the racial segregation of a wide variety of public spaces, including schools.

Plessy did not come out of nowhere. It was made necessary by a long series of African American challenges to segregation that took place both on the carriers and in the courts.

RACE AND SPACE ON THE ROAD DURING THE ANTEBELLUM ERA

From the advent of the iron horse, Americans frequently described their railroads as "republican," and loved to boast that "we have no second class cars for the inferior classes, because all of our citizens rank as gentlemen."[6] But in point of fact, all but the earliest American trains had at least two passenger cars, and railroad authorities usually divided their riders by class, race, and/or gender. What was republican, perhaps, was the nomenclature used to describe these cars, which generally made no mention of class. The railroads began selling middle-class travelers comfortable upholstered seats in passenger cars known as "chair cars" as early as the 1830s. But they also found space for less affluent travelers, who were typically accommodated in older passenger cars, freight cars, or even baggage cars, usually at a cut rate.

Despite their egalitarian claims, Americans of all classes rarely traveled together on any of the nation's earliest common carriers. The stagecoaches and steamships that preceded the railroads were expensive and typically catered to affluent passengers. Working-class and poor travelers usually rode in horse-drawn wagons or carts, or walked. If they managed to secure space on a steamship or stagecoach, they rode outside—paying a half fare for deck passage or a perch on the outside of a stagecoach. In the North, servants and slaves who traveled with their masters usually occupied these half-fare accommodations—as did free Black laborers. White southerners, who were used to living in close quarters with their house slaves, often preferred more egalitarian seating arrangements. One northern abolitionist noticed, "There is never any objection to mixing with colored people while they are slaves"; another maintained that "nothing is more provoking to the slaveholders themselves, than to exclude their colored servants from the inside of stage coaches, as is the villainous practice in New England."[7] Gender could further complicate the question of who sat where. On boat rides, female passengers of all classes and colors often shared a single ladies' cabin.

With the abolition of slavery in the North, the rise of a new class of elite Black travelers posed a new challenge to these already complicated arrangements. Members of the North's emerging Black middle class who were affluent enough to purchase full-fare tickets were not always welcome to travel on equal terms with members of the white middle class, regardless of what they paid for their tickets. The discrimination they met was neither customary nor mandated by law. It took shape haphazardly in the wake of the gradual abolition of slavery, and reflected white fears that Black freedom would undermine the antebellum North's social order, in which Blacks were traditionally slaves or servants. Well-dressed and respectable middle-class Black travelers were living symbols of emancipation's challenge to the status quo, and thus particularly unwelcome.

Such fears were evident in the urban legends that began to circulate among travelers in the 1820s and 1830s, which told of passengers on crowded stagecoaches who traveled in the company of a "lady, closely veiled," only to later realize that they had shared close quarters with "a very ebony colored individual of the female gender."[8] Actual African American travelers were still more problematic: some white travelers refused to share space with them. Stagecoach drivers and steamship captains usually deferred to the wishes of such passengers by forcing unwelcome Black passengers to sit outside—even if they had full-fare tickets. Some coach drivers and steamship officers even took it upon themselves to bar African American passengers from traveling anywhere but on the outside seats and decks of their conveyances. These men may have been worried that such passengers would alienate other customers, but many were hostile to Black passengers, even in the absence of complaints. Intent on preserving their own class status, they were reluctant to extend the courtesies normally provided to middle-class passengers to members of a group so strongly associated with servitude.

In 1833 a stagecoach driver refused to seat two visiting Liberian missionaries who wished to travel from Boston to Providence, Rhode Island. They had purchased full-fare tickets in advance, but when the driver saw them, he told them that he "would not carry *Niggers*! Unless they would take an out-side seat!" And in 1835 Black abolitionist David Ruggles was "forcibly ejected" from a stagecoach in New Jersey by a like-minded driver who told him, "It is against my rules to allow colored men to ride inside."[9]

Such policies could extend to women as well, denying Black women access to spaces traditionally set aside for women. Gender was the standard qualification for access to the ladies' cabins where women took shelter on boat trips, but the captain of the steamboat *Passaic*, which ferried passengers from Newark to New York City, did not allow Black women in his ladies' cabin. Described in the *Colored American* as "a rude, hard-favored [man] . . . selected from the lower walks of society," he could regularly be seen "driving or dragging pious educated females, and some of them as fair as himself, from the ladies' cabin and from seats not denied common prostitutes, and the most illiterate and vulgar pale faces." Female slaves and servants had long been welcome in the ladies' cabins on boats. But "colored females who are neither servants nor slaves" attracted the ire of men such as this 'rude, hard-favored" captain.[10]

This kind of discrimination was far from universal, but the fact that Black passengers could never tell when they would be permitted inside stagecoaches and ship cabins made travel all the more uncertain. Shipping clerks and stage-coach agents rarely refused to sell them full-fare tickets, which sometimes left African Americans wholly unprepared for the conditions they encountered. One case in point is the horrifying journey to New Hampshire endured by three teenage boys who all grew up to be Black nationalists—perhaps in part because of this miserable trip.

In the winter of 1835, Alexander Crummell, Henry Highland Garnet, and Thomas Sidney, who all lived in New York City, traveled from their homes there to Canaan, New Hampshire, where they were to attend an abolitionist high school. From middle-class families, the boys expected to make their journey in relative comfort. They (or perhaps their parents) had booked a cabin on a steamship that would take them as far as Providence, Rhode Is-land, and from there they planned to complete the final leg of their journey by stagecoach. They dressed accordingly, wearing their Sunday best. This proved to be a mistake. Barred from occupying a cabin on the steamship, the boys spent the night on deck, "bedless and foodless and exposed to the cold and storm." In Providence, matters only got worse. Their stagecoach driver refused to let them sit inside, so they ended up traveling the four hundred miles between Providence and Canaan "mounted on the top of the coach," where they suffered from both "cold and exposure" and "thirst and hunger," as "rarely would a hotel or inn give us food, and nowhere could we get shelter." They also suffered from sustained public humiliation.

"The sight of three black youths, in gentlemanly garb, traveling through New England was, *in those days, a most unusual sight*" which inspired "universal sneers and ridicule," Alexander Crummell recalled with some bitterness many years later. The young travelers were subject to "taunt and insult in every town and village, and ofttimes every farmhouse," and arrived in Canaan both exhausted and heartsick. It seemed "hardly possible that a Christian people could thus treat human beings traveling through a land of ministers and churches," Crummell reflected.[11]

African American leaders routinely sent irate letters to white abolitionist newspapers to protest the abuses experienced by Black travelers. They also aired their complaints in editorials and letters published in the Black press.[12] But their protests do not seem to have had much impact. Occasional calls for the boycott of a particular steamship line or stagecoach company foundered because such businesses were numerous and middle-class Black travelers were far too few to constitute a crucial market for any one company. This meant that African American travelers had little recourse: they could travel only on those transportation lines that did not discriminate, or forgo public transportation altogether: "If you have not horses and vehicles of your own to travel with, stay at home, or travel on foot," *Colored American* editor Charles Ray resolved in 1838. "Cease giving your money to men, who forbear not to degrade you beneath the dogs."[13] But even Ray himself could not follow his own advice. An abolitionist and minister as well as a journalist, Ray traveled extensively throughout the North, giving lectures and attending antislavery conventions.

By the late 1830s Ray had the option of making some of his journeys by rail, which initially seemed to offer a promising alternative. The Northeast was home to most of the nation's earliest railroads. Few covered more than fifty miles, but they were powered by steam engines that made them "object[s] of wonder"—and often alarm. Faster than any horse-drawn vehicle, they seemed to annihilate space and time, bringing once-distant places into close proximity.[14] In upstate New York, the Mohawk and Hudson Railroad, which was completed in 1831, reduced to a forty-minute ride the sixteen miles between

Schenectady and Albany, which had once taken travelers half a day or more. Ray, who tried this train in 1837, was among the many travelers impressed by its "tremendous" speed. Had he stuck his head out the window, he marveled, he would have most certainly lost his hat.

He was almost equally impressed by the Mohawk's democratic seating policies. "The proprietors of the Mohawk and Hudson Rail Road do not act upon the proscription principle," he wrote. "You receive your ticket at Albany, designating by the letter and figure, the car you are to take at Schenectady. On arriving, all having a ticket of the number and letter of yourself, take the same car, without reference to anything. I have seldom traveled so great a distance, when accompanying circumstances told that we were but men associated together."[15] On a subsequent train trip taken in 1839, Ray was likewise pleased to find "but one class of cars" on a train from Jersey City to New York City. He took his seat "among 'gentlemen of property and standing,' and among gentlemen not of property and standing—among white and among colored persons, as the case may be," he reported. "There is no other alternative. . . . [and] no one raising an objection, nor apparently thinking of any."[16]

But Ray's sense of satisfaction was short-lived. Traveling to Massachusetts in 1841, he met with discrimination on both the Nantucket steamboat and the New Bedford and Taunton Railroad. Even before then, the *Colored American* had begun to receive reports of discrimination on trains in New England. In the summer of 1838, David Ruggles reported being "forced" into "the pauper (or Jim Crow Car)" on the Stonington Railroad in Connecticut. Later that year, Massachusetts resident Henry Scott was outraged to be told that he must ride in the *"dirt car . . . on account of my color."*[17]

JIM CROW RIDES THE RAILS

The pauper car, dirt car, and Jim Crow car were all the same thing: half-fare coaches that railroad officials set aside for the poorest, most disreputable travelers. Also known as "refuse cars" and "emigrant cars," these cars were given names that reflected either the passengers they carried or the function they served. Soot-stained vehicles that rode directly behind the locomotive were known as dirt or refuse cars because they were used by railroad workers to store "almost all manner of dirty things." One Eastern Railroad passenger complained that the half-fare coach, in which he was forced to ride, contained "a buffalo skin filled with coal dust, and slippers, dirty rags &c."[18] Known as emigrant cars in regions where they carried newly arrived European migrants, such cars would come to be called Jim Crow cars on northeastern railroads that attracted numerous Black passengers.

How the name "Jim Crow" made the leap from the blackface minstrel shows of the 1820s and 1830s to the railroads remains unclear. But the name was apt. Jim Crow was a wildly popular theatrical character created by a white actor, Thomas Dartmouth "Daddy" Rice, who maintained that he modeled his blackface song and dance routines on the comical antics of a crippled, enslaved stable hand. But, as performed by Rice, minstrelsy's dancing Jim Crow figure above all mocked free Black aspirations to respectability and prosperity. The image was also a perfect avatar for a system that confined even middle-class Black travelers to the railroads' half-fare coaches. Invariably dressed in a crumpled top hat and tattered coattails, Jim Crow was a symbol of failed gentility, a vision of all the well-to-do Black passengers whom whites excluded from their presence.

As the development of the Jim Crow car testifies, segregationist practices transitioned easily from older forms of transportation to early railroads. In fact, their persistence was perhaps all but inevitable, given that the Northeast's railroads had close ties to its stagecoach and shipping businesses. The Eastern Railroad Company, for example, began as a stagecoach line and employed former stagecoach drivers as conductors. It gave these men license to continue segregating their passengers by enacting a regulation that stipulated that "all passengers upon the road are required to take such seats in the cars, and in such cars as shall be designated by the respective conductors; and all tickets are sold subject to this rule."[19] The New Bedford and Taunton Railroad was financed largely by local steamship companies, which also supplied its first president—Joseph Grinnell of the Martha's Vineyard Steamship Company. The railroad opened for business in 1840, and from the start it operated under a set of regulations that specified that all passengers had to "take such seats as may be assigned them by the conductor." The rule, Grinnell maintained, "was made to render the passage pleasant and convenient to passengers and the public. . . . [It] separates the drunken, dirty, ragged and colored people from the others."[20]

Incensed by such regulations, Black travelers sometimes refused to follow them. On an 1841 trip from Salem to Boston on the Eastern Railroad, Thomas Jennings, who "paid full price . . . and received a ticket directing him to a

Lithograph from the mid-1800s depicting a Jim Crow character.

first class car," refused to move when he was "ordered out" of that car. Only when "threatened with violence from the *conductor, baggage-master, brakeman, and one ruffian passenger*" did he finally retreat.[21] Frederick Douglass routinely refused to move into the Jim Crow car, even though he "was sometimes soundly beaten by the conductor and the brakeman" as a result. During an epic brawl on the Eastern Railroad in 1841, he retained a firm grasp on the seats around him even after the railroad's officials summoned "half a dozen fellows of a baser sort" to carry him out of the car. Defiant to the end, he managed to drag several seats with him on his way out.[22]

Irate Black travelers sometimes also challenged the railroads in court. Thomas Downing, another abolitionist who was physically forced out of a first-class car, sued the Harlem Railroad for assault and battery. But the jury that heard his case ruled in favor of the railroad, as did a Massachusetts judge in a similar case launched by David Ruggles the following month. The railroads, both judgments affirmed, were entitled to enforce their own rules.[23] The courts could offer "but little hope in the case of our people," concluded Charles Ray, the editor of the New York–based *Colored American*, after Downing lost. Black litigants were likely to be defeated by "corrupt public sentiment."[24]

In Massachusetts, Black activists sought to turn public sentiment around. With the support of white abolitionists such as William Lloyd Garrison, they circulated anti-railroad petitions and pressured the state legislature to force state railroads to change their policies. Massachusetts's constitution protected the equal rights of the commonwealth's inhabitants, they argued.[25] The sustained public protest eventually spurred state legislators to hold hearings on transportation discrimination and draft a law that would have made it illegal for the railroads to make distinctions in accommodations based on a "passenger's descent, sect or color." Defeated in the state legislature in January 1843, the new law never went into effect.[26] But the protests that led up to it succeeded nonetheless. In the spring of 1843, Massachusetts's railroads voluntarily abandoned their segregation policies. They could no longer take the bad publicity, the intransigence of prominent Black passengers, and the political pressure from abolitionist legislators, who threatened to revoke their charters of incorporation unless they revised their policies. Some conductors continued to discriminate against Black passengers even after that, but by 1855 Frederick Douglass was reporting that "the 'Jim Crow car'—set up for the degradation of colored people—is nowhere found in New England."[27]

But other, less straightforward forms of travel discrimination persisted throughout the Northeast. Harriet Jacobs, who fled from slavery in the early 1840s, was disappointed to find out that she had not escaped color prejudice. Traveling from Philadelphia to New York City by rail, she had enough money to buy a first-class ticket, but she quickly learned that "they could not be had for any money. They don't allow colored people to go in the first-class cars." Instead, she ended up traveling in what was probably the emigrant car. "A large, rough car, with windows on each side, too high for us to look out without standing up. It was crowded with people, apparently of all nations. There were plenty of beds and cradles, containing screaming and kicking babies. Every other man had a cigar or pipe in his mouth, and jugs of whiskey were handed round freely. The fumes of the whiskey and the dense tobacco smoke were sickening to my senses, and my mind was equally nauseated by the coarse jokes and ribald songs around me."[28]

According to Jacobs, the late 1840s and 1850s brought "some improvement in these matters."[29] Her assessment was echoed by William Lloyd Garrison. In an 1861 editorial, Garrison described Black men as once having had to "pace the deck all night amidst howling storms, with his wife and little ones, while going up and down on the rough tempestuous Sound" or sit among "drunkards and lewd, dirty persons in Jim-Crow cars, while passing from city to city." But conditions were different now, he noted: "Now railroads and steamboats are free to him."[30] As much as abolitionists liked to celebrate their victories, though, travel discrimination remained common throughout the North. Like the steamboats and stagecoaches that preceded them, both the railroad lines and the railroad personnel had many different policies. On the Old Westchester Railroad in southeastern Pennsylvania, Black travelers could expect to be "handed into a corner by themselves, unless they happen to be acting in the capacity of nurses or servants"; but the Reading Railroad, which operated nearby, made no such distinctions. They had only "high fare and low price seats." On some railroads, at least one frequent traveler maintained, the racial discrimination encountered by Black passengers had nothing to do with railroad company regulations: "it was the conductors, and not the Company, . . . that make so much ado."[31]

Ironically, the color line was less of an issue on antebellum southern railroads. For one thing, passenger travel by rail was far less extensive in the South. Built largely to carry freight, the region's early railroads connected eastern port cities with cotton and tobacco fields further west. Most of the

NEGRO EXPULSION FROM RAILWAY CAR, PHILADELPHIA.

Engraving from *The Illustrated London News* from September 27, 1856, showing
a Black man being expelled from a railroad car in Philadelphia.

region's railroad lines were short and offered limited passenger service.[32] They
did, of course, carry enslaved Blacks, but such passengers had little opportunity
to either choose seats or register complaints about the conditions under which
they traveled, which varied according to the reason they were being moved.
Slaves who were transported south for resale often traveled in what was called
the "nigger car," or the "negro car," which usually consisted of little more
than a box car outfitted with a bench on each side, or even just a few bales

of hay. On routes where the Negro car was not likely to fill up, it also served as "the smoking car, and sometimes the baggage car."[33]

The Negro car and the luggage car were a natural combination, because Blacks and luggage both traditionally rode in front of the railroad's regular passenger cars. Nineteenth-century railroads put their baggage cars up front to serve as a buffer between the passengers and the soot, cinders, and smoke that trailed their wood- or coal-burning locomotives, a placement that also provided passengers with better protection in the event of a crash. Negro cars and Jim Crow cars were typically positioned in front of other passenger cars for the same reason.

Still, racial segregation was far from universal in regular passenger coaches on antebellum-era southern railroads. Although some railroads adopted regulations discouraging passengers from seating their enslaved servants in these coaches, these regulations were often honored only in the breach. Northern travelers were often surprised by the degree of integration on the trains. "The railroad compan[ies] advertise to take colored people only in second class trains; but servants seem to go with their masters everywhere." wrote Frederick Law Olmstead, who took an extended tour of the South in the 1850s. When he offered his seat to a white woman and her family, he added by way of example, he was startled to see her fill it with "a stout negro woman" before taking an adjoining seat. "The rest of her party . . . consisted of a white girl, probably her daughter, and a bright and very pretty mulatto girl," he noted, and the foursome traveled together like old friends. "They all talked and laughed together, and the girls munched confectionery out of the same paper, with a familiarity and closeness of intimacy that would have been noticed with astonishment, if not with manifest displeasure, in almost any chance company at the North."[34]

Free Black travelers were less common in the first-class cars. Such travelers were relatively rare, given that free Blacks could not move around the antebellum South with ease. Prohibited from entering some southern states, free Black travelers had to be prepared to produce papers to document their free status, and could be "treated as vagrants and arrested when traveling outside their county of residency"—especially if they could not provide "proof of 'honest employment.'"[35] When they did travel, they were often relegated to the Negro car. "Free persons of color," as one nineteenth-century visitor to the region observed, generally joined the slaves in "the first half of the foremost car . . . unless they are females travelling with their mistress, when they sit by her side."[36]

White southerners were perfectly happy to travel alongside Black slaves or servants, but elite Blacks were another matter. One Mississippi steamboat owner set aside two first-class cabins for some wealthy Blacks with whom he did business, who were of mixed race and light skin. But even these "special people" were not permitted to mingle with white passengers in his ship's saloon.[37] The doors in their cabins that led to the saloon were locked from the outside. If they wanted to mingle with other passengers, they had to step outside and join the ship's other colored passengers on deck.

JIM CROW MOVES SOUTH

After emancipation, struggles over segregated transportation were increasingly concentrated in the South. Northern Blacks emerged from the Civil War having already won significant victories against Jim Crow travel on both the railroads and streetcars, and they effectively used the Union's victory to press for equal rights on all common carriers. Founded in Syracuse, New York, in 1864, the National Equal Rights League (NERL) called for full citizenship as a just recompense for Black military service in the Civil War. The NERL was made up of numerous state branches that took on travel segregation in the courts. In more than a dozen northern states, by the 1880s Black activism, in combination with liberal sentiments nurtured by the Union victory, had helped secure the passage of state civil rights laws granting all citizens equal access to common carriers, public amusements, and a wide variety of other venues. The NERL also spearheaded a five-year campaign to secure federal protection for Black civil rights, which culminated with the passage of the short-lived Civil Rights Act of 1875, which guaranteed African Americans equal treatment in public transportation and public accommodations and service on juries. Undaunted, the Black northern equal rights struggle continued even after the Civil Rights Act was ruled unconstitutional in 1883. As federal support for Black civil rights ebbed, Black activists across the region renewed their campaigns for state-level civil rights laws, securing the passage of more than a dozen such laws during the 1880s (see Table 1).[38]

Like the Civil Rights Act of 1875, these laws promised Blacks equal access to common carriers and public accommodations, but none were entirely

TABLE 1. States Enacting Public Accommodations Statutes

State	Date statute(s) enacted
Massachusetts	1865, 1866, 1885
Rhode Island	1885
Connecticut	1884
New York	1873, 1881
New Jersey	1884
Pennsylvania	1867, 1881
District of Columbia	1863
Ohio	1884
Michigan	1885
Indiana	1885
Illinois	1885
Iowa	1857, 1873, 1884
Minnesota	1885
Nebraska	1885
Kansas	1874
Colorado	1885

Source: Franklin Johnson, *The Development of State Legislation concerning the Free Negro* (New York: Columbia University Press, 1919).

effective. As subsequent chapters of this book will show, informal forms of segregation and racial exclusion remained common in the northern states well into the twentieth century. Still, overt racial discrimination in the post-emancipation North became less of a problem over time. Indeed, some observers marveled over the change: "Thirty years ago it was at the risk of his life that a black man claimed public privileges; sentiment was worse here than it is now down South," Frank Webb Jr. reflected with reference to "freedom loving" northern states such as Indiana and Ohio in 1892. "Here we have no separate coaches, or separate theater seats, the hotels are free from colorphobia; a man can sit in the finest hotel in America and order what he likes, although, his skin be as black as the ink that prints this page."[39]

The regional change was no doubt all the more striking because colorphobia skyrocketed in the post-emancipation South. The region had little history of strict segregation, but with emancipation, all forms of public space became contested racial terrain. In cities and towns across the South, even sidewalks were not neutral territory. Prewar social etiquette had required Blacks to abandon their place on the sidewalk to any white person with whom they crossed paths, but once the war commenced, African Americans began to stand their ground. Eliza Frances Andrews, a white woman who came of age in Washington, Georgia, during the war was stunned when she had to step "out into the dusty road" to get around a "group of Yankees and negroes that filled up the sidewalk, but not one of them budged. It is the first time in my life that I have ever had to give up the sidewalk to a man, much less to negroes!"[40]

The high level of mobility among Blacks in the postwar South made such encounters still more fraught. Starting in the summer of 1865, thousands of freed people crowded near railway lines, stations, and depots. Some came in search of family members, or news about family members, while others were looking for work. The Union Army had seized many southern railroads even before the war ended—destroying and then rebuilding the South's railway networks in an effort to immobilize Confederate troops and destroy Confederate supply lines, while shoring up its own transportation network. As a result, the postwar South's railroads, while still not extensive, were at least operational. And when the War Department established the Bureau of Refugees, Freedmen, and Abandoned Lands (known as the Freedman's Bureau) to oversee the South's transition from slavery to freedom, it located many of its offices in recaptured southern railway junctions and depots, making such locations a major draw for displaced Black southerners. During its years of operation between 1866 and 1872, the Freedman's Bureau also facilitated Black mobility. It supplied free transportation passes on US military railroads to freed people who wished to reunite with their families and travel to places where they had secured work.[41]

While Black southerners had many good reasons for crowding the South's roads and railways, whites were unnerved, and sometimes mystified, by the unprecedented Black mobility of the postwar years. Even northern reporters were surprised to see the freed people leave their homes in search of a future somewhere else. They must be "intoxicated with their newly acquired freedom," a reporter for the *New York World* observed with disapproval in 1865. The two freedoms that most appealed to the Negro, suggested this writer, were "first, freedom from work; second, freedom to come and go where he will."[42] Not surprisingly, the new Black mobility was even more alarming to southern whites. Unaccustomed to Blacks traveling freely, and all too aware that their region's economy had long depended on a captive labor force, white southerners moved quickly to limit African American freedom of movement wherever they could.

But the laws and practices that structured the South's system of Jim Crow segregation did not emerge overnight. In the wake of the Confederacy's defeat, many white southerners were eager to restore antebellum racial hierarchies of all kinds, and might well have codified Jim Crow earlier, if permitted. Indeed, shortly after the Civil War several southern states enacted "Black codes" designed to resurrect slavery in all but name. These measures included statutes that codified the informal system of segregation that had long relegated many antebellum Black travelers to the Negro car. Passed in 1865, Florida's and Mississippi's Black codes made it illegal for "any negro, mulatto, or person of color . . . [to] intrude . . . into cars set apart for the exclusive accommodation of white people," and Texas's 1866 code required its railroads to set aside "one car for the special accommodation of Freedmen" on every passenger train. But these laws did not last long.[43]

President Andrew Johnson had been willing to let the South reconstruct itself largely on its own terms, but the Radical Republicans who rose to power in the congressional elections of 1866 proved unwilling to cede control of the South to unrepentant Confederate loyalists. These congressional leaders embraced what at the time was an almost equally unthinkable alternative: they made Blacks into citizens. The Civil Rights Act of 1866 declared "all persons born in the United States . . . to be citizens . . . without regard to any previous condition of slavery or involuntary servitude," and promised them the "full and equal benefit of all laws and proceedings for the security of person and property, as is enjoyed by white citizens." The Military Reconstruction Acts of 1867 required the southern states to adopt new constitutions providing suffrage rights for African American men as a condition of readmission to the Union. Adopted in 1868, the Fourteenth Amendment offered citizenship and "equal protection" under the law to all persons "born or naturalized in the United States." And the Fifteenth Amendment, which was enacted in 1870, secured federal protection for Black voting rights.

Elected with the support of the region's newly enfranchised freedmen, the state governments that emerged during the period known as Radical Reconstruction wrote new constitutions that repealed the Black codes. Their members included Black legislators who pressed hard for "equal laws, equal legislation and equal rights."[44] In some states this agenda even translated into new legislation requiring common carriers to provide equal accommodations for all. "The pretended legislature of Arkansas," an Indiana newspaper editor complained in 1868, passed a law prohibiting the operators of common carriers, hotels, and public amusements from making "any distinction on account of race, color, or previous condition of servitude." Violators were subject to a fine of no less than $500 and no more than $2,000.[45]

Both the fact of Reconstruction and these state-level civil rights laws lent support to Black civil rights struggles. In Mississippi, which did not adopt civil rights legislation, enfranchisement alone encouraged Negro travelers to "strain the bounds of prudent freedom." Whitelaw Reid, who traveled through the state in 1866, reported witnessing "a handsome negro sergeant" take a seat in the first railroad car and not even deign to reply to "a young blood" who told him, "Get out of this car, you black puppy." Asked again to move by another white man, who quietly explained that no negroes were allowed in the ladies' car, the sergeant held his ground. "Ise paid my passage, same as de rest of ye," he replied. "Ise goin' on Government business, and Ise got as good right to what I pays for as anybody else." He was the only Black man in the car when he took his brave stand, and he finally moved after the conductor threatened to have him "pitched off the train." But Reid heard reports of "other cases, where several [Black] soldiers were together, in which they stood their ground."[46]

Although the civil rights laws enacted by Reconstruction-era legislatures sought to put an end to discrimination in transportation, the impact of these laws varied greatly from state to state. In Georgia in 1870, African American legislators managed to pass a law requiring that "all common carriers of passengers for hire in the State of Georgia shall furnish like and equal accommodations for all persons, without distinction of race, color, or previous condition."[47] But Georgia's Reconstruction ended shortly thereafter, and the law was never enforced. Instead, the state became notorious as a place in which all Black travelers, including those who held first-class tickets, could expect to be "compelled to ride in the Freedmen's Cars."[48]

The restrictions that Blacks faced in Georgia were all the more striking because in South Carolina, Georgia's neighbor to the north, such segregation was far less common. In 1868 African American legislators there pushed through a bill banning racial discrimination in public accommodation. Republican rule in South Carolina lasted until 1876, giving the law some chance to take effect. As a result, notes historian James M. MacPherson, Black travelers in the Palmetto State "reportedly suffered less segregation" than in many other southern states.[49] "The Negroes . . . are permitted to, and frequently do ride in the first-class railway car and in street railways cars," South Carolina planter and poet Belton O'Neall Townsend wrote in the *Atlantic Monthly* in 1877. "This liberty at first encountered much opposition from the railroad conductors and white passengers, and led to several fights, expulsions, and lawsuits," he further explained. "But it is now so common as hardly to provoke remark." Whites there remained reluctant to sit beside Blacks not traveling in "the capacity of servants, nurse, etc.," so "if practical," they left "a wide space" around any such "intruders."[50] But race relations on South Carolina trains were otherwise cordial. Traveling through the state in 1885, Black journalist Thomas McCants Stewart was amazed to find that he could ride in "first-class cars on the railroads" without difficulty and could even stop in restaurants and "drink a glass of soda and be more politely waited upon than in some parts of New England."[51]

The impact of Arkansas civil rights law, however, was decidedly mixed. Reconstruction there lasted until 1874, but many of the state's former rulers returned to power well before then. Hopeful predictions that the civil rights bill adopted by the state's Republicans would transform race relations in the state proved unfounded. The same reporter who called Arkansas's new state government a "pretend legislature" insisted that the state's steamboat companies would most certainly go out of business as a result of the new law. Who would ride their boats once they could no longer "refuse to give a negro couple berths in the ladies' cabin, or seats at the table with white passengers [?]" Could they really expect "white stewards and cabin boys . . . to wait on Negro passengers?"[52] These questions proved moot. Arkansas steamboats remained segregated.[53] But the law does seem to have had an effect on the state's railroads, which were operating in compliance with its civil rights law by the 1880s—having "dropped early segregated arrangements."[54]

In short, as of the mid-1870s, segregation in southern transportation was neither uncommon nor universal. It was an inconsistent patchwork of law and custom that varied by state, within states, and by form of transport. And with the passage of the Civil Rights Act of 1875, which remained in effect until 1883, this patchwork became still more complicated. Widely dismissed as a dead letter, the new federal law was ignored in some states, but it did offer some federal protection to Blacks who wished to claim their civil rights in others. Reconstruction's last great civil rights measure, the law was pushed through Congress by Massachusetts senator Charles Sumner.

THE CIVIL RIGHTS ACT OF 1875

An abolitionist before the war and a leading Radical Republican after it, Charles Sumner was convinced that African Americans could not achieve full citizenship without the elimination of all discrimination against people of color. While most Republicans were content to have made "the Negro a voting citizen," Sumner was all too aware that Blacks could exercise few other civil rights. The "doors of the Senate Chamber were opened" to Black elected officials such as Louisiana's lieutenant governor Oscar J. Dunn, but even Dunn's position as an elected official did not keep him from "being denied access to a first-class railroad car in his own state."[55] Sumner believed that the Fourteenth Amendment's promise of equal justice under the law should prohibit such discrimination not only on common carriers but also on juries and in public schools, churches, public amusements, restaurants, and cemeteries. As early as 1870 he began lobbying for the passage of a supplemental civil rights bill designed to secure these rights for Blacks. "The right to vote will have no security until your rights in the public conveyances, hotels, and common schools are at last established," he told the National Convention of Colored Citizens when it met in Columbia, South Carolina, in 1871. "Discrimination . . . weakens all other rights."[56]

Sumner's position put him at odds with most white Republicans, who were willing to leave questions of social equality alone. By 1870 Sumner was increasingly alienated from his own party and had trouble getting most of his fellow congressmen to even consider the legislation he proposed. His civil rights bill had widespread support among Black voters and legislators but virtually no support outside the African American community. It languished in the Senate's Judiciary Committee until a year after the long-ailing Sumner died of a heart attack in 1874. Shamed into taking action by his death, his fellow Republicans passed a watered-down version of Sumner's bill in March 1875. Stripped of any prohibitions against discrimination in cemeteries, churches, or schools, the final bill promised "citizens of every race and color. . . . full and equal enjoyment of the accommodations, advantages, facilities, and privileges of inns, public conveyances on land or water, theaters, and other places of public amusement," and barred courts across the nation from disqualifying jurors "on account of race, color, or previous condition of servitude."[57]

Passed as "an act of posthumous glory to Charles Sumner," the final bill was meant to be little more than a symbolic gesture.[58] The act made discrimination a federal crime, subject to a $1,000 fine and a jail sentence of up to a year. It also permitted victims of discrimination to seek civil damages of $500. But Ulysses S. Grant's administration displayed no commitment to enforcing the new law. Grant made no public statement on the bill, and his attorney general, George H. Williams, issued no instructions regarding its enforcement. He did not even circulate copies of the new statute to the US district attorneys who were supposed to enforce it.[59]

Meanwhile, the law's numerous opponents insisted it was both unnecessary and unenforceable. Blacks "were happy and content in the sphere God had intended for them," maintained the *Charlotte Observer*, while the *New York Times* was confident that Black New Yorkers would "hardly deem it prudent to force themselves into first class hotels or restaurants."[60] Moreover, the *Times* added, the law could not change their status because it claimed constitutional power "beyond even what the amendments warrant.[51] "Our duty is to ignore the law," said a writer for the *Atlanta News*, who predicted the legislation would soon be overturned.[62]

But those who predicted that Blacks would not take advantage of the Civil Rights Act were sorely disappointed. Signed into law on March 1, 1875, it inspired legal complaints that soon had US district attorneys across the country scrambling to secure more information about the bill. "Please send me without delay a duly certified copy of the 'Civil Rights Bill' as it exists as a law," the US attorney for western Tennessee wrote to Attorney General Williams on March 4. Williams received similar requests from US attorneys in Chicago, Savannah, Raleigh, New Orleans, and San Francisco later that month, and still more after that.[63] "To invoke the civil rights law is becoming very fashionable," observed a reporter for the *New York Times* in 1879, noting with some disapproval that recent cases had included a colored clergyman who was refused refreshments in a Jersey City ice cream saloon.[64]

The *Times* never supported the legislation and did its best to trivialize the rights it protected, but African American litigants used the law to secure access to public accommodations that were increasingly crucial to Americans of all races. Chief among these accommodations were travel services, which would figure prominently in the civil rights cases inspired by the law. Travel segregation, as we have seen, was widely contested even before the passage of the bill. But both state and federal courts had proved to be inconsistent, at best, in their support for the rights of Black passengers. They would remain that way, even after the passage of Sumner's civil rights bill.

TRAVEL RIGHTS AND CIVIL RIGHTS

Even though courts throughout the United States generally agreed that common carriers were required to seat all passengers, they did not always rule out racial segregation. In *Day v. Owen* (1858), the Michigan Supreme Court ruled in favor of a steamboat company that had refused to let Black passenger William Howard Day purchase cabin accommodations. "The Court held that while a common carrier could not have refused to transport Day," explains legal scholar Marilyn Hall Mitchell, "it could require him to conform to the reasonable regulations of the vessel. Regulations were reasonable if 'calculated to render the transportation most comfortable and least annoying to passengers generally.'"[65] Decided in the wake of *Dred Scott v. Sanford* (1857), a US Supreme Court decision that famously had ruled that Blacks were not citizens and "had no rights which the white man was bound to respect," the *Day* decision was hailed by proslavery observers as additional proof that Negroes were "not citizens of the United States, either at the North or the South."[66]

Black citizenship, once achieved, did not supply African American passengers with any guarantee of equal accommodations. In 1867, for example, the Pennsylvania Supreme Court overturned African American schoolteacher Mary Miles's lower-court victory against travel discrimination. Miles had sued the West Chester and Philadelphia Railroad for trespass after one of its conductors had expelled her from a train for refusing to move from her seat in the middle of the car to another seat in an area "set aside for people of her race." She won her suit and $5 in damages only to see the judgment overturned on appeal in a decision that held that common carriers had the right to divide up passengers by race.

In *West Chester and Philadelphia Railroad v. Miles,* Pennsylvania Supreme Court chief justice Daniel Agnew maintained that Miles had no real cause of action. The seat that she "was directed to take was . . . not inferior in any of these respects to the one she was directed to leave, so there were no damages to recover." The only legal question posed by the case was: Did common carriers have the right to "separate passengers . . . to preserve order?" Agnew had no doubt they did and cited the common practice of dividing passengers by gender as the most obvious example. "The ladies' car is known upon every well-regulated railroad, implies no loss of equal right on the part of the excluded sex, and its propriety is doubted by none." Railroad segregation regulations, likewise, aimed to "'prevent contacts . . . arising from natural . . . repugnancies, which are liable to breed disturbances by promiscuous sitting.'"[67]

Issued in November 1867, the court's ruling had little impact in Pennsylvania, which on March 22 that year—more than six months earlier—had enacted a new civil rights law barring its railroads from making "any distinction between passengers on the basis of race or color." In issuing his ruling, Agnew noted that it addressed the law only as "it stood when this case first arose."[68] But his judgment, which would be cited in *Plessy*, underscored that the law of common carriers did not prohibit racial segregation.

The US Supreme Court's ruling in *Hall v. DeCuir* (1877) offered even less support for Black travelers. The case originated with a boat trip taken by Josephine DeCuir, a Louisiana Creole whose husband, Antoine DeCuir, died in 1871. The DeCuirs had once been among the richest free Blacks in the United States. As owners of a vast plantation in south central Louisiana and more than 112 slaves, the DeCuirs were members of the antebellum era's free Black elite and had always been able to secure a first-class cabin on steamboats that chugged up the Mississippi River from New Orleans—making a convenient stop in Hermitage, the Louisiana town closest to the DeCuirs' Pointe Coupee Parish plantation, before proceeding on to Vicksburg, Mississippi. But by 1872 DeCuir was a widow, had lost her slaves to emancipation, and had been forced to auction off much of her plantation. Her reduced circumstances did not prevent her from booking her usual five-dollar first-class ticket aboard the steamship *Governor Allen* when it came time for her to travel home from New Orleans to Pointe Coupee that summer. When she boarded, the ship's steward refused to let her take a berth in one of the first-class cabins on the upper deck, which, he maintained, were "specially set aside for white persons." Instead, he directed her to a berth in the lower cabins. Usually located on the ship's steerage deck, and ticketed at discounted rates, such cabins were distinctly second-class accommodations. On the *Governor Allen* the cabins in what was known as the "colored bureau" were windowless and accommodated men and women alike. Whereas the boat's upper-deck cabins cost $5, those on the lower deck cost only $3.

DeCuir refused to move. She "passed the night . . . sitting in a chair in what is known as the recess back of the upper cabin"—a corridor used primarily by nursemaids and children. Once home, she sued the ship's owner, John C. Benson. DeCuir won her suit at trial and prevailed again when Benson took the suit to the Louisiana Supreme Court. In their ruling in DeCuir's favor, the justices pointedly noted that the state's 1869 civil rights law was "enacted solely to protect the newly enfranchised citizens of the United States, within the limits of Louisiana, from prejudice against them."[69] But the case did not end there. Although John C. Benson died while the case was still in court, his executor, Eliza Jane Hall, was unwilling to accept DeCuir's victory or to pay the $1,000 in damages mandated by the court. Instead, Hall filed an appeal with the US Supreme Court, which reversed the decision.

In *Hall v. DeCuir* (1877) the US Supreme Court not only rejected DeCuir's suit, it maintained that she had no grounds for filing suit. The decision did not engage the details of her case. Instead it held that no state law could outlaw racial segregation on interstate common carriers, because only Congress had the right to regulate interstate commerce. Although Josephine DeCuir's travels had taken place entirely within Louisiana, Thomas Waite, the Court's Chief Justice, maintained that her journey should still be seen through the prism of interstate commerce. Given that "the river Mississippi passes through or along the borders of ten different States," he explained, "its regulation is clearly a matter of national concern. If each State was at liberty to regulate the conduct of carriers while within its jurisdiction, the confusion likely to follow could not but be productive of great inconvenience and unnecessary hardship." Accordingly, "to the extent that it requires those engaged in the transportation of passengers among the States to carry colored passengers in Louisiana in the same cabin with whites . . . , Louisiana's statute Civil Rights Law is unconstitutional and void."[70]

DeCuir's boat trip up the Mississippi had taken place before the passage of the Civil Rights Act of 1875, so the new law offered her no protection. But the Court's decision in her case did not bode well for the survival of that legislation. Waite maintained that "if the public good" required legislation designed to protect the equal rights of passengers on common carriers, such legislation would have "come from Congress and not from the States." His ruling did not acknowledge that Congress had recently passed such legislation. Instead, it insisted "that inaction by Congress . . . is equivalent to a declaration that inter-state commerce shall remain free and untrammeled," and that "there was and is not any law of Congress which forbids such a carrier from providing separate apartments for his passengers."[71] As legal scholar Barbara Welke notes, the *Hall v. DeCuir* verdict's steadfast "insistence that Congress had not acted is somewhat peculiar," and suggests that the Supreme Court's Justices were maintaining a "studied distance" from the Civil Rights Act, "which the Court would later rule unconstitutional."[72]

Hall v. DeCuir all but endorsed segregation. Although the Court's decision rejected Louisiana's civil rights statute solely on account of "its effect upon foreign and inter-state commerce" and claimed to express "no opinion as to its validity in any other respect," the Justices made little attempt to hide their hostility toward any legislation that might interfere with the right of common carriers to separate their passengers by race. "Irrespective of the decisions of the State court," Waite mused in delivering the Court's verdict, "it might well be doubted whether the State statute in question does prohibit a steamer carrying passengers from having and maintaining separate cabins and eating-saloons for white and colored passengers, and whether the denial to a colored female of a passage in the cabin assigned to white female passengers is a denial of equal rights and privileges . . . provided the applicant was offered a passage in the lower cabin, with equally convenient accommodation." Justice Nathan Clifford, who offered a concurring opinion, made the same point in more emphatic terms. "Substantial equality of right is the law of the State and of the United States," he proclaimed, "but equality does not mean identity, as in the nature of things identity in the accommodation afforded to passengers, whether colored or white, is impossible . . . the laws of the United States do not require the master of a steamer to put persons in the same apartment who would be repulsive or disagreeable to each other."[73]

Both before and after the passage of the Civil Rights Law of 1875, judicial decisions about segregated transportation were far from uniform. Still, even when African American litigants prevailed in court, their victories were fragile and often came within the context of judicial rulings that underscored that racial segregation might well be legal—under the right circumstances. A case in point is Anna Williams's Illinois Supreme Court victory *Chicago & Northwestern Railway Company v. Anna Williams* (1870). Williams, a Black woman, had sued the Chicago & Northwestern Railroad Company after one of its conductors refused to allow her to ride in the ladies' car. Williams was successful in her circuit court suit and in defeating the appeal launched by the railroad to overturn her victory. But her favorable ruling was hardly a resounding triumph for Black civil rights. In ruling against the railroad, the court held that while racially segregated seating "might not be unreasonable . . . under some circumstances," in this particular instance the Chicago & Northwestern Railroad Company had a regulation separating passengers by gender, and no regulation separating passengers by race, making Williams's exclusion unreasonable.[74]

THE PROBLEM OF THE LADIES' CAR

As legal scholar Barbara Welke has observed, passengers who were both Black and female posed a particular challenge for the nineteenth-century judges who presided over travel discrimination cases, because on many common carriers, segregating the races was not just a matter of drawing a color line. "Railroads and steamboats had long divided passengers by class and sex to create privileged enclaves for women," she notes. Usually reserved for the exclusive use of "women traveling first-class and their escorts," ladies' cars were difficult to segregate because the law of common carriers extended the same gender privileges to Black women who could afford to pay for first-class seats as it did to white women. Both "the law and their own financial interest led carriers to allow respectable women of color to ride in first-class ladies' accommodations."[75] And when carriers did not, such passengers could sue, as Anna Williams did.

At issue in cases such as Williams's was not just race but the gendered parameters of first-class travel. By the second half of the nineteenth century, ladies' cars were increasingly common and all but synonymous with first-class travel. Modeled on the "ladies' cabins" on steamships, which had berths set aside for women, ladies' cars were first introduced in the antebellum era alongside another innovation in the technology of railroad passenger transportation: sleeping coaches. Initially these were little more than nonsmoking sleeping compartments set aside for women. But cars that offered female travelers refuge from the smoking and rowdy male passengers soon became popular among daytime travelers also.

Described by one appreciative traveler as "always the freshest car and most comfortable in the train," ladies' cars came into widespread use at a time when many trains pulled no more than two passenger cars, one of which was always a smoking car.[76] Open to female travelers and men who traveled with them, ladies' cars included amenities such as padded seats and water closets—and sometimes (but not always) required a first-class ticket. They were particularly popular in the South, where prior to the Civil War ladies had not customarily traveled "without a male escort, even when two or three ladies were in company."[77] The ladies' cars were designed as a safe space where even solo female travelers could expect to feel perfectly at ease—as they were supervised by conductors who were careful to "allow in it . . . only such men as will be agreeable to its fair inmates." Impressed by the gentility of the ladies' car, one English traveler observed that such cars made it possible for "modest girls" to travel "for hundreds of miles as undisturbed by rudeness as if they were at home."[78]

The security of the ladies' car was just as appealing to Black women as it was to white women—if not more so. Women, Black or white, who could afford train tickets tended to be middle class or elite, and ill-prepared to deal with the rough-and-tumble conditions in the smoking cars, where they were likely to be assailed by not only tobacco smoke, but snuff, spit, vulgar language, drunken revels, and unwanted male attention.

Traveling home from Oberlin College to Memphis, Mary Church, now sixteen, ended up in a Jim Crow car for the first time in her life, and found it terrifying. The year was either 1879 or 1880, and Church had a first-class ticket, which was supposed to supply her with first-class accommodations throughout her journey. But she was no longer traveling under the protection of her father, and when she changed trains in Bowling Green, Tennessee, she could not protect herself when the conductor refused to accept her ticket. "This is first class enough for you," he said as he directed her to a seat in what was known as a combination car—the front of which was used as a smoker for white men, while the rear accommodated Black passengers of both sexes. Church seated herself reluctantly and grew increasingly alarmed as her journey progressed. Night fell shortly after the train pulled out of Bowling Green, and the Jim Crow section of her car emptied out, leaving her alone and "at the mercy of the conductor or any man who entered." "As young as I was," she later recalled, "I had heard about the awful tragedies which had over taken colored girls who had been obliged to travel on these cars late at night."[79] Increasingly frantic with fear, she begged the conductor to let her move to the ladies' car. When that did not work, she threatened to get off at the next stop and wire her father, who would surely sue the railroad for making

Mary Church.

his daughter spend the night alone in a Jim Crow car—at which point the conductor finally let her move.

Other Black women were equally determined to ride in the ladies' cars and equally assertive in securing their rights—and often sued when they were prevented from traveling in those cars. For much of the nineteenth century, Black women filed "the vast majority" of suits challenging racial segregation on common carriers.[80] The cases they filed proliferated only after the passage of the Civil Rights Act of 1875—which reinforced the status of their claims. The late 1870s and early 1880s saw Black women win some previously unthinkable court victories affirming their rights to travel in the ladies' car. Among them was Millie Anderson, who sued the management of Houston & Texas Central Railway for denying her admission to the ladies' car on one of their company's trains in 1877. In his charge to the jury, the federal district court judge made it clear that so long as there was only one ladies' car on any given train, railway officials had to admit "female colored citizens" to that car. Had there been two such cars, he noted, both of which "afforded the same advantages, comforts and conveniences," railroad officials might not be liable. But they would have had to have offered Anderson a seat in a car as "fit and appropriate for white female citizens as for female colored citizens."[81]

Railroads were not prepared to attach more than one ladies' car to each train, so they did everything they could to resist such judgments. When Jane Brown sued the Memphis & Charleston Railroad after being ejected from a ladies' car in Corinth, Tennessee, in 1880, the railroad's lawyer insisted that her character rather than her color was what had made her unwelcome. She was "a notorious courtesan, addicted to lascivious and profane conversation and immodest deportment in public places," he maintained. What was the point of having a ladies' car "if whores and all other classes of improper characters, can gain admittance there?" D. J. Hammond, the Tennessee federal district court judge who presided over the case, made short work of this argument, pointing out that if every woman who purchased a railroad ticket had to go "on trial for her virtue with the conductor as judge . . . [it] would practically exclude all sensitive and sensible women from traveling at all, no matter how virtuous, for fear that they might be put into or unconsciously occupy the wrong car." He also charged the jury who heard the case to treat Jane Brown exactly as they would "a white woman excluded under similar circumstances."[82] The jury in *Brown v. Memphis* evidently took this charge to heart: they ruled in Brown's favor and awarded her $3,000 in damages.

Black women were able to secure victories like Brown's only for a limited time, and only if they traveled solo, as the legal liabilities associated with the ladies' car soon pushed the railroads to divide passengers by race rather than gender. And while white women were free to travel with their husbands or other male companions, Black women never had that freedom. African American men who attempted to ride in the ladies' car took their life in their own hands. Whereas railroad officials often took the lead in refusing to let Black women sit in their ladies' cars, Black male travelers who ventured into the ladies' car often faced mob violence.[83] In Georgia, for instance, the railroad conductors did not even need to eject Black male passengers from the ladies' car. They relied on white men at the railroad station or on the train to convince any Black man who seated himself in their ladies' cars that "the coach set apart for them was most comfortable."[84]

Among the Black men who learned this lesson was Dr. Walker J. Roberts, who made the mistake of seating himself, his brother, and his brother's wife in a ladies' car on a train departing from Atlanta, Georgia, in the spring of 1876. The railroad conductor gave him no trouble, but before his train even left Atlanta someone on it used a telegraph to summon armed men to the train's next stop—"negroes were in the ladies' coach" was the report. Twenty-four miles later, in Conyers, Georgia, Roberts and his travel companions were confronted by a white delegation that Roberts described as "a crowd of gorillas, with two or three six shoot Colters [pistols] buckled around their waists." Not surprisingly, they successfully forced Roberts and his travel companions out of the car.[85]

Local law enforcement authorities also helped the railroads eject Black men from first-class cars, leading many to wonder whether any state authority would enforce their rights. In 1877 William Jenkins was among a group of "several young ladies and gentlemen" who boarded a train in Montgomery, Alabama, bound for Selma. The group took seats in the train's first-class car "because they held first class tickets and could purchase no other," which convinced them they had "a right to ride in what was called the first class coach." But as soon as they were seated, they were "ordered into the 'Jim Crow Car,' which was a filthy hole full of bad tobacco smoke, and where men . . . are allowed to enter, drink whiskey, and smoke with impunity. A dumb brute would not have ridden in it if he had been given his choice." Not surprisingly, they "hesitated about changing our seats," but had little choice about doing so once "the conductor went out and soon returned with a great burly policeman," who stood by as Jenkins and his companions were hauled out of the first-class car by "two ruffians who were in the employ of the railroad company." When Warren Logan, who taught at Tuskegee Institute, refused to leave, he was "immediately assaulted by this great Colossus of a policeman." Jenkins was stunned by the incident. He described it in a letter to the *New York Freeman* in which he asked, "If the police officers who are supposed to protect us become the assailants, what are we to do?"[86]

The courts offered no help. The legal paternalism that allowed Black women some access to ladies' cars was waning by the late 1870s, and it had never protected the rights of Black men. African American men who ventured into the ladies' cars were subject to the kinds of violence that ensured that their misadventures rarely even ended up in the courts. And when they did, the courts were unsympathetic. In 1879, for example, Sallie J. Robinson and her nephew Joseph Robinson were refused entrance to a ladies' car in Grand Junction, Tennessee, by a conductor who asked: "Why do you people try to force yourselves into that car?" Sallie Robinson and her husband, Richard Robinson, were outraged and launched a civil rights suit against the Memphis and Charleston Railroad in federal court, but the case went nowhere.

The conductor managed to convince the court that it had all been a mis-understanding: The only reason he had been reluctant to let Mrs. Robinson enter the ladies' car, he explained, was that he initially assumed that her nephew, who was described in the trial transcript as "a young man of light complexion, light hair and light eyes," was a white man, and that Mrs. Robinson must therefore be "an improper character"—by which he meant a prostitute. In his experience, the conductor explained, "when young men travelled company with colored women it was for illicit purposes." It was an honest mistake, the conductor insisted, further arguing that once he talked to Joseph Robinson and found out that Mrs. Robinson was Joseph Robinson's aunt, he had allowed the couple to move to the ladies' car at the next stop. Robinson's attorney objected without success to much of the conductor's testimony, noting that the conductor's false assumptions provided "no excuse or justification of the defendant," but to no avail. In his instructions to the jury, the judge told them they could consider "the conductor's *bona fide* reason for excluding the woman from the car," in evaluating "the liability of the company."[87] The Robinsons lost their suit, and were equally unsuccessful on appeal.

THE CIVIL RIGHTS CASES

The Robinsons never got a fair hearing. Their appeal was one of the five cases the US Supreme Court selected to review in the momentous *Civil Rights Cases* suit of 1883, which ruled the Civil Rights Act of 1875 unconstitutional. The five cases were consolidated to resolve persistent legal debates over the constitutionality of the Civil Rights Act, and the discussion they inspired focused on the question of whether Congress had the authority to prohibit racial discrimination. In a decision that both nullified the Civil Rights Act of 1875 and greatly limited the federal protection offered Blacks by the Thirteenth and Fourteenth Amendments, the Court held that the Thirteenth Amendment did apply to private individuals, but only insofar as it prohibited people from owning slaves: it did not prohibit discriminatory behavior. And the Fourteenth Amendment's guarantees of national citizenship were likewise very narrow. The amendment prohibited only the denial of equal protection by the state. "Individual invasion of individual rights is not the subject-matter of the amendment," declared the Court: Congress had no power to address private acts of discrimination.[88]

The Court's decision was hailed by white southerners as "a Triumph of Law and Sense." In Atlanta, where the Supreme Court's verdict rebuffed a challenge to segregated seating in the city's opera house, the decision was announced onstage during the final act of a performance by Haverly's United Mastodon Minstrels—a blackface troupe. It was greeted by the most hearty and prolonged "thunder of applause . . . [ever] heard in the walls of the opera house." Only the "dusky inhabitants of the colored gallery" abstained, offering "not a note of applause." They sat in "solemn rows . . . silent and smitten with dumbfounded consternation."[89]

The reaction in the "colored gallery" was not unwarranted. The Court's decision further eroded federal protection for Black civil rights at a time when even northern Republicans no longer supported such protection. An editorial in the *New York Tribune* accurately predicted that the Supreme Court's decision was likely to be met with "the approval of a very large majority of Republicans." Most Republicans, the *Tribune*'s editors added, had never supported the civil rights bill, "not because they wish to see the colored people denied any part of their rights, but because they wish to see those rights fully enjoyed without controversy in every part of the land." Only a "change in public sentiment," the *Tribune* opined, could truly bring that about. While the *Tribune*'s editors were willing to wait for "the decay and obliteration of a prejudice which denies privileges to the colored man simply because he is colored," those on the receiving end of that prejudice were not.[90] African Americans had little reason to believe that such prejudices were declining. And now the Court had, as Frederick Douglass put it, left them "naked and defenseless against . . . malignant, vulgar, and pitiless prejudice."[91]

Both Black leaders and US Supreme Court Justice John Marshall Harlan, who dissented from the Court's decision, saw the right to travel freely as one of the most important of the Black civil rights left unprotected in the wake of the Supreme Court's nullification of the Civil Rights Act of 1875. Citing the eminent English legal theorist William Blackstone, Harlan wrote: "Personal liberty consists in the power of locomotion, of changing situation, or removing one's person to whatever places one's own inclination may direct, without restraint unless by due course of law. But of what value is this right of locomotion if it may be clogged by such burdens as Congress intended by the act of 1875 to remove?"[92]

Harlan found these burdens all the more egregious because he believed that the Court had sacrificed the "substance and spirit of the recent amendments of the Constitution to a subtle and ingenious verbal criticism." Railroads were "public highways," the use of which was no different from the right to "use the public streets of a city or a town, or a turnpike road, or a public market, or a post office." Whatever limits the Court chose to place on federal power over the states, Congress most certainly had the right to regulate the rights of its citizens "in public conveyances passing from one State to another." Yet the Court ignored Congress's well-established power to regulate interstate commerce when it decided for the railroad in *Robinson and Wife v. Memphis & Charleston Railroad Company.* Mrs. Robinson had purchased "a railroad ticket entitling her to be carried from Grand Junction, Tennessee, to Lynchburg, Virginia." Surely the Act of 1875 was at the very least applicable to "commerce between the States?"[93]

Frederick Douglass, who denounced the decision in one of the many indignant mass meetings held in Black communities across the United States after the Court's ruling, did not take up the constitutional issues it raised, which he saw as a "question for lawyers." But like Harlan, Douglass saw the decision as a "calamity" for Blacks. The Court's ruling, he maintained, was an embarrassment to all Americans insofar as it gave "a South Carolina, or a Mississippi, Railroad Conductor, more power than it gives to the National Government. . . . It gives to a hotel-keeper who may, from a prejudice born of the rebellion, wish to turn. . . . [a man's wife] out at midnight into the darkness of the storm, power to compel her to go." Because the law eliminated federal remedies for private acts of discrimination, Douglass suggested, even white women were compromised by its passage. Their rights, too, were no longer protected "by law, but solely by the accident of . . . color."[94]

The outrage and alarm that Douglass expressed were widely shared. T. Thomas Fortune, the editor of the *New York Globe,* a leading Black weekly, lamented, "The colored people of the United States feel to-day as if they had been baptized in ice water." The AME bishop Henry McNeal Turner maintained that the decision "absolved the negro's allegiance to the federal government" by making "the American flag to him a rag of contempt instead of a symbol of liberty."[95]

In response to the ruling, many ordinary African Americans rallied to express their opposition. Black communities from "Maine to Florida" held indignation meetings to protest the Court's decision and discuss what to do next, and African American newspapers were "flooded" with letters on the subject.[96] The *New York Globe* reported that it had received more letters about the *Civil Rights Cases* verdict than it could possibly publish. "We have really been paralyzed by the abundance of strong, manly protests and apprehension for the future which has reached us in the form of correspondence," its editors noted regretfully just days after the Supreme Court's decision was announced.[97]

Even as they mourned and protested the Court's decision, Blacks across the United States also scrambled to figure out how to secure protection for their civil rights in the wake of the Court's decision. Largely unenforced, the Civil Rights Act may have been a dead letter, but its symbolic importance could not be discounted—Frederick Douglass mourned the loss of an act that "though dead, did speak."[98] Once the Supreme Court struck down federal protection for civil rights, what legal means did African Americans have left to even seek such rights? "The Nation having failed the states will be appealed to, and not in vain," predicted the *People's Advocate*. This prediction proved accurate in many northern states, where the mid-1880s saw African Americans and their allies replace the Civil Rights Act of 1875 with new state laws protecting Black civil rights, but in the South such protections were impossible to secure.[99] Issued at a time when poll taxes and paramilitary violence against Black voters had begun to reduce the Black vote throughout the region, the Supreme Court's decision in *Civil Rights Cases* empowered southern whites to repeal state civil rights laws.

South Carolina legislators began to debate repealing their state's civil rights act as early as November 1883, although they did not take action at that time, largely for fear that an immediate repeal would make a bad impression on northern whites. Such legislation, one low-country newspaper predicted, "would probably create a strong hostile sentiment towards the State which would injuriously affect the chances of the Democracy in the Presidential campaign." Instead, the law, which was by then largely unenforced, was quietly repealed in 1889.[100]

In contemplating their status in southern states with no civil rights laws, Blacks had to ask, "What then, with this Act declared to be unconstitutional and void, is our condition?" Without additional federal protection, African Americans were "left to the common law, the [Civil Rights] Act of 1866, . . . [and] the Thirteenth Amendment," noted John Mercer Langston, an African American leader and a former Virginia congressman who insisted that such laws could still protect Blacks if they could secure the full support of the Republican Party. "We are not civil nondescripts. We are not quasi-foreigners. We are complete citizens entitled to the full measure of privileges and immunities as such." But Langston's bravado was fragile. He was all too aware that the Democratic Party supported no such interpretation of Black civil rights.[101]

So, too, was North Carolina congressman James E. O'Hara—one of the two remaining African American elected officials serving in the US House of Representatives in 1883. A man of mixed-race origins and West Indian descent, O'Hara was born in New York City in 1844 and moved to North Carolina in 1862. After training as a legal apprentice, he was admitted to the bar in the early 1870s and became an active member of the Republican Party. He ran for Congress twice before finally being elected to represent North Carolina's second congressional district in 1882.[102] Known among whites as "mulatto with cheek a plenty," O'Hara had celebrated the passage of the Civil Rights Act by "personally integrating that saloon of the famous steamboat, the *Cotton Planter*."[103] Elected to Congress a matter of months before a ruling in *Civil Rights Cases*, he continued to support equal rights for Blacks, but he faced an uphill struggle when it came to representing Black interests in a nearly all-white House with a Democratic majority. He nonetheless made a brave attempt to counter the nullification of the Civil Rights Act of 1875 during the first session of Congress in 1884 by introducing a resolution calling for the passage of another constitutional amendment to protect Black civil rights.[104]

Not surprisingly, his proposal went nowhere. A man not easily defeated, O'Hara then attempted to write similar protections into a bill concerning interstate commerce. First proposed in 1884, the Interstate Commerce Act of 1887 created a federal Interstate Commerce Commission (ICC) designed to regulate the interstate activities of railroads and other common carriers. It was created at a time when the railroads were very unpopular, especially among western farmers who believed that the railroads were charging them exorbitant rates for handling and transporting crops and other agricultural products. The ICC was charged with using the federal government's constitutionally mandated power over interstate commerce to eliminate discrimination and other forms of unfairness in the freight rates charged by railroads. O'Hara complicated the issue at hand by proposing an amendment to the bill that addressed other forms of discrimination.

James O'Hara.

On December 16, 1884, during a dry discussion of the exact wording of the bill and whether the ICC should be empowered to regulate pipelines and waterways as well as railroads, O'Hara interrupted to propose an amendment that would ensure that all interstate passengers were assigned accommodations according to the purchase price of their tickets. The draft of the bill then under discussion opened with a sentence specifying that all railroad charges "shall be reasonable," to which O'Hara suggested inserting the additional sentence: "And any person or persons having purchased a ticket to be conveyed from one State to another, or paid the required fare, shall receive the same treatment and be afforded equal facilities and accommodations as are furnished all other persons holding tickets of the same class without discrimination."[105]

In introducing his amendment, O'Hara noted with some sarcasm that Congress had already provided for the "dumb brutes" transported by the railroads with legislation requiring carriers that shipped animals to stop at least once a day to tend to the "rest, care and feeding" of such cargo. Surely it could protect railroad passengers as well as freight? No one could deny the "constitutional right" of Congress to regulate interstate transportation, he emphasized, making indirect reference to the Supreme Court's recent decision in

Civil Rights Cases. Congress had not only the right but the "imperative duty" to protect all interstate passengers, O'Hara maintained.[106]

O'Hara's amendment inspired limited enthusiasm except from South Carolina's Robert Smalls—Congress's only other Black representative. One Texas congressman suggested that it not even be considered on the grounds that "the subject of transportation of persons has never been considered by the committee."[107] When that maneuver failed, other southern congressmen rallied to strip O'Hara's amendment of any meaning. Georgia congressman Charles R. Crisp proposed an amendment of his own designed to make sure that the reworded bill would not interfere with racial segregation on the railroads in his state. The bill, he suggested, should also contain a sentence specifying, "Nothing in this act contained shall be so construed to prevent any railroad company from providing separate accommodations for white and colored persons."[108] When this disingenuous proposition was rejected, other members offered a series of modifications to O'Hara's language that had a similar effect. The final version of the bill contained an all but incomprehensible provision banning the railroad from charging "any person or persons a greater or less compensation for any service rendered, or to be rendered, in the transportation of passengers or property" and requiring "like and contemporaneous service in the transportation of a like kind of traffic under substantially similar circumstances and conditions." The Act also deferred to the concerns expressed by southern politicians such as Congressmen Crisp by underscoring that none of its provisions applied "to the transportation of passengers or property . . . wholly within one State."[109]

Deeply disappointed, O'Hara did not even vote for the final bill. But his legislative intervention had an enduring impact. Rather than regulating just railroad freight transportation and rates, the Interstate Commerce Commission was given the power to regulate the railroads' (and later, other common carriers') transportation of passengers. Despite stringent congressional efforts to avoid any clearly worded admission that the ICC might regulate racial discrimination, the commission would in fact become an important, if often disappointing, forum for complaints about travel discrimination. It began hearing complaints about racial discrimination on common carriers as early as 1887, and would continue doing so until the passage of the Civil Rights Act in 1964.

Admittedly, the ICC did little to eradicate discrimination. Especially during its early years, it steadfastly held that segregation did not violate the Interstate

Commerce Act so long as the color line was maintained "without disadvantage to either race." In fact, as historian Catherine Barnes notes, its rulings on this issue may well have "promoted Jim Crow transit" by suggesting "that Jim Crow laws could be adopted without risk of federal disapproval."[110] Even when the agency's commissioners identified cases of racial discrimination that violated the Interstate Commerce Act, their rulings had no effect. The ICC was a regulatory agency with a small staff and had no mechanism to enforce its rulings and regulations.

But the ICC nonetheless supplied some support to the long Black struggle against travel segregation. Throughout the agency's history, its commissioners were far more receptive to complaints about unequal travel conditions than were southern state courts, and they repeatedly ruled that Blacks could be assigned "to separate cars" only on "equal terms." These rulings were neither honored nor enforced, but they did help sustain African Americans' hopes of eventually securing a legal remedy to at least some forms of travel segregation.

LEGALIZING SEGREGATION: THE SEPARATE CAR LAWS

By the 1880s southern lawmakers were eager to pass legislation requiring racial segregation on the railroads. Although legally obliged to provide first-class ticket holders with first-class seats, the railroads were reluctant to add additional first-class cars for Black passengers. But with no federal protection for Black civil rights in place, the southern states were finally free to force the issue by enacting laws that made such arrangements mandatory. Tennessee led the way with a "separate car law" passed in 1881, a time when the Civil Rights Act of 1875 was at least theoretically still in effect but widely regarded as doomed.

Ineffectual or not, the federal law was notably unpopular with the Democratic legislators in Tennessee, who displayed their defiance to it less than a month after the act took effect by passing a law that abolished their state's common-law rights of equal access to transportation and public accommodations. At the crossroads of several of the South's largest rail networks, Tennessee was also home to a large Black middle class, whose refusal to accept second-class accommodations in the railroads' smoking cars clearly galled state legislators. "While the state legislature had no power to take away the rights granted by the federal act," the legal scholar Kenneth Mack explains, it could and did express its displeasure with the legislation by removing "any parallel rights that its black citizens might enjoy under state law."[111] Its 1881 legislation had a similar goal.

Tennessee's groundbreaking separate car act was developed after the state legislature's four Black Republicans led a protracted but ultimately unsuccessful campaign to secure equal accommodations for Blacks on the state's railroads. First they tried to repeal the law abolishing their common-law rights, and when that failed, they introduced "a bill that would have banned racial discrimination on Tennessee railroads." White legislators rejected this bill and proposed, by way of compromise, a new bill calling for separate but equal railroad cars. Entitled "An Act to prevent discrimination by railroad companies among passengers who are charged and paying first class passage," the bill addressed African American complaints about discrimination on the railroads by requiring the railroads to "furnish separate cars, or portions of cars cut off by partition walls, in which all colored passengers who shall pay first-class rates of fare, may have the privilege to enter and occupy." It also specified that the separate cars "be kept in good repair," "have the same conveniences," and be "subject to the same rules governing other first-class cars, preventing smoking and obscene language."[112] This was the nation's first separate but equal law, and it sailed through Tennessee's legislature—opposed only by its Black members.

Ambiguously worded, the law required the railroads to supply separate first-class cars for Black passengers, who were offered the privilege of riding in them, although they were not explicitly required to do so. But the segregation it suggested seems to have been mandatory rather than optional, and there is little evidence to suggest that the bill had any positive effect on the level of service offered to Blacks by the railroads.[113] Two years after it took effect, one traveler who complained about the treatment of Black passengers on southern railroads noted that on the trains between Nashville and New Orleans, Blacks were routinely "jammed into one coach," while whites on the same route were offered several [coaches] . . . and a Pullman Palace Sleeper."[114] That same year Ida B. Wells, who would later become a famous anti-lynching activist, was thrown out of the ladies' car on a Tennessee train on two different occasions. In neither instance did the train she boarded provide any first-class accommodations for Blacks.

Instead, on both trains Wells, who was then a young schoolteacher, was directed to the smoking car.

When Wells sued, Tennessee's courts made no reference to the egalitarian provisions in their state's 1881 separate car law in reviewing her suit. She won a fleeting victory in one of Tennessee's county courts. Judge James O. Pierce, the ex-Union soldier who reviewed her case, concluded that Wells was "a person of lady-like appearance and deportment, a school teacher, and one who might be expected to object to traveling in the company of rough or boisterous men, smokers and drunkards."[115] But when the railroad appealed Wells's victory, the Supreme Court of Tennessee dismissed Pierce's concerns. Its 1887 decision ignored conditions on cars, and instead attacked Wells. Abandoning the common-law tradition of the ladies' car in favor of the segregationist principles that animated the state's separate car law, the court insisted that the rear car was set aside for "white ladies and their gentleman attendants." Issued at a time when white southerners were becoming increasingly committed to segregation, the court's ruling accused Wells of filing suit only to "harass" the railroad company. Her "persistence" in the case, the court concluded, "was not in good faith to obtain a comfortable seat for a short ride."[116]

Disappointed and almost disbelieving in the face of the court's ruling, Wells wrote in an 1887 diary entry that she "had hoped such great things from the suit for my people generally." Prior to her verdict, she said, "I had firmly believed all along that the law and the world was on our side and would, when we appealed to it, give us justice. O God is there no redress, no peace, no justice in this land for us."[117] Wells's anguish was even more justified than she knew. By the end of the 1880s it would become clear that Tennessee's separate car ruling had provided a template for a region-wide series of railroad segregation laws that would grow increasingly repressive over time.

Florida's 1887 separate coach law was similar to Tennessee's in that it required railroad companies operating in the state to sell "respectable persons of color" first-class tickets and furnish them with first-class cars. But it also made segregation mandatory by requiring railroad officials to prevent Blacks from attempting to "ride, sit or travel in the car or cars set apart for the use of white persons traveling as first-class passengers."[118] Passed in 1888, Mississippi's "Act to Promote the Comfort of Railroad Passengers" made no mention of first-class accommodations for Blacks. It instead required only "equal but separate accommodations for the white and the colored races," and empowered conductors to refuse service to any passenger unwilling to "occupy the car to which he or she is assigned." Meanwhile, Texas's 1889 separate coach law made it a criminal misdemeanor for any passenger to ride in a coach "not designated for his race."[119] And in 1891 Tennessee updated its separate car act to strengthen its segregation requirements. Whereas the original required the railroads to provide Black passengers with first-class cars, the revised statute required only "equal, but separate accommodations for the white and colored races," and empowered conductors to "refuse to carry" any passenger who was unwilling "to occupy the car to which he or she is assigned." It also imposed fines on any railroad that did not enforce the law.[120]

Similar laws were passed in Louisiana, Alabama, Arkansas, Kentucky, and Georgia between 1890 and 1891, in South Carolina in 1896, in North Carolina and Virginia in 1899, in Maryland in 1904, and in Oklahoma between 1907 and 1908. North Carolina's law required separate but equal accommodations on steamboats as well as trains; Virginia added steamships in 1900, and South Carolina added ferries in 1904. Already the South's "most segregated form of travel," boats were segregated elsewhere by company regulations.[121]

The color line drawn by all these laws and regulations was broad but never absolute. Segregation remained most common in first-class cars and cabins, yet nurses and other servants were always permitted to travel in the "whites only cars" when they accompanied a white employer. Federal court judge David Key noted in 1885, "so long as a colored passenger occupies a servile position, he may ride anywhere. Let a woman black as midnight be the nurse of a white child," he wrote, "or a man equally as dark be the servant of a white man [and] there is never the slightest objection to their having seats in the ladies car or any other."[122] Only Blacks whose servitude was not clearly established were subject to segregation. Such distinctions had not been necessary during slavery, but by the 1880s and 1890s they became crucial.

THE TRIUMPH OF JIM CROW

The rising tide of white supremacy that fostered these laws was shaped by both local and regional forces. Tennessee's first separate car law, as we have seen, was developed to discourage Blacks from agitating for a complete ban of racial segregation on the state's railroads, while in Kentucky, where railroads were not segregated prior to the 1890s, a wave of public sentiment for a separate car law first developed in the aftermath of the shooting of a white woman by a "colored ruffian" on an integrated train.[123] Although the specific impetus behind the separate cars campaigns varied from state to state, the shifting tides of the South's regional politics were crucial to the creation and passage of such laws. The first wave of Jim Crow laws unfolded as "Redeemer" governments—state legislatures dominated by the white-supremacist Democrats who reclaimed the South from Republican rule—across the South struggled to contain an agrarian revolt that threatened to unite poor Black and white farmers. Both Black and white farmers were hard hit by the inflation, declining crop prices, and rising railroad rates of the 1880s and 1890s, and both were drawn to the Populist Party—an agrarian third-party movement that sought to raise crop prices and challenge the power of the railroads. But the biracial coalition created by the Populists was fragile. It was easily divided by white supremacists' campaigns that promised to "protect white women, ensure white supremacy, and spur progress for the white race."[124]

Segregation and Black disenfranchisement were central to these campaigns, which came at a time when white southerners were unnerved by the "uppity" behavior of a new generation of free-born African American men and women. Railroad cars and railroad stations were a central site for encounters between these groups, and the separate car laws and other segregationist measures provided a rallying cry for Democratic political campaigns dedicated to returning the South to "white man's government." "What white man wants his wife or sister sandwiched between a big bully buck and a saucy wench?" asked South Carolina's Eugene Gary, raising the reliably horrifying specter of an integrated ladies' car as he campaigned on behalf of white demagogue Ben Tillman in the 1890s.[125]

Plessy v. Ferguson, the 1896 Supreme Court decision most famously associated with the origins of segregation today, received only passing notice in the newspapers published by African Americans during the nineteenth century. The ruling came after all but a few southern states had already passed separate car laws, and it did nothing to check the further proliferation of such laws. It came on the heels of a number of similar legal defeats, the most widely lamented of which was the annulment of the Civil Rights Act of 1875 by *Civil Rights Cases* (1883).

Plessy originated in 1892 with an act of civil disobedience by Homer Plessy, a Louisiana Creole, who challenged Louisiana's 1890 separate car law by taking a seat in the white section of an East Louisiana Railway train and refusing to move. Neither Plessy's trip nor his act of civil disobedience was spontaneous. Plessy's trip was a test case organized by the New Orleans–based Comité des Citoyens to challenge the legality of Louisiana's separate car law. But such challenges were nothing new.

Black travelers had been challenging segregation on common carriers since the antebellum era, and the passage of the separate car laws only increased organized Black resistance to such discrimination. In the mid-1880s, Black professionals in Baltimore established an organization called Mutual United Brotherhood of Liberty in the United States. The organization first took shape around the lawsuit *Stewart v. The Sue,* in which Martha Stewart and several other Black women successfully challenged their exclusion from the ladies' car on the Baltimore-based steamship line. Established to expand upon that victory, the Brotherhood of Liberty was dedicated to using "all the legal means within our power to procure and maintain our rights as citizens in this country."[126] The African American League, a pioneering national civil rights organization founded in 1890, also tackled transportation segregation. It launched its first separate car test case in 1891, and planned several more after that—although all but one would fail to materialize due to the organization's chronic lack of funds. The early 1890s also saw Blacks in Kentucky organize an Anti-Separate Coach Committee and stage a test case designed to challenge their state's separate coach law.[127]

More important in hindsight than it was in its own day, *Plessy* solidified these legal losses by federally sanctioning the separate coach laws. In ruling against Homer Plessy, the US Supreme Court affirmed the constitutionality of Louisiana's Separate Car Act, which required "railway companies carrying passengers in their coaches in this state" to "provide equal but separate accommodations for the white and colored races."[128] The Court's decision provided an important and lasting precedent for a wide variety of municipal and state segregation laws, mandating "separate but equal" public schools, toilets, restaurants, hospitals, hotels, theaters, cemeteries, and public facilities of all kinds from 1896 through to 1954, when the legal doctrine of separate but equal was overturned by the Court's ruling in *Brown v. Board of Education.* But ironically, given the case's origins, the "separate but equal" legal doctrine enshrined in *Plessy* had a more limited application to travel segregation than it did to other forms of racial segregation.

Although its limits were rarely honored, *Plessy* applied only to "enforced separation of the races, as applied to internal commerce of the state." As a matter of law, the US Supreme Court had no authority over the regulation of interstate commerce, which is controlled by Congress. And the Court was careful to emphasize that fact in its ruling in *Plessy*, which notes that given that "the East Louisiana Railway [is] . . . a local line, with both its termini within the State of Louisiana," its ruling in the *Plessy* case would raise "no question of interference with interstate commerce."[129] Left unresolved by its ruling, however, was the status of Black passengers traveling across state lines, who would continue to be subject to segregation in many states, but would also continue to have legal grounds for civil rights litigation. Thus, the Supreme Court's verdict in *Plessy* brought no end to African American litigation against discrimination on common carriers.

Plessy also left unsettled the question of whether the accommodations that the railroads provided for Blacks were actually equal. The Jim Crow car sanctioned in *Plessy* was not a new piece of equipment. It was still the smoking car, and like the "dirt cars" Blacks were forced to ride in during the antebellum era, it was always the oldest, filthiest car on its train. As Chapter 2 will show, with the legalization of segregation and the modernization and expansion of long-distance travel by rail that started in the 1880s, the Jim Crow car would become an increasingly distinctive space. As trains grew longer, and railroad accommodations more lavish, Jim Crow accommodations rarely kept pace, making Jim Crow travel ever more uncomfortable, humiliating, and infuriating.

With the legalization of segregation, the Jim Crow car became a powerful symbol of the state-sanctioned degradation of all African Americans. For Blacks who grew up before the passage of the South's separate car laws, the Jim Crow car was a galling reminder of the rights that they had lost. A child of privilege, little Mary Church, whose misadventures on a train opened this chapter, would grow up to attend Oberlin College and marry a judge. But Mary Church Terrell's status as a traveler actually declined as she grew older. Her father, she later realized, had been able to defy the conductor who wanted her to move to the smoker at least in part because in the late 1860s there was "no law on the statute books" compelling Blacks in Tennessee and other southern states to ride in the Jim Crow car.[130] By the time Terrell was a parent herself, that was no longer true. When she traveled to Virginia with her own children in 1908, she could do nothing when a railroad conductor "rudely ordered my two little girls to go back to one of the rear seats where they belonged."[131] Segregation was by then required by law in every state in the South.

2

Traveling by Train

The Jim Crow Car

"DID YOU EVER SEE A 'JIM-CROW' WAITING-ROOM?" ASKED W. E. B. Du Bois in an essay he published in the *New Republic* in 1920. An excerpt from his autobiography, the piece sought to illuminate the everyday hardships of being Black in America. In it, Du Bois addressed a potentially skeptical audience, which included white friends who told him "You are too sensitive" and suggested that traveling to "places of beauty" might help ease his discontents.[1] His response to this suggestion crackled with rage. How can I take pleasure in travel, he fumed, when going anywhere involves discomfort and disrespect at every turn?

Black travelers, he explained, could expect to start their journey in a Jim Crow waiting room, where "there is no heat in winter and no air in summer." Furnished with "broken, disreputable settees," such waiting rooms were usually small and crowded with occupants, including "undisturbed loafers and train hands." Barred from entering the main waiting rooms of southern railroad stations, Black passengers shared only a ticket booth with whites. Located between the white waiting room and the colored waiting room, southern ticket booths typically had windows on both sides. Even these were not equal, as white passengers routinely took precedence over Black passengers. Just buying a train ticket was "torture; you stand and stand and wait and wait until every white person at the 'other window' is waited on."[2]

Once Black travelers finally managed to secure their tickets, they would have to make their way to the Jim Crow car. Invariably "the oldest car in service on the road," it was usually "caked with dirt" and crowded with

63

people. The railroads wasted no space on the accommodations they offered Black travelers. On many routes Jim Crow cars were "combination cars" that also served white smokers and doubled as the baggage car. As a result, Black passengers often had to share their accommodations with a "stream of white men" who came in to smoke, as well as "the white train crew from the baggage car," who used "the 'Jim-Crow' to lounge in and perform their toilet." Squeezed into "the smallest corner" of the train, Black travelers had little or no access to the dining car or any of the other amenities available to white passengers. "It is difficult to get lunch or clean water," Du Bois wrote. "As for toilet rooms—don't!" "There is not in the world a more disgraceful denial of human brotherhood than the 'Jim-Crow' car of the southern United States," he concluded.[3]

His contemporaries agreed. Most Blacks resented the Jim Crow car more bitterly than virtually any other form of segregation. They were forced to endure the Jim Crow car during what is now known as the golden age of American railroads, which extended from the late nineteenth century to the end of the 1920s, a time when railroads handled up to 95 percent of all intercity passenger transportation, as well as up to 77 percent of intercity freight.[4] At their peak, the railroads traversed more than 250,000 miles of track and served 85,000 stations. A period when everyone took the train, the golden age of American railroads is often remembered as a time when railroad passengers enjoyed plush seats, lavish sleeping compartments, and fine dining on board sleek modern trains, but these amenities bypassed most African Americans. As vividly illustrated in railroad advertising, which often featured Black Pullman porters serving white passengers, African Americans were never the target market for the luxurious accommodations and services offered by American railways in their heyday.

Instead, on the routes traveled by most African American passengers, railway accommodations actually declined over the course of the railroad's golden age. The passage of separate car laws, and the subsequent failure of state and federal courts to require truly equal accommodations, sent a clear message to railroads: conditions on board Jim Crow cars would never be subject to careful scrutiny. Railroads could and did continue to make Jim Crow cars out of their oldest rolling stock and force Blacks to share their compartments with railroad employees, drunk and disorderly whites, prisoners of both races, and sometime even livestock. On southbound trains, some railroads assigned Blacks to Jim Crow cars well before they reached the southern

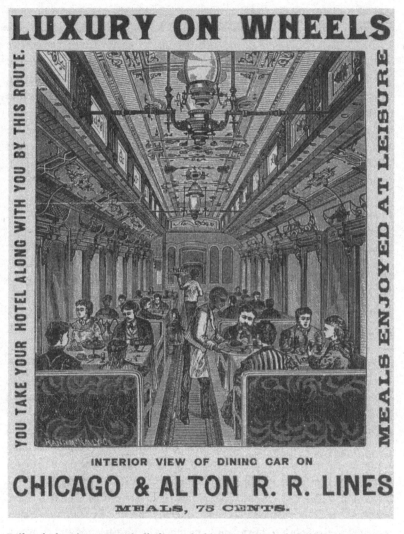

Railroad advertisements typically featured white passengers and Black servants, as can be seen in this 1880s print advertisement extolling the virtues of meal service aboard the Chicago and Alton Railroad.

states.[5] And despite the fact that the Interstate Commerce Commission (ICC) repeatedly held that "like accommodations shall be provided for colored passengers," Blacks could not count on being able to secure dining car service or Pullman sleeping car accommodations on numerous routes both inside and outside the South.[6] Conditions for Black passengers only grew worse during World Wars I and II, when overcrowding made Jim Crow car seats scarce and sparked racial conflicts among passengers over space.

Crowded or otherwise, the Jim Crow car became a defining feature of the African American experience because it was a space that few Blacks could avoid entirely. African American travelers could and often did stay with friends and family members to avoid segregated hotels and railroad station restaurants; they walked or traveled by buggy to avoid patronizing Jim Crow streetcars—which were segregated by law in southern cities in a series of ordinances passed between 1901 and 1910. But prior to the development of reliable automobiles and paved roads, few African Americans, regardless of their class or occupation, could avoid traveling by train.

The turn of the century saw more and more African Americans taking the train for the first time as they left the rural South for cities and towns elsewhere. During the years leading up to the First World War, this movement swelled into the Great Migration of rural Black southerners to cities across the North, Midwest, and West Coast. Its first wave was triggered by a labor shortage that allowed some migrants to travel North courtesy of employers who offered them free rail passes. But the Great Migration always included migrants who scrimped and saved to buy rail tickets, and some who jumped freight trains in the hope of traveling for free. By the 1930s, migrants would begin to travel north by car and bus as well as train, but the railroads shaped the first wave of the Great Migration and remained important after that. Southeastern migrants from Florida and the Carolinas typically took the Atlantic Coast Line up to Richmond to connect to destinations northeast, while Mississippi Valley residents took the Illinois Central to Chicago and other midwestern cities. Once settled in the North, many traveled by train when they returned to the South to bury family members or visit friends and relatives. During both world wars, the demands of the wartime labor market and military service increased the geographic mobility of all Americans, exposing even Blacks who remained in the South to long-distance travel by train.

Blacks could not escape the Jim Crow car, but men and women from all walks of life resisted its humiliations at every turn by a variety of means.

Especially during the early years of passenger travel by rail, middle-class and elite Blacks were more able to afford rail travel than were lower-class Blacks; and throughout the Jim Crow era, members of this group were far more likely to have the resources to challenge the railroads in court. But while affluent Blacks predominate in the court cases that historians have drawn on to chronicle the history of segregation, their complaints do not tell the whole story.

Discontented travelers came from all walks of life, and their discontents did not always end up in court. African Americans expressed their opposition to the Jim Crow car in myriad ways, which included writing to newspapers and civil rights organizations, lobbying the ICC for equal treatment, petitioning their state legislatures, fighting with conductors and railroad officials, and sometimes simply refusing to move. Prior to the 1940s their resistance had little lasting effect, and it is largely forgotten today. In historical accounts, African American resistance to segregation on railways tends to begin and end with *Plessy* and has never been fully chronicled. Black travelers' complaints and commentary are among the few records we have of the once-commonplace experience of traveling in the Jim Crow car. This chapter revisits that history.

"THE WORST ACCOMMODATIONS . . ."

The period spanning the end of the nineteenth century and the early twentieth is known as the nadir of African American history. A time when segregation was on the rise and lynching and other forms of anti-Black violence were at an all-time high, it was also when Black southerners lost the vote—along with virtually every other civil right they had gained during Reconstruction. Not surprisingly, this period was the nadir of Jim Crow travel as well. In the 1880s and 1890s a wave of separate car laws banished Blacks to Jim Crow cars, even in southern states where they had previously enjoyed more liberal travel options. This transformation came at a time when traveling by rail was increasingly common and essential to American life, and its negative impact on Black passengers became worse over time.

Enacted over the course of two decades, the separate car laws were hard to honor for many reasons, not least of which was that they sometimes took Black travelers by surprise. "In my travels North and South I've always traveled first-class in order to have no difficulty," one female public schoolteacher, who did not supply her name, reported to the *Christian Recorder* in 1889. Born and raised in New Orleans, she had also lived in Norfolk, Virginia, and "knew nothing of the North" prior to moving to New York City in the mid-1880s. But on a trip from New York to Mississippi at the end of that decade, she found herself traversing a new and different South where, when her train reached Birmingham, Alabama, rowdy young white men began pressuring her train's conductor to "make her git in the nigger car." She had passed through "this iron city of the South" without incident just a year earlier, and did not expect trouble because Alabama had yet to pass a separate car law. But the "backwoods ignorant white men" who boarded her train in Birmingham subjected her to a "mountain of threats and sauce," until the train's conductor finally intervened, telling them: "You dare to touch or insult that lady, and I will have the train stopped and put you off. If you are not satisfied, go into the smoker yourself; it will suit you better." The teacher made it as far as Meridian, Mississippi, without further incident, but was disheartened to find that she was lucky to have done so. Her hosts there told her that Mississippi had just adopted a "new law that had just gone into effect, that colored and white should ride in separate cars." On leaving Meridian, she would have no choice but to ride in the smoker.[7]

This teacher's experience would become the norm. As the South's separate car laws proliferated in the 1890s, the conditions Black travelers faced worsened. Southern railroads had long opposed the passage of Jim Crow laws because they were reluctant to take on the expense of adding the cars that would have been needed to separate Black and white passengers on equal terms. But once segregation was mandated by law, they found ways to avoid such expenditures. Most railroads did not add new cars. Instead they turned their oldest, dirtiest cars into colored cars. The cars they assigned to Blacks were usually "off-cast, or old coach[es]."[8] Many were originally built as second-class smoking cars, and they often accommodated both Black and smoking passengers.

Eager to avoid spending money on creating separate but equal accommodations, railroads that carried relatively few Black passengers typically provided only combination cars that included smoking sections, sometimes baggage, and Jim Crow accommodations, configured in a variety of ways. A Black minister who traveled extensively in the South explained that combination cars were divided by partitions and featured "a little apartment in the front for colored smokers," a middle compartment in which "colored ladies and gen-

Interior of a Jim Crow combination car with partition, St. Louis–San Francisco Railway, 1936.

tlemen were seated," and a "third part of the car, in the back end, [where] the white smokers are seated." The flimsy divisions used to create these three compartments, he added, did little to disguise the fact that "the railroad's first class colored car. . . . [was] nothing but an old smoker."[9] On the Chesapeake and Ohio Railroad in Virginia, conditions seem to have been even worse. Blacks were "cooped up in the smallest possible space in one end [of] the baggage car," and not even "allowed to fully occupy this limited space." Instead, they shared it with the newspaper vendor, who occupied "two seats in the Jim Crow corner," and the conductor, who took "two seats with his belongings usually just across from the newsboy."[10]

Such arrangements were not unusual, since these railroad employees typically used their train's Jim Crow cars as a work space and lounge. So did the train's fireman, engineer, and any other railroad workmen who happened to be on board. Other white men who often traveled in the Jim Crow car included white sheriffs transporting Black convicts or white convicts (who were supposed to ride in the whites-only car but were often put in the Jim Crow car)—as well as any white men who were too drunk or disorderly to be permitted in the whites-only car. "A *well-fitted Jim Crow car in the South* carries all the

Race people, the porter, the flagman, the conductor, the butcher boy [news vendor] and his boxes, the lanterns and signals, the deputy sheriff with five or six prisoners, all in handcuffs enroute for the state convict farm, and all the chickens, baskets, bags and acting suitcases that weary travelers may claim," wrote one Black traveler after completing a journey from Helena, Arkansas, to Mound Bayou, Mississippi, aboard the Yazoo and Mississippi Valley Railroad.[11]

Such conditions were unappealing for a variety of reasons, not least of which was that on some trains the Jim Crow car rarely had enough seats for the Black passengers. Those who could not secure seats stood in the aisle of the Jim Crow section or outside on the train's rear platform.[12] In fact, Jim Crow seating arrangements were so makeshift and uncomfortable that in states such as North Carolina, where railroad segregation was not the norm prior to the state's adoption of a separate car law in 1899, "there was a feeling that the Southern Railroad was trying to enforce . . . [the new law] in such a way to make it so unpopular that its repeal could be secured."[13]

However, in North Carolina as elsewhere, once the "law was seen to be permanent," the railroads had no incentive to improve on these arrangements.[14] Despite the legal language used in the separate car laws, which generally called for separate but equal accommodations for both races, southern lawmakers and courts put no pressure on the railroads to offer Blacks equal accommodations or service. The ICC was somewhat more sympathetic to Black complaints about the conditions aboard Jim Crow trains. It repeatedly ruled that segregation was permissible but carriers could not discriminate between Black and white passengers when it came to quality of accommodations. But the ICC had no power to enforce its rulings, and it typically accepted the railroads' claims that they were providing Black passengers equal although separate accommodations.

Ironically enough, the institutionalization of the Jim Crow car took place at a time when the railroads were beginning to provide their non–Jim Crow passengers an increasingly safe and comfortable ride. By the 1880s, railroads across the country had started to replace the oil lamps and coal stoves that once supplied light and heat to passenger cars with electric lights and new steam heating systems, which were both cleaner and far less flammable: "No more passengers burned alive," proclaimed one advertisement for a steam heating system.[15] But such improvements were rarely made to the Jim Crow cars. Although the Louisville & Nashville (L&N) Railroad began ordering new cars equipped with steam heating systems as early as 1902, the Jim Crow custom car it ordered in 1913 did not include this new technology. Instead the L&N's Combine Car Number 665, a combination smoking car and Jim Crow car with baggage compartment in the middle, was heated by two cast iron stoves. Air conditioning, which was available in some railroad cars as early as the 1930s, also rarely reached the Jim Crow cars.[16]

JIM CROW WRECKS

Bad as they were, uncomfortable seats, dim lighting, and smoky cast-iron stoves were not the most problematic of the Jim Crow cars' deficiencies, as far as the health and welfare of Black travelers was concerned. Usually the railway's oldest cars, Jim Crow cars became more hazardous the longer they stayed in service. This was especially true in the early twentieth century when the railroads began to replace their wooden passenger coaches with sturdier metal compartments. These steel cars were fire resistant and far less likely to be crushed in a collision than were wooden coaches. Railroads stopped ordering wooden cars as early as 1912 and over the next few decades phased out the ones they had in operation.[17] Although steel cars were designed to improve the safety of railroad passengers, their adoption often made traveling Jim Crow more dangerous. By the beginning of the twentieth century, the Jim Crow coaches were sometimes the only wooden coaches on the train. Sandwiched between heavy metal locomotives and the new metal coaches used to accommodate white passengers, Jim Crow cars were often collapsed like an accordion during collisions. Wrecks in which the casualties were limited to the Jim Crow car were not uncommon.

In fact, they were common enough to attract attention. Aware of the dangers of combining wooden and metal cars, the Interstate Commerce Commission lobbied throughout the 1910s, unsuccessfully, for the passage of federal legislation requiring the railroads to replace all their wooden coaches with steel-sided fireproof cars, only to be defeated by railroad owners, who were reluctant to take on the expense.[18] As a result, train crashes took on a racial logic that was obvious even outside the railroad industry. University of Louisiana professor W. O. Scruggs—a white man—first became aware of the potential risks involved in traveling Jim Crow after traveling on a train that "carried its white passengers in a steel coach and its negro patrons in a coach

Excursion train wreck, Hamlet, North Carolina, 1911.

of wood." Concerned, he raised the issue with another white passenger, who told him this arrangement was only logical: "It costs the road more to kill a white man than when it kills a nigger, so it takes extra precautions for us."[19]

Blacks in North Carolina reached the same conclusion after a head-on collision between a freight train and a passenger train in 1918 killed eight people—all of whom were Black, as were most of the several dozen passengers injured in the crash. The wreck decimated a Durham AME Church group whose members were on an excursion to Charlotte. They had been riding at the front of the train in wooden Jim Crow cars that were "old and frail and crumbled like pasteboard," while the rest of train, which carried 912 passengers, withstood the impact of the crash.[20] The tragedy came in the wake of an even more deadly collision in similar circumstances six years earlier, which had likewise resulted in "mostly" Negro fatalities.[21] In the aftermath of still another wreck in 1914, Black leaders from across the state petitioned the North Carolina Corporate Commission, which regulated the state's railroads, to protect the safety of Black passengers. "We do complain that we are not only assigned to the most dangerous portion of the train, but we are forced to ride the weakest coaches that made up the train. Because of this some of us have lost friends and kinsmen in wrecks, while other passengers on the same train, but in a stronger coach, were not damaged enough to need hospital attention."[22]

Great Train Wreck of 1918.

Their petition had no effect. Representatives for the railroads that operated in the state insisted that it was their "established policy" to treat their "colored patrons with equity and fairness," and the commission accepted their claims. Jim Crow train-wreck casualties continued to rise, both in North Carolina and elsewhere. The nation's deadliest train wreck, which took place in 1918, was a head-on collision between two Chattanooga and St. Louis Railroad trains that took place near Nashville and killed 105 people, 70 of whom were Black.[23]

The disproportionate number of Blacks killed in train crashes attracted virtually no attention from government officials, but it was obvious to the journalists who reported on these casualties. "Only Seven of Dead Are White Persons, as Majority Were Killed in Negro Compartment," a white Oklahoma newspaper noted without further elaboration in describing a crash that killed twenty-seven people in Kellyville, Oklahoma, on September 29, 1917.[24] The catastrophic wreck that took place near Nashville the following year elicited similar headlines, although no discussion of the Jim Crow car's dangers, from newspapers across the country. "100 Killed, 100 Hurt in Train Wreck: Fast Express and an Accommodation Train in Head-On Collision Near Nashville, Most of Victims Negroes," reported the *New York Times*.[25]

These fatalities received still more attention in Black newspapers. The Black press routinely tallied train crash fatalities by race, and sometimes made jubilant special note of the rare train crashes in which the Jim Crow car was spared. "Jim Crow Car Escapes in Ga. Wreck, January 1, 1927," was the headline in the *Baltimore Afro-American* after a crash in which a southern railroad's Jim Crow car somehow miraculously "resisted" under the force of the "heavy cars pushing behind," while the "'white folks' car' did not," resulting in a train wreck in which no Black passengers were killed or injured.[26] The report also noted that under similar circumstances most Jim Crow cars splintered.

The Black reporters who covered Jim Crow wrecks often expressed outrage over the conditions that produced so many Black casualties. "As a rule, the Jim Crow cars are placed next to the baggage cars which are immediately following the engines, as well as being about the poorest on the train," the *Cleveland Gazette* noted in a brief but bitter editorial on a train wreck that killed "six members of the race" in Johnson City, Tennessee, in 1907. "The result is that in accidents those of our people that are forced to occupy them are subject to the greatest risks. . . . More Southern 'friendship' for our people."[27] A decade later Roscoe Dunjee, the editor of Oklahoma's *Black Dispatch*, directed his editorial on the 1917 Kellyville crash to the state's corporate commission, which regulated its railroads. "Jim Crowism flowed, Gentlemen, at Kelly Ville!" he told them, "snuffing out the lives of . . . twenty helpless black men and women whose brains, arms and eyes were scattered like dung on soil of the land of the fair Gods, and there was brought to light the vile sort of accommodations furnished to black men by the railroads of Oklahoma."[28]

Not all Black reporters were as dramatic as Dunjee, but by the 1920s African American newspapers routinely described Blacks who died in train wrecks as casualties of Jim Crow. "Placed next to the Engine, Race Passengers Have No Chance to Escape as Trains Crash Head-On in the Fog," ran a headline introducing the *Pittsburgh Courier*'s account of a collision between two South Pacific trains in southeastern Louisiana on March 26, 1925. Nine of the thirteen passengers who died in the crash were Black, a reporter for the paper noted in an article that went on to contend that the train's colored casualties were "murdered in the name of law." The train's white passengers, "riding in their steel Pullman cars were little more than shaken up by the crash," while the Jim Crow coach in which its Black passengers were forced to ride was "old fashioned, made of wood, far different from the modern steel coaches now in general use." Although "easily flammable," it was "placed next to the engine to act as bumper in cases such as this."[29] The *Baltimore Afro-American*'s brief account of the same crash underscored that all of the people who perished in the wreck, whose fatalities included "a white engineer, a [white] fireman and a white news vendor," were riding in the Jim Crow car at the time of the crash.[30]

African American travelers were often cognizant of the special dangers they faced. In 1926 the Black writer J. A. Rogers rode from Wilmington, North Carolina, to Richmond, Virginia, "in an old wooden car placed between a modern steel luggage car and steel coach for whites." In the event of a crash, Rogers noted, the car that he occupied "would have been crushed to tinder." Unnerved by this arrangement, he was all too aware that it was deliberate. "The colored car is always placed ahead," he wrote, "so that in the case of a head on collision, the 'Negroes' will get killed first. This, by the way is the only instance in the South, where the black man goes first; in Jim Crow street cars he goes in the rear."[31]

Rogers survived the trip, but his safety worries were not unwarranted. Three years later eleven Blacks perished when a Frisco Railroad train ran off the rails near Henryetta, Oklahoma. The train's white engineer and fireman "were burned in the wreckage of the Engine," while the Jim Crow car's passengers, who rode directly behind the engine, were scalded to death by the steam that escaped when the engine's boiler burst. There were no deaths among the train's white passengers.[32] "Jim Crow car wrecks," as Black newspapers sometimes called them, persisted until the railroads finally retired their wooden Jim Crow cars in the early 1950s.[33]

". . . FOR THE SAME MONEY"

The resentment that African American railroad passengers felt over the dangerous and degrading conditions they encountered while traveling Jim Crow was frequently compounded by a sense of economic outrage. Although Jim Crow cars offered distinctly second-class accommodations, by the early twentieth century the discounted Negro car fares that had been common were largely a thing of the past. Black passengers now almost invariably paid what J. A. Rogers ironically termed an "impartial fare" to ride in the dilapidated wooden coaches the railroads set aside for their race.[34] In the late nineteenth century, railroads throughout the United States abandoned the dual-fare system that traditionally allowed passengers who planned to ride in the Negro car to pay second-class or half fares. This shift has received little attention from historians of the segregated South, who rarely pay much attention to the economics of segregated transportation. But ticket prices were a central issue in many Black protests against traveling Jim Crow, which actually grew more, rather than less, expensive as single-fare pricing became mandatory.

Fare prices varied from railroad to railroad, but during the antebellum era, passengers typically paid discounted rates for accommodations in the Negro cars. Travelers willing to ride in these minimally furnished cars paid half fares (or second-class rates), as did the employers and slave owners who purchased railroad tickets for their servants and slaves. These discounted fares persisted after the Civil War, but they eventually gave way to a single-fare system.

This shift was national rather than regional, and seems to have occurred at least in part due to the influence of the agrarian political movements that swept the country during the last three decades of the nineteenth century. The Granger Movement, the Farmer's Alliance, and the Populist movement—which were most active in the 1870s, 1880s, and 1890s, respectively—all represented the interests of cash-strapped farmers. One of the central concerns of these movements was the high price of transporting agricultural commodities by rail, which the leaders of all three movements attributed to price fixing by monopolistic railroads. Increasingly impoverished by a combination of rising freight rates and declining agriculture prices, members of these agrarian movements lobbied relentlessly for more regulation of the railroads by the state. The political influence of these farmers' movements was limited in other ways, but their demands for railroad regulation were successful. The late nineteenth century saw the creation of state railroad commissions empowered to regulate railroad rates in some states, and the passage of maximum rate laws in others. These measures generally resulted in the reduction of both freight rates and passenger rates, as well as the adoption of simpler rate schedules that abandoned first- and second-class fares in favor of a single passenger rate.

In the South this shift had the additional virtue of simplifying the practice of racial segregation. Single rates made it impossible for Black passengers to claim access to cars reserved for whites by virtue of having purchased first-class tickets—as they had in the past. Perhaps for this reason, the railroads in at least one southern state adopted a single fare well before they were under any pressure to change their rates.

In Georgia, where Blacks were forced to travel in the Negro car long before the passage of the state's first separate car law, the price Blacks paid for their tickets doubled after the Civil War. The change went largely unnoticed among whites, but unfair ticket pricing was the single most pressing grievance articulated by a delegation of prominent Blacks who crowded into a standing-room-only meeting at the state Railroad Commission in 1888 to petition for "equal accommodations for equal money." The delegation read a prepared statement that noted that, while Georgia's railroads had long accommodated Blacks in a "colored people's department in smoking cars, or whole cars for colored people as the travel might demand." during the "days of slavery . . . colored people had paid only one-half the fares that white people paid." After the war, by contrast, "the railroad still required colored people to ride in the second class car, but stopped selling them tickets at half prices. This state of affairs has existed for a half century." they added, with understandable temporal exaggeration, "despite loud and repeated complaints by colored people the [rail]roads have made no material change."[35]

Georgia's Railroad Commission ignored their complaints, and other railroads in the South began eliminating their second-class fares starting in the 1880s. In most states the shift came as part of a general movement to limit the power of the railroads. Alabama's railroads adjusted their rates shortly after the state established its first Railroad Commission in 1881. Founded with the support of the state's Granger Movement, Alabama's Railroad Commission was not empowered to change railroad rates, but it managed to exert enough pressure on the state's railroads to secure voluntary rate reductions. Anxious to retain their power to set their own rates, railroad companies throughout Alabama slashed their first-class passenger rates by more than a penny per mile during the commission's first year of operation while eliminating their second-class passenger rate entirely—on the grounds that once they cut their first-class rate, they would no longer be able to afford to offer reduced rates of any kind.

In Alabama, as in Georgia, the impact of the rate adjustment was far from race-neutral. Whereas Jim Crow travelers had previously been able to secure their second-class accommodations at second-class rates, now they would pay first-class rates for the same accommodations. In an unsuccessful effort to avoid reducing any of its rates, the president of the L&N Railroad raised this issue, warning the Railroad Commissioners that lowering its ticket prices might make it impossible for the railroad to divide up its passengers by race. "There is in your state, a class of travel," he told them, "to whom we sell second-class tickets at reduced rates simply for the purpose of forcing them to ride in the forward or second-class car." If the L&N lowered its ticket prices and elimi-nated such rates, he maintained, such divisions would surely disappear: "They [Blacks] would purchase first class tickets and occupy seats in the ladies car, greatly to the annoyance of your first class passengers."[36]

Even this dire prediction did not discourage the Railroad Commission from continuing to support lower passenger rates. Railroads throughout Alabama ended up reducing their rates and eliminating their second-class fares without ever changing seating arrangements. By the mid-1880s Alabama railroads sold only first-class tickets, but offered Black passengers only second-class accom-modations. "The railroads of Alabama do not provide as good accommoda-tion for colored passengers as those furnished for white passengers for the same money," wrote a young Booker T. Washington in an 1885 letter to the *Montgomery Advertiser:* "The fare is not first class as described on the ticket." In most cases "the smoking car and that in which people of color are put are the same," and sometimes Black people were put in the baggage car. No one could mistake the "coaches given to the colored people" for those given to whites. The former was "usually very filthy" and had "no carpet as in the first-class car." A man who would become famous in the 1890s for urging his fellow Blacks to acquiesce to segregation, Washington spoke out not to decry segregation per se but to demand equal service for equal rates. "If the rail-road will not give us first class accommodations, let them sell us tickets at reduced rates."[37]

In other southern states, the second-class rail fares were eliminated by statute or state regulation in measures that went hand in hand with the rise of the Jim Crow car. The region's state legislatures embraced both reduced railroad rates and separate cars, sometimes even incorporating them into the same statute. Kentucky's separate coach law is a case in point. Passed in 1900, it regulated rates as well as seating arrangements and specified that "after the

approval of this act, the rate for transportation passengers on all railroads . . .
shall not exceed three cents per mile . . . ; and such railroads shall not be required to have second class coaches or to sell second class tickets." The legislation abolishing second-class fares in Tennessee was less direct, but had
the same effect. The Separate Car Act of 1891 effectively nullified Tennessee's
rarely honored 1881 law requiring separate cars for "colored passengers who
pay first class fare." The 1891 law dropped this provision in favor of language
that required nothing more than "equal, but separate accommodations" for
Blacks and whites.[38]

Of course, the railroads' actual cars remained the same, so with the passage of the new law Black and white travelers in Tennessee paid "the same
money" to ride in very different cars. "The 'colored' car is not as good as the
'white' car," wrote a correspondent for the *Chattanooga Observer*, after traveling on the Nashville and Chattanooga Railroad the year the law went into
effect: "One is a cattle pen, the other is a car. . . . Drunken, puking white men
whose natural smell would turn an ostrich's stomach are put in the colored
car. White convicts yet smelling of jail, and with lice creeping on them, sit in
the colored car."[39]

Passengers would ultimately pay the same money to ride in very different
cars in North and South Carolina and Virginia as well. Although slower to
segregate their trains than many states, between 1898 and 1902 all three states
adopted separate car laws and revised their railroad passenger rates shortly
thereafter. South Carolina did not address rates in its Separate Car Act of 1898,
but the state's Railroad Commission abolished second-class fares that same
year. And in North Carolina, which enacted its Jim Crow law in 1899, a similar rate adjustment soon followed. In both states the new laws and new rates
were the result of a compromise between the legislators and the railroads in
which the latter, as the *New York Times* explained it, "abated their opposition to the 'Jim Crow' cars, with the understanding that the second-class fare
will be abolished." Legislators in Virginia, which had a weak railroad commission, seem to have negotiated a similar deal.[40] "Before the passage of the
Virginia Jim Crow law," reported a Baltimore paper in 1902, "the Norfolk and
Western sold second-class tickets to passengers who rode in the smoking car.
Now all tickets are for first-class passage." Once Virginia fell in line, Black
passengers throughout the South had to "pay the same fares as whites."[41]

"It's a system of robbery," maintained Atlanta resident Dr. R. H. Butler in
the Black newspaper the *Broad Axe* in 1904, "to charge more than . . . a second

or third-class fare for the present Jim Crow service . . . is nothing more than a swindle."[42] Butler's complaint was echoed by virtually all the major Black organizations of his era. To give just a few examples: The 1905 Declaration of Principles issued by the Niagara Movement, one of Black America's first national civil rights organizations, included a protest against the Jim Crow car, which "make[s] us pay first-class fare for third-class accommodations"; and so, too, did the "The Declaration of the Rights of the Negro Peoples of the World," issued by Marcus Garvey's Universal Negro Improvement Association in 1920. Pan-African in scope, the latter protested the European colonization of Africa and the British exploitation of the West Indies, but also listed high up among the grievances suffered by the race the fact that Blacks "in the Southern portion of the United States . . . are jim-crowed and compelled to accept separate and inferior accommodations and made to pay the same fare charged for first-class accommodations."[43]

But such protests had little impact. The elimination of second-class fares on southern railroads was a swindle that benefited not only the railroads but white passengers as well. Designed to appease populist discontent, the rate adjustments that eradicated the second-class fares paid by most Blacks often lowered the fares paid by many white passengers. In both North and South Carolina, for example, the elimination of the second-class fare of $2\frac{3}{4}$ cents per mile was accompanied by a reduction in the first-class fare—the only remaining fare—which dropped from $3\frac{1}{4}$ cents per mile to 3 cents.[44] The exploitative character of rate adjustment, which lowered the price for whites while raising the price that Blacks paid to travel Jim Crow, went wholly unnoticed among whites. One reporter for the *New York Times* took brief note of North Carolina's rate change, but insisted that the abolition of first- and second-class fares would help southern Blacks resign themselves to riding in the Jim Crow car. "It is well known that there is nothing connected with the race problem that so galls and cuts the negro as the policy of separate cars for the races. It is an unerring fact that the negro never goes into a second-class car if he has the money to pay for first-class accommodation," maintained this writer, who apparently believed relabeling the tickets sold to Blacks would solve the problem. This conviction rested on his false assumption that "the same accommodations are to be provided for the same money."[45]

Even though the separate car laws mandated equal accommodations, they legalized a system of segregation in which equal accommodations were both unnecessary and unlikely. The railroads' second-class cars had once served lower-class whites as well as Blacks. Once they became Jim Crow cars rather than smokers, they served a disenfranchised class whose comfort and safety was of little consequence to either the railroads or the state. Southern railroads saw segregating their passengers as an unwelcome expense, which they sought to minimize by crowding Black people into their most dilapidated coaches; and southern state governments embraced a doctrine of white supremacy under which Black people were both separate and unequal. As a result, Jim Crow facilities of all kinds were inferior to facilities set aside for "whites only." Segregation not only separated the races, it inscribed the logic of white supremacy onto the South's built environment.

JIM CROW JOURNEYS

The humiliations involved in traveling Jim Crow began before Black travelers even boarded their trains. By the beginning of the 1890s the proliferation of separate car laws had ushered in separate waiting rooms. Although before 1899 only Arkansas, Louisiana, and Mississippi had passed laws requiring the railroads to construct segregated facilities. colored waiting rooms were common across the South well before then. Writing in 1891, Black academic William Scarborough described one of the New South's most unpleasant innovations as "the novelty of three waiting rooms—one for ladies, one for gentlemen, and one for neither gentlemen nor ladies, but for 'negroes.'" That Negroes were "neither ladies nor gentlemen" was a point that could be inferred from the conditions in these new spaces. "The negro-waiting room is a dirty miserable place, with here or there a broken chair and [a] few miserable benches," wrote Scarborough of the accommodations that he had seen in Chattanooga, Atlanta, Macon, and elsewhere.[46]

Built and maintained by the railroads, colored waiting rooms were sometimes created as a result of new construction and sometimes added to existing structures; but they were almost always smaller, less comfortable, and less convenient than the facilities available to whites. Black novelist Charles Chesnutt noted in an article written in 1901, "If there is any choice of location" when it came to positioning such rooms, "the Negro always gets the worst room and it is seldom well lighted or clean."[47]

The "Colored Waiting Room" in Seaboard Air Line and Southern Railway Depot in Raleigh, North Carolina, provides one example of the kind of facility he had in mind.[48] Black travelers described it in a discrimination complaint filed before the North Carolina Board of Railroad Commissioners in 1898 as "the most poorly equipped room at the depot, being dark and ill ventilated," and "very inferior" to the waiting room used by the station's white passengers. Small and cramped, it seated only twelve people, and one of its rows of seats was located "within a few feet of its restrooms" and faced directly into these facilities. Travelers who sat in these seats had an unavoidable view of "people going in and out [of] the urinals and stalls," and were close enough to be able to smell the bathrooms as well. These busy bathrooms were used not just by colored travelers, but by railroad hands and "the public around the depot, *ad libitum*," so the stench that they gave off during warm weather assaulted not only the people in nearby seats, but everyone in the waiting room.[49]

Conditions in the station's colored waiting room were especially troubling to Black women passengers, whose race exempted them from the privileges usually accorded to female travelers. The Raleigh station had no ladies' waiting room for Black women, who were "not allowed to go into the general ladies' waiting room." They, too, had to occupy Raleigh's tiny, smelly "colored waiting room" and experience its bird's-eye view of the toilet. "Convicts and insane people" were among the travelers who used these rooms, the complainants charged, and "the seats are so arranged that when such people are in there, lady passengers must sit next to them or immediate back of them."[50]

Raleigh's small station was built nearly a decade before North Carolina passed its 1899 law requiring the establishment of separate waiting rooms for white and colored races, and may have had an especially cramped colored waiting room for that reason. But southern railroads designed with segregation in mind were often equally problematic. Completed in 1906, Atlanta's massive Terminal Station replaced an older station and provided more spacious accommodations for Blacks. The station it replaced had only two waiting rooms: a general "Waiting Room for Ladies and Gentlemen," and a smaller "Colored Waiting Room" that had once served as its "Ladies' Waiting Room."[51]

Still, most Blacks probably preferred the old station to the palatial new building. The "whole front" of the new station, according to journalist Ray Stannard Baker, "was given up to white people."[52] Its facilities included a grand main waiting room, several ladies' waiting rooms, a gentlemen's reading room, a gentlemen's smoking room, and exactly one waiting room for Blacks—a "small and dirty room" that had to be entered from the side of the building.[53] The size, location, and unkempt state of the Terminal's colored waiting room

Railroad station, Manchester, Georgia, 1938.

were the result of deliberate decisions made by the railroads that built and maintained the facility. Even the dirt served to underscore the racial hierarchies inscribed in the station's architecture. When asked why the room was so filthy, the Black porter explained he "was expected not to keep the Negro waiting rooms as clean as the one for whites The differential had to be maintained."[54] Differential access was also maintained. The only Blacks permitted to pass through the station's white waiting rooms were redcaps, servants, and porters. Black travelers who used the station had to enter and exit the facility through their "dirty little segregated room," which was situated on a side street more than a hundred feet away from the station's main entrance and taxi stands.

The stationmaster who imposed this policy was "no respecter of persons," according to Baptist minister Benjamin Mays, who lived in Atlanta for much of his life. "He treated all Negroes with equal disrespect," preventing Black celebrities such as Marian Anderson from passing through the station's front doors and even extending the ban to a white woman, Florence Reed, whom he considered "contaminated because she was the president of Spelman Negro College." Black college president Rufus E. Clement was even more unwelcome:

in the 1940s, a station policeman threatened to shoot him "for the heinous crime of having *walked through* the white room to the train to avoid having to walk outside in the rain as would have been necessary to get to the Negro waiting room."[55]

Although far larger than most southern railway stations, Atlanta's Terminal Station was not unusual in its design. Most stations built during the segregation era routed Black travelers through separate entrances. Completed in 1899, Forsyth Station, also in Georgia, was typical in its design. Its small colored waiting room was completely cut off from the rest of the station. It had a front door that opened directly onto the street, and a side door through which Black passengers could access the tracks, but no door connecting it to the station's main waiting room. The only space the station's Black travelers shared with their white counterparts was the station's ticket office, which had a ticket window that opened into the station's colored waiting room.

The fact that most railroads had a single ticket booth with segregated ticket windows was less innocuous than it might seem.[56] The railroad employees who worked the ticket booths served both windows, but routinely made African American ticket buyers wait until they had finished serving customers on the white side of the booth, regardless of how long their Black customers had been waiting. As a result, however early Black travelers arrived at the train station, they sometimes found themselves forced to purchase their tickets "moments before their train pulled out."[57] Sometimes the wait could be fruitless, for by the time the "tired ticket agent" began to serve Black customers, "often there was no time to buy [a] ticket and if they did not get them they had to pay extra on the train." Some unfortunate travelers waited so long at the ticket window that they missed their trains altogether, and even those who managed to secure a ticket could leave the window "burning with indignation and hatred."[58]

Such emotions were unlikely to abate as Jim Crow travelers progressed on to their destinations. White railroad station personnel were rude to Blacks, who rarely received assistance getting on or off the train and could not count on help carrying their baggage. Even at small stations with no platforms— where passengers typically disembarked "stepping on the narrow little stool placed under by the conductor"—Black women could not count on assistance from these officials, noted the Black writer Anna Julia Cooper in 1892. Instead, "gentlemanly and efficient" railroad conductors would hand "[white] woman after [white] woman from the steps to the stool, thence to the ground, or else

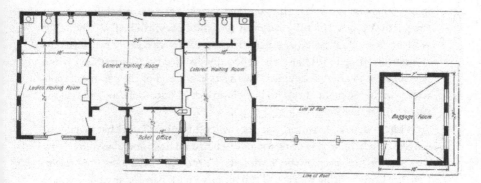

Plan of central waiting area of Georgia station at Forsyth, Georgia, 1900.

relieving her of satchels and bags and enabling her to make the descent easily."
But when "the Black Woman's turn came to alight," these men "would deliberately fold their arms and turn round."[59] And as the Jim Crow car became
entrenched, Black passengers lost access to the step. At small stations, according to W. E. B. Du Bois, southern railroads began to stop the Jim Crow
car, which was invariably the first passenger car, "out beyond the covering
in the rain or sun or dust," and require Black passengers to climb on and off
without even providing a step.[60]

African American travelers who boarded trains in the North often experienced similar rudeness well before they crossed the Mason-Dixon Line.
Cairo, Illinois, along with Cincinnati, Ohio, and Washington, D.C., were all
stops where conductors began to force African American passengers to move
from regular seats to seats in the Jim Crow car—often with no grace whatsoever. One Black traveler complained in a 1946 letter to the *Chicago Defender*
that when Illinois Central Railroad trains passed through Cairo, conductors
sometimes pushed "women and children around as if they were beasts," addressing them as "'nigger' girls and 'nigger' boys" and telling them they had
to move to "the 'nigger' coach."[61] Likewise, in Cincinnati and Washington,
conductors "hollered (under their breath of course) 'Every pig to his pen,' or
words to that effect."[62]

The rudeness continued inside the Jim Crow car. "The conductor appro-
priates two seats for himself and his papers and yells gruffly for your tickets
almost before the train has started," wrote Du Bois, describing race relations

in a typical Jim Crow car: "It is best not to ask him for information even in the gentlest tones. His information is for white persons chiefly." The other whites who made themselves at home in these cars were equally discourteous, at least according to Du Bois, who especially disliked the "impertinent white newsboy" who always occupied "two seats at the end of the car and importunes you to the point of rage to buy cheap candy, Coca-Cola, and worthless, if not vulgar, books."[63]

White rudeness, however, was not the most pressing issue that Black passengers faced. Colored waiting rooms often had no heat, and many Jim Crow cars had "no fire" even on the "coldest days." Food was even more of problem. Few Jim Crow waiting rooms had restaurants, snack bars, or any place where Black travelers could purchase "the refreshments to be found in the big main waiting room."[64] Nor could African Americans count on being able to buy food once on board the trains. First introduced on Pullman's Palace sleeping cars in the 1860s, dining cars by the beginning of the twentieth century were all but ubiquitous on long-distance routes. They were designed to offer travelers an attractive alternative to railroad station restaurants, where meals were often hurried and unappealing. But in the South, railroad dining cars were subject to state segregation laws that put them off-limits to Black customers.

While stationary restaurants were free to cater to an exclusively white or Black clientele, railroads and other common carriers were supposed to offer separate but equal facilities to Blacks and whites. They rarely did so, and would have faced insurmountable challenges had they tried to do so, as railroad food services were subject to both restaurant and transportation laws— which were not necessarily complementary or even compatible. On southern trains, any shared coach was to be "divided by a partition, designated for the race to which such passenger belongs," while restaurants were subject to still more stringent regulations.[65] In Birmingham, Alabama, for instance, facilities that served food could not accommodate Blacks and whites in the same room—unless, as the municipal legislators put it, "such white and colored persons are effectually separated by a solid partition extending from the floor upward to a distance of seven feet or higher, and unless a separate entrance from the street is provided for each compartment."[66]

The logistics of dining car service made it impossible to fit all of these requirements, and none of the railroads were willing to operate two dining cars. So they adopted a variety of ways to divide up Black and white diners, ranging from excluding Blacks from food services entirely, to creating segregated seating within their dining compartments, to seating African American diners only after all their white passengers had finished eating, to having waiters and other railroad food service personnel take food to the colored car.

In the South the worst of these arrangements usually prevailed. "It can be flatly stated that it is impossible for the Negro to get dining car privileges South of Washington," wrote Howard professor Thomas Montgomery Gregory after completing an investigation of travel segregation for the NAACP in 1916. Gregory came to this conclusion after traveling from New Orleans to Washington on a halting, roundabout trip that took thirty hours, while subsisting on nothing but Coca-Cola. Confined to the Jim Crow car, he had no access to his train's dining car and "the stopovers at stations were not long enough to procure food at the stations if any was provided there for Negroes." Furious, he concluded that "it is not sufficient to say that I should have to take food with me or that I should have lived on grapes and peanuts. If I am to have equal accommodations, I should be able to secure palatable food served in a proper manner."[67]

Gregory's experience was not unusual. Even when Black passengers could purchase food, their options were limited. William Pickens's experience on a ride from Lynchburg to Norfolk, Virginia, in 1920 was fairly typical. Barred from dining car service, his only hope of food came when the train made a twenty-minute stop in Petersburg to allow white passengers who were "too stingy to pay for dining service and tips" to grab a quick meal at the station's lunch counter. At the end of their meals, just as the train resumed its journey, the lunch counter's staff sent out a basket full of cold leftover food, "which could never be sold to white customers, in an effort to get rid of it among the colored passengers." The food they sent, Pickens noted bitterly, only added "indigestion to insult." For seventy-five cents, you could get "a quarter of an impenetrable dried hen fried the day before yesterday, old bread and a slice of musty pie," whereas "the white passengers in the lunch room may get a hot drink or a fried egg for a few cents." The passengers who bought the overpriced food could not even secure cutlery or any beverages with their meals, as railroad employees were not allowed to bring dishes or flatware into the colored car.[68]

When railroads crossing through the segregated states did open up their dining rooms to Black customers, they observed the requirements of segregation law either by holding a separate seating for Black diners after white diners had eaten, or by setting aside a small number of special tables for Black customers, partitioned off by a curtain—an experience that Blacks found truly humiliating. "The first time that I was seated behind a curtain in a dining car, I felt as if the curtain had been dropped on my selfhood," Martin Luther King Jr. recalled in his autobiography, describing it as one of the moments in which he realized, "I could never adjust to the separate waiting rooms, separate eating places, separate rest rooms, partly because the separate was always unequal, and partly because the very idea of separation did something to my sense of dignity and self-respect."[69] Dining in shifts was little better. The announcement "Negroes are now being seated in the colored car" invariably came only after train officials had been seating whites for several hours.[70] Not surprisingly, African American travelers often chose to bring their own food.

JUMPING JIM CROW

Although many African Americans resigned themselves to traveling Jim Crow, others went to great lengths to avoid it. One of the most common ways of doing so, for those who could afford it, was to secure seats in a Pullman sleeping car. Owned and operated by the Pullman Palace Car Company, these luxury sleeping cars were never segregated by law in most southern states. The brainchild of a Chicago-based engineer, George Mortimer Pullman, Pullman cars were "hotels on wheels," complete with carpets, drapes, upholstered chairs, pull-down sleeping berths, and a solicitous service staff of Black porters and maids.[71] Even though these cars were transported by the railroads, the railroads had no other jurisdiction over them. Pullman passengers paid a base fare to railroads, and an additional, entirely separate, fare to the Pullman Company—the Pullman surcharge, or extra fare, usually ranged somewhere from 30 to 70 percent of the ticket price.

Pullman service was limited to long-distance routes, and the Pullman Company's business was interstate everywhere outside Illinois, where the company had its headquarters. This made its accommodations difficult to segregate—at least officially. With passage of the Civil Rights Act of 1875, which occurred just as the Pullman Company was extending its business in the South, George Mortimer Pullman infuriated white southerners by announcing that he would comply with the law, so far as it was "applicable to the business of his company," and issuing orders instructing his conductors to accept Negro passengers.[72]

"The civil rights bill has become a dead letter in the south, except in the Pullman sleeping cars," fumed a writer for the *Atlanta Constitution* in an editorial published a few weeks after the new law took effect. "The courts, and that more powerful influence, public opinion, have robbed it of every other sting; and in the sleeping cars it would have been the source of no trouble whatever if Mr. Pullman had not almost instantaneously accepted this vile unnatural and unconstitutional law."[73] The editorial predicted that Pullman's policies would most surely result in the total abandonment of "Pullman's berth by white travelers. On some routes in Mississippi and other districts where negroes travel extensively," its writer maintained, Pullman's business was already dead: "Not a white man, it is said, takes a Pullman car. Short naps in the seats are preferable to long naps in the berths of such cars."[74]

However, there is little evidence that Pullman's southern business was seriously compromised by his policy, which he maintained even after the Civil Rights Act of 1875 was overturned in 1883. Pullman was an unlikely champion of Black civil rights. He staffed his Pullman cars with Black porters and maids, whom he hired both because they could be paid almost nothing and because he was convinced that former slaves had received the perfect training to "take care of any whim that a customer had." He also preferred Black workers who resembled the smiling slaves of southern legend—the company routinely hired "the blackest man with the whitest teeth" to evoke white southern nostalgia for antebellum times.[75] Yet even though Pullman had no trouble seeing Blacks in servile terms, he remained unwilling to segregate his cars.

The *Atlanta Constitution* denounced Pullman as an "extreme Republican" who had "no disposition to prevent the intrusion of negroes into the sleeping cars."[76] Pullman's motives for resisting segregation, however, appear to have been as practical as they were political. As the owner of a national business headquartered in Illinois, he would have to have been as concerned about defying federal laws and alienating northern legislators as with violating southern racial etiquette. He also had a pressing financial interest in avoiding segregation. Like the railroads, the Pullman Company could not refuse to carry Black passengers, so acquiescing to segregation would have meant having to provide separate cars for such customers, which would have been prohibitively expensive—given how few Blacks could afford Pullman service. The sleeping car tycoon, who died in 1897, never had much incentive to change his policies. During his lifetime, very few Blacks could afford Pullman service, which may help explain why the *Atlanta Constitution*'s prediction that the Pullman Company would lose its white ridership never came true.

Instead, traveling by Pullman quickly became the Black elite's preferred mode of transportation. "I assure you that from New York to our place you will not have the slightest trouble on the Pullman car," wrote Alabama educator Booker T. Washington to a prospective northern visitor in 1892. "I have traveled that route for 10 years and have never had the slightest intimation of any unpleasantness. You can get into a Pullman car in New York and come to our place without any change of train, and you can do the same returning and not a word said."[77]

The trouble, even before then, was that African Americans could not always count on securing Pullman tickets. "In the South, good accommodations are now given the colored people," one representative of several southern railroads told the *New York Times* as early as 1887, "except that they don't get into the Pullman cars very often. I don't mean to say that there is any positive order not to admit them to the sleepers, but it is not the custom. There is a sort of unwritten law against it, just as there is at some hotels, where the proprietors feel that they cannot afford to tread on the corns of a score of patrons for the sake of one."[78]

As separate car laws proliferated across the South, and as African American Pullman passengers became more numerous, Blacks would have more and more difficulty securing Pullman car accommodations. Although Pullman coaches were exempted from most states' separate car laws, between 1893 and 1907 Georgia, Arkansas, Texas, and Oklahoma all enacted "sleeping car laws" specifying that carriers "may haul sleeping or chair cars for the exclusive use of either race separately, but not jointly."[79] Even in the states where Black passengers were not barred by law from mingling with white Pullman travelers, the railroads and white passengers often devised ways to keep African American travelers from ever entering these cars.

Of the four state sleeping car laws, Georgia's was the most draconian, as it explicitly exempted carriers from any obligation to provide service to Blacks. Passed in 1899, it specified that "nothing in this act shall be construed to compel sleeping car companies or railroads operating sleeping cars to carry persons of color in sleeping cars or parlor cars."[80] The railroads enforced this law to the letter. In a widely publicized incident that took place shortly after its passage, African Methodist Episcopal Church bishop Henry W. Turner, who had recently suffered a stroke and remained gravely ill, was denied ac-

Modern Pullman steel sleeping car, ready to be made up for the night

Modern Pullman steel sleeping car during the day

Interior of a Pullman sleeping car, ca. 1917.

cess to a sleeping car on Georgia's Central Railway.[81] Despite several reports on this incident suggesting that "under the new law, the central and other lines will probably be compelled to provide two sleeping cars," nothing changed after that.[82] "In the State of Georgia. a negro cannot purchase a berth in a sleeping car, under any circumstances, no matter where his destination," reported Black lawyer Wilford H. Smith in 1903.[83] Such practices clearly violated the US Constitution's interstate commerce clause, but Smith doubted that anything could be done about it. "I fear the Commission would be powerless to grant relief," he wrote in a 1902 letter to W. E. B. Du Bois, who was then living in Atlanta and very troubled by the law. "It has not the power to declare a state law unconstitutional."[84]

Du Bois himself was equally pessimistic about the prospect of getting this "clearly unconstitutional" law overturned, but he launched a test case anyway. "Sheer self respect compels us to test the law if we can possibly afford the expense," he wrote, although he was convinced that should his challenge get to the US Supreme Court, the Court "would of course find it—constitutional."[85] Both men's doubts were borne out in 1905, when *W. E. B. Du Bois v. Southern Railway Company* was "indefinitely postponed" by the Interstate Commerce

Commission after a series of discussions and hearings that lasted over four years.[86]

Other early legal challenges to Pullman segregation were only slightly more successful. In 1897 Thomas W. Cain, a Black minister, won $100 in damages from the Pullman Company and the Great Northern Railroad Company after being ejected from a Pullman car in Longview, Texas, on a trip between St. Louis, Missouri, and his home in Galveston.[87] But Cain's victory in Texas's Civil Court of Appeals did little to discourage Pullman segregation in the state, or elsewhere. Indeed, such segregation was later upheld in the US Supreme Court case *McCabe v. Atchison, Topeka & Santa Fe Railway Company* (1914), a challenge to Oklahoma's 1907 separate coach law—and in particular its provisions regarding separate sleeping cars—which was rejected largely on procedural grounds.[88] African Americans would not begin overturning such laws until the 1940s, and Pullman car segregation persisted well after that.

Pullman car segregation persisted, at least in part, because the measures that railroad employees used to prevent Blacks from securing Pullman accommodations rarely relied on state law. Ticket agents in Texas and other states that later passed segregated sleeping car laws excluded Blacks from Pullman cars well before then by doing everything they could to keep Blacks from buying tickets.[89] When Milton A. Baker, a Black man, asked a ticket agent in Texas for sleeping car tickets on a train to Chicago for himself and his wife on a Monday in 1891, he was told that they were "all taken." What about Thursday?, he asked, only to be given "the same answer." "He then suggested Wednesday," at which point the agent said "they had been booked all week." On hearing this, Baker, who had already threatened to lodge a complaint with the Pullman Company, said he was prepared to "wait and go the first day the berths were not all taken." But he still could not secure a ticket until he returned a few days later to press his case again. Anxious to "avoid trouble and possibly a lawsuit," the ticket agent finally relented, selling him two tickets.[90] Railroad agents throughout the country used similar methods to discourage Blacks from traveling by Pullman anywhere in the South, usually with more successful results. "If a Pullman ticket should be purchased by a negro in Kansas to New Orleans, it would carry him thro[ugh]," a railway agent for a major southern railroad told a northern visitor to New Orleans in 1898: "the interstate-commerce act requires that a through ticket be honored." However, he further noted that his railroad did not actually sell Pullman tickets to Blacks in Kansas or New Orleans: "When a negro came to buy a Pullman ticket," he explained, "the car is always full." In the 1920s, white sociologist Hannibal Gerald Duncan found a similar system at work in Ohio, where ticket agents "refused to sell Pullman tickets to Negroes on trains going south from Cincinnati."[91]

None of these systems of rebuffing Black passengers were foolproof, and Black travelers who had the means to travel by Pullman car foiled them whenever they could. Among those who took advantage of the Pullman Company's willingness to sell tickets to Black passengers was Booker T. Washington, whose tolerance for segregation rarely extended to traveling Jim Crow. As an associate noted in 1916, the Tuskegee Institute principal routinely "'violated' the law of whatever State he happened to be passing through . . . when not an interstate passenger."[92] The most prominent Black leader of his day, he traveled all over the country and used Pullman services even in the South, where his celebrity status seems to have allowed him to purchase Pullman accommodations long after other southern Blacks lost that privilege.

On the rare occasions when he could not secure such accommodations, Washington used his wealth and power to avoid traveling in the "colored car." Refused a Pullman sleeper on a ten-day speaking tour in Texas in the fall of 1911, he called upon "the colored citizens of Texas" to provide him with a whole separate railroad car for his trip. According to one news report, the porter was "the only other occupant of the car." When critics in Austin suggested that he "avoided his race" by refusing to travel Jim Crow, the normally accommodating Washington was unabashed. "No one could possibly endure ten days of constant travel," he told the *Washington Post*, ". . . without some provision for sleeping at night."[93]

Most Black travelers lacked Washington's wealth and influence and had to secure Pullman tickets by more devious means. One of the easiest ways for an African American to purchase Pullman car accommodations was to convince the railroad station's ticket agent that they were buying the ticket for someone else. On at least one occasion, Black minister and educator Benjamin Mays managed to secure a Pullman ticket in Birmingham, Alabama, by the simple expedient of telling the ticket agent that he was buying the ticket for "Mr. Mays." "Remember," he explained in his autobiography: "Negroes are not supposed to call themselves Mr., Mrs., or Miss when speaking to a white man."[94] But this subterfuge was not always successful in the South, where station agents often asked Black Pullman ticket buyers, "Are these for your own use?"[95]

So other ruses developed. Blacks who were light-skinned enough to pass as white simply entered through the white waiting room and purchased their tickets there, while others enlisted white helpers. "In the South the black man who desires pull reservations seldom applies directly to the ticket agent," one Baltimore newspaper editor noted in 1929. "He finds a local colored man who [in] turn can get some white friend of his to 'straighten it out' so that he may secure a ticket."[96] Clarie Collins Harvey, a civil rights activist, noted that when she first started traveling outside her native Mississippi in the 1930s and 1940s, the only way she could obtain a Pullman reservation was to have a "doctor or attorney friend" of her parents call up the stationmaster and say, "My friend's daughter has to go to such and such a place and it is too long for her to sit up. Let her have a booth."[97]

African Americans who traveled frequently, however, did not always have the time or connections to take advantage of such arrangements. When traveling in the South on NAACP business in 1914, the organization's secretary, William Pickens, who had no connections in Louisville, had great difficulty figuring out how to get a Pullman ticket from Louisville to Birmingham. First he explored the possibility of having a "white Negro" or a messenger boy buy a ticket on his behalf, but he found out that this approach would not work because the local station agent insisted that Pullman tickets "must be gotten by the 'party' as the party enters the train." He then managed to reserve a ticket by phone, taking advantage of the fact that "they could not tell the color of my voice and made the reservation quite politely." But he still had to find a way to pick up the ticket and get on the train, which he ultimately managed to do only by enlisting the help of his white NAACP colleague Joel Spingarn. Spingarn accompanied Pickens to the station and walked him onto the train, where he claimed "Mr. Pickens's" ticket, while Pickens trailed behind him, carrying his suitcase. Both men managed to board the train without a hitch, as "the conductor and the porter politely admitted us—heeding not me the burden bearer"—at which point Spingarn slipped quietly off the train. By the time the conductor figured out what had happened, the train was moving and Pickens was secure in his berth. "You ain't the one that asked for this reservation at the door," the Pullman conductor then complained to Pickens, but he made no attempt to dislodge him from his berth.[98] Pickens was able to sleep all the way to Birmingham, but he could not help but resent the amount of time and effort he had put into getting his berth.

Such dodges were made possible, at least in part, by the fact that the Pullman Company continued to be more willing than the railroads to offer Blacks non–Jim Crow accommodations. Exempted from the Jim Crow laws of most southern states, the company had berths to fill and no hope of making money off passengers the railroads relegated to the Jim Crow car. So, while Pullman officials do not seem to have interfered with the railroad agents who refused to sell Pullman tickets to Blacks, they admitted those Blacks who managed to buy tickets, and sometimes even sold Pullman tickets to Blacks who were unable to secure them at the station.[99]

The Pullman Company's disregard for Jim Crow laws was an ongoing irritant to white southerners, who sometimes sued the company for forcing them to travel with Negroes. Company representatives were polite, but uncooperative, in the face of a 1914 complaint from the South Carolina Railroad Commission, which maintained that even though there was "no law upon the South Carolina Statutes Books requiring the separation of the races by the Pullman Company," the company "should defer to the wishes of our people on this important matter." By way of reply, "the Pullman people" told the commission, as one of its members reported, that while they were sympathetic to its "effort to enforce railroad segregation, both upon railroad cars and Pullman cars, . . . their service is entirely interstate and any effort on their part to meet this righteous demand by our people would bring them into conflict with National Law."[100]

Still, the Pullman Company did make substantial concessions to white prejudices in its handling of such passengers. As historian Catherine Cocks has noted, "while instructing its conductors to abide by the law requiring equal access regardless of race, the Pullman Company also advised them to seat passengers with consideration for whites' racial prejudices."[101] In practical terms, this meant that Pullman conductors were careful to keep Black passengers as far from white passengers as possible, which usually meant assigning them to a berth in an empty section of their car or giving them a special compartment known as the "Lower 13."

The Lower 13 was a private drawing room with a bed and bathroom located at the end of Pullman cars, which typically held twelve regular two-person compartments with upper and lower berths and one drawing room suite. Roomier than the other compartments, the Lower 13 typically cost more, except in the case of Black passengers, who were routinely assigned to this compartment to keep them away from other white passengers. Such assignments were

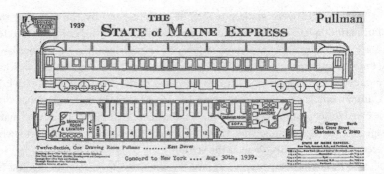

A Lower 13 compartment can be seen in this diagram of a 1939 State of Maine Express Twelve Section, One Drawing Room Pullman car. The drawing room, which is not numbered, is the Lower 13 compartment.

"one of the few instances in which it pays to be nonwhite," noted Stetson Kennedy in his 1959 *Jim Crow Guide to the USA*, "for in such circumstances you can get a private drawing room for a lesser price than a simple berth."[102] The poet Langston Hughes relished these rare moments of Black privilege, and wrote jubilantly about the palatial accommodations he enjoyed on a trip from New Orleans to Jackson, Tennessee, in a Pullman car that contained only two other passengers—both white. While his fellow passengers were assigned to ordinary Pullman berths, he crowed, he enjoyed a "private bedroom . . . complete with a private washroom and toilet" that would have cost him twice as much had he been charged for it—"Anything to keep the Negroes segregated!"[103]

But other Black travelers resented the enforced isolation imposed on Blacks in the Lower 13. A historian and activist who was a member of Franklin Delano Roosevelt's Black cabinet, Howard University professor Rayford Logan was so deeply opposed to segregation that he sometimes refused to accept Lower 13 accommodations. But he conceded that, given the dangers Blacks faced in some parts of the South: "a Negro traveler must know when it is best to get the 'Lower Thirteen' . . . to keep from . . . being seen."[104]

African American Pullman passengers could not always count on securing this unintended privilege, because they were assigned to the Lower 13 only when these compartments were empty. If they were already occupied, Black passengers who had paid for Pullman tickets could find themselves traveling in the Jim Crow car. As a court case against the Gulf, Mobile and Ohio Railroad in the early 1940s revealed, Pullman employees were not supposed to "sell Negroes space in the open section of car, that Negroes must be confined to enclosed space." Not surprisingly, the dining car employees on the same railroad were also under instructions "not to serve colored passengers when white passengers were in the diner."[105]

BLACK CHALLENGES TO THE JIM CROW CAR

By the twentieth century, travel by rail had become broadly affordable and was no longer a form of transportation reserved for middle-class and elite Blacks. But lower-class Blacks also found traveling Jim Crow degrading. In the fall of 1911, Cincinnati resident Mrs. Suzie Givens wrote to NAACP member Carrie Clifford asking for her help in dealing with the regular humiliations she faced when traveling South by rail. Employed as a private cook by a club that sent her out to a variety of different employers, Givens was "compelled to travel the L. & N. . . . two or three times each week" and found her travels almost intolerable.[106]

The L&N crossed into Kentucky right after it left Cincinnati, which was one of its few stops north of the Mason-Dixon Line. Headquartered in Louisville, Kentucky, the L&N served southern cities such as Memphis, New Orleans, and Pensacola, Florida, and forced all of its Black passengers to travel Jim Crow. Suzie Givens could not get used to it: "I have been offended so often that I can't stand it anymore; so a friend told me to write to you," she wrote. Chief among her complaints was that while L&N trains had special smoking cars for passengers who wished to smoke, "if there is no room in the smoker they don't have to go out." Instead, the train's conductor directed any smoker "to ride with us" in the Jim Crow car. As a result, more often than not, Givens had "to sit with dirty old white men and they smoke and spit at will." On one of her recent trips home from Kentucky, the car was so full of "white and black men" that Givens and "two other girls" had trouble squeezing in and tried to go into the "ladies' coach" instead. But before they could enter, "the flagman ordered us back in a very rough manner." When Givens objected, he threatened them with "an unlawful weapon, called a slingshot."[107]

Givens complained to the railroad and was told that "if it happened again . . . they would put a stop to it." But she was not satisfied. "I am against the Jim Crow car because they don't treat us right," she told Clifford. "I am only a poor working woman, but I want my rights, and if there is anything I can do or say that will do away with this car law I will do it for it certainly is humiliating. Hoping to hear some encouraging word from you soon."[108]

Carrie Clifford could not offer her the encouraging news she hoped to hear. Early twentieth-century race leaders were having no luck reforming the railroads. As we have seen, Booker T. Washington detested traveling Jim Crow and rarely did so himself, but the accommodations philosophy that gave him power and influence among whites made it difficult for him to mount an effective public opposition to travel segregation. Instead he lent secret support to legal challenges to transportation discrimination, while publicly decrying "the bitter vague and futile cry against the Jim Crow Car" issued by his more radical contemporaries.[109] Not until 1912 did he finally begin to address the issue openly, and even then he condemned "not the separation, but the inadequacy of accommodations," which he sought to improve by launching a "Railroad Days" campaign in 1914. Directed at the railroads, rather than the courts or the states, Washington's initiative designated June 7–8, 1914, as "Railroad Days," and called for Blacks across the nation to mark the occasion by flooding railroads with letters requesting "better accommodations on all the lines."[110] The campaign had little impact on travel conditions, and he dropped it after 1914.

Washington's campaign may have been too polite, but African American leaders who offered more forceful challenges to transportation discrimination made no greater headway. R. H. Boyd of Nashville, Tennessee, the founder and head of the National Baptist Publishing Association, used his press to publish and distribute a sixty-two-page pamphlet containing a complete compilation of the separate car laws passed in every southern state. Entitled *The Separate or "Jim Crow" Car Laws or Legislative Actions of the Fourteen Southern States* (1908), Boyd's book was designed to enable Black travelers to claim their rights on the railroads.[111] While Boyd believed that these laws were passed "for the purposes of humiliating and degrading the Negro race in the eyes of all the civilized world," he was also convinced that if the various state separate car laws "were properly enforced or executed by the courts, or obeyed by the railroads" there would be "no jim crowism"—at least as far as the comfort of Black travelers was concerned. After all, all of these laws "required the railroad companies to furnish separate but equal accommodations. Every accommodation on coaches or in waiting rooms that is provided for

white passengers is required by these enactments to be furnished for colored
or Negro passengers paying the same fare." He believed, following the logic of
his mentor Booker T. Washington, that Blacks just had to find a way to secure
these equal accommodations. Boyd's book offered "Negro passengers . . . an
opportunity to read and understand these laws," and "see to it that the railroad companies give them the accommodations required by these laws." He
urged travelers to familiarize themselves with "legislative enactments of the
fourteen states" and to sue any "agent, receiver, or company" that did not
comply with them. But Boyd's campaign was doomed from the outset.

Boyd's campaign was inspired at least in part by the ICC's ruling in *Georgia
Edwards v. Nashville, St. Louis and Chattanooga Railroad Company* in 1907.
However, that case, contrary to Boyd's hopes, ended up doing very little to
"promote the comfort of colored passengers."[112] Edwards was a Chattanooga
resident who filed a complaint with the ICC after being forced to ride in a
"filthy" Jim Crow car on a trip from Chattanooga to Dalton, Georgia, and she
had received some support for her complaint. After reviewing her case, the
ICC once again held that the segregation of white and colored interstate passengers was reasonable and permissible, but it took note of the limited amenities available to Edwards after she was moved into the Jim Crow car and
issued a ruling requiring the railroad to provide Black travelers with equal
accommodations. In particular, the commission specified that "where the defendant provides a washbowl and towels in coaches devoted to the use of
white passengers, and a separate smoking car for such passengers also, . . .
similar accommodations should be provided for colored passengers."[113]

The ICC's ruling left Boyd jubilant and convinced many whites that railroads would now have to "furnish equal accommodations to Negro passengers . . . even down to the smallest details." Indeed, one reporter for a white
magazine noted with alarm, "If Pullman cars are operated for whites, then
the Negroes must have them. If the whites have a smoking car, so must the
Negroes. If lavatories with soap and water and towels are furnished for the
whites, they must be furnished for the Negroes also. If the seats in the cars
for the whites are nicely upholstered, cane seats cannot be furnished to the
Negroes. If the whites have a dining car, the Negroes must have one, too."
The new ruling would create an "awkward predicament," this writer predicted, for the railroads: they would either have to double the length of their
trains to provide equal accommodations for both races, or "take away all the
luxuries from whites."[114]

In the end the ICC's ruling changed nothing. The railroad ignored the order even after President Theodore Roosevelt took up the issue the following year in a public letter insisting that colored passengers were entitled to receive accommodations "as good as those furnished to white passengers."[115] Two years later an investigator for the ICC found that the Nashville, St. Louis and Chattanooga Railroad Company along with virtually "all others in the south [had] failed to follow the directions of the commission."[116]

Other Black attempts to challenge transportation in the courts were also unsuccessful—at least in the short term. The first decade of the twentieth century was a generative period in the history of the Black freedom struggle, with the rise of a new generation of radical Black leaders who rejected all forms of segregation, denounced Booker T. Washington's accommodationist leadership, and worked hard to create an enduring national civil rights organization. Founded in 1909, the National Association for the Advancement of Colored People (NAACP) had a number of predecessors, the most immediate of which were the National Afro-American Council (1898–1907) and the Niagara Movement (1905–1909). All three were committed to challenging segregation and other forms of racial discrimination in court, and all three had great difficulty raising enough money to make much headway.

Alexander Walters, who was a bishop and the president of the National Afro-American Council, vowed to fight segregation on the railroads "until the last Jim Crow car has passed into oblivion."[117] But his organization never succeeded in raising the money it would have needed "to test the disenfranchising laws and Jim Crow cars that oppress the Negro race in this land of ours." Supporters dreamed of amassing a "national defence fund reaching into hundreds of thousands of dollars for a hundred different purposes," but the Council never managed to raise more than a few thousand dollars, most of which went to attempts to regain voting rights in states that had disenfranchised Black voters.[118]

The Niagara Movement, likewise, proved overly ambitious in its hope of using "a systematic bringing of suits" to undermine segregation by challenging the southern states to "enforce the federal court mandate that separate accommodations on public conveyances must be 'equal in quality and convenience.'" During the Niagara Movement's four years of operation, its Committee on Legal Defense and Civil Rights won only one case. In 1906 it overturned a Virginia court's judgment against Barbara E. Pope, a Washington, D.C., resident who had been arrested and fined $10 for refusing to move into the Jim Crow car on a trip to Virginia. Unfortunately it was a pyrrhic victory—as would often be true of travel cases. In reviewing the case, Virginia's supreme court avoided litigating "any real Jim Crow issues," conceding only that state segregation laws "did not provide for criminal penalties to passengers who refused to change rail cars." As historian Paul Nelson points out, Pope's victory "had no consequence except saving Barbara Pope ten dollars."[119] It also left the Niagara Movement's legal committee in debt.[120] By 1909, which would be its last year, its legal department was "unable to do anything owing to lack of funds except to offer advice and assistance in preparation of briefs that have come to us."[121]

The NAACP encountered similar challenges in its early days. Although its finances were less dismal than those of the National Afro-American Council and the Niagara Movement, its legal bureau founded in 1912, began its work at a time when Jim Crow laws were proliferating so rapidly that it was difficult to know where to start. "The past year has been characterized by a flood of discriminatory legislation," the organization told its members in its annual report for 1913: "anti-intermarriage bills, 'Jim Crow' bills segregation ordinances in cities and segregation in the Federal departments at Washington. Everywhere we have witnessed efforts to officialize caste."[122] These developments ensured that the organization had a variety of legal concerns that were more pressing than challenging travel discrimination in the courts; these included identifying test cases that could be used to challenge "the grandfather clause," poll taxes, and other measures used to sustain Black disenfranchisement, and securing anti-lynching legislation. By the mid-teens, the NAACP was wary of transportation test cases. It was difficult to get such cases past southern state courts—as seen in Barbara Pope's case—and the US Supreme Court had repeatedly refused to revisit the principles it had laid down in *Plessy*. In 1910 the Court even expanded the scope of the travel discrimination it had authorized in *Plessy*, by ruling in *Chiles v. Chesapeake and Ohio Railway* that state segregation laws could be applied to interstate passengers.[123]

Not surprisingly, given the difficulties they faced in challenging travel segregation in the courts, turn-of-the-century Black civil rights activists sought to secure federal legislation banning Jim Crow on the railroads. The early twentieth century saw the federal government exert increasing power over the railroads in ways that seemed poised to create opportunities for outright abolition of Jim Crow. The first such opportunity came in 1902, when, in the face of continuing public complaints about railroad rates, Congress moved to strengthen the regulatory power of the Interstate Commerce Commission by passing a measure to increase the ICC's control over rate regulation that would ultimately become known as the Elkins Act. When Congress began to deliberate on this measure, a delegation from the National Afro-American Council visited Republican congressman Edward de Veaux Morrell of Pennsylvania.[124] The Council's representatives persuaded Morrell to propose an amendment that would put an end to segregation on the railroads. Reportedly drafted by Daniel Alexander Payne Murray—a member of the Council, an assistant librarian at the Library of Congress, and a well-known expert on African American affairs—the Morrell amendment to the Elkins Act would have compelled the railroads "to furnish identical accommodations for all persons paying the same fare" and prohibited them from "separating passengers on the basis of color."[125]

Morrell's amendment had the full support of the National Afro-American Council, whose members solicited letters from Blacks across the country urging Congress to pass the measure. Council members also sent a delegation of eminent Blacks to testify in its favor before the Congressional Committee of Interstate and Foreign Commerce. The men who spoke on the amendment's behalf included former congressmen George H. White, who, prior to declining to seek a third term in 1901, had been Congress's last remaining African American member; Jesse Lawson, a lawyer and sociologist; Cyrus Fields Adams, an assistant registrar of the treasury; and Walter H. Brooks, a prominent Baptist minister. Speaking as "citizens of the Republic," they appealed to the committee for "simple unalloyed justice."[126] But their testimony does not seem to have had much of an impact. The committee members they spoke to expressed little interest in what they had to say, and went on to pass the Elkins Act without ever seriously considering Morrell's amendment.[127]

Black activists were equally unsuccessful in making the Hepburn Act of 1906 into a measure to stop Jim Crow. Designed to increase the regulatory power of the Interstate Commerce Commission, the Hepburn Act expanded the ICC's membership from five to seven members, gave the ICC's rulings the force of law, and empowered the ICC to determine the maximum "fair, just, and reasonable" rates that railroads could charge for their services. The act therefore provided another potential opening for eliminating racial discrimination on the railroads. Seizing on this opportunity, George White and other Black leaders once again lobbied members of Congress to insert into pending legislation an amendment forbidding racial discrimination. They managed to secure the support of Ohio senator Joseph B. Foraker. But in formulating his proposed amendment, Foraker ignored the advice he received from George White and Archibald Grimke, who told him that any amendment he introduced should "not only forbid discrimination but separation, as well, knowing that whenever there is separation the Negro never gets equality of service."[128]

Designed to win the acceptance of white Senate members, Foraker's amendment did no such thing. Instead it required only that railroads provide Blacks with facilities that "were the same or equally good" as those provided to whites. George White and other Black leaders were horrified. Foraker's measure—which became known as the Foraker-Warner Amendment after it was modified by Senator William Warner of Missouri to better emphasize that "segregation was not an issue, only equality of facilities"—seemed to give federal sanction, as White lamented, "to all the discriminations now practiced in all the southern states where the Jim Crow is now in full force."[129] White and Grimke joined forces with Du Bois and other Black radicals to oppose the amendment and eventually managed to get Foraker and other Republicans to rescind it.

World War I provided yet another opportunity for decisive federal action against racial discrimination. As the war approached, the nation's railroads were on the verge of going out of business. Regulatory measures such as the Hepburn Act had kept rates down, but they had also helped make it all but impossible for the railroads to earn enough revenue to meet their expenses at a time when many were still adding terminals and tracks and upgrading equipment. Railroad companies also faced increasing demands for shorter hours and higher pay from their workers. By the mid-teens, many were bankrupt and others faced threats of a massive strike. With World War I making unprecedented demands on the nation's transportation infrastructure, Congress had little choice but to take over the railroads. It began the process by passing the Adamson Act, a 1916 law that helped resolve the railroad's labor disputes by mandating an eight-hour workday, and completed it with the Federal Possession and Control Act (1917), which nationalized the railroads.

This gave Congress a prime opportunity to eradicate the South's Jim Crow car system. But President Woodrow Wilson's administration had no interest in doing so. Born in Virginia and raised in Georgia and South Carolina, Wilson was a southerner who favored segregation. During his first year in office he authorized his cabinet to resegregate the federal civil service—which had been desegregated during Reconstruction. And in presiding over the federalization of the railroads, he paid no mind to Black leaders who asked him to "take down Jim Crow signs and begin democracy at home." Instead he maintained the status quo by appointing his son-in-law, Secretary of the Treasury William G. McAdoo, to be the director general of the newly formed United States Railroad Administration (USRA).

A southerner from Tennessee, McAdoo had presided over the segregation of the Treasury during his term as its secretary, and he brought little change to the railroads. Under McAdoo and his second-in-command and eventual successor, Walter Hines, the USRA fielded discrimination complaints by making modest attempts to improve the Jim Crow facilities on southern railroads. Both men had trouble justifying the actions of railroad conductors, who drove Black officers and enlisted men out of Pullman cars and other accommodations, but neither was willing to recognize Black men's civil rights. Racial discrimination on the railroads involved "two apparently irreconcilable factors," Hines wrote in a 1918 memo to McAdoo. On the one hand, discrimination was incompatible with "the settled policy of the government in favor of equality," especially in "view of the equal participation of the colored race in the war." But on the other hand, "the local conditions in the South which have brought about the separate cars laws" made segregation necessary. Throughout the region, he opined, "the tendency to disorder and disturbance is much greater where large numbers of colored passengers are mingled with white passengers."[130]

White southerners mobilized similar arguments to block racial reforms in the fall of 1919, as the government prepared to transfer the railroads back to private ownership. At that time Congressman Martin B. Madden of Illinois proposed an amendment to what would become the Esch-Cummins Act (1920), which dictated the terms of the transfer. This act was crafted in collaboration with a number of D.C.'s most influential Black leaders, including Arthur Wergs Mitchell, who, as a congressional representative, would later make his own flawed but consequential legal challenge to train segregation in 1937 (as will be seen in Chapter 7). Madden's amendment would have required the railroads and other common carriers to supply Blacks with "equal and identical rights, accommodations and privileges," and explicitly banned them from discriminating against passengers on "account of race, color, or previous condition of servitude."[131]

Madden's proposal outraged representatives from the South. "Bloodletting would follow the abolition of separate cars," maintained William Stevenson of South Carolina, who claimed that Madden's bill was unnecessary because "accommodations for white and colored passengers in the South were equal." Other southern delegates insisted that southern Negroes had a strong preference for separate accommodations. "Our Negroes down South know that they were not welcome in the white man's coach," explained Jared Sanders of Louisiana, "and they do not want to go in there."[132] The debate was followed by extensive testimony to the contrary by four Black leaders, who described the discomforts of traveling Jim Crow and laid out the long history of African American attempts to secure equal accommodations. Their testimony fell on deaf ears. Congressmen sat in silence as the Madden amendment's southern opponents offered their dubious rationalizations for rejecting the bill and had no questions for the Black men who testified that the conditions in Jim Crow cars were "dangerous and unsanitary."[133] Few were interested in seeing legislation designed to return the railroads to private ownership delayed by a deadlock over segregation. And few were interested in doing anything about segregation.[134] Madden's bill was defeated by a vote of 142 to 12.

If anything, segregation on the trains would only get worse after the war—or at least it felt worse in the aftermath of a war that African Americans had hoped would secure their civil rights. Traveling through Texas in 1923, William Pickens could not even get a "day coach ticket." The "morning train is only Pullman and colored folks are made to wait twelve hours longer for the train that carries the Jim Crow compartment." While he waited, he was confined to an unkempt twenty-by-twenty-foot Negro waiting room "away off in one corner of the station like a place of quarantine or veritable hole in the wall." The main waiting room would accept "any foreigner or foreign spy who happens to be loose in the land," he reflected as he waited, "but not the mothers, wives or sisters of the black Americans who fought and died in France."[135]

Throughout the South, African American travelers would continue to occupy cramped waiting rooms and Jim Crow cars through to World War II, despite an ever-rising chorus of Black protest. As we will see, it was not until the 1940s and 1950s that Black legal challenges to segregated transportation would finally begin to make headway in American courts—and even after that, the desegregation of the nation's trains and other common carriers would be slow and hard-fought. Ironically, by the time these victories arrived, the golden age of the American railroad was long over. Starting in the 1920s and 1930s, the railroads began competing with cars and buses for passengers, and by the 1940s and 1950s they were losing passengers to airplanes as well. All of these alternate forms of transportation would hold a special appeal for African American travelers, who were all too ready to turn their backs on the Jim Crow car.

3

Traveling by Car

Race on the Road in the Automotive Age

JACK JOHNSON LOVED TO DRIVE. A BIG BLACK MAN WHO CARRIED himself with swaggering self-confidence, Johnson, in 1908, appalled much of the white world by becoming the first man of color to win the heavyweight championship of the world. His mastery of boxing's "sweet science" was a challenge to white masculinity, as was his penchant for consorting with white women. So was his love of cars. Far too proud and hotheaded to be comfortable traveling Jim Crow, Johnson began buying automobiles as soon they became available.[1] By 1909 he owned five cars, which he drove everywhere. "His command of cars," as cultural critic Paul Gilroy notes, "drew hostility, harassment, and an introjected, covetous admiration from the police wherever he went."[2] Johnson received tickets for speeding, reckless driving, obstructing traffic, and other moving violations whenever he drove, which discouraged him not at all. He parked his cars on the sidewalk in Chicago, and once told a judge that his constant speeding "was simply done for 'advertising' purposes."[3] Johnson also toyed with the idea of a career in car racing, and offered $5,000 to any driver who could beat him in a race.

Johnson's offer was clearly designed to muscle his way into a new field. Membership in the motor sports division of the American Automobile Association (AAA) was limited to whites, and the AAA's Contest Board refused to license him or sanction any race in which he participated. Johnson's efforts almost failed: AAA drivers were all but unanimous in decrying Johnson as too ignorant of "the mechanical end of an automobile" to be a worthy opponent. However, in 1910 world champion racer Barney Oldfield defied the AAA Contest Board's color bar to beat Johnson in a race—and found himself banned from the circuit for over a year as a result.[4] AAA racing would remain an all-white sport for many years to come.

Still, Johnson did not need to win races, or even drive particularly quickly, to attract attention as a driver. One of the few Black men of his era to own even one car, Johnson was once arrested while cruising slowly down Broadway in New York City for driving a car with Chicago plates. Disgusted to be stopped yet again, he said, "I goes fast they arrest me and now it seems like if I go slow they does the same. Next thing, somebody'll arrest me for being a brunette in a blond town."[5]

As Johnson was clearly aware, his race was responsible for much of the outrage and anxiety that his driving inspired. Both the police who harassed him and the AAA drivers who refused to race him drew on a variety of racial stereotypes when they questioned his ability to own and operate a car. At the start of the twentieth century, car ownership was largely limited to very wealthy whites, so Johnson's multiple car purchases disrupted established hierarchies of class and color. His mere act of driving was equally problematic. Often barred from skilled jobs, Blacks were also widely held to lack mechanical aptitude. But Johnson drove with ease, and even took on white champions.[6]

As Johnson's experiences suggest, the technological transformations of the automotive age offered African American travelers both new forms of mobility and new sites of racial contestation. Cars were a symbol of freedom and mobility for all Americans. Many whites waxed eloquent about how cars offered every driver the opportunity to be "his own stationmaster, engineer and porter, with no one's time to make up but his own," and freed passengers from traversing "the same old scenes again and again."[7] Blacks no doubt appreciated these advances as well, but they above all saw automotive technology as a potential escape from the degrading segregation of the Jim Crow car. As early as 1924, Black newspapers such as Atlanta's *The Independent* were encouraging their readers to "buy a car of your own and escape jim-crowism."[8]

Jack Johnson was not the only African American to embrace the new technology. Other well-to-do Blacks, such as doctors, ministers, businessmen, and entertainers, also welcomed the freedom and status that automobile ownership conferred, and working-class African Americans worked as chauffeurs and mechanics. During the World War I era, as cars became cheaper, even some Black farmers and sharecroppers bought them.

African Americans both rich and poor hoped that cars would bring greater freedom and autonomy. But automotive technology would only go so far in

Boxer Jack Johnson sitting in the driver's seat of one of his cars, early 1900s.

allowing Blacks to escape Jim Crow. Privately owned cars would provide those who could afford them with a small space in which to escape some of segregation's humiliations. But traveling by car is not private. Driving any distance involves entering what sociologist John Urry has described as a "system of automobility" defined not only by its users' commitment to cars as their major means of transportation, but also by their reliance upon industries and services that make car ownership useful. Almost too quotidian to list in full, these include "road-building and maintenance; hotels, roadside service areas and motels; car sales and repair workshops; suburban house building; retailing and leisure complexes; advertising and marketing; urban design and planning." Urry emphasizes that within this system, the car is never just a car. For most car owners, a car is the "major item of *individual consumption*" after housing. The car also functions as a symbol. Its design, make, and model communicate its owner's or user's status (or lack thereof) through "sign-values (such as speed, security, safety, sexual desire, career success, freedom, family, masculinity)," some of which can also attract the attention of the "criminal justice systems."[9]

As I will show in this chapter, the "system of automobility" that took shape in the United States between the twentieth century's first decade and the Second World War was deeply racialized in a variety of ways. (The ongoing effects of this phenomenon are discussed in the Epilogue.) From the invention of the automobile onward, whites debated whether Blacks should own cars and what kind of cars they should own, and often treated with suspicion and hostility African Americans who drove expensive cars. The service stations, roadside restaurants, motels, auto camps, and other businesses that took shape around the car were rarely designed with Black travelers in mind. Instead, many such establishments were segregated by law in the southern states, and off-limits to Blacks as a matter of custom in many other states. Likewise, the state regulation of driving was rarely race-neutral. Frequently targeted for traffic violations, African Americans were also subject to a variety of largely unwritten traffic laws in southern states, where even parking could be segregated.

In other words, technology alone, as Black travelers would find in boarding buses and planes in later decades, was not able to destroy segregation. Rather than offering an escape from Jim Crow, instead the invention of the automobile introduced new and complex forms of traveling Black.

THE CHAUFFEUR PROBLEM IN BLACK AND WHITE

As the twentieth century opened, stereotypes about Black technological incompetence led many early auto enthusiasts to question whether Blacks could become drivers. Such prejudices would later be replicated in early white resistance to African Americans learning how to pilot another new technology: airplanes. But with automobiles, observers were eager to highlight not just Black incompetence, but a graceful departure from the need for Black workers at all.

"The coach and pair is fast giving way in old Virginia to the chauffeur and the toot of his horn," proclaimed a writer for the *Washington Post* in 1909. "The trained mechanic with duster and gloves, his cap and goggles, has passed by the time honored Southern Negro, who almost invariably filled the role of the driver and coachman in the South." Skilled white chauffeurs had to be paid twice as much as the coachmen they replaced, the writer noted, but progress was subject to "the law of political economy," which "like water seeks its own level, sends the darky to other work."[10] African Americans lacked the capacity to master complicated machinery, proclaimed another reporter that same year, which made chauffeuring "a very dangerous occupation for them."[11]

The idea of putting a Black man in charge of a car raised other objections as well. As skilled laborers in command of expensive vehicles, Black chauffeurs threatened to overturn the racial hierarchies around which many American communities were organized. In 1911, South Carolina governor Cole L. Blease went so far as to suggest that "a law should be passed prohibiting any negro from driving an automobile, because my experience is that it makes them impudent and the fact that they are driving a machine for the white man puts it into their heads that they have the right of way of the road, and that everyone and everyone should give way for them."[12] Although no such law was ever passed, similar sentiments were strong enough to discourage the hiring of Black chauffeurs in some areas. The Miami Chamber of Commerce banned Negro chauffeurs prior to World War I. "Auto driving is in Miami, and should be elsewhere," one local explained in 1916, "a white man's occupation."[13]

The ban was enforced by Miami's white chauffeurs, who became so notorious for mobbing African American drivers that whites from other states who employed "colored chauffeurs" grew hesitant about visiting Miami. In 1916, New Jersey resident George C. Miller, who was contemplating making Miami his base for a winter holiday, wrote to the *Miami News* to inquire whether his driver would be welcome there. He had heard, he said, that Miami's residents "have a strong feeling against colored motormen. It is true? For I think a good deal of my man and would not submit to his being badly treated."[14] Unwitting visitors to Miami, such as millionaire Edward L. Stone of Roanoke, Virginia, who toured the South with his Black driver in 1915, experienced the problem more directly. White chauffeurs protested the presence of Stone's driver, Charlie Shultz, by tooting their horns and blockading the tourist attractions that Stone attempted to visit, forcing Stone to send Shultz home by train and hire a white chauffeur.[15]

Not just in Miami but across the country, white chauffeurs were some of the most energetic and enduring opponents of Black chauffeurs. Anxious to define driving as a high-paying form of skilled labor that only white men could master, New York's white chauffeurs did their best "to prevent the employment of a negro in driving capacity" by refusing to patronize parking garages that accommodated Black drivers and by sabotaging cars driven by Negro chauffeurs.[16] "They . . . put mothballs in our gasolene [sic] tanks, shortcircuit our ignition system and throw the carbureter [sic] out of adjustment," one African American chauffeur complained in 1912. These practices were sufficiently widespread to make many garage owners reluctant to rent space to anyone who employed a Black chauffeur. "I would not dare to have such a car in my garage," one told a motorist who was having trouble finding a berth for his car. "Not only would a number of white drivers withdraw their cars, but goodness knows what would happen to the colored driver's car, and I might have to stand the damages." Outside New York City "the warfare against the colored chauffeur" was "less open, but . . . none the less vigorous in general."[17] In many cities, white chauffeurs formed unions that did not admit Blacks, in the hope of reserving their line of work for their own race.

Outside of Miami, which retained its ban on Black chauffeurs until 1917, white chauffeurs were unsuccessful in barring Black men from their profession for several reasons. By 1910, rapid advances in automobile technology and the spread of garages, many of which offered both parking and automotive maintenance and repairs, had transformed the chauffeur's job. Early automobiles required weekly oil changes, frequent valve changes, and careful engine maintenance, and many of the nation's first chauffeurs were trained machinists. But by the late 1910s, most cars could run for many months with few repairs or adjustments, and could be taken to garages for repair. Chauffeurs no longer commanded premium wages, nor did they have to be trained in auto mechanics. And some employers had begun to have mixed feelings about the mechanically minded young white men who initially monopolized chauffeur jobs. "The free-born American mechanic, turned chauffeur," one employment agency explained to the *Literary Digest* in 1912, is "more trouble than other servants." Too often, such chauffeurs thought that they "outranked the butler, the coachman, and the gardener, and . . . [were] in comparison to the housemaid, an exalted being." They spent their spare time joy-riding and picking up girls, and typically refused to do "any work outside the garage." As a result, motorists had begun to avoid hiring such men: "The chauffeur today is no longer coming from the mechanic class. People want him not only to be a servant, but to know he is a servant. Former coachmen are more and more in demand. So are foreigners."[18]

Nevada lawyer Key Pittman, who was abused by his political opponents during his unsuccessful 1910 run for state senate for "having a colored boy driving his car," offers one real-life example of a motorist who wanted his driver to be a servant. Pittman refused to fire his driver, and sent out a chain letter notifying Negro voters that he retained his Black chauffeur as a matter of fairness to their race—and soliciting their votes of support on that account.

But his real reasons for keeping his driver were far less noble. "As a general rule," he wrote in a private letter, "unions among chauffeurs . . . don't amount to much. My boy is getting just as much pay as any of them, and he works at my house when he is not running the automobile. I took him for that reason as most chauffeurs would not do anything but run a car. . . . I am going to keep this coon in my employ and there is no use arguing the matter."[19]

By 1914, scholars of Negro labor were reporting "a steady demand for both white and colored chauffeurs," which eased racial tensions within the profession. The demand was created, at least in part, by the advent of World War I, which reduced white European immigration, making jobs more plentiful. But it also reflected the fact that Black workers had managed to claim a place within this new profession—often because they did more work for less money. Although many white automotive schools did not admit Black students, most African American chauffeurs had "a working knowledge of the machine they operate[d]," and could "keep a car out of a repair shop unless there is some serious trouble."[20]

Black chauffeurs' expertise not only belied white racial stereotypes that held that Blacks had no mechanical aptitude; it also documented the quiet rise of an African American "network of automotive knowledge and services."[21] The network's participants included former coachmen and butlers, who sometimes received their training from their employers, or from the company that had manufactured the car they drove (some car companies offered a small number of classes set aside for colored chauffeurs). The 1910s also saw the emergence of a small number of automobile schools that catered largely to Black students. In New York City, where African American attempts to enroll in the West Side YMCA Auto School were unsuccessful, the Cosmopolitan Automobile School on West 53rd Street welcomed Black students between 1910 and 1911, and possibly thereafter—its history is documented only by the advertisements it ran in *Crisis* magazine when it first opened.[22] Meanwhile, the Imperial Employment and Repair Auto School opened in Pittsburgh in 1911, and was successful enough during its first year to force "one white school to open its doors to colored students." It may not have survived the competition. The school's ads, which urged students "Don't be Jim Crowed. Come here where you can exercise your race pride and be a gentleman," disappeared after 1912.[23]

Not surprisingly, given their precarious access to automotive training, many early Black mechanics were largely self-taught—"I am mechanically

inclined also with the advantage of a course with the International Correspondence School in Automobile," one Black southerner who sought work in
Chicago noted in a 1917 letter to the *Chicago Defender*.[24] Some mobilized
their skills to build successful businesses. Most remarkable in this regard,
perhaps, was African American entrepreneur Frederick Douglass Patterson.
A lifelong resident of Greenfield, Ohio, Patterson converted his father's
carriage-making business into an automobile factory in the early 1900s and
produced 150 Patterson-Greenfield cars. In 1920 he retooled his factory to
produce bus bodies, having decided not to continue competing with Detroit's big automakers. His new venture, the Greenfield Bus Body Company,
which built buses and trucks that ran on a Ford or GM car chassis, flourished for over a decade. But after Patterson died in 1932, the Great Depression gradually eroded the business he had built.[25]

Just as World War I signaled changes to the nation's trains, it also greatly
increased demand for skilled labor of all kinds and briefly opened up new
opportunities for Black automotive education. With the passage of the Selec-
tive Service Act of 1917, the US Army quickly discovered that its draft pool
lacked "the technicians required for ordinary military operations." Most recruits entered the army with no vocational training of any kind; meanwhile,
both voluntary enlistment and the draft made matters worse, because students departed technical schools before they finished their training. Accordingly, in 1918 the War Department contracted with 157 schools and colleges
to establish National Army Training Detachment units designed to train col-
lege-age draftees in critically needed trades that ranged from carpentry and
blacksmithing, to electrical and mechanical work of all kinds, and included
driving instruction. Later expanded into a Student Army Training Corps,
which trained officer candidates as well, the program established vocational
training units at thirteen Black colleges.

Although these programs ended with the armistice in 1918, almost all of
them offered the ten thousand Black students who completed them courses
in truck driving and auto mechanics. The war years also opened up similar
training opportunities to Black women for the first time. Recruited for work
in "every kind of possible factory devoted to the production of war materials," many women worked on assembly lines, but some received training
in "motor mechanics and truck driving."[26]

Once the war ended, unemployment soared and white men resumed their
traditional jobs, pushing many Blacks back into unskilled labor. But stereo-

types about Blacks being unable to operate any vehicle more complicated than a horse and buggy did not survive the war's end. Instead, the mobilization of Black drivers solidified a new stereotype, reassuring to many whites, of the African American driver as a servant. A 1919 discussion of the increasing importance of motor trucks to "the nation's industrial progress" in *The Outlook* magazine summed up this new racial script. Commenting on a picture of Black workers loading a truck with freight, its writer observed, "Thus the old Southern darky with his span of 'ornery' mules gives way to the *up-to-date Negro chauffeur*."[27]

"IT IS THE NEGROES WHO ARE BUYING CARS": BLACK CAR OWNERSHIP

African Americans bought and drove their own cars, of course, although prior to 1910 the high cost limited automobile ownership to the rich. The fact that cars were closely associated with wealth and power made them especially appealing to affluent Blacks, whose wealth did not exempt them from traveling Jim Crow. African Americans rushed to purchase automobiles precisely when railroads were doubling down on segregation, even as the degradations of traveling by rail—including the danger of being in a Jim Crow wreck—were intensifying.

Affluent Blacks had limited access to many of the luxuries enjoyed by other wealthy Americans and were unwelcome in high society. So they embraced automobiles as symbols of citizenship and class. Such symbolism was particularly important to wealthy Black celebrities, who, as scholar Lerone A. Martin has noted, "had few other means of setting themselves apart from other people." In a world that offered little recognition or respect to prominent Black performers and athletes, Martin argues, "an extravagant vehicle was one of the few canvases on which Black celebrities could depict and proclaim their celebrity for all to see."[28] Little wonder, then, that Jack Johnson referred to his speeding tickets as "advertising."

Other Black celebrities seem to have had a similar relationship to their cars. Early Black car owners in New York included the dance team of Avery and Hart, whose drives through the city captured the public imagination. "Old New Yorkers tell me," recorded Langston Hughes, "they were among the first to be seen speeding up Broadway in long open cars, all occupants dressed in linen dusters to keep the rush of air from blowing their garments into dis-array." And of course Jack Johnson did the same when he visited the city. Johnson was known not only for his driving but also for the flashy luxury cars he favored. They included a canary yellow roadster and possibly even an armored car—which he was rumored to have purchased because he was not satisfied with owning only "ordinary" automobiles.[29]

By the late 1910s, however, the use of cars was no longer limited to wealthy motorists and their chauffeurs, which further complicated race relations on the road. First introduced in 1908, Henry Ford's mass-produced Model T was a sturdy, inexpensive vehicle that grew cheaper over time. Priced at an all-time low of $260 in 1925, it was as reliable as a mule and cheaper than a good horse.[30]

The mass production of the Model T transformed African American life in at least two important ways. First, as remains well known today, Ford was one of the first industrial giants to employ African Americans, and the man-ufacturing work generated by his revolutionary car helped trigger the Great Migration of Black southerners to northern cities such as Detroit.[31] Second, and largely forgotten, the Model T put car ownership within the reach of or-dinary African Americans. In this sense, the Model T was both a catalyst and a tool by which the Great Migration occurred: a reason for African Amer-icans to leave the South, and a means for them to do so.

The transportation revolution ushered in by Ford's "Tin Lizzie" crossed race and class lines, opening car ownership to ordinary Americans, both Black and white. The Model T and the other affordable cars soon produced by Ford's rivals opened up car ownership to the Black middle class and some members of the working class, creating new hierarchies of race and class on the road that varied widely from place to place.

Roadways themselves were part of the revolution. When the Model T was first introduced, most of America's rural roads were unpaved dirt or gravel pathways that became muddy and impassible when it rained and were very dusty during the dry months of summer, making long car trips an ordeal. Starting in the 1910s, a "good roads" movement, which dated back to the 1870s and first took shape around bicycles, finally began to transform America's roads into pavement. Initially funded by state and local governments, the good roads movement received much-needed federal support when Woodrow Wilson signed the Federal Road Aid Act in 1916, which led to the creation of interstate roads such as the Lincoln Highway, which stretched from the East

Coast to the West Coast, and the Dixie Highway, which ran from Canada to Miami.

In the South, road work was largely assigned to Black convicts, who were so ubiquitous in this line of work that one Florida lawyer described this as a logical remedy for states that had "too many Negroes and not enough roads."[32] But this forced labor did not ensure African American access to these roads. When Henry Watson, a well-to-do Georgia farmer, used his new car to drive his daughter into town in 1917, he and his daughter were forced out of the car by an angry mob of white men who poured gasoline on the car and set it on fire. "From now on, you niggers walk into town," the men told the Watsons, "or use that old mule if you want to stay in this city."[33] And that same year saw several other automobile owners in Georgia dragged out of their cars and beaten.[34]

The hostility encountered by Black physician Joe Griffin of Bainbridge, Georgia, who used his car for medical calls, was more genteel, but nonetheless striking. During the influenza epidemic of 1918, Griffin was in considerable demand among white patients, but his car was not. One of the only doctors in his area known to offer an effective treatment for influenza, Griffin was called to come treat white patients who lived as far away as Florida. Even in their time of need, however, the whites who summoned him were unwilling to have him drive up to their homes in his Model T. Instead, they would send their own cars to drive him back and forth from his office.[35]

Such incidents reflected the white South's long-standing hostility to any display of Black wealth. The region's racial hierarchies, notes historian Jason Chambers, led many southern whites to look for "hard evidence of their superiority in the division of material goods." They asked (and taught their children to ask), "If you aren't any better than a nigger, who are you better than?"[36] And cars—as a highly valuable and visible symbol of conspicuous consumption—could easily provoke such questions of superiority from southern whites.

For this reason, some Black men who drove expensive cars wore a chauffeur's cap "to avoid offending whites," while other middle-class Black car buyers chose their cars with an eye to white opinion.[37] "So offensive to white sensibilities was a black driving an expensive car," writes historian Jerome Packard, "that even well-to-do African-Americans kept to older models so as not to give the dangerous impression of being above themselves."[38] They also chose the make of their cars carefully. James Weldon Johnson, executive secretary of the NAACP, noted in 1927 that in some parts of the South the "possession of any car other than a Ford by colored people is frowned upon."[39] More than thirty years later, writer William Styron, who grew up in the South, found similar car-buying strategies still in place. Revisiting the region in the 1960s, he discovered that while Black southerners were far more prosperous than they once were, they still favored "decent late-model Fords" over "new-model Buicks." "The Southern man's strictures against Negro ostentation remain intimidating," Styron concluded.[40]

And yet, owning even a modest vehicle remained a point of pride among members of the Black southern middle class, because car ownership allowed them to avoid traveling Jim Crow. Black travelers directly connected their embrace of cars with the deplorable conditions on the railroads described in Chapter 2. For example, one "Arkansas Traveler" in 1927 noted that railway segregation was instituted at least in part to "humiliate the better class of Negroes." But now, he continued, such Negroes were "beating the white man at his own game"—"[they are] owning cars that take them wherever they wish to go."[41]

Such freedom was an improvement on the humiliations even the wealthiest railroad traveler might face, whether in purchasing a ticket, eating a meal, or being allowed to move about the train. And Black travelers relished that freedom. Consider what a well-to-do Black North Carolinian told sociologist Charles Johnson, who researched segregation in the 1940s: "Of course Negroes ride in the Jim Crow here. . . . But I don't ride in it. I just don't ride the trains now. I use my car to drive anywhere I want to go. That's one reason I have a car."[42]

Outside of the South, evading Jim Crow was less of an issue, and so, too, were questions of ostentation. In the North and West, African Americans often used their choice of cars to signal their wealth and status. City dwellers for the most part, middle-class African American northerners generally had access to public transportation; but like many other Americans, they embraced car ownership all the same. Among Blacks throughout the United States, the *Negro World* reported as early as 1924, "The motor car is regarded as a necessity rather than a luxury . . . even among small families of modest means."[43] The *California Eagle,* another Black newspaper, noted that Black automobile ownership was no longer a "curiosity"; instead, "the automobile is a necessity to everyone."[44]

In discussing specific Black car owners, however, both newspapers tended to present car ownership as less a necessity than an emblem of Black economic success, and in doing so chronicled the growing importance of luxury vehicles among middle-class Blacks. Black car owners often "put prosperity . . . on parade" by buying elegant vehicles, the *California Eagle* noted; the *Negro World* maintained, "It is a common experience to see a Negro or a member of his family driving a high-powered automobile." By way of example, the paper cited the recent conventions of Black Masons and Elks in Pittsburgh. The meetings hosted by these middle-class fraternal organizations drew "Negroes [who] drove their Cadillacs, Pierce Arrows, MacFarlans, and Buicks from every state east of the Rocky Mountains." The reporter's list underscores that African Americans drove high-end cars.[45] (MacFarlans, which ceased production in 1928, were once known as the "American Rolls Royce," and even Buick was once a luxury brand—like all the other cars on the list.) The *California Eagle* likewise celebrated the growing prosperity of its readers by publishing an "Exhaust" column that functioned as "a social register of automobile owners . . . who bought new cars and who took automobile vacations."[46]

Such purchases may have been especially popular among African Americans, Gretchen Sullivan Sorin suggests, because even relatively affluent Blacks often found themselves shut out of the housing market. Throughout the nation, racially restrictive covenants, redlining, and other discriminatory measures made it difficult for even middle-class Blacks to secure mortgages and buy housing. "Middle class African Americans had discretionary income but fewer options than whites," when it came to spending money. "Purchasing a car was considerably easier than buying a house."[47]

By the 1920s, car ownership was not limited to the middle class—especially among rural Blacks. Cars were tremendously popular among farmers of all classes, who used them for agricultural work as well as transportation. Designed with the needs of farmers in mind, the Model T could be easily used to power threshers, bucksaws, balers, water pumps, grain elevators, and electric generators. Farmers also used them in the fields to pull hay rakes, mowers, grinders, and other light equipment. And they also transformed them into tractors by purchasing conversion kits such as a Sears Thrifty Farmer Tractor kit, which contained lugged steel wheels, a rear frame, tractor gears, and engine and cooling system upgrades that made it possible to use the car for plowing and other heavy work.

Not surprisingly, then, African American farmers were quick to purchase cars when they could afford them, and their purchases heightened the racial tensions that divided the South during the World War I era. These years saw good crops and high prices in many parts of the Mississippi Delta, enabling modest numbers of Black sharecroppers, tenants, and small farmers to buy cars for the first time. Hard numbers on just how many rural Black southerners bought cars during these years do not exist, but the phenomenon was significant enough to attract the notice of automobile industry magazines, which reported dramatic sales increases in the South, and noted, "It is the negroes who are buying cars."[48]

Southern journalists responded with amazement—and disapproval. "Negro farmers are buying automobiles who were content a year ago to ride behind an oxcart, or, at best, in a new red buggy behind a $150 mule," the *Savannah Press* noted sourly in 1916.[49] "Never before in the commercial history of Jefferson County have negro farmers aspired to be automobile owners until now," a reporter for the *St. Louis Star* commented in 1917. Wartime prosperity had caused them to "splurge in reckless and sensational abandon."[50]

The rising levels of car ownership among rural Black southerners were particularly troubling to white landowners, who denounced African American automobile ownership as a needless extravagance. White farmers might well make such purchases, reported Bradford Knapp, an official in the US Department of Agriculture, but "that a *negro* farmer should purchase a six-cylinder, high-powered *automobile* becomes a story to bandy from mouth to mouth, because everybody knows that while the Negro had money and actually bought the machine, he could not afford to do so. . . . The negro probably owned no land, had a poor house, had no livestock and had no capital behind him." They were wasting money that might be better spent on "land, stock, tools, and above all better homes."[51]

Such complaints were disingenuous. Southern white landowners had no interest in seeing Blacks buy land or amass capital. Instead, as historian Nan Woodruff writes with reference to planters in Mississippi, they worried that "car ownership gave African Americans the mobility to drive wherever they pleased, back and forth across the Mississippi River, in search of higher-paying jobs."[52] And with the Great Migration leaving many planters shorthanded, some worried that Blacks might use their cars to leave the region altogether (as was already occurring on the railroads, which despite being segregated still carried Black travelers away from the South).

One enterprising planter in Natchez, Mississippi, thought cars could be a solution as well as a problem: he tried to keep his workers at home by buying "twenty-eight Ford automobiles to sell on easy terms to his tenants with the hope of contenting them."[53] But most landowners saw Black car ownership as far too dangerous to be encouraged. African American automobility threatened to upend the region's labor relations and patterns of consumption. Sharecroppers and tenants could use their cars to shop outside the plantation commissary, which had long been a major source of profit for landlords. Blacks who once spent all their "surplus coin" at home, southern newspapers reported, were now patronizing "the city merchant, the supply house and the automobile man."[54]

Such complaints did not keep rural Blacks from continuing to buy cars. Indeed, the strong-minded sharecropper Ned Cobb, whose life is chronicled in Theodore Rosengarten's *All God's Dangers*, bought his car at least in part to defy white opinion. "There's a heap of my race," he told Rosengarten, who "didn't believe their color should have a car, believed what the white man wanted them to believe." Cobb used his car to haul lumber, and he lent it to his sons to use for work and for fun. His white landowner disapproved, but Cobb embraced car ownership as a measure of his freedom: "I bought it to serve my family, and I knowed that I had title [to] anything I wanted if I had the means to get it."[55]

Other rural Blacks in the South and Southwest did the same, often on a minimal budget. Born in 1922, Edmund Threatt grew up on a 160-acre farm in Oklahoma in a family so poor that he and his eleven brothers and sisters never ate anything that they had not raised themselves—"just what was on the farm was all we had." But one day his father vowed "he was going to buy him a Model T if we raised a good crop" and the next year the family raised a record crop and became the proud owners of a Model T.[56]

Poor Blacks typically bought used cars, making their purchases on credit when they could get it. Social scientist John Dollard, who conducted research in Mississippi in the 1930s, noted that the cars owned by Blacks there often underscored their poverty. They were typically "one eyed cars, or cars without tail lights, or cars without any lights at all," which could often be seen by the roadside "stalled or changing tires." Arthur Raper, a sociologist who conducted fieldwork in rural Georgia during the same years, likewise observed that many of the cars owned by rural Blacks were "literally rattletraps" that could be kept moving only by dint of frequent repairs.[57] On the weekends,

A used car dealership in Belzoni, Mississippi, 1939. Marion Post Wolcott, who took this photograph, titled it "Many Negroes Spend Their Cotton Picking Money on Used Cars."

when their owners used them to go shopping and attend church, such cars could be seen along the roadside "surrounded by their undisturbed occupants," who were "undisturbed because they expected to stop along the way, patch a tire or two, change a spark plug, adjust the carburetor, find a short circuit, tape an exposed wire."[58]

Still, the presence of such cars on southern roads underscores that while the post–World War I surge in automobile ownership was most remarkable among white farmers, it never excluded Black farmers. The 1930 census, the earliest source of any remotely comprehensive figures on car ownership by race, reported that 1 in 2 white farmers in the South owned an automobile, as compared to 1 in 4.7 Black southern farmers.[59] Even in the lean years of the Great Depression, the region's sharecroppers still put any money they could spare into cars. Indeed, automotive dealers counted on it. "We have so many automobile salesmen and second hand automobiles scattered around out front that it reminds one of a dead mule with a lot of buzzards coming in for a feast," Mississippi plantation manager A. F. Toler complained to one of his neighbors in 1933. "We are doing everything possible to discourage the purchase of automobiles, but in spite of this, a few Negroes are buying."[60]

As Toler no doubted suspected, African Americans remained interested in cars even in bad times because mobility gave them some chance of surviving the South's "crumbling economic order." The Depression saw increasing numbers of sharecroppers who owned nothing but a car. During the period's worst years, reflected a writer for *Crisis* magazine, thousands of Black families abandoned the Delta to follow "crops across the south, uprooted from the soil, but somehow determined to cling to it." They were "farmers without land, without farms, tools, or animals, without homes, without any moorings whatever except a broken-down jalopy," who kept moving until they found work and eventually "spilled over California and the West."[61] A 1940 congressional hearing on "Interstate Migration of Destitute Citizens" underscored the growing importance of cars when it concluded that "the coming of good roads and cheap automobiles on easy credit terms, together with modern communication devices, have added to the mobility and restlessness of the farm geared [*sic*] and racially proscribed southern Negroes."[62]

A group of Florida migrants on their way to Cranberry, New Jersey, to pick potatoes. Currituck County, North Carolina, 1940.

"THE RACIAL RIGHT-OF-WAY"

When African American southerners first began to buy cars, some whites called for "Jim Crow highways"; others correctly predicted "there will be no Jim Crow highways since it will require the combined assets of both races to construct even one set of highways worthy of the name."[63] But although Blacks and whites ended up sharing the same set of roads, were those roads open to all?

The evidence is mixed, and varies by region. Black northerners may have experienced some sense of equality on the road; but in the South, rising levels of Black car ownership did little to quell the hostility that whites felt toward Black drivers. Racial power struggles played out on the road in ways that would shape the experiences of all Black drivers who traversed the region.

Cars, which were available to anyone who could afford to buy one, challenged the Jim Crow South's carefully regulated social order. Unlike trains, they allowed African Americans to move freely and share space with whites on potentially equal terms. Cars empowered Black drivers while provoking resentment among whites, which could endanger Black drivers and complicated the process of traveling Black.

The empowerment was transformative, according to some close observers of the region. Arthur Raper was convinced that the automobile gave rural Black southerners a new sense of importance and power. Cars were coveted by even the poorest Black sharecroppers, he maintained, because "the feel of power, even in an old automobile, is most satisfying to a man who owns nothing, directs nothing, and while producing a crop literally begs food from his landlord." To Raper, automobility was a democratic force that allowed Black travelers to avoid the "irritations of unequal transportation facilities," and transformed even day-to-day encounters between Blacks and whites in the rural South. "In automobiles on public roads," he argued, members of these groups met "on terms of equality" for the first time. "Prior to the coming of the automobile, when the landlord met the tenant, or when the Negro met the white man, each knew the relationship to each other and acted accordingly. But today when the landlord, speeding down the road at forty miles an hour, sees an old automobile coming he doesn't know whether he is meeting his tenant or the richest planter in the country who takes pride in his ability to go as fast in his old car as a neighbor in a new one."[64]

To Raper, the fact that cars allowed Blacks to travel without being easily recognized was important. Not only did automobiles spare rural Blacks from always meeting on unequal terms, they also allowed them to escape white surveillance. "Incognito" once they got some distance from home, African American car owners could make more choices about where they shopped, worked, traveled, and sought recreation. Cars took both rural Blacks and rural whites out of their immediate communities, "providing the mechanical means for greater self-direction and self-expression."[65]

Black sociologist Charles S. Johnson, who also conducted research in the Black belt during the 1930s and 1940s, was far less confident that the impact of the automobile was wholly democratic. An African American driver himself, he recorded the emergence of a new mode of traveling Black. "The automobile is a technological innovation which has disturbed many of the traditional patterns of association, caused some modification of established mores, and presented new problems of interracial etiquette," wrote Johnson in 1943. Having conducted research in the Black belt for almost two decades, Johnson was able to trace these changing mores over time.

"At first," he noted, "Negroes were expected to operate automobiles for whites, but not own them. Later ownership by Negroes was tolerated, but they were not supposed to own large or pretentious cars." By the 1940s, he explained, "Negro ownership of any type of car is no longer questioned except in small towns." But driving had its own racial etiquette, which had also changed over time. When Black drivers were almost exclusively chauffeurs, "they were identified with whites and accorded the rights of the road." But as greater numbers of African American car owners hit the road, a new system evolved in which Blacks who drove their own cars "were expected to maintain their role as Negroes and in all cases, give right-of-way."[66]

In practical terms, the historians Stephen and Abigail Thernstrom explain, the racial right-of-way was "a rule of black deference to white drivers, especially white women drivers, without regard to which car arrived first at an intersection."[67] Passing white drivers was also problematic. "In some Southern communities," James Weldon Johnson wrote in 1927, "it is a breach of social code for a colored man driving an automobile to pass a white."[68] In Mississippi, historian Neil R. McMillan writes, local custom "forbade black drivers to overtake white drivers on unpaved roads." As one Black Mississippian understood this custom: "It's against the law to pass a white man because the black man might stir up dust that would get on white folks."[69] In some counties in the Deep South, "racial right-of-way" rules remained in place through the 1950s. Folklorist and activist Stetson Kennedy's *Jim Crow Guide to the U.S.A.*, first published in 1959, offered instructions for driving through "segregated territory" designed to help visitors follow these rules. "The only time you can safely claim right-of-way in segregated territory," wrote Kennedy, "is when the other motorist is also nonwhite; while if you are white, you can claim not only legitimate right-of-way in encounters with white motorists, but also racial right-of-way over nonwhite motorists."[70]

Additionally, parking could also be subject to segregation: many southern towns reserved the parking spots on their main streets for whites, and some workplaces had segregated parking.[71] At the Firestone tire plant in Memphis in 1941, Black workers could not park on the paved lot (the "white lot") directly outside the plant. Instead, they had to be sure to park a little farther away on the gravel parking lot (the "Black lot"). "Even after the plant was integrated," one Black worker remembered, "it was just unwritten law that you just didn't do certain things" such as park in the "white lot."[72]

Segregated parking was fairly straightforward, but many of segregation's road rules were unworkable. On the highway, as Charles Johnson noted, the racial right-of-way was impossible to honor: no one could identify the race of the driver "without further investigation." "Usually you are by before they know you are colored anyhow," a North Carolina educator told Johnson. "If I have the right-of-way, I take it."[73] And likewise, sociologist Arthur Raper acknowledged that the car was a more democratic force at higher speeds: "Effective equality seems to come at about twenty-five miles an hour or above."[74]

Even on local roads the racial right-of-way system conflicted with the law and logic of traffic regulation in ways that made it impossible for Blacks to follow it. An African American driver who gave several white drivers the right-of-way could hold up other white drivers, and would surely end up offending somebody. "Some of them don't like it when you don't wait for them to get away first," Johnson was told by one Black informant who largely disregarded white claims to superiority of the road. "But where there is a lot of traffic you can't bother with them because you tie up traffic and that would be worse."[75]

Blacks generally resisted racial right-of-way whenever they thought they could get away with it. Several informants told Johnson that it was possible to "bluff people out of the way" by driving quickly and aggressively. Johnson described such practices in detail. "With white men the Negro may sometimes indulge in 'bluffing' in traffic," he wrote. "He may appear to be driving with minimum of caution, when in reality he is employing a great deal of skill. He attempts to obtain his traffic right of way by innocently driving his rickety car very close to the white man's shining automobile. They both know that in the event of collision about all the white man can get is personal vengeance, which might give him a measure of satisfaction, but will not repair his car."[76] Almost twenty years later, Stetson Kennedy noted that such calculations, and the "bluffing" they inspired, were still commonplace. "One of the best forms of protection for nonwhite motorists in the South is a dilapidated car," he noted. "White motorists are less likely to impose upon the driver of such a vehicle, it being assumed (1) that the brakes are no good, (2) that the owner will care but little if it is wrecked, and (3) that the owner is financially unable to pay for any damage done the white car."[77]

However, both Johnson and Kennedy underscored that Blacks had to be far more careful when driving anywhere near a white woman, whose racial right-of-way was absolute. Several informants told Johnson that white women drivers made them nervous because "many of them pay little attention to traffic regulations when a Negro is involved." One man said: "These white women act like these brakes is colored too and just naturally stop dead still when they sees a white woman busting into the open highway without stopping. They look up and see you colored and keep going like it is a disgrace to stop at a stop sign to let a nigger pass."[78]

Even in the rural South, racial right-of-way was never universal. "In some places whites did maintain normal driving rules," writes historian Jerome Packard. "But in others, Jim Crow was more important than highway safety." African American travelers who ventured into unfamiliar territory often pulled aside for white drivers as a "precautionary measure," stayed on interstate highways if they could, and sometimes drove on back roads only at night in the hopes of avoiding any confrontation with white drivers.[79]

African American drivers had other reasons to avoid such confrontations: when it came to insurance, they faced another kind of racial right-of-way if they got into any kind of accident. In the South, as Johnson wrote, custom dictated that "if there is a collision, the Negro does not expect to get paid for damages to his own car, whether entitled to them or not."[80] The North seems to have had a similar custom. African Americans throughout the country had a great deal of trouble getting automobile insurance. The history of automobile insurance policies and their regulation varies by state and has received virtually no historical analysis. But both the African American newspapers and the NAACP records reveal that throughout the interwar years many automobile insurance companies refused to insure African American drivers, on the grounds that they would always be held at fault should they get in an accident and find themselves in court.

"It is generally understood that insurance companies do not want Negroes as risks," an underwriter for the Saugus Insurance Company told one Boston resident when he applied for auto insurance in 1933.[81] A year later, another insurance company canceled all of its African American policyholders' accounts "due to the fact that if a Negro and a white man are in an automobile accident, the Negro is blamed regardless of the circumstances." Commenting on this news, an insurance agent said that Blacks, especially in the South, should expect to find it increasingly "difficult to obtain automobile liability insurance . . . because litigation in several cases has shown a Negro defendant or plaintiff cannot expect to get justice in the courts if a white man is his opponent." Other insurance agencies were more welcoming, if not enthusiastic. Equitable Building told a reporter for the *Baltimore Afro-American* who investigated the subject in 1933: "Our company as a general rule does not accept colored business, but when they are in business and in a profession it makes a difference and they are considered as any other risk."[82]

African Americans who wished to insure their cars (automobile insurance was not compulsory in most states prior to the 1950s) were limited to a few often underfinanced companies—some of which were Black owned. But such firms were hard to find. A court-ordered investigation into automobile insurance company practices in Illinois, conducted in 1939, looked into the practices of forty-seven insurance companies and found that forty-four of them "refused to insure Negroes" and three said "they would do so 'under certain circumstances.'"[83] Not surprisingly, in the 1930s the NAACP received regular correspondence from members looking for a list of insurance companies willing to sell insurance policies to Blacks, and it began challenging state lawmakers in several states to address the issue.[84] But in states where insurance was not mandatory or linked to other driving privileges, such as securing a license or registering a car, this discrimination was hard to fight. In 1940, Travelers Insurance Company canceled the policy held by Thurgood Marshall, an NAACP attorney and future Supreme Court Justice. Marshall could do nothing about it. The insurance company's official reason for canceling was

Club Headquarters 5305 BAUM BLVD.	AUTOMOBILE CLUB OF PITTSBURGH · INCORPORATED 1903 ·	Downtown Branch 440 OLIVER AVE.

I hereby apply for membership in the AUTOMOBILE CLUB OF PITTSBURGH, (AAA), and agree to abide by all Club regulations.

Date _____ 194 ____

NAME _____ Age _____ Phone _____

PLEASE PRINT

Residence
Address □ _____ City _____

Business
Address □ _____ City _____
(CHECK ADDRESS T...   YOUR MAIL SENT)   ZONE

Occupation _____ ...yed by _____

Make of Car _____ Style of Body _____

Name of Beneficiary _____ Relationship _____
       Check payable to Automobile Club o...   ...uld accompany this application.

Proposed by _____   Club
Representative _____

Address _____

DUES FIRST YEAR $12.50 · RENEWAL $10 EACH YEAR THEREAFTER : INCLUDES 12 Months Subscription to the Pittsburgh Automobilist. Membership open to White Race.

Follow the Arrow— Here's the application used for membership in the Automobile Club of Pittsburgh, Pa., which has been rapped for its anti-racial policy. The arrow points to the words which bar Negro memberships. Despite the so-called precautions taken to insure the "pure" angle, the club has a Negro member, Charles Harris, well-known Pittsburgh Courier photographer. AAA officials in Pittsburgh have made no statements indicating intentions to modify their policy.

This application to join the Automobile Club of Pittsburgh appeared in the *Pittsburgh Courier* on March 8, 1947. It illustrated an article on discrimination in the automobile insurance business and drew attention to the fact that the Automobile Club of Pittsburgh accepted only white members.

that Marshall "'lived in a congested area,' meaning Harlem and 'not' because I am Negro," which made it "practically impossible to work out a court case."[85]

RACE ON THE ROADSIDE

Despite such challenges, many African Americans still preferred driving over traveling in the railroads' Jim Crow cars. Indeed, by early 1929—only ten years after the return of the nationalized railroads to private companies, and the government's failure to desegregate the railroad cars—W. E. B. Du Bois was reporting that the "Jim Crow cars are usually empty." In hindsight, this state of affairs may well have foreshadowed the looming Depression that would become official with the stock market crash later that year. But Du Bois viewed the many "empty cars" he witnessed on a journey across the South in February 1929 as unalloyed good news. "The automobile is certainly bringing just retribution upon the silly profiteering of Jim Crow," he crowed. "All over and everywhere people are traveling in their automobiles."

That said, Du Bois was a special traveler. On a tour of educational institutions in the South during which he covered "1399 miles by Pullman, 841 by Jim Crow, and 531 by Auto," Du Bois did not have to worry about accommodations.[86] Welcomed by a variety of different collegiate hosts, he avoided one of the major problems faced by Blacks who drove any distance by car: how to find a place to stay.

Du Bois did, however, encounter what would become a common problem encountered by African American drivers, especially in the South: discrimination at the gas station. Largely a product of the post–World War I era, these specialized outlets for the sale of gas and motor oil reflected the growing use of the automobile for traveling long distances; they were only one of the new retail industries that took shape around the American consumer's growing automobility. Much like railroad dining cars and sleeping cars, gas stations were a travel amenity that quickly became the site of conflict over who was permitted and encouraged to travel freely.

In the early days when cars were scarce and bad roads constrained motorists to short trips, drivers had to look for gas in a range of outlets: general stores, hardware stores, grocery stores, drugstores, bicycle repair shops, automobile dealers, and other establishments that sold petroleum products largely as a sideline to other business activities. By the 1920s, though, motorists could buy gas without even leaving their cars, thanks to an ever-growing number of "drive-in" filling stations. However, not all of these establishments welcomed African American customers. "A filling station on the Jackson-Daytona Road had a sign 'For Whites Only,'" reported Du Bois, describing the sign as the "only discrimination" he experienced on the road during his 1929 southern tour.[87] Du Bois was not especially worried by this new manifestation of the color line. He "passed the station four times and saw no single car there." The station seemed to be an absurdity. "These crackers persist in being fools," a friend told him.[88]

But Du Bois and his friend were proved wrong: gas stations would in fact become a problem for Black drivers, in ways that seemed to grow worse over time. Throughout the segregation era, African American travelers could not be absolutely sure that they would be welcome at gas stations—or on what terms. A small number of stations, such as the one Du Bois passed, refused to serve Blacks altogether; many others barred Blacks from using their rest-rooms, snack bars, and other amenities.

The discriminatory policies adopted by southern service station owners grew at least in part out of Jim Crow laws requiring segregated restrooms and dining facilities. Unable to accommodate both races without building two sets of restrooms or two eating areas, some station owners refused to serve Blacks, while others followed the spirit rather than the letter of the South's segregation laws by simply limiting the use of these facilities to whites. But the mistreatment of African American customers at gas stations extended be-yond the South and was shaped by economic motives as well.

Faced with the challenge of selling largely indistinguishable products such as motor oil and gasoline, early service station owners sought to create a wel-coming, homelike environment that would ensure consumer loyalty, in an era when consumers were most often imagined to be white. Accordingly, their efforts were informed by ideals of white middle-class domesticity, and were designed to appeal to the nation's growing population of white female drivers. To that end, beginning in the late 1920s Shell, Standard Oil, Sunoco, and Texaco began to build "English-cottage-style stations," complete with chim-neys, gabled roofs, shuttered windows, and flower boxes. "Dress your sta-tion up with Flowers, Here is how to go about it," advised *Petroleum News*—the industry's main journal.[89] Service station chains also advertised "Home Clean" restrooms, to use Shell Oil's catchphrase, which Texaco countered by intro-ducing a "White Patrol" of forty-eight inspectors who crisscrossed the country inspecting the company's facilities.[90] Unfortunately, the domestic ideals that the White Patrols policed were *white:* Black people had little to no place in the sheltered, homelike environment early service stations sought to create.

Du Bois would not be the only Black traveler to encounter discrimination at the gas station. In the mid-1930s, members of the Ohio NAACP threatened to pursue legal action under their state's civil rights laws to get a station near Cincinnati to take down its "We serve whites only" sign. Meanwhile, their contemporaries in Norfolk, Virginia—a state with no civil rights laws—could do little more than complain about a local filling station that pursued a sim-ilar policy. Located on the way to the Ocean Breeze Beach, a popular Black vacation spot, the Norfolk area station posted no segregation sign. But its policy was well known to locals, and communicated verbally to those not in the know, who would pull up only to be told, "We don't cater to colored." Attorney Walter L. Davis, who was one of those turned away, tried to take the matter up with the oil company affiliated with the station, but found that the station was privately owned. Its oil supplier promised to investigate, but also insisted that it had "no authority to act in the matter."[91]

Filling stations that belonged to national chains were often better, but even the chains had trouble keeping track of the practices of their various franchisees.[92] By the 1930s Standard Oil had a policy that "there would be no distinction whatever made with respect to the use of the Standard Oil [restroom] facilities." But this policy did not keep African American customers from being refused the use of the restrooms at some of its stations. Moreover, station restaurants seem to have been exempt from its policies: for example, the restaurant at Standard Oil's Myers station near Joliet, Illinois, greeted travelers with a large "We do not cater to colored" sign. This sign remained on display until 1948, when Illinois state representative Corneal Davis finally persuaded the company to have it removed.[93]

While Shell Petroleum Company was willing to issue an official apology for a notorious incident of discrimination—in which Blanche Calloway, Cab Calloway's sister, was arrested for attempting to use the restroom in a Shell Station in Yazoo City, Mississippi, in 1937—it offered no assurances that such racial slights would not recur. Instead the company warned that "its New York office did not have absolute control over all its territory in the United States and can only suggest what might be done by the regional distributors."[94] African American complaints about being barred from gas station restrooms and restaurants grew along with the expansion of these facilities. Many early gas stations sold little more than gas and motor oil, and seem to have served Blacks on a more equal basis than they would later on.

But even as problems at the pump escalated, they paled in comparison with those involving roadside accommodations. Black travelers found it was even more difficult to find sleeping accommodations on the road than it was on the rails. African Americans who traveled by train were able to secure bunks in Pullman cars in some states, and even the Jim Crow cars' wooden benches provided Black travelers with serviceable, if uncomfortable, sleeping accommodations. But motorists of all colors who traveled long distances had to stop and sleep somewhere, and prior to World War II very few roadside motels and hotels served Black travelers. Even the auto camps, which predated many of these more formal accommodations, were generally off-limits to Black travelers. Created to meet the needs of America's growing motoring public, these inexpensive camps were popular throughout the interwar years, and gave

Roadside Gulf gas station billboard advertising segregated ladies' rooms along US-1 in Lexington County, South Carolina, 1956.

travelers the freedom to stop whenever they got tired. Many were little more than an open field where drivers could pull off the highway to park and pitch a tent, or sleep in their cars, although some featured small cabins that evolved into motels. But even the most modest of these establishments tended to welcome only whites, although some tourist camps for colored clientele eventually emerged in the South. No such camps existed in New England, but the region's camps were less rigidly segregated than most: Blacks could patronize them with "only occasional question."[95]

The trouble was, these camps were not always appealing—especially when traveling through New England in the wintertime. So, when Du Bois made

Tourist cabins for "Colored," South Carolina, 1945.

plans for another car trip that would take him from New York City to Boston in 1929, he had to confront what was emerging as one of the biggest challenges to face African Americans who traveled by car: finding roadside accommodations.

His search for overnight accommodations in New London, Connecticut, began well in advance of his departure with a letter to George Crawford, a friend who lived in New Haven. He would be passing through New London on November 14, Du Bois wrote Crawford two weeks before his trip: did Crawford know of a place where he could spend the night? "I do not know of anyone in the business in New London to whom I could refer you for overnight lodging," Crawford replied on November 6. But he did know someone in New London. Perhaps Mrs. Sarah D. Harrison, secretary of the Negro Welfare Council, could "take you, or make arrangements for you," he suggested. "Mrs. Harrison is the granddaughter of the late Bishop Tanner."[96] Two days later, Du Bois wrote Harrison to ask her if there was "a colored boarding house in New London."[97] Harrison, who sometimes let her spare bedroom, wrote back offering him a place there, and finally he had a place to stay—although he subsequently had to cancel his trip, which required another letter to Harrison.

In short, even the eminent W. E. B. Du Bois could not travel to an unfamiliar town and assume he would be able to find a place to stay. His problem was a common one that was very much on Sarah Harrison's mind. Indeed, when she received his letter, she had already begun work on a solution by creating *Hackley and Harrison's Hotel and Apartment Guide for Colored Travelers* (1930–1931). The product of a collaboration between Harrison and Edwin Henry Hackley, who was a Black attorney and civil rights activist, *Hackley and Harrison's Guide* was the first of a variety of guides designed to help African Americans find roadside accommodations and other travel amenities. Published between the 1930s and 1960s, these works included: *Grayson's Guide; The Negro Motorist Green Book* and the *Negro Traveler's Green Book* (1936–1966); *A Directory of Negro Hotels and Guest Houses* (1939, 1941); *Go: The Guide to Pleasant Motoring* (1952–1959); *Bronze American National Travel Guide* (1961–1962); and *Travelguide* (1947–1963).[98]

Hackley and Harrison's Guide addressed the problem Du Bois faced—and included a copy of his letter to Harrison as an endorsement. In writing Harrison, it began, Du Bois had "unknowingly" illustrated "the practicality of the service herein supplied." Its listings bear out this claim by further underscoring just how difficult it was for Black travelers to find accommodations. Although national in scope, the *Guide* listed few hotels or other easily identifiable commercial establishments. Instead, the predominant form of accommodations it proposed would have been hard for any stranger to find without local assistance: they were mostly informal arrangements such as Sarah Harrison's guestroom, which the *Guide* described as "private accommodations available conditionally," rather than "rooming houses."[99]

However valuable it might have been, *Hackley and Harrison's Guide* was short-lived. It appeared just as the Great Depression decimated the travel market, and co-author Edwin Henry Hackley died shortly after its publication. Unable to keep it going by herself, Sarah Harrison published only one updated edition, the following year, which she retitled *The Traveler's Guide* (1930).

But the need for such a guide lived on. In 1933 Alfred Edward Smith, a Black journalist, teacher, and recent Howard University graduate, called for "the compilation of an authentic list of hotels, rooming houses, private homes catering to the occasional traveler, tourist camps, and every type of lodging whatsoever, including those run by members of other races and open to Negroes." The Arkansas-born Smith, who would soon go on to become an administrative assistant and staff advisor in the Federal Works Progress Administration and a member of Franklin Delano Roosevelt's Black cabinet, was familiar with *Hackley and Harrison's Guide*. But he also knew it was outdated and no longer in print. He lived, he said, "in hope that some individual, organization or publication in his command" would attempt a list.[100] As it turned out, he would need one.

Newly married in the summer of 1932, Smith drove cross-country with his wife, Lula J. Smith, exploring the country from Washington, D.C., to Colorado. He wrote about his trip in the magazine *Opportunity* the following year, chronicling his trip in a lyrical, plaintive, and sometimes funny article titled "Through the Windshield." An avid motorist, Smith clearly hoped to wander across the country, "gypsying" along its transcontinental highways.

"Good roads beckon to you and me," began Smith's article; "daily we grow more motor-wise. The nomad in the poorest and the mightiest of us sends us behind the wheel, north, south, east, and west, in answer to the call of the road." By the early 1930s the kind of rambling road trip that Smith envisioned was fairly common. The nation was still recovering from the Great Depression, but there were 160,000 travel trailers on America's highways and enough paved roads, gas stations, auto courts, and other travel accommodations to allow motorists to wander cross-country—traveling, as Smith put it, "whither and when we will."[101]

Accounts of such journeys had become a new genre of nonfiction, which celebrated the freedom to be found on the open road. Popular works such as Winifred Hawkridge Dixon's *Westward Hoboes: Ups and Downs of Frontier Motoring* (1921) described the highway as America's last frontier. "Fords have replaced prairie schooners, and Indians are less interested in one's scalp than in one's pocketbook, yet overland travel still furnishes adventure," wrote Dixon, whose book chronicled a cross-country drive taken by Dixon and her friend Katherine in a Cadillac Eight. Both recent graduates of Wellesley College, the two women made their way from Massachusetts to California, exploring the West's tourist camps and other roadside stops. The romance of the road was open to all, Dixon promised. To experience it fully, all you had to do was "leave behind limousine and liveried chauffeur, forswear palace hotels, and get out and rub elbows with folks."[102] Other enthusiastic travelogues included government publications designed to promote

Alfred Smith, ca. 1930s.

the nation's first transcontinental highways, which made similar claims in even more hyperbolic terms. A Department of Agriculture press release, issued in 1928, announcing the completion of Route 40, which ran from Atlantic City to San Francisco, invited drivers to cruise "westward on the path of empire, along the routes traversed by the pioneers of America from the Atlantic to the Golden Gate."[103]

Smith was likely familiar with such texts, for his article also invoked the language of exploration, conquest, and pleasure. In addition to feeling the "call of the road," he writes, "there is propulsion. . . . It's mighty good to be the skipper for a change, and pilot our craft whither and when we will. We feel like Vikings."[104] But he broke away from the all-American road narrative by adding: "What if our craft is blunt of nose and limited of power and our sea is macadamized; it's good for the spirit to just give the old railroad Jim Crow the laugh." Few other writers who sang in praise of traveling on America's open road made any reference to Jim Crow. There's a simple reason for this: almost all were white. African American bards of the open road typically worked in another genre altogether, singing the blues. Smith's article helps illustrate why.

After celebrating the relatively recent advent of good roads, good cars, and good tires, Smith has to admit that "there is still a small cloud that stands between us and complete motor-travel freedom." The Smiths are able to wander, but they are not totally carefree. By the afternoon that little cloud has begun to cast "a shadow of apprehension on our hearts and sours us a little. 'Where,' it asks us, 'will you stay tonight?'" It's a question "of no consequence . . . to our Nordic friends," Smith recognizes. "But to you and me, what peace-destroying world of potentiality."[105] Black travelers could have great difficulty finding food and accommodations on the road, Smith lamented. And while staying with friends could sometimes solve this problem, navigating from friend to friend was not always easy or convenient. "We have a friend in Atlanta and another in Jacksonville, so what?" he asked. "So we must be off like a rocket at break of dawn from Atlanta and drive like fiends and fanatics to reach Jacksonville before midnight. Or maybe it's Cincinnati and St. Louis, or Dallas and El Paso. We must not tarry, cannot; to see the wonders that thrust themselves at us 'round each bend.'" Yet the alternative was undeniably worse. "The Bugbear" was always "the great uncertainty, the extreme difficulty of finding lodging for the night, a suitable lodging, a semi-suitable lodging, an unsuitable lodging, any lodging at all, not to mention an eatable meal."[106]

Finding accommodations was "hard" in large cities, "a gigantic task" in small towns, and "sheer luck" in anything smaller, Smith added. And the problem was by no means limited to the South: "In spite of unfounded beliefs to the contrary, conditions are practically identical in the Mid-West, the South, the so-called Northeast, and the South-southwest."[107] He was not exaggerating. In the early 1920s, the music magazine *Billboard* compiled a list of "stopping places available to the Negro traveler," which consisted of six hundred establishments nationwide. But they were unevenly distributed and even less numerous than this list would suggest, according to a reporter for the *Pittsburgh Courier*, who studied the list. Some were flophouses, which turned away nobody; others offered their guests little more than a bed; while many listings recorded "the names of private home keepers" willing to accommodate "race traveler[s] who would not otherwise be cared for." No more than one hundred of the *Billboard*'s list entries were for "bona fide hotels operated for the accommodation of the colored travelers," and taken together they made it clear that "the race can boast adequate hotel accommodations in less than one third of the larger cities in the nation and in very few small towns."[108] In 1930 another report in the *Courier* presented a still more negative assessment of accommodations for Blacks, especially in the South. They were dismal throughout the region, *Courier* columnist Jesse O. Thomas contended, and Black travelers who looked for a place to stay in Memphis were more likely to be directed to a "hootch joint" than an actual hotel.[109]

Not surprisingly, Blacks who traveled frequently, such as vaudeville players, musicians, and other performers, often did not even try to find hotels. Most traveled by train and slept on the train when they could, or looked for colored rooming houses whenever they had to stop somewhere overnight.[110] But such establishments were not an easy alternative to staying in a hotel. They were not commercial enough to advertise, so it was hard to secure travel accommodations in advance. This meant that entertainers and other Blacks who traveled by train would often start their quest for accommodations by asking the porters working on their train. Those who entered unfamiliar communities by car would have to "drive into town and find the black community . . . [and] find the boarding house."[111]

As the Smiths soon found out, in some parts of the South not even rooming houses were an option. They were sometimes directed to the home of a local resident and told it was "folks stay sometimes," with mixed results. On occasion they ended up in "a really nice home," but they also came across places that had "sewage but no indoor toilet or bath, water pipes but no running water, feather beds to trap the unsuspecting, minute bed inhabitants, no screens, and so on."[112] Such establishments catered to a small market of Black travelers who had few other options and were not always the primary customers of the run-down lodgings to which they were directed. Some travelers would eventually realize that the home or "rooming house" in which they found accommodations was actually a brothel or speakeasy—often not until their hosts began entertaining noisy late-night visitors who made sleep impossible.

The accommodation problem was so pervasive that when Duke Ellington toured the South with his orchestra in the 1930s, he made his manager hire several private Pullman cars, which they used not only to get from place to place, but also as hotels. "We parked them in each station and lived in them," Ellington later remembered. "We had our own water, electricity and sanitary facilities."[113] Toni Stone, who traveled the South in the 1940s and 1950s as one of the few women ever to play in the Negro Baseball leagues, came up with a different solution to the accommodations problem. As a woman traveling with a team of men, she was routinely taken for a prostitute and sent off to the local brothel. With few other options, Stone eventually gave in and met a warm welcome among the "sporting girls," who were happy to offer her a clean bed and warm meal. They also knew of other places where she could stay and helped her find regular accommodations at "a network of brothels throughout the South."[114]

As Stone's experience suggests, Blacks could only secure minimal access to hotels and motels, even as roadside accommodations for white Americans became ever more plentiful. Hotel segregation was required by law in many southern states and became increasingly common throughout the nation over the first half of the twentieth century. In 1910 Du Bois observed that "colored men could be maintained in the best hotel in Cleveland, New York, and Chicago." But by 1934 "there was not a single Northern city, except New York, where a Negro can be a guest at a first-class hotel. Not even in Boston is he welcome; and in New York, the number of hotels where he can go is very small."[115] This assessment remained true well into the mid-1950s, when a market survey of more than twenty-five hundred hotels and motels (which excluded the southern states because of their "state laws prohibiting the intermingling of the races") revealed that Negroes were "not welcome" in 94 percent of them.[116]

And so it was that the Smiths encountered their "old Bugbear" in the West—albeit in a new and slightly different form. Tourist camps with guest cabins were the most common roadside accommodations in Colorado and Utah, and these informal establishments initially struck the Smiths as perfect places to stay. Their parking lots revealed that they housed a clientele that included families who rattled down the road in "flivvers" (old beat-up cars) as well as more elegant motorists who drove Rolls Royces, which led them to hope they would also welcome Black travelers. And they did—sometimes.

But the Smiths were frustrated to find that they could never tell when they were going to be told that the camp in which they had hoped to stay was "*full* for the night," or be led to a cabin that was "second rate in appearance." They received a warm welcome at camps run by the Mormons and the Utah Indians, but had their spirits crushed at a Colorado camp owned by an emigrant from Texas who assured them that there were "no accommodations to be had to 'us' within fifty miles."[117]

The Smiths were usually able to find a "better camp" nearby each time they were turned away, but such slights only compounded over time. "It would seem that our sensibilities would be somewhat dulled by the continuous hurts they receive in this land of ours; but not so," Smith noted as he reflected on the trip. Viking no more, as he looked to the future he no longer dreamed of car trips spent roaming "whither and when we will." Instead, he called for a travel guide that could supply him with an entirely different sort of freedom. He was convinced, he wrote, "that within the area of every fifty square miles of the more frequently travelled sections of the United States there are lodgings to be found at all times." Freedom would be knowing "exactly where they were, what a world of new confidence would be ours."[118]

Among Smith's readers might have been Dudley B. Luck of Conoco, one of the earliest Black executives in the automotive services industry. Owned by the Continental Oil company, Conoco operated both a line of gas stations and a travel service bureau, which supplied its customers with maps and travel guides. Luck, who was hired with "the idea that Negroes in the public relations division may produce new business for the company," quickly moved to promote Conoco among Blacks by mobilizing its travel services to meet their needs.[119] Starting in 1933, Conoco announced that it was placing "its free travel service . . . at the disposal of all Negro motorists." Those who signed up for the Conoco Travel Club would receive not only customized maps and travel information outlining the attractions and "routing most desirable for the contemplated trip," but also a "complete list of Negro hotels, tourist homes, Y.M.C.A.s, Y.W.C.A.s in the United States and Canada." "The only directory of its kind," according to Luck, it included "some 1600 or more accommodations for Negroes." Luck continued to work at Conoco through the 1930s, but no record of Conoco's much-vaunted Black directory exists today, and it is not clear that it was ever widely distributed or advertised.[120] Certainly, African American travelers such as the Smiths do not seem to have been familiar with the Conoco Travel Bureau's efforts to make their "travels more comfortable and attractive."[121]

THE *GREEN BOOK*

Such efforts would continue, most notably with the publication of *The Negro Motorist Green Book*. Published annually between 1936 and 1966 (except during the war years of the mid-forties), this far better-known travel directory supplied much of the information sought by travelers such as Smith. It was the brainchild of Victor H. Green, a forty-four-year-old Black New Yorker, who lived in Harlem and worked as a mail carrier in Hackensack, New Jersey.

As a lifelong northerner, Green might seem to be an unlikely originator of a book now best remembered for helping African Americans navigate the

South's Jim Crow landscape. But Blacks encountered travel restrictions in the North as well, and as a mailman Green had probably fielded many inquiries from travelers who were looking for a place to stay. (African American mailmen routinely were asked for this information, as they invariably knew the locations of all the colored boardinghouses, hotels, and other Black businesses on their postal routes.) A gregarious man and member of the postal workers union, Green also collected information from other mailmen. He knew "postal workers everywhere," remembered civil rights leader Julian Bond, and "used them as guides to tell him: 'Well, here's a good place here, a good place there.'"[122]

Green's personal life also contributed to the venture. A World War I veteran, he was no stranger to travel, and he acquired family ties to the South when he married Alma Duke of Richmond, Virginia, in 1918. How often the couple traveled south cannot be determined, but Green's publication most certainly made use of Alma Green's knowledge of the region. Alma Green, historian Gretchen Sorin writes, was the "driving force in his publishing business."[123] An advisor from the beginning, she took over from Green as publisher of *The Negro Motorist Green Book* when Green retired in 1952. Victor Green also employed his brother, William Green, who was a partner in the family business between 1937 and 1945 and may have received valuable input from his brother-in-law, Robert Duke. Duke was a musician, whose career Victor Green managed for a time, and whose line of work would have given both men access to the wealth of information contained in the stories of good and bad experiences on the road that circulated among Black musicians.[124]

Designed "to give the Negro traveler information that will keep him from running into difficulties, embarrassments and to make his trip more enjoyable," the *Green Book* started out focusing exclusively on "reliable business places and resorts" in New York State, but soon expanded.[125] It was modeled on two very different publications: the *Automobile Green Book,* a road guide to the East Coast published by the Automobile Legal Association, which dated back to the 1920s, and New York City's *Kosher Food Guide.*[126] Published quarterly, the latter was primarily designed to "serve as a guide to observant Jewish Women desiring to uphold dietary laws." But in addition to listing approved packaged foods, *The Kosher Food Guide* also enumerated hotels, summer resorts, and camps that catered to Jewish travelers.[127] *The Negro Motorist Green Book* combined features of both publications, offering road information and travel tips, together with geographically organized listings of hotels, restaurants, taverns, drugstores, service stations, beauty parlors, and barbershops that welcomed Black customers, as well as advertisements for some of the businesses it listed. Many of the businesses were owned by African Americans, but the *Green Book* also listed and advertised white-owned establishments that welcomed Black travelers.

By 1937 the *Green Book* had attracted the attention of Charles McDowell, an expert on Negro Affairs for the United States Travel Bureau (USTB) who would help Green expand his book. Both the Bureau and McDowell's position in it were novel. Established in February 1937, the USTB was an agency within the Department of the Interior that promoted the nation's tourist industry with campaigns such as the "Travel America Year" (1940) and "Travel Strengthens America" (1941). Its mandate also included getting more Americans to travel by distributing travel information, serving as "a national clearing house for valuable tourism related information," and promoting travel among "groups unaccustomed to leisure travel."[128] African Americans were one such group, and McDowell was hired to reach out to them. He did so by supplying Green with information to publish in *The Negro Motorist Green Book*, which starting in 1937 began to include national listings drawn from federal resources such as the US Department of Commerce's collection of information on Black businesses. And he also used these resources to compile a government publication entitled *A Directory of Negro Hotels and Guest Houses in the United States* (1939).[129]

Although it could be obtained for free from the government, the USTB's *Directory* never posed any real competition to the *Green Book*. The government's *Directory* was shorter and less comprehensive than the *Green Book*, which was never very expensive and continued to prepare its listings "in cooperation with the United States Travel Bureau"—as the cover of its 1940 edition proclaimed. The *Green Book* also contained much more information than the *Directory*, which listed only lodgings. Travelers could consult the *Green Book* to find places to eat, shop, and service their cars. And finally, the *Green Book* remained around longer and was updated more often. New editions appeared annually until 1963, except during World War II when gas rationing made driving vacations unlikely. The Interior Department eliminated the USTB for good in 1941, the same year it published the second and final edition of the *Directory*.[130]

The *Green Book* also had a few commercial competitors during its early years, but none lasted very long. *Smith's Tourist Guide of Necessary Information for Businessman, Tourist, Traveler and Vacationist* (1940), which I have been unable to locate, went through only one edition, while *Grayson's Guide to Hotels, Cafes, Resorts, and Motels Where Civil Rights Are Extended to All* was more successful. Published by Burt E. Grayson, a journalist whose previous experience included "writing a travel column for the Negro Press," it first appeared in 1936 and was updated at least twice. The last edition I have been able to locate a reference to appeared in 1946.[131]

Grayson's Guide included nightclubs as well as hotels, and may have been directed primarily at businessmen rather than tourists. Less upbeat than the *Green Book,* it opened with a brief preface that seemed to address the exhausted business traveler rather than the carefree vacationer. Grayson drew attention to "the exceedingly large number of accidents on our public highways," and stressed that colored travelers were involved in more than their share. "Sixty-six per cent of the accidents on the highways attributed to colored drivers is said to be due to the driver falling asleep at the wheel," noted Grayson, before going on to reassure readers that such accidents "could have been avoided had the driver stopped for relaxation or refreshment before becoming completely exhausted." With the purchase of a *Grayson's Guide,* he promised, drivers no longer had to endure "the weariness often caused by lack of information about suitable places of accommodation."[132] "Every Business Should Have One," proclaimed one of Grayson's advertisements, but his *Guide* did not seem to find its audience. "The majority of the black travel guides," historian Gretchen Sullivan Sorin suggests, "were unsuccessful because they did not have sufficient circulation or advertising revenue to maintain them."[133]

The *Green Book* may have defied the odds at least in part because it was more useful than other guides. While the USTB's *Directory* and *Grayson's Guide* focused primarily on hotels—although the *Directory* also included colored YMCAs and YWCAs—the *Green Book* included extensive information on "tourist homes" whose owner-occupants were willing to rent out their spare rooms. Sarah Harrison's 73 Hempstead Cottage, in New London, can be found in some editions of the *Green Book.* Such listings may have been particularly valuable to travelers seeking safe, well-maintained lodgings during the segregation era. More difficult to find than commercial establishments listed in business directories or phonebooks, tourist homes were more private, spacious, and family-friendly than room options at the YMCA and YWCA, and had advantages over colored hotels as well. Many such hotels were seedy

GRAYSON'S GUIDE

A NATIONAL DIRECTORY OF

✦ HOTELS   ✦ CAFES   ✦ RESORTS   ✦ MOTELS

WHERE CIVIL RIGHTS ARE EXTENDED TO ALL

TELLS WHERE TO STAY — EAT AND PLAY

IN OVER 300 CITIES AND RESORTS

PRICE   ONE   DOLLAR

Associated Negro Press's office
copy of *Grayson's Guide.*

and run-down, a by-product of segregation, which gave their proprietors "a mcnopoly over a limited clientele."[134] They were also a concession to segregation that many Black travelers were not eager to support.[135] Tourist homes, by contrast, fit comfortably within Black traditions of organizing trips around visits to friends and family.

The *Green Book*'s circulation was also boosted by the fact that it was sold at Esso stations rather than being available only by mail, like the other travel guides. Although a subsidiary of Standard Oil, the Esso Marketers chain, which operated in New York, New England, and the Upper South, was unusually progressive: it offered franchises to African Americans and actively sought Black customers. As a result, Esso became a popular choice among Black drivers, who appreciated the fact that Esso stations offered them "more courteous and accommodating" service than other stations. They also appreciated the company's policies when it came to Black employment and franchising opportunities.[136] In 1935 Esso decided to build on its strong record among Black consumers by hiring a Black executive, James "Billboard" Jackson, to "conduct research and promotion work in the Negro market."[137]

Born in 1878, Jackson started out his business career in the Negro Department of the New York–based music magazine *Billboard*, where he got his nickname, followed by a six-year stint in the US Department of Commerce shortly before joining Esso. Both of these experiences made him uniquely qualified to appreciate the *Green Book*. Musicians traveled more than virtually any other African Americans, which may explain why he first started compiling a list of accommodations for African American travelers when he was at the Department of Commerce. That list may have served as a starting point for the USTB's *Directory*. Jackson was also the likely compiler of a similar list kept in the office of *Billboard* during his tenure there.

Jackson himself was a tireless traveler, and he must have included his own road experiences in the information he compiled. A popular speaker and determined researcher, he logged 20,000 to 40,000 miles a year while working at the Commerce Department in the early 1930s, and he kept up a similar schedule when he joined Esso, traveling more than 250,000 miles and making "thousands of speeches" during his twenty-one years with the company.[138]

Intimately familiar with the difficulties that Black motorists could encounter, Jackson promoted Esso stations by publicizing in the Black press the company's policy of offering "all of its services without discrimination to all customers," and making sure that Esso stations sold a travel guide that Black customers could actually use.[139] Triple A travel guides, the more common option at most stations, were all but useless to African American travelers, as the company readily acknowledged. "We are returning your application for membership and check for the Automobile Club of Virginia and the national AAA," one of the organization's representatives wrote to Black driver A. G. Brodax in 1947, explaining that "hotel and motor court reservations at official AAA recommended places" were a "major part of AAA benefits . . . it would be embarrassing to offer this service to you when we could not deliver on it."

Jackson's promotional activities helped generate African American loyalty to both Esso stations and the *Green Book*, which further strengthened the ties between the travel guide and its corporate supporter. By the 1940s Esso was one of the *Green Book*'s major sponsors and the *Green Book* included an endorsement from Jackson. "If there had been a publication such as this when I started traveling back in the Nineties," he wrote in an article that ran in a

1947 edition of the *Green Book*, "I would have missed a lot of anxieties, worries, and saved a lot of mental energy."[140]

Jackson's endorsement may have run alongside advertisements for "Happy Motoring . . . with Esso Products and Services," but travelers with no stake in the book expressed similar sentiments. "At last," a frequent traveler from Cleveland wrote in 1939, "a directory of hotels, taverns, restaurants, service stations and beauty parlors covering the entire nation from Maine to California. . . . It is the most complete directory covering our side of the fence that it has ever been my privilege to see."[141] Updated over time, the *Green Book* continued to receive high praise throughout its history: Black Chicagoan Earl Hutchinson, who first purchased a *Green Book* in 1955 for a trip to California, remembered it as "the Bible of every Negro highway traveler in the 1950s and early 1960s."[142]

Yet the *Green Book*, as Victor Green readily acknowledged, was not a real solution to the problems Black motorists faced. "There will be a day sometime in the near future when this guide will not have to be published," he predicted in the preface to some of its editions. "That is when we as a race will have equal opportunities and privileges in the United States . . . [and] can go wherever we please, and without embarrassment."[143]

So long as that day remained elusive, the *Green Book* testified to the many uncertainties faced by Black drivers, and the care they had to put into planning their routes. Those who bought it could hope to avoid travel nightmares such as sleeping in their cars for lack of accommodations, but its listings were not always useful or up to date. Its 1946 edition, one Cleveland reader complained, contained many Cleveland listings with inaccurate addresses and included hotels "whose memories are nostalgic, but alas gone with the wind of the late twenties."[144] Travelers could use it to find Cleveland's Black business district, but that was about it. But the more serious problem it faced was that no travel guide could do much about the limited options available to Black travelers. Hotels, motels, and other establishments that welcomed them were so scarce that none of the travel guide authors made any real attempt to say anything about the quality of the accommodations and services they listed.

As a result, all of the travel guides for colored motorists disappointed Alfred Smith, the intrepid would-be Viking who had once had such high hopes for them. Revisiting his travel dilemmas sixteen years after his first cross-country trip, Smith found such books "informative and useful," and conceded "it is a good idea to own one," but he was troubled by the fact that they only

The Negro Travelers' Green Book, 1956.

added to "the chief bugaboo of the colored traveler," which he described as "our uncertainty." Cruising into an unfamiliar town, he explained, the owner of such a book might be confronted with a choice of "Mack's Hotel, Bill's Hotel, Joe's Rest and Ollie Mae's Tourist Home." But how was he to know which one of these places "is the modern building with clean rooms, with clean baths, service and reasonable prices (we can dream can't we) and which is the joint over the Elite Pool Room in the tough district?" So, guide or no guide, African American travelers still had to "ask our way around as we have always done or take our chances with those white managers."[145]

AFRICAN AMERICAN AUTOMOBILITY

African American travelers like Billboard Jackson and Alfred Smith had once dared to hope that cars would allow them to "enjoy personal liberty and go from one city or state to another unrestrained."[146] But by the 1940s it was all too clear that automobility would involve a variety of compromises and constraints. Although less humiliating and uncomfortable than traveling in the Jim Crow cars of segregated railways, traveling by automobile exposed African Americans to racial slights from white drivers, as well as a variety of forms of discrimination in many of the roadside establishments that serviced America's increasingly mobile car culture. No guide could hide the fact that Black travelers' choices were limited, or keep these limited choices from shaping every aspect of travel. Cautious travelers mapped their routes out in advance, consulting friends and relatives for up-to-date information about Black-owned filling stations and the best places to stay.

While some frequent travelers had little choice but to hunt for lodgings in a segregated marketplace dominated by "fourth-place room and board accommodations at first-rate prices," many avoided commercial establishments altogether.[147] Looking back on the segregation era, Black psychiatrist Price M. Cobbs remembered that prior to the 1960s, his family mostly traveled to places where they could stay "in private homes with friends, or friends of friends, relatives, colleagues of my father, or church people we knew or who had been told of us. Sometimes we would be asked to pay, sometimes not."[148]

African American drivers experienced a form of distinctive automobility, even on the blacktop itself. Like African American train travelers, who often boarded their trains stocked with everything they might need while on the train, Black drivers learned to assemble Jim Crow kits before driving any distance. They loaded up their cars with food, water, and maps—so they would not have to stop and ask for directions—and carried amenities such as toilet paper and "pee cans," assuming that they would not be able to use roadside restaurants. Many filled their gas tanks before leaving home, and carried additional gas in the trunks of their cars.[149] If they had to stop for gas, they tried to time their trips so they could get their gas in major cities.

The travel experiences that resulted from all these precautions could be equally distinctive. While white drivers negotiated an increasingly seamless world of commercialized travel choices filled with opportunities for roadside camaraderie, Blacks were generally confined to their cars. John Hope Franklin, an African American scholar, memorably captured this stark isolation in his account of driving from Charleston to Raleigh on December 7, 1941—the day the Japanese attacked Pearl Harbor. News of the attack had been broadcast shortly after 2 p.m., but Franklin and his wife, Aurelia, knew nothing of it until they reached Raleigh that evening. Their car had no radio, and, like most "black families motoring through the Jim Crow South," the Franklins had "packed box lunches to avoid the humiliation of being turned away from restaurants . . . and relieved themselves in roadside ditches because service-station restrooms were often closed to them." Occasionally they would be lucky enough "to come upon a black-owned service station." But "you could drive from Charleston quite nearly to Baltimore before finding one."[150]

As we will see, Black drivers would continue to make such Jim Crow journeys well beyond the 1940s. The postwar period, although often remembered as the golden age of the American family vacation, saw rising tensions over Black civil rights that only made southern roads more complicated and dangerous for Blacks. Car ownership was a source of African American agency that often exposed Blacks to new forms of discrimination. Freedom from the Jim Crow car, for those who could afford another kind of car, came at the price of having to navigate a new landscape of segregated gas stations, motels, and roadside attractions and contend with discriminatory auto insurance policies and road rules that invariably favored whites. These trade-offs would only intensify as the Black freedom struggle over segregated transportation escalated during the 1950s and 1960s. Car ownership would be vital to the success of civil rights initiatives such as the Montgomery Bus Boycott, but throughout the civil rights movement Black activists who owned cars were subject to many forms of segregationist resistance, including the cancellation of their insurance policies and arrests for trumped-up moving violations.[151] As the day-to-day Black struggles against Jim Crow led to the bus boycotts and Freedom Rides of the 1960s and met with a rising tide of resistance to desegregation by white southerners, the roadside segregation and many other dangers that African Americans faced when traveling by car would become worse before they got better.

4

Traveling by Bus

From the Jim Crow Car to the Back of the Bus

IN AUGUST 1905, BLACK INVESTORS IN NASHVILLE POOLED THEIR assets to buy a fleet of automobiles "to furnish a passenger service where there will be no lines drawn between the whites and the blacks."[1] Determined to resist Tennessee's new law requiring segregation on streetcars throughout the state, they founded the Union Transportation Company, one of the nation's first autobus companies. The city's Blacks had already begun to boycott the streetcars, and the company's founders were determined to help them stay off the cars indefinitely. Investors included longtime foes of transportation segregation such as R. H. Boyd, a Baptist minister who was also a very successful businessman.[2] Boyd saw the boycott as an opportunity to stimulate the "cause of the automobile as common carrier" while also getting around the "nefarious law of Jim Crow street cars."[3]

Although initially successful in helping Nashville Blacks sustain their streetcar boycott, the Union Transportation Company did not survive long. Its first fleet consisted of five steam-powered automobiles, which cost the company $5,000 but proved unable to travel up Nashville's hills without slowing to a crawl. The company then invested another $20,000 in electric cars, which were faster but unreliable due to battery problems. Nashville struck back by passing a law imposing an annual tax of $42 on electric cars—which was, of course, designed to cripple the Union Transportation Company's fledging venture. The streetcar boycott cost the Nashville Transit Company $500 a week in September 1905, but less than a year later the Union Transportation Company was all but bankrupt. With no reliable transportation alternative, Nashville's Black workers slowly and reluctantly returned to the streetcars.

In the summer of 1906, Union Transportation cut its losses by selling off its vehicles and ceased operating. Still, Black Nashville's early attempt to use buses to defy segregation on their city's streetcars underscores the fact that buses, much like cars, were initially welcomed by African Americans as a new technology that might allow them to escape traveling Jim Crow.

That moment is now largely forgotten even among historians of segregation, who rarely discuss the history of the bus and have described the transfer of Jim Crow rules and customs from railways to new forms of transportation as a seamless extension of existing practices. C. Vann Woodward, one of the few historians to even reference the advent of segregation on buses, sums it up in a matter of sentences in *The Strange Career of Jim Crow*. "Jim Crow kept step with the march of progress in transportation and industry, as well as with the changes in fashion," he writes. "The advent of the cross-country buses as serious competitors of the railways was marked by the extension of the Jim Crow train law to the buses in all particulars, including seating arrangements, waiting rooms, toilets, and other accommodations."[4]

But Woodward offers no direct evidence to support this claim, and such evidence is hard to find. Codified several decades after the passage of the separate car laws that governed seating arrangements of the railroads, the rules governing segregated seating arrangements on buses were never identical to those on trains. Railroad segregation laws generally called for two or more passenger cars on each passenger train, or for dividing the cars by a partition to secure separate accommodations, whereas many bus segregation laws required only "equal but separate seats for white and colored."[5] Designed to seat Blacks at the back of the bus, rather than to create separate cars, such laws were not really an extension of Jim Crow train laws to buses: they have a history of their own, which has yet to be told.

Like the history of the bus itself, the history of Jim Crow buses is rooted in what an early automotive magazine once called the "muddled affairs of municipal transportation."[6] Long-distance travel by car and bus alike remained all but impossible until most of America's main roads were paved. The nation's first buses competed with other forms of urban public transportation, such as streetcars. The emergence of regional bus lines, which eventually consolidated into an expansive interstate system, did not begin until the 1920s.

Large automobiles, such as those purchased by the Union Transportation Company, were among the nation's first buses. But cars were not cheap or reliable enough to successfully compete with streetcars, or any other form of municipal transportation, until the World War I era—when car-based buses, known as "jitneys," suddenly flooded the streets of American cities and towns.

Jitneys provided those who operated them opportunities for entrepreneurship and offered their riders an affordable alternative to the streetcar. They were particularly popular among southern Blacks, who had never resigned themselves to, as one reporter put it, "being seated at the rear ends of streetcars."[7] Black-owned and -operated "Jim Crow jitneys" proliferated during the jitney craze, and for a brief time it seemed like Black and white southerners might establish dual transportation networks.[8] But urban jitneys did not last long. Despised by municipal leaders and streetcar companies alike, these unregulated vehicles were a major source of traffic problems and accidents, and they quickly inspired enough licensing and liability regulations to become unprofitable where they were not banned outright.

Intercity jitneys were another matter. They survived and even spawned successful bus companies like the Greyhound Bus Corporation—the most enduring survivor of the jitney era. The course of racial segregation on buses followed a twisting path shaped by these developments. Small, unregulated, and usually owned and operated for either Blacks or whites, jitneys were rarely subject to any formal segregation laws. In areas where African Americans were numerous, jitneys were survived by Black bus lines, which for a brief time seemed like they might supply African Americans with their own separate but equal form of transportation. These Black bus lines were crucial to the communities they served, because many early intercity bus lines operated by whites, like the jitney bus businesses that preceded them, refused to carry Blacks. But Black entrepreneurs never had enough customers or consumers to take advantage of the economies of scale that propelled the rise of the bus industry's most successful companies.

Black bus lines all but disappeared by the 1930s, at which point African Americans had to fight to secure seats on most bus lines. The Jim Crow laws that relegated Blacks to the back of the bus first emerged within the context of such struggles. The new laws were modeled on the streetcar segregation laws of the early twentieth century, and were equally unpopular among Blacks. (After all, one reason Black travelers had switched from streetcars to buses in the first place was to evade segregation.) The streetcar segregation statutes empowered the cars' conductors to "increase or decrease space for each race" and "require any passenger to change his or her seat as often as it may be necessary or proper"; now, two decades later, the new laws gave

similar powers to bus drivers. Some states' segregation laws even designated streetcar conductors and bus drivers "special policemen," who could
arrest any passenger who disobeyed their seating instructions. And all
states gave the white men who operated these vehicles the power to determine when, where, and whether any Black person could secure a seat on
their buses.[9]

White passengers were routinely seated first on southern intercity buses,
and only after they were accommodated could Black passengers take seats on
the bus—if there were any seats left. The humiliation involved in being assigned to the back of the bus was far from purely symbolic: the backseats of
most early buses were uncomfortable and poorly ventilated. Bus companies
made matters worse by assigning African American passengers to Jim Crow
seats even outside the South, and roadside restaurants and other facilities
added insult to injury by refusing to serve Black passengers.

Blacks contested all these forms of segregation from the outset, taking their
complaints to the courts, the government, the media, and the NAACP, without
ever managing to greatly improve their experience on Jim Crow buses.
And yet the struggle against segregated buses can be seen as a culmination of
struggles—against segregated trains, streetcars, and roadside services—that
equipped Black travelers and Black organizers with tools and experience for
fighting segregation more generally. As we will see, the boycotts and freedom
rides of the civil rights era were not the beginning, but rather the end, of a
long history of Black resistance to Jim Crow buses.

"THE JITNEY IS THE NEGRO'S CAR"

In 1915 at the height of the "jitney craze," the *New York Times* explained that
"the jitney bus is an automobile of any kind, operated at the rate of 5 cents. . . .
As long as there is room in the jitney bus any one may board it at any place."[10]
Or almost anyone, the reporter might have specified. In point of fact, these
private unregulated vehicles served only whichever passengers the jitney
driver chose to pick up, and generally catered to either Black or white passengers but not to both. In many southern towns, white drivers did not pick
up Black customers, but many such municipalities were also home to Jim
Crow jitneys, which, like Nashville's Union Transportation Company, were
owned and operated by African Americans.

A New York jitney ca. 1915.

Jim Crow jitneys did more than allow African Americans access to this new form of transportation. They offered southern Blacks a second chance to boycott a form of segregation they despised: the segregated streetcar. When streetcar segregation laws were enacted in cities across the South during the 1910s, they met widespread resistance. The years between 1900 and 1906 saw well over twenty streetcar boycotts in thirteen states, some of which lasted many months. Such protests took place in virtually every city where streetcar segregation was imposed. Neither streetcar segregation nor Black resistance to it was unprecedented: streetcars of various kinds had operated in American cities since the antebellum era and had long been sites of racial conflict. But streetcar segregation was abandoned in northern cities after the Civil War and was successfully contested by Black southerners during Reconstruction. By the end of the nineteenth century, Black streetcar passengers rode alongside whites even in Georgia, which in 1891 passed but did not fully enforce a separate car act that applied to streetcars and railroads.[11]

But in the early years of the twentieth century, states and municipalities across the South passed a wave of segregation ordinances requiring the separation of Black and white streetcar passengers; and municipalities where such laws already existed, such as Savannah and Atlanta, began to enforce them. These measures were an expression of the New South's deepening commitment to maintaining strict racial segregation in every aspect of public life, and they came at a time when rapid urbanization was making streetcar systems across the region increasingly crowded and when the region's Blacks were all but politically powerless as a consequence of disenfranchisement. The new laws required the streetcar companies to "make provision, rules and regulations for the separation of white passengers from negro passengers by separate cars, or fixed divisions, or movable screens, or other method of division."[12] Just as, in coming decades, automobile filling stations, restrooms, lunch counters, and so on would move from being racially open to being racially segregated, so too did streetcars.

African Americans across the South adamantly opposed the new laws. Throughout the region, urban Black southerners saw the segregation of the streetcars as an alarming new incursion on their freedom. "After 40 years of freedom and during all this time of indiscriminate passage through the thoroughfares of the great cities of the state," Black protesters in Memphis complained, the state of Tennessee was now imposing "obloquy and shame upon those of her citizens whom she should encourage and lift up."[13] Black businesswoman and philanthropist Maggie Lena Walker of Richmond also spoke out. Jim Crow was no longer "confined . . . to long distance travel," she noted with dismay. "'Jim Crow car' is now upon every steam and electric line in the state." She urged Richmond's Black community to join her in protesting "loss of citizenship."[14]

Walker and other African American streetcar riders resented not just the segregation of the cars, but the insulting and unequal status the new measures imposed on Black passengers. The new laws were a result of a compromise between southern lawmakers and the streetcar companies, which had long insisted that any law requiring them to run a separate set of Jim Crow cars for Blacks would be "ruinously expensive." In crafting the new statutes, most state legislators addressed these concerns by permitting the streetcar companies to use partitions or screens to divide up their existing cars. Virginia required its electric railroads to assign Blacks and whites to a separate "car or coach [or] a portion thereof, or certain seats therein"; Arkansas called for its streetcars "to operate separate cars or separate white and colored passengers in cars operated for both." These statutes, which allowed for far more complicated seating arrangements than did separate coach laws, also included

detailed measures to address the logistical problems such seating arrangements might face. Louisiana specified that streetcar companies should use
"wooden or wire partitions . . . to secure separate accommodations between
the white and colored races"; Texas required no more than "a board or a
marker placed in a conspicuous place."[15] Other states left the location of the
dividing line entirely up to the conductor.

In practice, segregation partitions or markers were always movable, and
the real arbitrator of who rode where was the conductor—who was invariably white. Segregation laws throughout the South recognized this fact and
gave streetcar conductors the power to determine how much space would be
allotted to Black passengers and to white, as well as the authority to "require
any passenger to change his or her seat when and as often as it may deem
necessary or proper." Blacks had no trouble foreseeing the abuses that could
(and would) result from these laws. Conductors would be free to ask Black
women to stand to make room for white men, pointed out John Mitchell of the
Richmond Planet, and Black passengers might have to give up their seats
repeatedly during the course of a single trip.[16]

None of the streetcar boycotts undertaken by African Americans in Richmond, Nashville, Memphis, or any other city were successful. Streetcars held
a virtual monopoly over urban public transportation, making it difficult for
Blacks to stay off them for long. Many protesters had long walks to work.
Black hack (horse taxi) owners and draymen helped sustain the boycott in
many cities, both by picking up protesters and reducing their fares, but their
hacks and wagons were not numerous enough to replace the streetcars. When
boycott leaders managed to establish new transportation companies using
hacks or horse-drawn omnibuses in several cities, local officials shut down
these operations by threatening to prosecute their proprietors for "working
old, worn out animals from early morning until late at night and [for] . . . only
half feeding them."[17] R. H. Boyd and other Black leaders in Nashville clearly
hoped that their use of autobuses might exempt them from white harassment,
but they had trouble getting the local power company to supply them with
power for their electric cars. And transportation alternatives were not the only
issue. Even in Montgomery and Richmond, where Black protesters managed
to sustain their boycotts long enough to force the streetcar companies to
abandon their segregation policies, victory was fleeting. Municipal officials
came back with new laws forcing the streetcar companies to reinstitute
segregation.

But the battle was not over. Although forced to accept streetcar segregation, Black southerners avoided streetcars whenever they could. The seating patterns adopted under the new laws were both unpredictable and insulting. On most streetcar lines, explained North Carolina lawyer Giles Thomas Stephenson in 1910, "the colored passengers . . . are seated in the rear in order—to give the reason as stated by the mayor of Birmingham, Alabama—to do 'away with the disagreeable odors that would necessarily follow the breezes.'" But even this configuration could vary. In some cities, "the two rear seats are reserved for smoking, so the colored passengers begin to sit on the third seat from the rear."[18] Alabama's Jim Crow laws required segregation, but unlike the laws of the Carolinas and Virginia, they did not "specify whether the negroes shall occupy the front or the rear of the car."[19] So Birmingham's streetcars reversed the usual seating arrangements, putting "colored passengers . . . in front so as to give the white passengers the rear for smoking." In the end, "it isn't important which end of the car is given to the nigger," one Alabama resident explained. "The main point is that he must sit where he is told."[20] And regardless of where they were supposed to sit, white southerners felt free to take over Jim Crow seats when the streetcars got crowded, although they were sometimes unhappy to find Blacks there. "Whites Ride in Jim Crow Section, Then Complain of Presence of the Race" was the *Chicago Defender*'s ironic summary of an Alabama public service meeting held to discuss such complaints.[21]

Not surprisingly, then, Black southerners remained eager to avoid the streetcars. Affluent Blacks bought cars at least in part to avoid the day-to-day humiliations of the segregated streetcar, and those who could not afford cars embraced Jim Crow jitneys. Jitneys of all kinds proliferated during the economic depression of 1914, when enterprising automobile owners in Los Angeles began to pick up passengers for a "jitney"—a nickel fare. (The word "jitney" is of obscure origin. It likely originated from *jetnée,* a Louisiana French Creole word for a small coin, which was slang for a nickel in some parts of the South.) Propelled by the drop in car prices that followed the introduction of Ford's Model T, jitneys took the nation by storm. "San Francisco had over 1,500 on their streets four weeks after the first one appeared," noted one automotive trade journal, adding that the craze had left "automobile dealers at the Golden Gate . . . relieved of every automobile in their possession."[22] Just one year later there were more than 65,000 jitneys in operation in virtually every state of the Union.[23] Jitneys offered many Americans their first opportunity to enjoy a car ride, but novelty was not the only source of their appeal. They competed with the streetcars, often trolling the same streets in search of passengers. One reason jitneys caught on so quickly is that they had significant advantages over the streetcars. Not tethered to rails, they could be hailed on the street and taken beyond the trolley line. "Take you anywhere and stop at any corner for a jitney," was their slogan. They also made fewer stops than most trolleys, which allowed them to travel up to twice as fast.[24]

For Blacks in the urban South, jitneys had other advantages. Few historians have taken note of the African American participation in the jitney craze, but it attracted widespread attention during the winter of 1915 when journalists across the country were following the story with interest. "Jitneys Beat Jim Crow" proclaimed one widely circulated local report, which pointed out that jitney services for "the exclusive use of Negroes" had been introduced in Austin and several other Texas cities. "Owned and driven by race men," the cars attracted so many riders that "the new service . . . [had] the effect of greatly reducing the receipts of the streetcar companies," added the reporter, who noted that Blacks in Texas had previously boycotted the streetcars "to show their disapproval of the race separation laws."[25] "At last the Jim Crow question is solved," a reporter for the *Wall Street Journal* likewise noted after observing that Blacks in Charlotte had abandoned local streetcars in favor of a jitney bus labeled "For Colored Only." As the jitney craze expanded, "colored jitneys" could be found in many towns. "Even aristocratic Richmond, with its streetcar partitioned off with the front for whites and the rear for colored, may be relieved of the burden of having its conductors remind the public they are at the wrong end of trains and streetcars."[26]

Of course, there were cities, including Los Angeles, where the phenomenon first started, in which jitneys initially did not pick up Blacks, or carried them only with other Blacks. "The Jitney Buses inaugurate Jim Crow," reported the Black *California Eagle* newspaper in 1914, in an article that urged Blacks to stick to the city's streetcars.[27] But outside the South, racial restrictions on jitney passengers did not always survive legal scrutiny. One of the very first municipal ordinances the City Council of Los Angeles passed to regulate the jitneys decreed that "as a public utility," jitney buses could "make no discrimination against the negroes and Chinese as passengers."[28] The St. Louis courts agreed. In February 1915 six Black protesters successfully challenged the whites-only policies on the jitneys in St. Louis. They boarded a car and refused to move. They were arrested but soon vindicated in the city's Police Court, which ruled that the city's jitney buses "could not draw the color line."

Although one West Virginia court decreed that all jitney drivers had to pick up Blacks, segregation went otherwise unchallenged in the southern states.[29] In Atlanta the first jitneys were "for whites and not for colored passengers." "Every man who owns a 'Ford' thinks it is too good for the colored citizens," complained one Black commentator. But he was able to take comfort in the possibility that Blacks would soon begin to "operate some jitney buses for our own benefit." This option seems to have eased the sting of exclusion for most Black southerners. Black-owned Jim Crow jitneys were popular in many Black communities, whose residents appreciated them both as a symbol of Black enterprise and as an alternative to the streetcar. The jitneys' popularity made them rewarding for their owners, whose businesses sometimes took in "more money than those for white people."[30]

Over time, a dual system of jitneys emerged in most cities in the South. By 1922 most jitneys, as *Electric Railway Journal* noted at the time, were "either a 'white' jitney or a 'colored' jitney," although heavily Hispanic cities such as El Paso also had Mexican jitney drivers who served their own people.[31] The jitney color line was largely informal, although Austin's jitney ordinance specified that "any Jitney operated for the carrying of white persons shall not be required to carry any person of the negro race, nor shall any Jitney operated for the carrying of members of the negro race be required to carry any person of the white race and by the term 'White Race' as used herein is meant any person not of the negro race."[32]

In most cities, however, the jitney craze did not last very long. Untaxed and unregulated, these vehicles cut into the revenues of streetcar companies, contributed nothing to municipal coffers, created traffic havoc, and quickly became associated with accidents. City councils across the country had little choice but to regulate jitneys, and in doing so often bowed to political pressure from the streetcar companies to "legislate the jitney out of business."[33] Some cities banned jitneys altogether, while others imposed permits, licensing fees, taxes, and route restrictions that effectively drove them out of business. The jitney craze was largely over in most cities by 1918.

But Jim Crow jitneys persisted in some Black communities well after that—largely because they served neighborhoods with no other form of public transportation. When municipal officials in Norfolk, Virginia, first tried to restrict the operation of the city's "colored jitneys" in 1921, the Black community there managed to maintain them for a time. Given that the Virginia Power and Railway Company, the local streetcar company, did not serve Black areas, the city's Black neighborhood jitneys, Norfolk Blacks protested, were "the only means of transportation that the colored people have of getting into the business section of the city."[34] Norfolk had developed a "dual transportation system" in which "blacks rarely patronized white carriers."[35] In 1925 the city of Norfolk unified the two systems by introducing new restrictions that put the Black buses out of business. Events in Atlanta followed a similar course. The Colored Jitney Bus Association, a privately owned Black bus company, served several Black neighborhoods in Atlanta between 1922 and 1925. Created to help African Americans escape the discrimination, overcrowding, and inadequate service they had long faced on the Georgia Power Company's streetcars, the company's sixteen buses ran the same routes as the streetcars until it was finally put out of business by the city council.[36]

The longest-lived of these Black jitney operators was the Safe Bus Company of Winston-Salem, North Carolina. It was incorporated in 1926 by Black jitney owners, who for more than a decade had already been providing the African American residents of Winston-Salem with their only form of public transportation. "The company was formed out of necessity," notes one recent account of its founding. Before the first Jim Crow jitneys arrived in Winston-Salem, "Negroes had to walk halfway to town before they got to a carline."[37] Duke Power, the city's streetcar company, did not serve its Black neighborhoods. With no utility company to compete for its business, the Safe Bus Company prospered, surviving until the Winston-Salem Transit Authority took it over in 1972.

Other forms of transportation that survived the municipal crackdown on jitneys of the early twentieth century included unlicensed jitneys that continued to operate in some Black neighborhoods for much of the twentieth century. Most often found in neighborhoods where both cabs and public transportation were scarce, jitneys flourished on the South Side of Chicago through the 1970s. "They look like cabs but they behave like buses," a *Chicago Tribune* reporter noted in 1971. "You can ride as far as you want between 29th and 63rd."[38] Jitney service still survives in Pittsburgh, where it is reportedly "illegal, but thriving."[39]

"NO PLAN TO PROVIDE SPACE FOR NEGROES": FROM EXCLUSION TO SEGREGATION

Even though the jitney craze would not last long, its service model shaped the racial arrangements of the long-distance bus companies that emerged in the 1920s. Intercity buses, the most enduring survivors of the jitney craze, generally started out serving a racially homogeneous clientele. Governed by

the same rampant individualism that had characterized the jitney movement, they remained largely unregulated throughout the 1920s. The most
famous example is Greyhound Bus, which began in 1914 as a jitney service
that carried Scandinavian miners from their work in Hibbing, Minnesota, to
nearby Alice—a town less than two miles away. Founder Carl Eric Wickmam
was a Swedish immigrant who had once worked in the Hibbing iron mines
and began the business after being laid off from the mines. He soon found
that he could make good money driving miners to work and back, and still
more by carrying them to destinations farther afield. Within a few short
years Wickmam's single bus had become the Mesaba Transportation Company, and Wickmam had begun to partner with other regional operators to
create a fleet of buses that traversed several states. This loose association of
bus operators became the Greyhound Bus Corporation in 1930. A "white
jitney" by virtue of its Minnesota origins, Greyhound continued to operate
like one for many years—accepting Black passengers only reluctantly.

The 1920s also saw the emergence of a number of small Black-owned intercity bus lines, which were "operated by Negroes for Negroes."[40] Examples
include the John M. Drew Bus Company, whose founder, John Drew, decided
to take action when he realized that many of the Black domestics who, like
him, lived in Darby—a township outside Philadelphia—had trouble reaching
their jobs in Philadelphia and other nearby towns. The Drew Bus Company
started with two five-passenger Ford Touring cars and remained in operation until 1930, when it was bought out by the Philadelphia Suburban Transportation Company—which was later purchased by SEPTA, the current
public transit authority for Philadelphia and surrounding counties.[41] Other
Black bus lines included the Brooks Bus Company, which Blacks in Alexandria, Virginia, founded in 1921 in an effort to "avoid Jim Crow regulations
on the white lines," and a line that ran between Jacksonville, Florida, and
Miami in the late 1920s.[42]

But such bus lines were never numerous, and they began to disappear altogether when travel dropped precipitously during the Great Depression,
wiping out many of the bus industry's small carriers. By the mid-thirties,
the intercity bus business was dominated by two large operations: Greyhound
and the National Trailways Company—an amalgamation of the remaining independent carriers. Both were owned and operated by whites.

Like the jitney operations that preceded them, many of the early bus lines
simply did not accept Black passengers. "With the increase of bus transpor-

tation systems throughout the United States has come a new problem for Negroes," reported the *Pittsburgh Courier* in 1929. "Whereas they have long been jim crowed in streetcars and passenger trains across the South, they are now in numerous instances barred altogether from the swift shining buses that speed up and down the hard surfaces for which Negroes have helped pay."[43] A few years later a reporter for the Associated Negro Press noted that "the buses are not only employing all the methods of ill treatment practiced by the railroads but, in many cases, have gone still further by denying the right of any accommodation at all to Negro citizens."[44]

This color bar often extended to local bus lines as well. In Portsmouth, Virginia, Blacks were both "barred from riding the bus lines . . . and not permitted to establish a bus line of their own"; and whites in Norfolk refused to allow "Negroes . . . to ride in the same busses with white folks because it would bring about race friction."[45] Blacks could never be sure whether they would be allowed to ride Baltimore's local bus line, which was run by United Railways. Some managed to board its buses, but in 1924 the city's Black newspaper reported that "hundreds of persons, men, women, and children, have been embarrassed by the United Railway employees who have refused to take fares from Negroes and ordered them off the buses."[46] The bus line had no official policy against admitting Blacks, but some conductors chose not to admit them. When in 1929 the *Baltimore Afro-American* sent out two female and two male reporters to investigate the matter, the women were able to board the buses, but the male reporters were refused admittance to three of the four buses they attempted to board. One bus driver refused to stop, another shoved them off, and a third barred them from entering his bus. The fourth admitted them only after an argument.[47]

At issue on both municipal and intercity buses in the South was, of course, the matter of segregation. "When intercity buses were first introduced to the South," recalled sociologist Charles Johnson in 1943, "there was apparently no plan to provide space for Negroes. In some places, they accepted white passengers only."[48] This oversight seems to have extended to municipal services such as Baltimore's United Railway buses as well—which accepted some Blacks but not others, largely because its conductors had different interpretations of the company's basic policy requiring them to "tell Negroes they can't ride but don't put them off."[49] On intercity buses, the situation was, if anything, more confusing.

News Item.—United Street Railway Company sued for refusing to haul colored passengers in Baltimore.

This editorial cartoon showing a Baltimore United Street Railway bus refusing to take Black passengers appeared in the *Baltimore Afro-American* on August 8, 1924.

By 1931 the "general impression that the cross-country busses are intended and available to white persons alone" was so persistent that the South Carolina Motor Vehicle Department had to issue a public ruling correcting the "mistaken idea that only whites can use the bus lines." "Negroes have as much right to ride in the buses traveling over the state highways under class 'A' certificates of public conveniences and necessity as have white people," the ruling clarified, "and operators of busses are required to carry Negro patrons when they apply for transportation as well as white passengers."[50]

The new bus segregation laws enacted in the southern states during the 1930s were necessitated, at least in part, by African American attempts to gain access to intercity buses. North Carolina passed new regulations requiring buses to provide "separate but equal" transport only after Blacks there teamed up with white liberal allies and waged a long and ultimately successful battle to open up all bus transportation in the state to Blacks.[51] It began when Berry O'Kelley, a wealthy Black businessman who lived in Method, North Carolina, protested his exclusion from an intercity bus running between Method and Raleigh in 1925. A reporter from Raleigh's white newspaper, the *News and Observer*, dismissed his complaint as utterly groundless. "If public busses are to haul negroes as passengers then there must be separate automobiles to carry them," it opined. Until the bus companies had "facilities for hauling colored fares, they are not required to do so." If Raleigh's African Americans were unhappy, the reporter suggested, they could always take the matter to court, but they would be better off just waiting for "separate cars for Negroes."[52] Four years later, however, most bus lines in North Carolina were still refusing to accept Black passengers.[53]

As it turned out, North Carolina's legislation did not class buses as common carriers, which are bound by law to serve the general public. The state legislators had deliberately left their status unresolved in order to allow the bus companies to refuse to take Black passengers. In 1929 the North Carolina Interracial Commission asked the State Corporate Commission, which regulated buses, to take Black passengers, only to be told that it did not have "the authority to declare buses common carriers." Not until 1930, when the state's Supreme Court issued a new ruling clarifying the status of buses as common carriers, was the matter finally resolved.[54]

Blacks in Texas also had to fight to get on board most of the buses in their state. Texas was home to several successful intercity Black bus lines in the 1910s, but none survived the crash. By 1929 Black residents of Austin and several other Texas cities were petitioning the Texas Railroad Commission to require "all holders of [bus company] certificates to transport Negroes on their lines."[55] In Texas, as elsewhere, the ban on Black passengers sometimes applied to local buses. In 1925 W. H. Mitchell was arrested for simply trying to board one of the Houston Electric Company's buses.[56] Likewise, in Portsmouth, Virginia, "colored persons" were "barred from riding on the bus lines."[57]

Early bus lines shunned Black passengers in the North as well, as Mrs. Helen Dorsey found out when she attempted to board a Blue Goose Bus bound for Louisville, Kentucky, in Evansville, Indiana, in December 1927.[58] Mrs. Dorsey had telephoned ahead of time to arrange to board the bus at a street corner near her home, where Blue Goose buses frequently stopped to pick up white passengers. She was waiting, along with a travel companion, at the "designated corner when the bus approached." The bus slowed and pulled up to the curb, but on "recognizing the racial identity of the awaiting passengers, [the bus driver] put on more speed and drove hurriedly away, despite many attempts to stop him." Dorsey sued, and although the outcome of her case is not on record, it is possible she may have won. Earlier that year Laura Fischer of Richmond, Indiana, won $500 in damages from a bus company after one of its drivers forced her to sit in the back of the bus. There "are no Jim Crows in Indiana," the judge had noted in announcing this verdict.[59]

Three years later, similar pressure was required to persuade William H. Provost, the ticket agent for the Yankee Stages bus line in Springfield, Massachusetts, "to sell tickets to Negroes." Provost insisted that he normally did so, except when other customers had made prior reservations in Hartford, in which case "a bus sometimes leaves Springfield without being filled." But few local Blacks were convinced. They complained to Springfield city council member Alford H. Tavernier, who insisted that the Yankee Stages buses should be barred from stopping in Springfield until the matter had been resolved. Such practices were not in keeping with the spirit of Massachusetts, declared Tavernier, who was "unalterably opposed to making Springfield like Jacksonville, Fla. or Jackson, Miss., or any other Southern city."[60]

Yet even in the South, Jim Crow laws rarely supported the complete exclusion of Blacks from buses. Both municipal and intercity buses were defined as common carriers under US law, and were therefore legally bound to carry any passenger who bought a ticket. Blacks could be assigned to segregated or separate buses, but they had a right to receive service. By the beginning of the 1930s most bus companies were bowing to this reality. But Blacks would not ride on equal terms. Instead, in the 1930s most southern states revised their segregation statutes to include buses.

The laws that relegated African Americans to the back of buses were modeled on streetcar segregation laws rather than the separate car laws that had created the railroads' Jim Crow cars. Like buses, streetcars were typically single vehicles, and the streetcar companies had already waged a successful battle to establish that segregation could be achieved by separate compartments rather than separate cars. While some white southerners might have hoped for separate buses, no state seriously considered requiring bus carriers to run them. Instead they simply crafted new segregation statutes regarding motorbuses. North Carolina simply extended its existing segregation statutes regulating "street and interurban railways" to "motor busses used as common carriers." Oklahoma passed a new law requiring motor carriers to provide "separate compartments . . . for the accommodation of the white and negro races," and Arkansas took pains to note that segregation on buses should involve signs directing "all the white passengers to seat from the front of the vehicle . . . and all colored passengers . . . [to] seat from the rear of the vehicle forward." But like the streetcar statutes, all the new state laws empowered bus drivers to designate the "amount of space set apart for either race" and to reseat passengers at will.[61] And likewise they all levied fines on both passengers who refused to take the seats they were assigned and operators who failed to segregate their vehicles.

Although most of the new statutes did not specify which part of the bus should be set aside for colored passengers, seating Blacks at the back of the bus must have seemed logical from the outset, given that it was very much in accordance with the logic of segregation. One of the central tenets of the South's Jim Crow society was that the "separate but equal" accommodations assigned to Blacks were invariably inferior to those assigned to whites. The seats located in the rear of early buses filled this bill: they included all of these vehicles' most uncomfortable seats, or more specifically the seats located over the rear axle, which were noisy, and sometimes so much higher up than other seats that their occupants could not rest their feet on the floor; and the last row of seats did not recline. "Buses weren't very well cushioned those days," civil rights activist Lyman Johnson noted, recalling the discomfort he experienced traveling out of the South by bus in 1931. "Every time we hit a pothole in the road . . . the people in the back were bumped up and down. It was rough as riding an old mule." These undesirable rear seats, which might have otherwise been difficult to fill, were assigned to Blacks even when other nearby seats were available—a fact that the Black passengers often noticed and resented. Johnson, for example, "would not have minded sitting in the back of the bus—even when the roads were bumpy—if that's where the only seats were. . . . But I didn't like having to pass empty seats in the front to go [to] colored seats in the back!"[62]

It is worth noting that the specific character of the segregated seating arrangements on southern buses could have been even worse. Both Georgia and South Carolina briefly experimented with seating arrangements that had African Americans riding backward. "Divided in the middle of the bus," the seats faced different directions: whites faced forward, while Blacks looked out onto the road behind them. These arrangements were a recipe for motion sickness and so appalled African American passengers in Charleston, South Carolina, and Savannah, Georgia, that they contemplated forming their own bus line rather than going along with the new seating arrangements.[63]

The *Chicago Defender* came to their defense, blasting the practice in a notably xenophobic cartoon that complained "the Chinaman, Indian, Turk, Eskimo and German ride comfortably in the front part of the bus with the white man, while you ride in the rear, over the springs, FACING BACKWARD and courting certain death in case of a disastrous rear-end collision."

This uncomfortable arrangement did not last long. Bus company officials in Georgia and South Carolina turned the rear seats forward after receiving a petition protesting the practice from their African American passengers. The petitioners enclosed the *Chicago Defender*'s cartoon, inspiring the Black newspaper to crow, "Cartoon corrects vicious practice." But the *Defender* also noted that the correction was no more than a "half victory," and vowed: "The battle will continue until Jim Crow seating is abolished."[64]

African Americans across the country made good on this threat. When Texas finally opened up its buses to Black passengers in the early 1930s, the legislature initially forgot to pass segregation regulations.[65] But they were quickly forced to correct the omission after a "negress," Sadie Patillo, "at-

STUDY this picture closely. It shows the latest method of humiliation adopted by bus lines operating IN THE SOUTH, and its object is to keep you forever in the background. You are full-fledged citizens when CLOUDS OF WAR necessitate a CALL TO ARMS, but when peace comes you are STIFLED, SUBJUGATED, SUPPRESSED. You are told to "stay in YOUR PLACE"—and that place, the South says, "is in the REAR." Your VISION, your OUTLOOK, is supposed to be BACKWARD—toward oblivion and defeat; while your white brethren and all races not considered non-white, face FORWARD and ride onward to HAPPINESS, PROSPERITY and OPPORTUNITY. The Chinaman, Indian, Turk, Eskimo and German ride comfortably in the front part of the bus with the white man, while you ride in the rear, over the springs, FACING BACKWARD and courting certain death in case of a disastrous rear-end collision. JIM CROW RAILROADS did segregate you, but at least you rode FACE FORWARD. The SOUTHERN bus lines have gone the railroads one better and not only SEGREGATE you, but compel you to ride BACKWARD. It's their answer to your record of PROGRESS and ACHIEVEMENT which you have made, not BECAUSE of them, but IN SPITE of them.

Editorial cartoon depicting "A New Method of Jim Crow."

tempted to ride in the front of the bus in 1932." Charged with riding in a compartment of the bus reserved for whites, Patillo was initially convicted and fined $10 for "violating Jim Crow law." She challenged her conviction and won. Texas's Jim Crow laws "did not apply to motor buses," the appellate court ruled, rather reluctantly, in a verdict that also noted that such segregation "might be desirable."[65] Texas legislators agreed, and wrote new legislation specifying that all commercial vehicles must maintain "separate coaches or compartments for the accommodation of white and negro passengers." Passed in 1935, the new legislation was further updated in 1943 to clarify that in vehicles without separate cars or sections, Blacks must "take seats in the back or rear end."[67]

"IS NOBODY GOING TO STOP IT?"
SEGREGATION ON NORTHERN BUSES

In the southern states that had remembered to issue new regulations requiring buses to provide "separate but equal" accommodations for Black passengers, segregated seating was almost impossible to challenge in court. But outside the South, African Americans waged a relentless, often frustrating, war against Jim Crow buses. The North and the West had no segregation laws, so in those regions segregation on buses was never as ubiquitous as it was in the South, and people who challenged discrimination on those buses in court were often successful. But their lawsuits rarely changed bus company policies. Nor did the bad publicity that bus segregation engendered, which was largely confined to the Black press. The segregation (and sometimes exclusion) that Blacks encountered on northern buses diminished only modestly over time.

In 1927 the *Chicago Defender*, which issued a steady stream of editorials, articles, and cartoons attacking all forms of Jim Crow, commissioned a devastating exposé on the segregationist practices on Chicago's intercity bus lines. It hired Albert Libby, a white reporter, to visit the city's bus lines, posing as a southerner who did not want to sit next to a person of color. He found that one of the bus lines refused to carry African American passengers, while others limited their number, and all but one of the intercity bus lines then serving Chicago seated Black passengers in the back of the bus.[68]

Most repressive was Ni-Sun Bus Company, whose ticket agent assured him: "We never under any circumstances sell a ticket to a Negro. We sell some tickets to Mexicans, but only if they are well dressed and clean, and then they sit in the rear. But we intend to keep Negroes out." When Libby asked the agent what he did to discourage African Americans who wanted to buy tickets, he explained that he simply told all Black passengers that the tickets for whatever bus they wished to ride were "all sold out!!"[69]

Vendors at the city's largest carrier, an amalgamation known as the Purple Swan-Greyhound-Oriole Bus line, were slightly more accommodating, accepting "a maximum of four" Black passengers per coach. The Inter-State Bus Company had a straightforward policy, which the ticket agent described without mincing words: "We seat niggers in the back." Ticket agents at Shoreline Bus Company took a more polite approach, which they were happy to share with Libby. Following a script provided by their boss, they told African American ticket-seekers that although their company was "compelled by law to sell transportation" to all comers, Black passengers would not "be permitted the use of the restroom . . . [nor] be allowed refreshment or use of the lavatories." On hearing this news, Black customers invariably lost interest, a young female ticket agent cheerfully told Libby: "They get offended . . . and go away."[70]

In Chicago, as elsewhere, protests succeeded in improving Black access to the buses, but they did not end segregation on board or at rest stops. In the summer of 1928, a year after Libby's exposé, the *Chicago Defender* issued a jubilant assessment of the outcome of its campaign against segregation on the intercity buses running in and out of Chicago. The paper's efforts, combined with those of "the determined people of Chicago," who had filed a number of "successful suits," it proudly proclaimed, had resulted in "another victory for civil rights." Whereas Black Chicagoans had previously been "denied all service on roads running to and from Detroit, St. Louis . . . [and] other points . . . all passengers now enjoy full freedom of the coaches."[71]

But the victory was either short-lived or overstated. Discrimination continued even in Chicago, where on September 28, 1929, the local NAACP felt compelled to "declare war on bus companies that practice discrimination." "We've had far too many reports . . . to permit it to go unchallenged," said association president Herbert A. Turner, who worried that segregation was moving north. By way of example, he cited the experience of Chicago resident William A. Roberts, who had boarded a Greyhound bus bound for St. Louis the previous week. When he boarded, "the driver directed him to take a seat in the rear." Roberts responded that "he would sit where he wished, since his ticket was first class." But the driver did not back down. Instead, he told Roberts that "the Greyhound bus company runs these buses and you will sit wherever we want you to sit." Roberts then called for the station manager, who backed the driver. The official was happy to refund Roberts's bus fare, but not willing to allow him to seat himself in the front of the bus.[72] Roberts took his refund, but also filed a complaint with the NAACP.

Complaints against bus companies abounded and not just in Chicago. The Nevin Bus Company, which was based in New York City with lines extending up and down the East Coast, is a case in point.[73] In 1929 Rolland Fallin, who rode Nevin buses regularly, testified that it was the company's practice to "put colored people on the seats numbered 21 to 27, or the last seats back." He had taken Nevin buses to Washington, D.C., Philadelphia, New York City, and Atlantic City, he explained, and had been asked "to use seat number 21 every time but once"—when he was asked sit in the back row.[74] The segregation on the Nevin buses was blatant enough to be detected even by those who had not experienced it personally. Harry Miller, of Burlington, New Jersey, who "never had occasion to use a bus belonging to this company," was troubled by the seating arrangements he had witnessed on its buses as they passed through his town. "I invariably see colored passengers on the rear seats—and only on these seats on [Nevin] busses," he wrote in a letter to the editor published in the *Baltimore Afro-American* in 1929. "Now just what are we going to do about public carriers in the north forcing segregation on colored patrons?" Miller asked, "Is nobody going to stop it?"[75]

Miller was not alone in his outrage. The *Baltimore Afro-American* had already sent reporters to the bus line to investigate its practices. But the paper's attempt to follow up on the complaints went nowhere. Representatives for the bus company insisted that Nevin did not practice "any discriminatory seating."[76] Still, complaints continued. When Beatrice Washington of Brooklyn tried to take a seat with a travel companion in the front of a Nevin bus traveling to Princeton, New Jersey, the driver told them that it was out of the question. "White people did not want to sit with Negroes and did not want to see them on the front seats," he said. "Only one other passenger, an elderly white man, occupied the bus at this time," noted Washington, who submitted a complaint about the incident to the NAACP.[77] In 1932 the company was forced to admit that at least one of its drivers practiced segregation when twelve students from Lincoln University, a historically Black institution in Chester, Pennsylvania, attempted to board a Nevin bus in

Baltimore only to be kicked off because they "refused to be Jim Crowed by a driver who insisted that they sit in the rear seats."[78]

Nevin fired the driver in question and promised to do the same to any other employees who tried to impose segregation on its passengers—"except in the South, where the law compels us to."[79] But Black travelers continued to report troubles on the Short Line buses, which served New York State; the Great Eastern System buses, which went up and down the East Coast; and bus companies in the West and Midwest as well.[80]

Seating was not the only problem. Securing tickets and seats could be an ordeal because bus companies typically ticketed and seated whites before opening up any space to Black passengers. Jesse O. Thomas, the southern field director of the Urban League, outlined the practical effect of these practices in a 1931 letter to the Norfolk *New Journal and Guide*, which described the challenges faced by African American passengers who had to transfer from one bus to another in New Orleans. On arriving at this transportation hub, Black passengers who needed to make a connection to another bus were compelled "to stand aside and wait until every white passenger is seated." Only after "the luggage of said passengers" was safely stowed away would African American travelers finally find out whether they would be able to secure a seat or be "sent in a separate bus." Louisiana laws might require segregation, he complained, "but there is no reason why a colored passenger should be embarrassed . . . [and] humiliated by having to wait indefinitely to find out if the space is to be occupied by white people and their luggage before he can be given a seat."[81]

Greyhound Bus Lines, which operated fleets all over the country, was particularly notorious for its segregationist practices. Its drivers routinely seated African American passengers in the back of the bus, even in the many states where segregation was not required. In New York City, complained one Black attorney in 1932, Greyhound ticket agents and bus drivers used a special ticketing system to make sure that all Black passengers ended up at the back of the bus. Ticket agents sold white travelers numbered tickets that assigned them to seats in the front of the bus, while Blacks who bought tickets had theirs marked with a check instead of a seat number. "When the bus driver collected all the tickets, he separated the ones marked by a check, all of which were held by colored people, and showed these passengers to rear seats."[82] In other cities, African Americans were simply "forced in rear seats."[83]

By the early 1930s the NAACP was receiving more complaints about segregation on buses than it could possibly address on a case-by-case basis. The
Greyhound Corporation, which commanded an ever-increasing share of the
bus transportation marketplace, figured prominently in such complaints. A
consolidation of more than a hundred early bus lines, which incorporated in
1930, Greyhound outlived its competitors largely through mergers, and appears to have exercised little control over the segregation policies in place
among the many lines under its control. Confronted with complaints, the corporation's executives routinely claimed to be unaware of any discrimination
on their bus lines, which may have been at least somewhat true. In its early
years Greyhound's management was largely focused on keeping the corporation afloat. Travel revenues plummeted during the Great Depression, almost
bankrupting Greyhound, which was heavily in debt from its rapid expansion.[84] Also during these years southern legislatures introduced Jim Crow
laws that made bus segregation mandatory in some states—and levied fines
on carriers that failed to segregate their passengers. With such pressures in
play, Greyhound's management may well have regarded complaints about discrimination as the least of its problems.

"NOTHING HAS SUCH A SALUTARY EFFECT AS
A SUIT FOR DAMAGES"

The NAACP, by contrast, began the 1930s poised to launch an all-out assault
on discrimination in education and interstate transportation. In 1930 it received a grant of $100,000, which was to be paid out over four or five years,
from Charles Garland, a wealthy and idealistic young Harvard graduate. The
chronically underfunded civil rights organization, which had never previously been able to afford even one staff lawyer, planned to use the money to
fight discrimination in the courts and commissioned Nathan Mangold, its first
in-house counsel, to craft an ambitious legal agenda that focused on education and transportation. Unfortunately, Garland's grant was invested in se-
curities, which all but evaporated when the stock market crashed. Instead of
$100,000, the NAACP ended up with $20,000. The reduced amount still allowed the organization to employ a full-time counsel, but virtually no money
was left to fund its legal cases. After Mangold stepped down in the early 1930s,
the NAACP was able to secure the services of Howard Law School dean Charles

Hamilton Houston, who reluctantly concluded that the organization's budget would not allow it to take on "two issues as large as discrimination in education and discrimination in transportation." A "concentration of effort" was required, he explained in a 1934 memo that proposed a "revised program of litigation" focused entirely on education.[85]

Houston's program was adopted, but the NAACP never abandoned its hope of attacking transportation segregation as well. Houston described one of the primary goals of the NAACP's legal department as "to arouse and strengthen the will of the local communities to demand and fight for their rights"—and NAACP staffers did just that in their responses to travel discrimination complaints.[86] Nathan Mangold had hoped that the NAACP would challenge the constitutionality of travel segregation directly by mounting a series of test cases designed to overturn *Plessy*, but during the Depression years NAACP staffers had to settle for encouraging discontented Black travelers to challenge the bus companies on their own. "The association is not at this time prosecuting any damage suits against bus companies for alleged discrimination," NAACP assistant secretary Roy Wilkins told one prospective litigant in 1932, while also encouraging her to put her case in "the hands of a competant attorney for legal action." At present, he explained, the organization was staying out of the courtroom, in favor of collecting information that "could be used in taking up the matter directly with the buslines."[87] But Wilkins had strong encouragement for anyone who was willing to sue the bus companies in civil court. "Nothing has such a salutary effect as a suit for damages," he told another correspondent. "The bus companies pay more attention to damage suits they lose than to all the protests ever written."[88] Thurgood Marshall, who joined the NAACP as an assistant special counsel in 1936, was more frank with another potential litigant: "We are planning an attack on the Jim-crow laws in the south surrounding the trains and bus transportation, but have not as yet been able to put our plans into effect because of our very limited budget."[89]

Even though it could not afford to litigate cases, the NAACP did use the information it gathered to take on Greyhound Bus Corporation outside the courts, staging an ambitious campaign in 1932 designed to force the struggling corporation's management to take discrimination more seriously. That spring Roy Wilkins began to sort through the many letters of complaint the organization had received, looking for complaints about the Pennsylvania Greyhound Company while also soliciting testimony from anyone who had experienced discrimination on their buses. Because the NAACP lacked the resources to address reports of discrimination on Greyhound buses across the country, its leadership had decided to put all the pressure they could muster on one strategically chosen branch of the bus company's emerging empire. "There are a half a dozen branches of the Greyhound lines all over the country," Wilkins told one correspondent. "We are concerning ourselves with the Pennsylvania Greyhound Lines because that is the key company and is affiliated with all the others."[90] Greyhound's Pennsylvania branch was key, he further explained, because 50 percent of its stock was owned by the Pennsylvania Railroad, which also held significant amounts of stock in other Greyhound bus lines across the country. The Greyhound Corporation had plans for expansion on the East Coast, which made its Pennsylvania branch particularly vulnerable.

The NAACP targeted Greyhound just as its new routes were under review at the Pennsylvania Public Service Commission in Harrisburg. In the spring of 1932 Wilkins appeared before the commission to "oppose the granting of new routes to the company on the grounds that the company was violating Pennsylvania law in Jim-Crowing passengers." The NAACP had received "complaints from colored patrons of the Greyhound lines in all points of the country," and they all reported that "Negroes travelling on Greyhound buses have been obliged to occupy rear seats, and seats over the wheels, to their discomfort, when better seats are available."[91] Wilkins convinced the commission to schedule another meeting to hear from African American travelers who had experienced discrimination on Pennsylvania Greyhound buses, and even managed to enlist the support of the Philadelphia branch of the Elks in his campaign.

But despite clear evidence of discrimination and the attendant public outcry, Greyhound bus lines still received its "certificate of public service." Confronted with the NAACP's long list of complaints, Greyhound manager J. E. Walker maintained that "it most certainly is not our general policy to discriminate against colored passengers." The complaints were the result of the actions of "individual bus driver[s] rather than any matter of company policy." Walker promised to address such complaints by issuing a "special bulletin to our regional managers, instructing them to advise all drivers and ticket agents under their jurisdiction that under no circumstance are colored passengers to be unduly discriminated against, and that they are to be given every consideration as passengers."[92]

Greyhound's assurances seem to have satisfied the Pennsylvania Public Service commissioners, but they were not reassuring to Wilkins, who told Walker he was troubled to see Greyhound issuing a bulletin stating that colored passengers should not be "unduly discriminated against." If individual drivers were the cause of past incidents of discrimination, why continue to let bus company drivers and officials use their own discretion in determining "what constitutes undue discrimination" in "the treatment of colored passengers"? Greyhound employees from different regions were likely to have very different opinions on that subject. "The only fair and just way of dealing with this problem," Wilkins concluded, "is to hand down a general order that no discrimination is to be practiced against colored passengers solely because of their color."[93]

When Greyhound proved unwilling to issue any such order, the NAACP tried to get the company's drivers to comply with state laws in the North by appealing to Blacks who rode the company's buses to "stand firm against bus 'Jim Crow.'" Taking the Greyhound Lines manager J. B. Walker at his word on the causes of discrimination on the company's buses, the NAACP issued a press release explaining that "most bus discrimination in the Northern States exists because a few prejudiced employees of the company make rules of their own, ignoring state laws." When confronted with such employees, the NAACP told Black readers across the country, "colored passengers should insist on their rights." Neither bus company officials nor the police were legally entitled to "herd" African Americans to the back of the bus, and if they lay "a finger on a regular passenger who is quietly insisting on his or her right, suit can be filed against the company and damages collected."[94]

Some passengers complied with the NAACP's request, but defying Greyhound bus drivers was not for the faint of heart. Ernest O. Boone successfully defended his right to ride in the front of a Pickwick Greyhound bus in Missouri in 1933, and even won $500 in damages, but only after a tense standoff in which three policemen boarded the bus in an attempt to force him to change seats.[95] When Isabella Smith refused to move to the back of the bus on a trip from Princess Anne, Maryland, to her home in Philadelphia in the fall of 1934, she ended up in jail. She had taken a seat in the center of the bus and traveled undisturbed until the bus stopped to take on additional passengers in Salisbury, Maryland, at which point the bus driver "ordered her to move to the rear and give a white passenger her seat." When she refused, the driver told her, "You will move or I'll kick you out of that seat." He also told her,

"We lynch colored people down here when they don't obey orders given by whites." Smith continued to stay put until she was dragged off the bus by the driver and a local policeman he had summoned to help eject her. The policeman arrested Smith, who was detained overnight until a Maryland court judge discharged her. She could "go back to Philadelphia," he told her. "Maryland jim crow laws do not apply to interstate customers."[96]

Bessie Nelson and Mamie Kinchlow had an even more terrifying experience when they stood up for their rights on a Greyhound bus. In the summer of 1932 the two women ended up on the same Virginia-bound Greyhound bus. Kinchlow, a Black New Yorker, who was traveling to Norfolk to attend her mother's funeral, got on first; Nelson, a New Jersey resident who was also headed to Virginia, appears to have boarded in Trenton, New Jersey. Although they were traveling into the segregated South, the two women had reason to believe that they would be able to remain comfortably seated on the same bus until they reached their destination. "Go 'Greyhound' all the way," proclaimed an advertisement Kinchlow had seen in the bus company's New York City terminal—which promised passengers "no inconvenience in changing from one bus to another." The sign was a relief to Kinchlow, who had been anxious enough about the trip to double-check on these seating arrangements with the ticket agent, who assured her that she would travel the entire trip on "the same bus and have the same seat."[97]

But the bus went no further than Washington, D.C., when its passengers had to transfer to a new bus for the last leg of their journey. Both Nelson and Kinchlow did so, and were seated beside each other in one of the bus's rear seats when the driver asked them to get up to make room for two white passengers. Kinchlow was outraged, and refused to move—as did Nelson. "There is no place for me to sit, do you want me to sit on top of the bus?" she asked the driver, who had both women removed and arrested as soon as the bus arrived at its next stop in Alexandria, Virginia. There they were both fined $25 plus court costs and put in jail. Worried that she would miss her mother's funeral, Kinchlow pleaded with the Virginia officials to let her go, but to no avail. She was detained for two days and missed the funeral.[98] Nelson fared no better. Instead of going to Fredericksburg, where she was headed, she was convicted of being "a disorderly person" and assigned to a work detail in an Alexandria municipal hospital laundry that lasted "almost a week."[99] Both women sued Greyhound and lost. After a legal battle that lasted five years, the District Court of Washington, D.C., rejected their suits.[100]

By 1935 it was amply clear that many Greyhound drivers continued to seat all Black passengers in the back of the bus. Maude Louther, a New Yorker, won a $150 judgment for being forced into the back of the bus by an Eastern Greyhound driver that spring, and in October 1936 the Peninsula and Greyhound Bus lines, headquartered in Baltimore, admitted that "their drivers were instructed to segregate colored passengers in interstate traffic, putting them over the wheels." Greyhound's response to this revelation was both evasive and dishonest. "Service between Washington and Annapolis," a company spokesperson told the *Baltimore Afro-American,* "was controlled by the Peninsula Lines"—an entirely different bus line. But reporters for the *Baltimore Afro-American* found that both companies could be reached at the same phone number.[101]

The Chicago NAACP's assault on bus discrimination in their region was equally unsuccessful. Their declaration of war on this form of discrimination in 1929 was quickly undermined by economic woes caused by the Great Depression. While complaints multiplied, they could take few to court, and their first legal victory did not come until 1935—though they may have settled some earlier cases out of court. In 1935 an Illinois jury awarded $60 plus court costs to Callie Stevens, a Chicago woman who had been refused a seat in the front of a Safeway Company bus. The damages were disappointingly small, but NAACP lawyers William H. Temple and Irwin C. Mollison did their best to put a positive spin on the case's outcome. "While the amount of damages in this case was not large," they reported, the verdict was still "significant because of the stubborn fight put up by the Safeway Bus Company," which had brought in witnesses from as far as Cleveland. Given that the NAACP had other cases pending against Safeway, Temple and Mollison's success in persuading an Illinois jury that the bus company had violated the Civil Rights Act was a good sign. So, too, was the fact that some members of the jury had favored a verdict of $300 plus costs. The lawyers also managed to get Safeway employees to admit that Blacks were routinely assigned the worst seats on their buses, and that "race people were usually given either seats over the rear axle or in the rear where seats did not permit the space for reclining." African Americans had to be relegated to these out-of-the-way seats, one white witness explained, because "wives of white men objected to riding beside colored people for a distance of 1,000 miles."[102]

Any regional reforms inspired by the NAACP's modest victory appear to have been purely rhetorical. When W. N. Cash of Omaha, Nebraska, inquired at his local Greyhound office about the "treatment a colored passenger might expect" during the summer of 1935, he received a gracious but confounding answer. "Please be advised that we make no discrimination in the handling of colored passengers except we maintain a right to seat them the same as we do with white people," a company representative told him, before promptly adding: "It is generally understood tha[t] colored people will choose seats to the rear of the coach and we cannot say that we have experienced any difficulty in this regard."[103]

Although the NAACP was largely defeated in its quest to end Jim Crow on northern buses, its staffers continued to collect complaints about discrimination on buses, trains, and other common carriers. They told most of the correspondents who wrote to them about travel that "the NAACP always prefers to have complainants engage their own attorneys to sue for damages," but they also routinely investigated and documented such complaints. In addition to filing their own queries with transportation companies that their correspondents complained about, they also helped their correspondents figure out whether they had legal grounds for a lawsuit and supplied prospective litigants with detailed legal advice.[104]

The NAACP also continued to publicize transportation discrimination and made pointed efforts to warn Black travelers about the Greyhound Bus Corporation's notorious record when it came to segregation. Roy Wilkins issued regular press releases announcing that the NAACP no longer used Greyhound services when it contracted buses to bring members to its annual meetings. He also notified the public that the NAACP "did not advise its members to use the Greyhound lines." Greyhound was still moving African American passengers from "the front and center of the buses into the rear seats," he warned all potential travelers, and there was no sign this was about to change.[105]

"NO ACCOMMODATIONS FOR NEGROES": DISCRIMINATION ON THE ROAD

African Americans who traveled by bus faced forms of discrimination that went well beyond segregated seats.[106] Henry Shepard, a labor organizer, was one of many Blacks who wrote to the NAACP about this problem. On a trip from San Francisco to St. Louis in 1931, Shepard encountered discrimination at "all the stations or cafes owned or controlled by the Pickwick Greyhound line." At some places, he noted, the servers "told Negro patrons that they would have to eat in the kitchen or take their food in a paper and eat it out-side," while other establishments were even less welcoming: their proprietors simply informed Black customers "that they did not serve Negroes."[107] Grey-hound's Omaha office presented prospective customers with a more upbeat account of why people of color did not eat in its restaurants. Even though Greyhound "imposed no restrictions relative to meals being served to colored people . . . we find that most do not wish to be seated at tables or counters, but prefer to obtain their food and eat it while being seated elsewhere in the terminal."[108]

Greyhound was not alone in failing to provide Black passengers with un-restricted access to food and other basic necessities. The Shoreline ticket agents in Chicago who discouraged African American passengers from buying tickets by warning them that they would not be "allowed refreshment or use of the lavatories" were, in fact, describing conditions that Black passengers encoun-tered while traveling on many different bus lines and on private buses.[109]

Finding food was often a problem for Black musicians and other per-formers who spent extended stretches of time on the road. While traveling bands and theatrical troupes had long traveled by train, by the late 1920s quite a few had begun to travel by bus, which was cheaper and allowed touring musicians to visit places not easily reached by train. In 1927 the popular blues singer Ma Rainey bought a "luxurious touring bus" with her name emblazoned on it. Count Basie's band, which performed 250 to 270 "one nighters" a year during the 1930s, traveled in uncomfortable "old-time buses" that Basie rented from a company in New Jersey.[110] While these pri-vate buses enabled performers to avoid the degradation of riding in the Jim Crow car, they often encountered problems when they stopped to eat. Harry Sweets, a trumpeter who toured with Basie during those years, told a re-porter from *Jazz Times* in 1997 that when it came time to eat, "the white bus driver had to go to the market and get us sandwiches, because as black men, we couldn't go into the grocery stores or restaurants."[111] Even in the grocery stores, ordering prepared food would have meant going "around the back of the grocery store," so the whole band stayed on the bus. On the road with white jazzman Artie Shaw and his band in the late 1930s, Billie Holiday often ended up eating sandwiches on the bus. "Some time it was a choice between me eating and the whole band starving," she recalled in her autobiography. "I got tired of having to make a federal case about breakfast, lunch and dinner."[112]

Even though ordinary bus passengers did not have to endure months on the road, they were usually less prepared to navigate the challenges involved in securing food on the road than performers who toured regularly. Touring musicians knew the road and could choose their own stops, or depend on white or white-looking band members, or get their bus driver to help them get food. But ordinary bus passengers rarely had such options. Then, as now, buses offered no meal service on board. But they did schedule stops at roadside cafes or restaurants at meal times. Often located inside bus terminals, and sometimes owned and operated by the bus companies, such facilities were promoted by bus companies as enhancing the safety and comfort of the travel experience. Greyhound Bus Corporation assured passengers that its chain of Post House restaurants was dedicated to "supervising the sanitary conditions of the Greyhound stops and helping toward the constant improvement of the food offered Greyhound passengers."[113] But many Blacks who attempted to eat at any of the bus company's roadside restaurants—both inside and outside of the South—were told to eat in the kitchen.

On a Union Pacific bus from Chicago to San Francisco, James W. Martin was utterly mortified to be relegated to the kitchen at a rest stop in Rawlings, Wyoming. The only Black person on the bus, Martin had "been treated OK" before the stop in Rawlings. He had even become friendly with several of his fellow passengers. So when he sat down at the Luxe Café's lunch counter with several of his new acquaintances. he was not expecting trouble. In fact, when the café's cashier came over to him and told him in "a low but firm voice, we'll take care of you in the kitchen," Martin "didn't quite catch the drift of what he said and had to ask him to repeat himself." When he did, Martin walked out and was able to get a good lunch at a café nearby, but he did not soon forget the very public slight. "Mr. White, it was really embarrassing," he wrote, describing the incident to Walter Francis White, the head of the NAACP, "and it would be doubly so to a girl or a young woman." White was sympathetic but explained that it was "difficult to attack segregation at lunch counters where busses stop unless there is a specific law that is violated by such a procedure."[114]

The color lines at southern rest stops were more clear-cut but no less humiliating. The white waiting room in Tuscaloosa's bus station featured a café where white passengers could enjoy breakfast, lunch, or dinner. Its "Colored

Greyhound bus passengers stopped at Greyhound Post Road Hotel and Restaurant on
Florida's Overseas Highway, 1948.

Only side," by contrast, had no food. "There was a window on the side of the
bus station where Colored people could ask to buy a sandwich. The sandwich
might never appear depending on the whim of the colored cook or the direction given by a white cafeteria supervisor." To add insult to injury, "the smell
of bacon, coffee, or fried chicken, unfettered by Jim Crow laws," wafted into
the "Colored Only" side of the bus station "and penetrated black noses causing
Colored mouths to salivate."[115] Built in the 1950s, the Greyhound bus terminal
in Montgomery, Alabama, had better dining facilities for Blacks—but even
these were hardly equal. The station had two Post House restaurants: a spacious one with a U-shaped Formica counter at the front of the building for
whites, and a small lunch counter at the rear of the building for Blacks.[116]

   Waiting rooms and restrooms were no better. Colored waiting rooms were
usually small and dingy. Some were so disgusting that they inspired complaints to the NAACP. College student Cassie Lewis was so appalled by the

At the bus station, Durham.
North Carolina, 1940.

bus station in her hometown of Chester, South Carolina, that she wrote to
Walter White to describe conditions there. On entering the station, she told
him in a letter written in 1939, Black passengers were directed down a narrow
alleyway to a colored waiting area that was "filthier (and that is putting it as
simply as I can) than a dog house. . . . Garbage bags, boxes and everything
we might mention can be found on the floor."[117]

The colored waiting room in the Florida Motor Lines bus station in Tampa
was still worse. It inspired so many complaints that the NAACP New York
branch asked the Tampa NAACP to investigate conditions there. Tampa branch
president W. D. Williams visited the station and fired off a strong letter to the
bus company president, D. G. Howe, reminding him that "Florida law provides
for separate but equal accommodations," and asking him to give "this discrimination in their waiting room" his "immediate attention." The station's colored
waiting room was not even an actual room, Williams told Howe. It was nothing
more than a "little space . . . in a dingy greasy corner, where your bus parks
and where grease, oil and other rubbish are kept." The baggage room "had
better facilities than the colored waiting room. Said baggage room," he suggested, "could be used as a waiting room for said passengers."[118]

Bus station bathrooms were even more problematic. The colored restrooms
in southern bus stations were notoriously uninviting. Black bus passengers
routinely complained that "the toilet facilities for colored people were grossly
inadequate and colored men and women were forced to use the same lava-
tory."[119] Civil rights activist Pauli Murray came home from an "extended
trip" on the Trailways bus system in 1939 reporting that "where there are
separate restrooms at the rest stops, facilities for Negro patrons are more than

inadequate. No effort is made to provide supplies for the rest rooms or keep them clean and sanitary."[120] Her observations are seconded by Joice Lewis, who grew up in Tuscaloosa, Alabama, during the 1940s and 1950s. The "Whites Only" bathrooms inside the Tuscaloosa bus terminal, she recalled, were always "spotlessly clean having been washed and wiped, and mopped and maintained by Colored janitors, who were not allowed to clean the Colored restrooms for fear of cross contamination." By contrast, the "Colored Only" restrooms "were too filthy to enter unless nature could not be denied." They were "cleaned once a week by a part-time janitor who did not work in the 'White Only' areas."[121]

Worse still were the bus stations that had no restrooms for Black travelers. Prior to the 1950s, long-distance buses did not usually have bathrooms on board, so passengers had to make use of the facilities inside bus stations and other rest stops. But some of these establishments refused to accommodate Black passengers. Black bus travelers kept largely quiet about how they navigated such indignities, but some returned from their trips too outraged to remain silent. Willamette Brown told the *Cleveland Call and Post* that she was "not permitted to use the restrooms provided for lady passengers" between Cincinnati, Ohio, and Knoxville, Kentucky, on a Pennsylvania Greyhound Bus trip she took in 1934; and that when she filed a complaint about her experience with the Greyhound office in Cleveland, where she bought her ticket, the company's agent and claims adjuster told her that "the company did not advertise in Negro newspapers and that was a clear indication that it did not desire the patronage of Negroes."[122]

Likewise, when Ada Montgomery got sick after being barred from using the bathroom at the Greyhound Company's rest stop in Parkersburg, West Virginia, on a trip between Wythehill, Virginia, and Pittsburgh, she was not too embarrassed to complain. She contacted the NAACP, asking for help in figuring out how to "carry a suit." She explained that when she tried to use the "comfort room" in Parkersburg, "the matron stoped [sic] me at door said no colored ladies allowed to use the comfort room. I ask why and she didn't answer my question." Montgomery appealed to the bus driver for permission to use the restroom. Although he informed her that "they was supposed to accommodate me," Montgomery did not get "accommodation" until the bus arrived in Wheeling, Virginia—its next stop. The experience left her physically ill, she reported: "I was sick in bed for 6 days, and still in care of a Dr. from not being able to use the comfort room."[123]

Ada Montgomery had traveled alone and could offer no witnesses to her exchange with the matron, which made the NAACP initially somewhat dubious as to whether she had strong enough evidence to file a suit, but Walter White and Charles Hamilton Houston were troubled enough by her story to investigate further. Was there a custom of "excluding Negroes from the comfort station at Parkersburg?" they wondered. If so, perhaps they could find witnesses to testify on the general "practice of the bus company" and would not need anyone to testify on Montgomery's experience in particular. Houston reached out to T. G. Nutter, the president of the NAACP's Charleston, West Virginia, branch, to find someone in Parkersburg who could answer these questions, and quickly heard back from J. Rupert Jefferson, a professor who taught at West Virginia State University, a Black college located in Parkersburg.[124]

Jefferson was not familiar with the bus station's policies, but he was happy to help. He wasted no time in going to the station to investigate and quickly found out that "it is an *actual fact* that there is absolutely no accommodations for Negroes and that they ARE refused use of the restroom and toilet facilities et cetera." The bus station, he explained, was located in a local hotel that catered to whites only. Representatives of the bus lines said that "they make no difference in accommodation as to passengers, but that the Hotel Owners are to blame." But regardless of whether the bus station or the hotel was at fault, added Jefferson, who collected his information from Black workers employed at both, "there seems to be no secret about the matter."[125]

After hearing back from Jefferson, Houston moved cautiously toward involving the NAACP in the matter, and asked Homer Brown, a Pittsburgh lawyer and NAACP member, to investigate further. The organization was loath to take on a case it could not win, both because it was perennially underfunded and because its lawyers were anxious to avoid any verdict "that will be more harmful to our present situation." So before taking the case, Brown traveled to West Virginia to investigate conditions at the bus station himself and establish whether "Miss Montgomery is the type of person you would want as a plaintiff in a case of this kind." He also enlisted Professor Jefferson to secure "two (2) responsible citizens to seek rest room accommodations [at the bus station] so we will have witnesses to testify as to the general situation."[126] The Black bus company porters who had spoken freely to Jefferson were "not willing to come to court because of the probable loss of their jobs."[127] In the end, the case did not go to court. Greyhound settled, accepting Brown's proposal that the matter could be resolved with a monetary settlement of "$300.00, if accompanied by an expression of apology and regret, and of future policy in accordance with the law of the land."[128]

As in the past, Greyhound was courteous in its response to a Black customer's complaint of discrimination, but unwilling to take any responsibility for the unpleasantness that those passengers experienced. "We appreciate our colored patrons and have endeavored to be fair and courteous to them in our service," Greyhound's attorney wrote to Montgomery's lawyers, before going on to explain that "we were not aware that any discrimination existed at the Parkersburg station against colored patrons and have taken the necessary steps to correct that condition, because it is contrary to our policy."[129]

Houston appears to have been ambivalent about the settlement. He had thought that Montgomery's case might help the NAACP "establish a general custom of bus companies to ignore the comfort requirements of Negro passengers . . . [and] serve as a spearhead for our attack on discrimination in transportation." Although the organization also had complaints on file about trains, he noted that "in the depression, more and more people are riding buses," and therefore bus travel might be the best focus for the NAACP's limited resources. "It seems to me from the standpoint of the masses to be more important to strike at discrimination in busses than to spend the same money on discrimination in Pullmans."[130]

As Houston's remarks reveal, segregation on buses had grown almost as rapidly as the bus industry itself. While bus travel was initially embraced by Black travelers as a possible alternative to Jim Crow, by the end of the 1930s it had become the worst of all forms of Jim Crow travel. Black educator and journalist William Pickens was convinced that "bus Jim Crow" was segregation at its "most horrible." "Jim Crow is bad enough on the trains," he wrote, "but it is at least more roomy than on the bus, it is wider and longer on the trains, but narrow, cramping and torturous on the bus." Pickens said he "avoided the Jim Crow bus as I would the devil, sometimes paying more for private automobile transportation rather than take it." He was also willing to "take the longer way around on the dirty trains to avoid the bus."[131]

The writer Ralph Ellison was still more eloquent in his condemnation of bus segregation. Ellison grew up in Oklahoma but did not fully realize how much he hated Jim Crow buses until he moved to New York City in the mid-1930s and found himself preoccupied with the city's bus system. Subways were new to him, Ellison recalled in an essay written half a century later, but their "noise and tension" were familiar; the real surprise was New York's buses, where Black and white people intermingled in ways that were unimaginable to him. Ellison found it so hard to believe that African Americans could sit anywhere they liked on New York City buses that he "experimented by riding all *over* New York buses, excluding only the driver's seat—front end, back end, right side, left side, sitting or standing as the route and the flow of passengers demanded." Only after completing this experiment was he finally convinced that "no questions of racial status would be raised by where I chose to ride," at which point his fascination finally began to subside. He also began to understand the toll that segregated buses had taken on his psyche.[132]

New York City buses, he concluded, were "simpler" than buses in the South: "They were merely a form of transportation . . . which one took to get from one place to another"; whereas southern buses "were places of hallucination . . . especially for Negroes." A rolling theater of segregation at its most unpleasant, the "Southern bus was a contraption contrived by laying the South's social pyramid on its side . . . and rendering it vehicular through the addition of engine, windows and wheels." A recent innovation, buses, unlike trains and most streetcars, had only one entrance and thus seemed to allow Blacks to "enter the section that had been—in its vertical configuration—its top." But "any semblance of upward mobility" ended then and there. "The motorized mobility of the social pyramid did little to advance the Negroes' efforts toward social mobility." Instead, Black passengers "were sent, forthwith, straight to the rear, or horizontalized bottom," where they were suspended like a "painted ship upon a painted ocean." Even as the "engine chugged, the tires scuffed, and the scenery outside flashed and flickered . . . they themselves remained . . . ever in the same old place."[133]

And that place was not a safe place. "Almost *anything* could happen" to Blacks on southern buses, Ellison stressed. As they made their way down the "haunted, gauntletlike passage" to the back of the bus, and even after they sat down, Black passengers were subject to aggressions that ranged "from push to shove, assaults on hat, heads or aching corns, to unprovoked tongue lashing from the driver or any white passenger, drunk or sober, who took exception to their looks, attitude or mere existence."[134]

While the railroads' Jim Crow cars were far from comfortable, William Pickens and Ralph Ellison were both convinced that Jim Crow buses were worse. Jim Crow railroad cars were shabby and dirty, and the Black passengers who rode in them often shared their space with luggage, news vendors, and white men who came into the car to smoke, but they offered African American travelers at least some small claim to their own space. On trains, as understood in Ellison's metaphorical terms, African Americans might occupy a space that was at the bottom of their society's social pyramid, but they did not have to enter through the top, or fight their way through a "gauntletlike passage" to its base.[135]

Traveling by Jim Crow bus was also worse than traveling by car. Drivers had to contend with segregated roadside restaurants and accommodations, but they could choose when and where to stop. They could load up their vehicles with provisions and do their best to chart routes that took them to roadside establishments that welcomed their patronage. Within their own cars, African Americans chose their own seats and did not have to share their space with white travelers, or move on the command of a white bus driver. Growing up in Tuskegee, Alabama, during the Jim Crow era, Wilhelmina Baldwin and her siblings were shielded from segregation by her parents, who kept their children out of "segregated places," such as stores where Blacks were not permitted to try on clothes or shoes. They were equally careful to keep them off the bus. "Going wherever we had to go out of town, they took us." Baldwin recalled, "We never went to the bus station for anything."[136]

But many African Americans could not avoid traveling by bus. Although both railroads and bus lines reduced their fares during the Great Depression, it was always cheaper to travel by bus than by train. Buses were often the only affordable option for low-income travelers, whose business the bus lines courted with promotional slogans such as "Of course it Costs Less . . ."; "Fare For all Trips Average Lower than other First Class Transportation."[137]

Concerns over the discrimination and danger on Jim Crow buses only accelerated during World War II. All forms of transportation were in short supply, making buses attractive to a wider range of Americans. Wartime gas rationing forced even affluent car owners to use public transportation, and the railroads were running above capacity carrying troops and supplies. Buses set new records in passenger transportation during these years, doubling their passenger miles from 13.6 billion in 1941 to 26.9 billion in 1945.[138] Black southerners who had migrated north in search of industrial work during World War I had traveled by train, but during World War II they increasingly traveled by bus. During these years, buses also carried soldiers of all races between their homes and the military bases and camps where they were stationed.

Transportation of all kinds was a "principal racial trouble spot" throughout the war, and no form of transportation generated more complaints among African Americans than buses.[139] With travel space at a premium, the fact that buses had no separate Jim Crow cars, and no fixed line of any sort dividing the seats between the races, made it nearly impossible for African Americans to get seats on some routes. Southern custom dictated that whites board first, and "as the number of people using the buses expanded during the war, Blacks were often left waiting for hours, sometimes days for another bus." Some bus lines in Georgia refused to "permit Negro passengers to ride the main line buses, adding worn-out, seldom used vehicles for the care of their colored riders," which of course forced Black travelers there to endure even longer waits.[140]

Black soldiers were not exempt from this insulting treatment, as Corporal John W. Childs discovered when he attempted to take a bus from Macon to Savannah in the summer of 1944. First the ticket agent had him wait an hour and a half to buy a ticket in order to ensure that any white person who might wish to ride the bus would be able to secure a ticket. Childs protested, to no avail. "I'll wait on you when I damned please," the ticket agent told him. When Childs finally secured a ticket, he had to wait in line again to get on the bus. Among the other passengers were three white soldiers, who were addressed as "Soldiers" and permitted to board the bus first. They passed by Childs, who recalled that he was "forced to wait until all the seats were taken and was addressed as 'boy' even though I had on a United States Army uniform."[141]

Race relations on board buses were explosive. The army compounded the insults experienced by Black soldiers by instructing them to "observe and conform to the local laws of the community in which they are stationed."[142] But Black soldiers and civilians alike were often unwilling to accept the discrimination and rude treatment they encountered on buses in segregated territory.

Bitterly aware that they were being called to support a war dedicated to securing freedom abroad when they faced discrimination at home, many African Americans embraced a "Double V campaign" that called for "victory over our enemies from without" and "victory over our enemies within." Promoted by Black newspapers, the Double V campaign encouraged African

Preferred Death to Jim Crow

JAMES GLOVER MORROW, 29, of 434 Orchard Street, Baltimore, who preferred death to riding from New York to Baltimore in a jim-crow seat on the Greyhound Bus lines. He was shot it is said, by a New York policeman in the Fifty-first Street Station when he refused to ride jim-crow and the body was brought to his home here for burial Sunday. Seating of passengers by color is not lawful in interstate traffic.

The passing of James Glover Morrow was commemorated in the *Baltimore Afro-American* on March 16, 1942, under the headline "Preferred Death to Jim Crow."

Americans to protest discrimination, and insisted that Black protests such as challenges to segregation on buses were an integral part of the war effort. James G. Thompson, whose letter to the *Pittsburgh Courier* launched the campaign, maintained that true patriotism involved fighting for democracy both at home and abroad. Blacks might feel no more than "half American," he maintained, but "things will be different for the next generation; colored Americans will come into their own, and America will become the true democracy it was designed to be. These things will become a reality in time; but not through any relaxation of the efforts to secure them."[143]

As African Americans rallied to fight on two fronts, the number of transportation complaints filed with the NAACP soared. So did the organization's membership, which increased tenfold between 1940 and 1946 as Black servicemen and other Double V freedom fighters "joined the organization in droves."[144] This legal action was accompanied by physical action. Increasingly unwilling to put up with Jim Crow, African Americans fought segregation on buses, although such resistance put them at risk of being arrested, assaulted, or even killed. "Preferred Death to Jim Crow" was the headline of the short, but heartbreaking, news item that announced the passing of James Glover Morrow in the winter of 1942. Morrow was killed when refusing to "ride jim-crow" on a Greyhound bus from Baltimore to New York City. "He was shot, it is said," the *Baltimore Afro-American* reported, "by a New York policeman in the Fifty-first Street Station . . . and the body was brought to his home here for burial Sunday." The paper offered no additional details about the conflict that led to Morrow's death, other than to note: "Seating of passengers by color is not lawful in interstate traffic."[145] That summer a Black soldier was shot and killed in Mobile, Alabama, by a white bus driver, while at least two others were shot by Texas police "for riding in white section of the bus"—as the *Chicago Defender*'s headline put it.[146]

As the tragedies multiplied, the NAACP could no longer put off tackling travel segregation head-on, and it took on a series of cases that quickly eroded the shaky legal foundation of segregation on interstate transportation. This litigation led to *Irene Morgan v. the Commonwealth of Virginia* (1946), a landmark Supreme Court ruling that state laws requiring the segregation of interstate passengers violated the interstate commerce clause of the US Constitution. Segregation on interstate buses—which seemed to defy all legal restraints—continued, especially in the South, and so did African American resistance to it. Both would play a central role in the birth of the modern civil rights movement, which took shape, at least in part, around a series of protests against segregation on buses.

5

Traveling by Plane

Segregation in the Age of Aviation

"AIRPLANES FLYING ACROSS THE LAND AND SEA," SANG THE BLUES man Josh White in 1941. "Everybody flying but a Negro like me / Uncle Sam says, 'Your place is on the ground, / When I fly my airplanes, don't want no Negro around.'"[1] Written in the year the United States entered World War II, White's song protested the continuing segregation of African American soldiers in the US military. But it also took pointed note of the emergence of yet another form of travel that promised soaring freedom and resulted in bitter disappointment. Having conquered the roads and the rails, Jim Crow would quickly establish itself in travel by air.

The forms of segregation and discrimination that African American passengers encountered when they traveled by plane are complicated and little known, even among historians. C. Vann Woodward gives the subject less than a paragraph in his classic work *The Strange Career of Jim Crow*. "The arrival of the age of air transportation appears to have put a strain upon the ingenuity of the Jim Crow lawmakers," he notes. "Even to the orthodox there was doubtless something slightly incongruous about requiring a Jim Crow compartment on a transcontinental plane, or one that did not touch the ground between New York and Miami. No Jim Crow law has been found that applies to passengers while they are in the air."[2] While Woodward gets his facts right, his fleeting assessment of the impact of Jim Crow on air travel does not capture the full story of flying Jim Crow.[3]

Law or no law, various forms of segregation did occur in the air, and they began early. Like most Americans, African Americans were excited to see humankind take to the air. They also had some of the same hopes for air travel that they had once had for driving. Flying would provide a new "way to avoid Jim Crow cars," some suggested.[4] However, especially during the early years of aviation, Blacks had extremely limited access to either airplanes or air-fields. The first colored pilots took flight during World I, but well into the 1930s white aviation experts insisted that Blacks were racially unfit to master the complex technology involved in flying a plane. Blacks were barred from military aeronautical training for many years, and were also unwelcome at many flight schools and airfields. Like the first generation of Black drivers and auto mechanics, they were excluded from opportunities to master the technical details of the craft, and vilified as unworthy users of the new technology.

Even though aviation was never subject to any official Jim Crow laws or regulations, African American passengers encountered a variety of now-forgotten forms of segregation and exclusion. During the 1930s some airlines refused to carry Black passengers, and prior to the early 1950s many airlines assigned Black passengers to segregated seats. When it came to changing planes or securing or keeping seats on crowded flights, African American travelers were subject to the same slights they experienced on other forms of transportation. Although never anywhere near as numerous as white flyers, Blacks who traveled by air were generally the first to be bumped off their flights when space was needed.

The indignities they encountered on the ground were more numerous and persistent. In the eyes of many southern municipal and state officials, Jim Crow laws did apply to airports, even though these statutes all but invariably violated nondiscrimination clauses attached to the federal grant funding that was crucial to the construction of most airports. Accordingly, white southerners found creative way to segregate airports, which most often involved using municipal or state funding to create segregated airport restaurants, waiting rooms, and bathrooms. Segregation was still more pervasive in the ground transportation to and from airports. Airport buses and cabs that catered to whites rarely served Blacks, who in many southern cities were assigned by law to their own "Jim Crow cabs." Such forms of discrimination ensured that even when African Americans managed to escape segregation in the air, they encountered it on the ground.

"NEGROES CANNOT FLY":
AVIATION ACROSS THE COLOR LINE

Although flying seems almost mundane today, aviation was once hailed as humankind's greatest achievement. The pilot Charles Lindbergh said that flying sometimes "feels too godlike to be attained by man." The first successful flying machines were preceded by so many failures that flight could also be understood as a testimony to human genius and persistence.[5] "Aviation is proof that given the will, we have the capacity to achieve the impossible," claimed World War I ace fighter pilot Eddie Rickenbacker, who went on to found Eastern Airlines.[6]

The technology of the airplane, which had its first great successes in Europe and the United States, was widely hailed as a triumph not so much for all humankind as for a particular branch of the human family. Acclaimed by many as Western civilization's greatest achievement, aviation became a measure of the racial greatness of white Westerners. In 1928 the US Congress commemorated the twenty-fifth anniversary of the Wright brothers' first successful flight as one of "the latest and most far-reaching achievements of Anglo-Saxon civilization." Even the inhabitants of Kitty Hawk, North Carolina—the small coastal town where the Wright brothers launched their first flight—received racial credit for their achievement. Largely fishermen, the town's residents were commended during the ceremony for possessing some of the "purest Anglo-Saxon blood on the American continent."[7]

Such sentiments ran high in the wake of Charles Lindbergh's pathbreaking solo flight across the Atlantic in 1927. Blond, handsome, and largely unknown before his famous flight, Lindbergh became an instant emblem of white racial achievement when he succeeded in flying from Long Island, New York, to Paris, France, that spring. A crowd of more than one hundred thousand people thronged his plane when he landed at Le Bourget Airport after a 33½-hour flight, and the US Navy dispatched a destroyer to carry Lindbergh and his plane back to New York, where he was greeted with the largest ticker tape parade in the city's history. Celebrated as a quintessentially American hero, writes historian Jennifer Van Veck, Lindbergh was also hailed as an "idealized racial type—an embodiment of transnational whiteness. Coming at the end of a decade marked by immigration restrictions, rising white supremacism, and cultural concerns about the very boundaries of whiteness, Lindbergh's flight seemed, to many observers, to confirm the vitality of the white race." Journalists and biographers celebrated not only his achievement, but his racial heritage, describing him "as a lanky six-foot blond Viking type" who "seemed to be composed of a mixture of the traits of his English and Swedish grandfathers."[8]

Lindbergh did nothing to disavow these connections between aviation and race. He titled the autobiography he published shortly after his famous flight *We* (1927) to underscore the collective character of his pioneering achievement, but clearly felt that not all Americans were fit to fly. On the contrary, Lindbergh's condescending descriptions of his encounters with African Americans while barnstorming in Mississippi in the early 1920s, suggests aviation historian Robert J. Jakeman, reinforced white stereotypes of Blacks as people who were "overwhelmed by the technological complexity of airplanes and possessed an inherent fear of flying." Lindbergh's accounts included a comedic sketch of an elderly Black woman who asked him, "Boss! How much you all charge foah take me up to Heaben and leave me dear?" and a mocking depiction of a brash Black passenger who lost all his confidence once he boarded Lindbergh's plane.[9] In an article published in *Reader's Digest* in 1939, Lindbergh gave full voice to the racial convictions that informed his vignettes. "Aviation seems almost a gift from heaven to those Western nations who were already the leaders of their era, strengthening their leadership, their confidence, their dominance over other peoples," he wrote. "It is a tool specially shaped for Western hands, a scientific art which others only copy in a mediocre fashion, another barrier between the teeming millions of Asia and the Grecian inheritance of Europe—one of those priceless possessions which permit the White race to live at all in a pressing sea of Yellow, Black and Brown."[10]

Lindbergh was also anti-Semitic and would eventually fall into disrepute as a Nazi sympathizer. But his conviction that aviation was a racial talent that some races possessed and others did not was widely shared. "Negroes cannot fly," Kenneth Brown Collings, a fellow aviator and war correspondent, wrote in the *American Mercury* in 1936: "even the bureau of Air Commerce admits that." As a trained pilot, Collings was anxious to dismiss the then-popular claim that any "man or woman who can drive an automobile can safely fly an airplane." Flying required highly developed physical and mental abilities, he maintained, seen in "only a very small percentage of Americans."[11] African Americans were not among them.

FOR THE SUNNY SOUTH.
AN AIRSHIP WITH A "JIM CROW" TRAILER.

African Americans figure as comically unlikely flyers in a cartoon that appeared in a February 1913 edition of the American humor magazine *Puck*.

Both Lindbergh's and Collings's assessments of Blacks as wholly unfit to fly were echoed by American military leaders. Although Blacks began applying to join the United States Air Service—the branch of the military that later became the US Army Air Corps and then the US Air Force—on its founding in 1917, none were ever considered for admission. Instead they were told that their applications could not be accepted because "colored aero squadrons were not being formed 'at the present time.'" They would hear back "later on," should such squads ever be formed. But "later on" never came. By 1930 the War Department's leadership had managed to convince itself that the absence of Negroes in the Air Corps reflected Negroes' lack of interest in flying. "As a rule, the colored man has not been attracted to this field in the same way and to the same extent as the white man," a War Department official wrote to NAACP executive secretary Walter White in 1931, after receiving a letter from White pressing the Department to allow Blacks to enlist in the Air Corps.[12] White found this reply galling, given the Army's long history of rebuffing Black aviators. "It is obvious that colored men cannot be attracted to the field of aviation 'in the same way or to the same extent as the white man' when the door to that field is slammed in the colored man's face," he shot back.[13]

As White's comment underscores, the history of segregation in air travel precedes the establishment of commercial airlines. Barred from military aeronautical training for many years, African Americans were also unwelcome at flight schools and sometimes even on airfields.[14] These restrictions forced most of the nation's earliest Black pilots to train abroad. Some of their exploits were widely promoted in the United States, where they generated a widespread interest in aviation among African Americans.

Black applicants who had been turned down by the Air Corps included at least one skilled aviator: Eugene Bullard. Born in Columbus, Georgia, Bullard was in France at the beginning of World War I and enlisted in the French Foreign Legion to fight against the Germans. Initially he served as a machine gunner, but in 1916 he joined France's air service and became a fighter pilot. His extensive combat record in the Aéronautique Militaire earned him a Croix de Guerre, a Médaille Militaire, a Croix du Combattant Volontaire 1914–1918, and a Médaille de Verdun. When the United States entered the war in the spring of 1917, Bullard attempted to transfer to the American Air Corps, but was not accepted. "American doctors cited his flat feet as the reason; Bullard informed them that those feet had walked all over France while he was in the infantry," writes Judy L. Hasday. "Next he was told he had large tonsils; Bullard is said to have replied that he was lucky he wasn't an opera singer. . . . The United States armed services were not integrated, so there was no unit for Bullard to join." Bullard spent much of the rest of his life in France, and remained largely unknown in his home country, despite having earned numerous French military awards.[15]

The same cannot be said of Bessie Coleman, another early Black pilot who trained abroad. Known as "Brave Bessie," the Texas-born Coleman became famous for performing "heart thrilling stunts" at airshows.[16] A migrant who left the Jim Crow South for a better life in Chicago, Coleman was working as a manicurist when she decided she wanted to become a pilot. Her race was a drawback at first, she later recalled. She could not find anyone in Chicago who would teach her to fly, and she had to move to France to study for a pilot's license.[17] But when she returned to the United States in 1922, she became both a "curiosity" and a sensation, whose flying attracted large audiences and received extensive coverage in the Black press. Coleman was killed while rehearsing an aerial stunt in 1926, but her influence lasted far longer than her meteoric career.

After her death, Bessie Coleman Aero Clubs proliferated across the country. Black pilots remained rare—unsurprisingly, few air schools admitted Black pupils. Still, there emerged small groups of (largely male) African American aviators, including William J. Powell and John Robinson, who fought their way into aeronautics schools. Prejudice could make life difficult even for those who managed to secure a pilot's license. Dr. A. Davis Porter of Kansas City, who received his license in 1932, had little difficulty enrolling in a local aeronautical school; but when he bought a plane for his own use, he could find no place to put it. One flying field declined his patronage with "no explanation"; at a second field his plane was vandalized; and the management at a third asked him to leave because his plane "attracted too many colored people."[18]

Such obstacles did not prevent African Americans from becoming "airminded," to use a now-obsolete term that once meant "having enthusiasm for airplanes, believing in their potential to better human life, and supporting aviation development."[19] Even African Americans who themselves had little interest in flying began to see aviation as crucial to the future of their race. Lindbergh's famous flight only upped the ante, reviving the memory of Bessie Coleman and inspiring the new question, "What will the Negro contribute to aviation?"[20] Some wondered if Blacks lacked "the stuff of which Lindberghs are made," as one letter writer put it in a missive to the *Chicago Defender*. "Most of our young men spend their time hanging around pool rooms by day and cheap dance halls by night. We are too house-bound," maintained "A Woman Reader," who clearly thought aviation was incompatible with the increasingly urban character of Black life. But many air-minded African Americans remained confident that "we have within our race the same daring and untried ability as any other race." They emphasized that the establishment of flying schools that would supply Blacks with "knowledge of aviation" was crucial to sustaining "the pride of race."[21] Writing in the *Pittsburgh Courier* in 1931, Black journalist Harry Levette captured the connections that African Americans drew between race, masculinity, and aviation in a poem entitled "The Call of Wings," which challenged Black men to honor Bessie Coleman's memory by conquering the sky:

Black men! List to the call of the wings,
As the myriads of ships course the skies!
Each an Argonaut venturing brings,
Golden fleece from the land where it flies
High over white peak, angry sea,
Man is fearlessly conquering the air,
History making. The entry is free—
Black men! Say, why are you not there?

Are you cowardly, spineless, and weak,
That your feet cling closely to the earth?
Rise from your lethargy; this new field seek!
You've won others; in this, prove your worth.
A mere girl pioneered for the Race,
But our men let her sacrifice fail.
Fly! Fly! With the nations keep pace!
Let the sun glint your silver sail.[22]

Among those who answered this call were Black aviators who vied to match Lindbergh's achievement with long-distance flights of their own. In 1932, J. Herman Banning and Thomas C. Allen flew from Los Angeles to Long Island in a plane constructed from junkyard parts. As underfunded as it was ambitious, their trip required just forty-two hours aloft, but took twenty-one days because they left without enough money for gas and oil and had to raise money along the way. Their slow progress may have helped build enthusiasm for their trip. When they landed in Pittsburgh, just 313 miles from their final destination, the city's Black newspapers celebrated their achievement with the front-page headline "DARING AVIATORS NEAR GOAL: Making Glorious History." Banning and Allen were "suntanned editions of the 'Lindy' of yesteryear . . . the type of men around whom history is made. . . . Lindy's feat of spanning the Atlantic at a single hop required no more courage than is [sic] the flight these men are making."[23]

A round-trip from Atlantic City to Los Angeles and back the following year by Charles Alfred "Chief" Anderson and E. Albert Forsyth attracted similar accolades. "The longest air trip ever made by members of the Race," proclaimed the Chicago Defender, "this flight . . . [brought] more recognition,

Thomas C. Allen and J. Herman Banning.

good will, accomplishment and prestige to the race than any other venture has been able to in such a limited time and at such a small cost."[24]

Anderson and Forsyth went on to fly from Atlantic City to Montreal and back in 1934, becoming "the first American Blacks to plan and execute a flight across international borders." Just a few months later they attempted a still more ambitious journey: a Pan-American Goodwill tour of South America, the Caribbean, and Central America. The tour was dedicated to "spreading [interracial] goodwill and winning respect for American Negroes," and its sponsors included the Tuskegee Institute. Flying a new plane named *The Booker T. Washington,* Anderson and Forsyth planned to visit twenty countries.[25] But they were grounded before they ever reached South America. Their plane clipped a grove of bamboo shortly after lifting off from an improvised airfield in Georgetown, Trinidad, stalled, and then crashed. Both men survived the crash, but their plane did not. Their abortive trip was widely publicized, though, and helped promote Black participation in aviation.

So, too, did the remarkable career of John Robinson, a Tuskegee Institute graduate, who began his aviation career as a janitor at the Curtiss-Wright

Aeronautical University in Chicago in 1929. Denied admission to the school, which did not admit Blacks, Robinson secured a cleaning job there and learned the fundamentals of aviation by "cleaning classrooms during lecture times" and staying after hours to copy the class notes and equations posted on the instructor's blackboard. Robinson's determined efforts eventually convinced the school to admit him, and he graduated "at the top of his class" in 1931.[26] Appointed as an assistant instructor at Curtiss-Wright immediately after he graduated, Robinson persuaded the school to admit other Black students and began training a new generation of Black pilots. Together with his students, Robinson went on to establish the Challenger Aero Pilots Association, a Black flying club. And in 1933, after the only Chicago-area airport open to Black pilots closed abruptly, Robinson opened his own airport in Robbins, a Black town located just outside Chicago.

But what Robinson became nationally known for was his leadership of the Ethiopian air force during the Second Italo-Ethiopian War (1935–1936). A Pan-Africanist who believed in Black self-determination, Robinson volunteered his service to Ethiopian emperor Haile Selassie in the spring of 1935, after a chance meeting with Malaku E. Bayen, a member of the Ethiopian royal family who was completing his medical training at Howard University. Bayen was rightly convinced that Italy, which had begun to build its forces on the borders of Ethiopia in Eritrea and Italian Somaliland, was poised to expand its overseas empire into Ethiopia, and he began to enlist African Americans to help defend his country's independence. Convinced that the "American Negro, through racial kinship, is duty bound to support Abyssinia," Robinson volunteered his services and ended up in command of Ethiopia's fledgling air force.[27]

With only a few trained aviators and a handful of aging aircraft at his disposal, Robinson ended up spending most of the war training Ethiopian recruits and repairing his fleet. But he flew dozens of reconnaissance missions for Selassie's government, braving Italian bombers as he ferried information and medical supplies between Addis Ababa (Ethiopia's capital) and the war's front lines. Wounded twice and also gassed, Robinson continued his missions until Ethiopia's warriors were overpowered by Mussolini's much larger and more modern army in the spring of 1936. Hailed by the Black press as the "Brown Condor of Ethiopia," Robinson returned home a hero and attracted large crowds of African American fans in both New York City and Chicago. His exploits were widely covered in the Black press and had made him into a "bona fide hero" as well as living proof that Blacks could excel in aviation.[28]

Robinson and other early African American pilots kept the dream of flight alive in African American communities that were otherwise largely excluded from aviation. The immense attention these popular figures received in the Black press helps explain why the "campaign for admission of Negroes to the Air Corps" was, in the words of military historian Ulysses Lee, "the most widespread, persistent, and widely publicized of all the prewar public pressure campaigns affecting the Negro and the Army."[29] It may also help explain why, even before the desegregation of the Air Corps, African Americans had begun to think about air transportation as an escape from Jim Crow.

ONE WAY TO AVOID JIM CROW CARS?

During World War II, the world of aviation seemed as if it might finally open up to admit African American flyers and passengers. By 1939 civil rights leaders had successfully lobbied to secure Black participation in the Civilian Pilot Training Program (CPT), a federal program created in 1938 to increase the number of civilian pilots in the United States. Renamed the War Training Service in 1942, the program was designed to prepare young Americans for service in the Army Air Corps, which also opened to Blacks in the late 1930s—albeit on a segregated and experimental basis. Still, both the admission of Blacks into the CPT, and the recruitment and training of roughly one thousand Black pilots at the new Tuskegee Army Air Field established in Tuskegee, Alabama, between 1941 and 1946, renewed African Americans' hopes that they might find a place in the white world of aeronautics. Whites continued to wonder whether Negroes could really fly airplanes. But the Tuskegee Program had the high-profile support of Eleanor Roosevelt, who visited the Tuskegee airfield on April 19, 1941. Intent on disproving the myth that Blacks were not capable of piloting planes, Roosevelt even abandoned her secret service agents to take an hour-long tour of the skies of Alabama with Tuskegee flight instructor Charles Alfred "Chief" Anderson.

The 1930s and 1940s also saw African American passengers take to the air. With the advent of regularly scheduled commercial airline flights that crisscrossed the United States, travel by air was no longer limited to pilots. It was expensive, often uncomfortable, and largely unavailable to nonmilitary per-

Eleanor Roosevelt (center) and Charles Alfred "Chief" Anderson (right) at Tuskegee
Army Air Field, 1941

sornel during the war years. But it was faster than any other form of transportation, and its speed attracted several different types of Black passengers.
Black journalists, entertainers, athletes, and other professionals whose jobs
required them to cover a lot of ground quickly began to do at least some of
their traveling by plane in the 1930s and 1940s. Other early flyers, both Black
and white, included travelers hurrying to join a sick loved one. And airlines
also attracted a small class of wealthy Black travelers who wished to travel in
style. The high-flying comings and goings of Black celebrities and the Black
elite were frequently featured in Black newspapers in news pieces that usually extolled the speed and convenience of flying and seemed to herald a better
day for all African American travelers. A *Baltimore Afro-American* photograph of the elegant young "Miss Gloria Northcross, daughter of Dr. Daisy
Northcross," boarding a Nashville-bound plane in Detroit ran under the headline "One Way to Avoid Jim Crow Cars."

Such headlines underscore that commercial aviation held a distinctive al-
lure for Black travelers because it presented a possible alternative to traveling
Jim Crow. "Calls are coming in from all over America from Negroes who are

One Way to Avoid Jim Crow Cars

MISS GLORIA NORTHCROSS,
daughter of Dr. Daisy Northcross, boarding a plane at the City
Airport in Detroit for Nashville, Tenn., where she entered her
junior year at Fisk University. By traveling in the plane from
Detroit to Nashville, Miss Northcross was able to avoid the jim-
crow system of the South.—Photo by Russ J. Cowans.

African American newspapers took
note of the journeys made by early
Black flyers, as can be seen in this
photograph of Gloria Northcross,
which appeared in the *Baltimore
Afro-American* on October 10, 1936.

interested in entering the aviation business," William Powell, a pilot based
in Los Angeles, wrote in 1934. "They want to establish airlines owned by Negroes. They are tired of being segregated on the railroads and buses."[30] On
his return from Ethiopia in 1936, John C. Robinson himself joined this chorus,
promoting the establishment of "an airline in the southern states, manned by
race pilots." "Negro passengers are for the most part prevented from traveling by air on Southern lines," he told a New York audience. "Such a service
would aid the entire section as well as give qualified pilots regular jobs."[31]

But the airline industry that emerged in the 1930s was not open to Black entrepreneurs. America's commercial airlines first took shape around the business of carrying mail rather than passengers. The nation's largest carriers received most of the lucrative federal airmail contracts that subsidized the development of America's aviation industry by paying carriers more per pound for carrying mail than could be earned by transporting passengers.[32] Even after the airmail scandal of 1934 (in which it was revealed that federal funding for airmail went to just a few large companies) opened up more business to small operators, and the advent of larger planes such as the DC-3 made carrying passengers more profitable, the capital investment involved in offering regularly scheduled flights continued to favor large operators. Pilots like Powell and Robinson could imagine small airlines owned and operated by Blacks. But from the 1930s onward, the airline business increasingly consolidated around five major lines: Pan American, TWA, United Airlines, American Airlines, and Eastern Airlines.

Still, African Americans' hopes for full participation in the airline business rekindled as World War II came to a close. During the war years "the number of black pilots in the United States had increased from a handful in the 1920s and 1930s to approximately two thousand."[33] Decorated fighter pilots such as Tuskegee airman Lieutenant William Ellis came home optimistic about the future of commercial aviation and the place of Blacks in it. "Air Travel will simply squeeze the Jim Crow out of the transportation system in this country," Ellis predicted in 1945. "There is not enough room in the air for backseats, people will simply have to travel closer together."[34] But Ellis, who also anticipated that he and other African American airmen would be hired to fly the planes, proved overly optimistic.

"I don't mean to hurt your feelings young man," A. N. Kemp, the president of American Airlines, told a reporter for the *Pittsburgh Courier* as early as 1943, "but I don't believe that Negroes will be used as pilots in the immediate world of post-war aviation." "Suppose I placed a Negro Pilot on our Memphis Tennessee run," he explained. "All the white passengers would refuse to fly on a plane being piloted by him and wait for a plane being piloted by a white man." Blacks still had to prove themselves and "would have to become more cultured," before they could enjoy "the fullness of American life."[35] Other airline officials were more discreet and told Black veterans that they had "no openings." The end result was the same. The nation's major commercial airlines did not hire a single Black pilot until 1963, when air force veteran Marlon Green's landmark Supreme Court case against discrimination in the airline industry forced them to drop their color bar.[36]

The postwar years also saw attempts to circumvent white prejudices by establishing a Black airline. Founded in 1944 by William H. Hawkins, a florist in the Washington, D.C., area, the Union Air Line aimed to provide "opportunities [to] colored flyers trained during the war." It was launched with great fanfare at a ceremony in Griffin Stadium, where five hundred people gathered to watch the christening of its first plane. The plane was a five-passenger Waco plane named after Mary McLeod Bethune, the president of the National Council of Negro Women, who was on hand to do the honors. In addition to "smashing [a] bottle of champagne on the nose of the flag ship," she also hailed the establishment of "the race's first commercial airline" as evidence of Black economic progress. "Colored people must become part of the progressive ideas and ideals of this country to achieve a stable economic status," she told the audience.[37] Businesses such as the Union Air Line were clearly a step in the right direction.

But there is no evidence to suggest that either the Union Air Line or Universal Skyways Inc., a "second Negro airline" incorporated shortly after the first, ever made money—or even flew any regularly scheduled flights.[38] Both were small businesses that had virtually no hope of surviving in a high-tech field that required large capital expenditures. Hawkins started the Union Air Line with one plane and hoped to add more later, while the G.I.s who filed the papers to establish Universal Skyways planned to fund it with a "'pooled' fund from army pay" and do not seem to have ever raised enough money to buy a plane.[39] Both ventures were an expression of Black hopes of becoming full participants in the world of aviation during the postwar period, and both sought to provide jobs for Black pilots, but neither ever got off the ground.

Both before and after the Second World War, the airline industry as a whole remained overwhelmingly white. In the early 1930s the New England and Western Airways briefly experimented with hiring African American male flight attendants in the hope that they would invoke "the familiar atmosphere of the Pullman car" and thereby make "flying seem less strange."[40] But this experiment was short-lived, as airline executives soon realized that luring passengers away from Pullman travel would require offering a distinctive brand of service. Instead the airlines settled on white male attendants, who were later replaced by white female attendants. Their job, a 1942 guide to careers

Participants at Christening of Union Air Line Flagship

Mrs. Mary McLeod Bethune, top photo, is shown christening the airplane, named for her, at a dedication ceremony sponsored by the Union Air Lines in Griffith Stadium, in Washington, on Sunday afternoon. Lower photo shows the drum and bugle corps of the James Reese Europe Post, American Legion, as they paraded in prechristening exercises. Photo at right shows Mrs. Bethune, seated in plane, and William H. Hawkins, president and general manager of the air lines.

Union Air Line photo spread in the *Baltimore Afro-American*, November 18, 1944.

in aviation explained, was to make flying "an exceedingly pleasant mode of travel."[41]

Airlines hired only white flight attendants, explains historian Kathleen Barry, and did not permit them to accept tips, because they "had special incentives to distance their stewards from any hint of servitude"—a characteristic traditionally associated with George, the nameless obsequious Pullman porter.[42] Unlike passengers on a train, airline passengers would never be confronted with service workers "holding a whisk broom in one hand and holding the other, Gypsy like, waiting to be crossed with silver." Instead, airline executives decided very early on that "they would let George, the Pullman porter, collect the quarters and the half dollars; stewardesses must not accept tips, and this rule is a strict one."[43]

Especially during the early years of commercial air, airline personnel had to provide passengers with the "basic reassurance that the transport being sold was fundamentally safe." White flight attendants "did what racial stereotypes would not allow black male attendants to do: Signal to fearful travelers that they were safely in the hands of those able to master the new technology of flight." The first generation of female flight attendants were nurses, whose professional expertise was meant to provide passengers with further reassurance that they were in the competent hands of highly trained professionals. Such employees were instructed to "meet every passenger with a smile . . . and on a more or less personal basis of genial good fellowship," and they offered airline passengers a "'fellowship' of whiteness," argues Barry.[44]

African Americans had little place in this fellowship. Black workers were rare even in fleet service work prior to the 1960s. Their exclusion may well have been dictated at least in part by the orderly image the airlines sought to project. "The terminal ramp is a stage upon which the ramp personnel appear as actors representing the inner workings of the Maintenance and Operations Departments," one Pan American Airways customer manual noted. Fleet service workers had to work "industriously and efficiently" at all times, and be careful to avoid "shouting, boisterousness, horse play, profanity, or any other action which will detract from the good impression we're trying to make on the passenger."[45] Blacks were not considered part of that good impression, and as of 1940 Blacks comprised only 3 percent of the nation's air transport industry, and were typically limited to jobs as janitors, airplane cleaners, and luggage handlers. Starting in the late 1940s the unionization of airline ground service workers slowly began to open up more jobs in that sector to Blacks. But American Airlines did not hire its first Black reservation clerk until 1955, and airline flight crews remained exclusively white until 1958, when Mohawk Airlines, a regional carrier based in New York, hired a Black steward. Most of the nation's major carriers did not follow suit until the 1960s, and opened these jobs to Black women only after losing a series of discrimination lawsuits.

EXCLUSION

Not surprisingly, the all-white world of flying did not welcome Black passengers. Much like the bus lines, some early airlines refused to carry Black passengers—at all. In 1929 Dorothy Lyles, a Cleveland resident, sued Northern Airlines and University Airlines after she was not allowed to take one of their $5 "pleasure trips." In declining Lyles's ticket, the airlines' representative told her "that she could not ride on one of the aeroplanes because of her color, and that this was the order from headquarters."[46] Blacks were sometimes excluded from regular flights as well, as African American clarinet player Wilton Crawley found out when United Artists Theatre asked him to fly from El Paso, Texas, in 1932 to Los Angeles to play in one of its productions. Crawley was initially unable to buy a ticket. He was informed that the "company drew the color line"—a challenge he ultimately overcame by putting on a turban and traveling as "a Hindu gentleman . . . carrying a clarinet case."[47] Undertaker John T. Rhines had a similar experience when he tried to get a seat on an Eastern Air Transport plane flying from Atlantic City to Washington, D.C. The plane was not full, but Rhines "was refused," he reported, "not because he was carrying a bomb, not because he was intoxicated, but because he was a Negro."[48] So was Walter L. Carter, another Black man who tried to take the same flight. Both men sued for $50,000 each.[49]

There is no record of the outcome of these suits, but in refusing some Black passengers, some early airlines may have held that they were not common carriers and therefore were allowed to turn away unwelcome customers. Private carriers, as one classic legal text notes, can turn away passengers "for a bad reason or no reason at all."[50] Some early airlines printed "private carrier" on their tickets, possibly to underscore that right. But by the early 1930s a series of accident liability cases had pushed the courts toward classifying airlines as common carriers, regardless of what they printed on their tickets.

The airlines' obligations toward people of color, however, remained unresolved. In a 1932 article in the *Journal of Air Law,* Frank Quindry, a Braniff Airlines executive who was also a leading expert in aviation law, theorized that airlines could still legally exclude Black passengers. In sections of the South where "close contact between persons of opposite races might lead to endangering the security of all the passengers and also the plane in which they are riding . . . the airline has the right to protect its property and it has the duty to protect its passengers by appropriate regulation."[51]

With the passage of the Civil Aeronautics Act of 1938, such arguments were increasingly untenable. A measure that transferred federal responsibilities for nonmilitary aviation from the Bureau of Air Commerce to a new, independent agency, the Civil Aeronautics Authority, the Aeronautics Act included a nondiscrimination clause. Designed "to put airlines on a regulatory footing similar to rail and bus transportation," it used language drawn from the Interstate Commerce Act of 1887, which had long been used to challenge racial as well as economic discrimination. "No air carrier or foreign air carrier shall make, give, or cause any undue or unreasonable preference or advantage to any particular person, port, locality, or description of traffic in air transportation," the act stipulated, leaving the airlines little room to exclude African American passengers.[52] Yet even after its passage, no law prohibited airlines from segregating their passengers, as Charles S. Mangum Jr., a University of North Carolina legal scholar, noted in his book *The Legal Status of the Negro* (1940). Given that neither southern Jim Crow laws nor northern civil rights laws addressed "aerial transports," Mangum maintained, "the commercial air lines would practically always be permitted to make their own regulations for seating passengers in their planes. They may mix or segregate the races as they wish. There are very few Negro passengers and hence the problem has not arisen."[53]

The fact that so few Blacks traveled by air made it possible for airlines to develop a variety of unobtrusive approaches to discouraging Black passengers—which never ended up in court. While interviewing airline personnel for his book *Eagle: The Story of American Airlines,* Roderick Serling discovered that during the 1930s American Airlines routinely instructed its telephone agents to tell callers who sounded Black or supplied home addresses located in Black neighborhoods that all their flights were full.[54] Scattered evidence suggests that other airlines used similarly indirect strategies to discourage African Americans from flying. Pittsburgh resident

Ethel Gillespie, for example, made arrangements to travel from Washington, D.C., to Florence, South Carolina, for a funeral in the summer of 1937, only to find that once "it was discovered she was colored," she no longer had a reservation.[55]

It is impossible to tell how many Black passengers were turned away by the airlines, especially because such slights were not systematic—or always effective. Ralph Matthews, the managing editor of the *Washington Afro-American*, was almost barred from boarding an Eastern Airlines flight from Washington, D.C., to Charleston, South Carolina, in the fall of 1938, not because the airline had a policy against carrying Black passengers, but because one Eastern Airlines employee objected to Black passengers. The *Washington Afro-American* had used Eastern Airlines for many years, and Matthews had flown across "the entire East and South for the past ten years" without ever being "refused accommodations" on any of its planes, so he was surprised to encounter an Eastern Airlines ticket agent who "arbitrarily refused" his ticket "upon seeing I was colored."[56] The agent freely admitted "that there were plenty of seats available," but told Matthews that he just "could not" take him. Matthews had to "threaten legal action" to finally secure his ticket. On returning, Matthews wrote a letter of complaint to Eastern Airlines chairman E. V. Rickenbacker, describing the incident and naming the employee. He had nothing but praise for the airline, which, he noted, had always served him well in the past. His letter simply warned Rickenbacker that one of his employees was refusing to accept paying customers. The fare of $27.25 might "seem like a small amount," he acknowledged, but over time the actions of an "employee who wishes to indulge his feelings of racial superiority" would add up and prove costly to the airline's business.[57]

Matthews's generally positive experience underscores that while some airlines and airline personnel did not welcome African American passengers, such discrimination was far from ubiquitous and seems to have grown less common over time. Indeed, I've found virtually no reports of airlines refusing to board Black passengers after the end of the 1930s. More welcome on planes than trains, many early Black flyers took to the air with enthusiasm. "Breakfast in Kansas; dinner in Los Angeles!" reported J. A. Rogers, a novelist who worked as staff correspondent for the *Pittsburgh Courier*, in 1936. "Colored youth take notice! The airplane will someday supercede the railroad as the latter did the covered wagon."[58] But flying would prove less ideal than many hoped, at least when it came to avoiding Jim Crow.

SEGREGATING SEATING

During World War II, the travel needs of military personnel—Black or white—took priority over those of all other passengers. In these years the airlines also began to experiment with various forms of seat segregation that either confined Black passengers to certain seats, or made sure they all shared the same row. How common such practices were is difficult to determine, given that Black passengers were not numerous and the airlines made no public commitment to segregated seating. But in 1945 the Chicago and Southern Airline (one of Delta's precursors) admitted that it practiced Jim Crow seating on its Dixie-bound flights.

"It is true that Negro passengers are requested to assume the forward seats on the airplane," an official for the airline wrote to Theodore Allen, a Black federal government employee who protested when one of the airline's stewardesses made him reseat himself in the front of the plane, after he and the white man with whom he was traveling had taken seats in the middle of the plane. The airline's representative was unapologetic about the practice and suggested that "from the standard of personal comfort, these [forward seats] are the most desirable seats in the aircraft. Thus it should be made clear that the practice rather than one of discrimination is one of offering Negro accommodations and facilities which are equal or superior to those offered other passengers."[59]

Langston Hughes was familiar with the Jim Crow forward seats, and actually agreed with this positive assessment. A well-known poet and playwright, who described himself as "half writer and half vagabond," Hughes was an early and enthusiastic advocate of air travel.[60] In a 1946 *Chicago Defender* column celebrating the advantages of "Planes vs Trains," he wondered why "everybody does not travel by plane." Faster and cleaner than trains, planes held additional advantages for "colored travelers in the South." "As yet, there are no Jim Crow planes," he also noted, before qualifying this claim by saying that he had heard that "colored travelers in Dixie are sometimes given the No. 1 seat," and admitting that "once in Oklahoma I was most courteously assigned to the No. 1 seat." But he had no objections to this seat assignment, as he was convinced that the No. 1 was "really the best seat, being at the front with lots of leg room and a wonderful view unobstructed by the wing."[61]

Not all travelers shared Hughes's enthusiasm for the No. 1 seat. Commercial airlines in the 1940s typically used propliners, or propeller-driven planes,

A TWA Douglas DC-3 propliner airplane, 1940

which were powered by propellers located in the front of the plane. These planes varied somewhat by model, but their front seats tended to be noisy. First-class seating on propliners, if available, was invariably located in the rear, which was not only quieter, but easier to enter and exit—given that these planes were entered through doors located on the tail of the plane. Far from being universally regarded as the best seat on the plane, the propliners' No. 1 seats may have struck many as the worst. In addition to enduring extra noise, passengers in these seats found themselves sitting disconcertingly close to the powerful turbine engines that drove such planes' propellers, which gave off plumes of flame, especially when first fired up—and a steady stream of exhaust thereafter.

Because most Blacks flew infrequently, if at all, during the 1940s, those who did were probably unaware that they were being relegated to any particular part of the airplane—and also unaware that other seats might be better. Horace Cayton, an African American journalist and politician, was on his third flight to the South before it became clear to him that there was a reason he always ended up seated in "the same place." He figured it out at least in part because of a slip on the part of the airline's personnel, who allowed

Cayton to hear their whispered references to him as a "CX passenger" when he called to confirm his booking. Cayton promptly asked what a "CX" passenger was and received an answer that only made him more suspicious. The airline clerk he was grilling stuttered for a second and then claimed "those are my initials." "Never in all my life had I known an individual whose last name started with 'X,'" thought Cayton. When he boarded the plane and was once again greeted by a stewardess who ushered him to the plane's "front single seat," his suspicion only mounted. The "CX" had to be a special Jim Crow seating code. Cayton confirmed his suspicions by refusing to be jim-crowed. He seated himself in the middle of the plane and refused to move even after the stewardess came back to say, "I asked you to take the front seat, sir." After a brief standoff, the stewardess retreated and later offered him a shamefaced explanation of her actions, mumbling "something about it being a rule of the company with colored people or something like that."[62]

Cayton seems to have spent his flight too upset to be much concerned about cabin noise or the view from his seat, so he had nothing to say about whether he actually preferred his middle seat. Instead he remained "restless and slightly angry" long after his initial confrontation with the stewardess. Unable to concentrate on the newspaper he had planned to read, he could not stop thinking about the petty slight he had suffered. "It was so foolish," he thought, his mind racing. "She was going to serve all of us; no one had paid the least bit of attention to me; if the plane had fallen we would have all gotten killed together—why one special seat just for me?" "It's the little hurts that get us," he later concluded in a column he wrote describing the incident. "The little calculated acts of humiliation—those aimless, pointless bits of stupid and brutal prejudice, not serious enough to take a great stand on, or to endanger a life or limb, but enough to throw us off step, making us angry and irritated for the rest of the day."[63]

Jim Crow seat assignments were more immediately obvious to African Americans who were traveling with whites. Paul Evans, a soldier who boarded an American Airlines flight in Burbank, California, in the late 1940s with his squad—a dozen soldiers traveling "under U.S. orders"—is one example. By the time he arrived in New York City, he and the squad's one other Black soldier were sitting by themselves in the front of the plane. The squad had switched flights in Texas, transferring to a Delta Air Lines flight, and when they boarded, the "Delta Hostess ordered the two of us to take a seat behind the engine. Although our captain objected, she insisted saying 'It is the policy of our company.'"[64]

Over time the airlines seem to have adopted less obvious forms of segregation. By the late 1940s, better soundproofing, fully pressurized cabins, and turbo jet engines had greatly reduced the cabin noise in most commercial airliners—which may help explain why Black passengers were no longer asked to take the forward seat. But they were still assigned to segregated seating—at least some of the time. American Airlines, for a time, seated Black passengers in the single row seats on the right side of its planes, and then, as its planes grew larger and such seats were eliminated, the airline began using a secret code to segregate Black passengers. Delta instructed its hostesses to avoid integrated seating by assigning Blacks who traveled alone to a "solitary seat," and several airlines reportedly "trained" their phone operators to "identify Negro voices in order to assign them only specific seats on specific flights."[65]

Such practices were too covert to be easily challenged in the courts. The "practice of segregation in air transportation" was very difficult to address, NAACP lawyer Robert Carter told Jacob W. Rosenthal, chief of the Civil Aeronautics Board, in a 1949 letter outlining the various forms of discrimination African Americans encountered when traveling by air. Not only was it "not uniform in southern states," but it was hard to figure out how it worked. "Segregation on the airplanes themselves" seems to "rest within the discretion of the stewards or hostesses themselves," speculated Carter, who was clearly unaware of the airlines' secret codes and seat policies.[66]

In the fall of 1951, however, some of the airlines' Jim Crow tricks would be revealed in a criminal complaint filed against American Airlines. Gabriel Gladstone, a twenty-two-year-old Jewish New Yorker, had begun a job as a reservations agent in the American Airlines office at LaGuardia earlier that year. But after working there for two months, he was dismissed for refusing to follow the airline's "special instructions on how to handle Negro passengers." As a trainee, Gladstone "was instructed to mark reservations with a symbolic E-111, if the passenger was a Negro, or in the case of a telephone reservation, was presumed to be Negro." These codes, he was informed, would be used to implement the airline's policy of "segregating Negro passengers on flights and preferring white applicants for airplane accommodations on waiting lists." When Gladstone began taking reservations, a supervisor observed him failing to mark "a reservation with a code even though the applicant had a southern accent," and fired him on the spot. Gladstone reported his experience to the American Jewish Congress, which helped him file a complaint charging American Airlines with violating the New York civil rights law.[57]

American Airlines initially denied Gladstone's allegation, insisting that "there is no discrimination of any kind practiced by our company" and "some of our best employees are Negroes." But the special instructions Gladstone refused to follow were then located in a copy of the American Airlines' training manual, at which point the airline's executives began backpedaling. The company's attorney, Thomas Holden, said the "practice had not been used recently" and was an "inadvertency" in the training manual; while another airline spokesman described it as a "stupid oversight." The Queens County district attorney disregarded their excuses and condemned the airline for failing to protect "the American way of life." He also issued a public memorandum ordering American and all other airlines operating within Queens County (which was home to both La Guardia and Idlewild airports) "to cease and desist if they practiced any kind of racial discrimination."[68]

Gabriel Gladstone's complaint underscored that Black flyers suffered indignities that went beyond segregated seats. American Airlines' policy directed its employees to put Negro passengers "on waiting lists for reservations," a practice that appears to have been widespread. Black travelers were first in line for any kind of travel disruption, and were sometimes bumped to make room for white passengers. According to one post–World War II letter writer who wondered whether American democracy was worth fighting for, such interruptions could involve something as direct as an "airline agent saying 'I'm sorry but your reservation has been postponed due to an unexpected request from a white passenger.'"[69]

The inconvenience imposed on Black passengers by these abrupt cancellations and delays was often compounded by discrimination within the airport itself. For instance, Dan "Chicken" McMullen found himself waiting until 2 a.m. for American Airlines to honor his reservation for an afternoon flight from Dallas to Chicago while watching the airline sell tickets on an earlier flight to white passengers who had just arrived at the airport. The insult was compounded by the fact that the terminal's restaurant refused to serve him.[70]

Not even well-known African Americans were spared such slights, as Jackie Robinson and his wife found out when they traveled from Los Angeles to Daytona Beach, Florida, in 1946. Hired to play for the Montreal Royals that year, Robinson was due to begin spring training as the first Black player ever to play major league baseball. Excited to be traveling in style, the couple arrived at LAX dressed to the nines for their American Airlines flight, and were embarrassed when Robinson's parents saw them off with a supply of sandwiches that seemed more suited to a cross-country journey in the Jim Crow car. But the food came in handy. The Robinsons were bumped from their first flight during a layover in New Orleans, and ended up spending twelve hours at the New Orleans airport, which did not serve Black customers in its coffee shop or restaurant. When they were finally allowed to resume their journey to Daytona, they were ordered off the plane in Pensacola, Florida, where their flight stopped to refuel. The airline needed to make room for three white passengers. The Robinsons finished their journey by Greyhound bus, on which they were forced to ride in the back, and they could not eat at the roadside restaurants along the route. By then their sandwiches were long gone, and they were too insulted to order food to go, so they sustained themselves on that twelve-hour leg of the journey by eating apples and candy bars.[71]

Likewise, jazz singer Ella Fitzgerald was bumped off a plane in Honolulu in 1954. On her way from San Francisco to Sidney, Australia, for a concert tour, Fitzgerald was traveling with an accompanist and her secretary, who were also African American, when her journey was cut short. After getting off the plane when it stopped to refuel in Honolulu, Fitzgerald and her companions were not allowed to reboard, not even to retrieve the clothes and other personal items they had left behind. They then had to wait three days before they could get another flight. Pan American Airways claimed that they were bumped through "inadvertence," but Fitzgerald sued the company for racial discrimination and won, receiving $7,500 in damages.[72]

Although settled out of court, *Fitzgerald v. Pan American World Airways, Inc.* "established the existence of a civil remedy based on the antidiscrimination provision of the Civil Aeronautics Act of 1938," which may have discouraged United States–based airlines from bumping other Black passengers.[73] But it is not clear that such practices disappeared altogether. In 1959, C. B. Powell, publisher and editor of the *New York Amsterdam News*, insisted that he was forced to give up his seat to a white passenger on a Singapore-bound British Overseas Airways flight.[74]

AIRPORT SEGREGATION

Black passengers also experienced segregation in airports, which varied from place to place and changed over time. Some early airports had no segregation policy but did not expect African American passengers, as William Pickens found when he traveled to Bakersfield, California, on NAACP business in 1932. When some local affiliates came out to meet him, airport officials were convinced that they must be there by mistake, and "did not want to let them into the field." "Nobody's coming on this plane whom you would want to meet," they assured the Pickens delegation.[75]

As more Blacks began to fly, southern segregation ordinances were eventually extended to airports, but the process was piecemeal and took some time, producing discriminatory practices that varied from airport to airport. "Segregation in air transportation is not uniform in Southern areas," NAACP lawyer Robert Carter noted in 1949, "principally because it is a new means of transportation and age-old customs and usages do not immediately take hold."[76]

Congressman Charles C. Diggs of Michigan, who was an early Black frequent flyer, actually witnessed the development of segregation at airports. When he first began flying in the late 1940s, he was "heartened to see that this newer mode of conveyance was not into the old pattern of segregation and discrimination established by railroads and bus lines." But this sense of satisfaction did not last long. He was soon disappointed to find that "undemocratic practices" were becoming common in airports, as he noted in a 1955 complaint to the president of Continental Airlines. In southern airports, he routinely encountered waiting rooms marked "for whites only," separate water fountains, "the refusal of limousines and taxi companies to carry Negroes . . . [and] discrimination and/or segregation against Negroes in airport restaurants."[77] Just as Mary Church had watched trains become segregated in the nineteenth century, and automobile drivers saw filling stations and rest stops turn toward segregation, so too did air travelers see the promise of flight pulled down to earth by segregation.

One of the places where Diggs encountered segregation was Washington National Airport, which was operated by the Civil Aeronautics Authority (CAA) and owned by the federal government. Completed in 1941, the airport was built on the mudflats of the Potomac River, which had been underwater before the airport was constructed. Whether this land was actually located in the District of Columbia became an open question shortly after the airport was built and remained unresolved until 1946, when Congress passed a bill conceding that D.C.'s claims to the Potomac River did not extend past the river's original eastern shoreline, putting the airport in Virginia. Congress also noted that the airport was under federal jurisdiction. Its terminal services,

however, were another matter. Air Terminal Services, Inc., private conces-
sionaires who ran the airport's restaurant, snack bar, and cafeterias, considered their businesses to be subject to Virginia law, and insisted on operating
them in compliance with Virginia's segregation statutes. They refused to serve
Blacks—even congressmen—and told African American patrons that they "could
get service downstairs with the help."[78]

Aggrieved passengers soon complained. In July 1941, shortly after the
airport first opened, Edgar G. Brown, the president of the United Government
Employees Union and a member of Franklin D. Roosevelt's famed "Black
Cabinet," staged a "one man sitdown strike" in the airport's main coffee shop
after being denied a cup of coffee there. When that did not work, he went
home and filed a civil suit.[79] What became of his suit is unclear, but the complaints kept coming. They highlighted the logistical difficulties of running
an airport that did not open its facilities to all of the passengers who traveled
through it. Washington National, as Charles Hamilton Houston noted in 1948,
was one of the many southern airports that made absolutely "no provision
for colored passengers" in its dining room, which meant that Black passengers who had to stay there for any length of time had no place to eat. But all
passengers had to eat somewhere "when planes are grounded en route because
of weather or mechanical trouble." Airlines often handled this problem by
sending "colored passengers by taxi, free, to eat at some colored restaurant."[80]
But American Airlines, the major airline flying in and out of Washington
National, does not seem to have made consistent provisions for its Black passengers, as attested by the experience of the Southernaires, a Black gospel
group based in Jackson, Mississippi.

The Southernaires arrived at Washington National Airport at 7 a.m. on December 18, 1941, intent on nothing more than returning home to Jackson
from a performance in Williamsburg that had been hosted by John D. Rocke-
feller. When they went to check in, they found that their plane had been
grounded due to bad weather, and they were given meal vouchers by their
carrier, American Airlines. But when they entered the restaurant, although
they were seated and given glasses of water and menus, no one came to take
their order. They soon discovered that the restaurant's assistant manager had
"stopped the waitresses from taking their orders" because Virginia law did
not allow "whites and Negroes to eat in the same dining room." According
to the report the group filed with the NAACP, after an hour-long wait the
assistant manager finally offered them the option of eating downstairs "in the

dining space . . . provided for Negro employees of the airport." The group's members initially acquiesced to this plan, but as they followed him down to "this proposed eating place," they had second thoughts. They soon found themselves in the airport's basement, where they were led through a door marked "no admittance," which opened onto a "dark hallway . . . littered with debris and dirty scrub buckets, "at which point they refused to go any further."[81] Instead, they returned to the airport's main dining room and remained there until they caught their flight, three hours later—still unfed.

The NAACP's hope of suing the airport on the Southernaires' behalf seems to have foundered on the question of jurisdiction, as the issue of whether the airport was located in Washington, D.C., or in Virginia remained unresolved until 1945. The airport was owned and operated by the federal government, but Donald B. Connelly, the CAA administrator who supervised its management, refused to get involved in the matter. The federal government controlled only the public spaces at the airport, Connelly told the NAACP: The use of "the space occupied by the restaurant" was under the control of Air Terminal Services, Inc.[82]

Five years later the airport restaurant remained segregated, and the airline continued to send unwitting passengers there. "The space on the memo insert found in the seat pocket of your planes is not large enough [for me] to tell you what happened to me while a passenger on August 7, 1946," Mamie E. Davis reported to the president of American Airlines in a letter written the next day. Booked on a flight to New York City that was delayed by two hours, Davis was issued an American Airlines voucher entitling her to a dinner at the National Airport's restaurant or coffee shop "not to exceed ($1.50)." But when she tried to use her voucher in the airport coffee shop, the waitress insisted, "This is Virginia and I can't serve you." When Davis went to the American Airlines desk to complain, the employee there also informed her, "This is Virginia." And when Davis replied, "It is also government property" and threatened to sue, the airline representative was dismissive. "Oh, you won't get anything," she said. "Others have sued and it made no difference." Davis lingered at her desk, still pressing for a meal, and was finally ushered into a back office, where she was given a box lunch valued at 95 cents. American Airlines forwarded Davis's complaint to the Department of Commerce, where government officials insisted, "We do not have the authority to compel the company operating these restaurants to ignore or violate the laws of the state of Virginia."[83]

Such complaints continued until shortly after the end of 1948, when the CAA ordered the desegregation of all eating facilities at Washington National Airport. The airport's concessionaire, Air Terminal Services, Inc., initially defied the order, but finally desegregated the following year, after the government threatened to take it to court. The CAA took no action on segregation in the terminals at other airports, but Washington National was a special case, serving, as it did, the nation's capital and seat of government. Subject of a series of lawsuits, the whites-only facilities were also an ongoing outrage to Charles Diggs and several other members of Congress who had to navigate these segregated facilities whenever they flew into and out of D.C. on government business.

Newly reelected president Harry Truman expressed sympathy for these protests. Truman had secured his second term at least in part on the strength of having won 77 percent of the Black vote, and he came into office with a civil rights agenda that included the desegregation of "interstate transportation and all facilities thereof" and the prohibition of discrimination and segregation in all "public and publicly supported" facilities in the District of Columbia.[84] He neither pursued nor achieved all of his civil rights goals, but he did pressure the CAA director into desegregating the Washington National Airport. The airport was a federally owned and operated "point of entry for many visiting foreign dignitaries," including nonwhites from Asia and Africa, which made segregation there an ongoing source of potential embarrassment to the federal government.[35]

Other airports were also problematic in this regard, but they were not under the direct control of the federal government, so airport segregation persisted throughout much of the South until the beginning of the 1960s. The Federal Airport Act of 1946, which provided federal grants to support the construction and expansion of airports across the country, included a nondiscrimination clause, which ought to have prohibited such segregation. It called for all grantees to "promise that the airport to which the project relates will be available for public use on fair and reasonable terms and without unjust discrimination." But prior to 1961 the CAA allowed southern municipalities to build "segregated facilities provided the cost of that facility was excluded from the computation of project cost for federal aid purposes."[86]

Some airports took advantage of the grants to actually introduce segregation in the 1950s. Built in 1939, Virginia's Norfolk Airport had no segregation until the early 1950s, when it received $1,750,000 in federal aid to complete a new terminal, and installed a segregated restaurant. The new terminal's design initially included segregated restrooms as well, but the city's African American leaders successfully lobbied "to have the toilet facilities . . . made available to all without designation."[87] Ironically enough, Norfolk's segregated Azalea Room Restaurant offered Blacks far better accommodations than many other airport restaurants. Although split into two rooms by a curtain that separated Black and white diners, its main dining room was open to all. Some airport concessionaires allowed African Americans to patronize their snack bars or cafeterias, but not their restaurants; others offered Black patrons still more limited options, advising those who requested meals that "they could only be served in the kitchen or manager's office." A Black Air Force officer who stopped for a drink at the New Orleans airport's bar in 1955 was greeted by an attendant who informed him that "the only way. . . . [he] could be served was if he agreed to take his drink outside the building."[88]

International incidents continued to be a source of considerable embarrassment to the government. Asked to move into a small private dining room set off from the Houston airport's main dining room, India's ambassador Gaganvihari Lallubhai Mehta and his secretary, B. A. Rajagoalan, initially thought they were getting "deluxe treatment reserved for special visitors."[89] When the truth came out, both the State Department staffers and Secretary of State John Foster Dulles scrambled to apologize, while Indian embassy officials refused to comment on the "possibility of the incident being used as material for anti-American propaganda."[90]

The segregation of foreigners and VIPs was embarrassing to airlines too. Pan American Airways, which operated regular flights to both the Caribbean and Latin America, had a nondiscrimination policy at its Miami airport terminal. But when Haiti's president, Sténio Vincent, came through Miami en route to Washington for a meeting with Franklin Delano Roosevelt in 1939, the airline had to confine him to their terminal. Its executives had planned to put Vincent up in a luxury hotel room while he waited to complete the final leg of his journey, but "no white hotels would accept him for the night." In the end, rather than subject "the sixty-year-old Vincent to cramped downtown lodging" at one of the city's "colored" hotels or rooming houses in the "Central Negro District," Pan Am executives, local officials, and agents of the US State Department decided to make sure he did not stay overnight in the city. To that end, they staged a reception for him in the lobby of the Pan American Airways terminal before shuttling him to a private railroad car.[91]

Other airlines had no nondiscrimination policy—even in their own terminals. Delta Air Lines' Atlanta terminal housed the Dobbs Restaurant, where
segregation remained common until the beginning of the 1960s. Even after
an "embarrassing incident when the Indian ambassador was invited to dine
in the jim-crow section," the airline did nothing to discourage it. In 1958
African American columnist Alice Dunnigan stopped for breakfast at the
Dobbs Restaurant only to be met at the door with the question "Are you colored?" Startled and humiliated by the question, Dunnigan concluded, "Now,
Southern hostesses play it safe. They ask brown customers outright if they
are colored before inviting them to eat behind the colored curtain."[92]

However unpleasant segregated restaurants might be, the most problematic for hungry travelers were the airports in which all dining facilities were
reserved for whites only. In Louisville, Black travelers complained that "they
were denied dining privileges in the snackbar, the dining room, and the cock-
tail lounge." Airport segregation could be humiliating even to Black passengers who never experienced it directly. On planes that stopped to refuel in
the South, white passengers were told "to depart for lunch in the terminal's
restaurant," while "Blacks were instructed to stay on the plane and eat boxed
lunches because blacks were not allowed in the terminal's restaurant."[93]

Segregation was not limited to cafés and restaurants. As Charles Diggs
noted, it could extend into restrooms, waiting rooms, and other amenities,
and was notably inconsistent from place to place. Some airports had segregated restaurants, waiting rooms, restrooms, and water fountains, while others
had colored restrooms, but no other segregated facilities—or vice versa. In
the Chattanooga airport, for example, Diggs was astonished to find that Blacks
were free to eat in the restaurant but could not use its toilet. "It appears that
we can consume food and beverages in the same place, but must eliminate
same in a separate facility."[94] Atlanta's airport segregation included not only
its restrooms, but also its barbershop and shoeshine stand—which did not
admit Blacks. When Ross Cowans, the *Chicago Defender*'s sports editor, sought
a shoeshine in the Atlanta airport, he was surprised to find that he would
have to take his shoes off and remain standing while they were shined.[95]

The forms of segregation in place in airport waiting rooms were likewise
variable. According to Black journalist Carl Murphy, the Dallas and Houston
airports both had waiting rooms that were "reserved for lily-whites only. Colored people are supposed to stand around outside after they have bought
their tickets and stowed their baggage." Other airports had separate waiting

The white waiting room at the Dale Mabry Field airport in Tallahassee, Florida. The entrance to the colored waiting room is on the right.

rooms or rows of "colored" seats.[96] "Out Texas way," one observer noted, "the 'colored' waiting room is two small benches facing each other in the general waiting room."[97] The Dale Mabry Airport, which was accurately described by the writer James Baldwin as Tallahassee's "shambles of an airport," was so small that it only had five seats in its white waiting room. But it still managed to set aside a separate space for Black travelers in a still smaller "alcove . . . with 'Colored Waiting Room' printed above it."[98]

Still more problematic for Blacks who traveled by air were the segregated ground transportation services and airport accommodations. No one flies from door to door: you have to get to and from the airport. And airport accommodations can be equally essential. Like all travelers, Black passengers sometimes ended up on planes that were detained overnight due to bad weather or mechanical problems. Segregation on the ground often made matters worse.

For Blacks, accessing the region's airports was complicated by the fact that from the 1920s onward many southern cities, and at least one southern state

(Mississippi), passed laws requiring cabs and limousines to serve either white or Black passengers only. These laws made it impossible for African American airline passengers to ride in the cabs and limousines that, early on, airlines hired to carry their passengers to and from the airport.

The airlines sometimes supplied Black passengers with colored taxis, but such arrangements typically required advance notice. "In too many Southern cities Negroes are not allowed to use the regularly furnished transportation," a columnist for the *Atlanta Daily World* warned his readers. Black travelers to Houston, New Orleans, Miami, Jackson, and Memphis could not use the taxis and buses used by other passengers on their flights to reach these cities. They had to secure "special service, airport to city," which was likely to involve ordering and paying for their own "colored taxi"—which might take some time to arrive. The savvy traveler could avoid this expense and inconvenience, the well-traveled journalist noted, by insisting that their airline take care of such arrangements. But this had to be done before boarding, and involved asking your airline to call ahead to order "special" service on arrival.[99]

Such arrangements required Black travelers to be in the know about the local Jim Crow laws and customs in any city they planned to visit. Few

A "colored only" taxi, Birmingham, Alabama, 1963.

travelers could manage to be so prescient. Instead, flying Black often involved unpleasant surprises, such as getting in a cab hired by your airline to take you to your flight, only to be told by your driver, "You'll not ride in this cab. I don't haul no colored people. You'll have to call a colored cab."[100] Segregation could also extend to airport bus services, as singer Muriel Rahn found out the hard way on a 1946 trip from Jacksonville, Florida, to New Orleans when she tried to board the bus "commissioned by the airlines to convey passengers to the airport from the city, and vice versa." "No n—r passengers," the driver told Rahn, "when she asked to go along with the rest of the passengers."[101]

Complaints from aggrieved African American passengers appear to have had little impact on such practices. When William H. Gray, the president of Florida Agricultural and Mechanical College, a historically Black institution, wrote to G. T. Baker, the president of National Airlines, in the fall of 1947 to ask him whether his "office was familiar with the practices taking place in many southern communities of denying Negro passengers service on the regular and established buses and taxi lines which meet your planes at various airports," he received a one sentence response: "In reply to your letter of September 4th we have no control, financially or otherwise, over ground transportation."[102] Gray's identical letter to Eastern Airlines received a more gracious answer, which said much the same thing: "We make arrangements with cab companies to meet our planes," Eastern Airlines vice president Stanley de J. Osborne wrote, "but do not in any way control their operation unless they operate in an unsafe or undependable manner."[103]

A writer for the *Pittsburgh Courier* observed that Black travelers tried to avoid "the problem of Jim Crow at airports by meeting incoming friends or relatives with their automobiles so there is no necessity for using the 'separate but equal' facilities."[104] But air travel was filled with uncertainties that were less easily remedied, like weather delays or mechanical problems that forced travelers to stay overnight in a place they had never planned to visit. Then, as now, such travelers would usually end up spending the night in a hotel. But hotels that accepted Black travelers were few and far in between, so these passengers could end up at "some colored person's house for lodging while the white passengers are put up at the best hotel in town."[105]

Or worse, they could end with no place to stay at all. Singer Muriel Rahn's ill-fated trip from Jacksonville to New Orleans in 1946 got even worse after her flight got stranded in Tallahassee and the plane's passengers ended up having to take a bus, which broke down near Pensacola. The rest of the flight's (white) passengers were able to take shelter at a nearby roadside inn, but not Rahn: "The Florida Inn proprietor ordered her out of his place and she was forced to go back to the bus and sit eight hours in the cold."[106] Likewise, African American opera singer Ruth Wyatt ended up spending the night in the lobby of the Albuquerque airport when her TWA plane was grounded there "due to inclement weather." Her fellow passengers were "given reservations to hotels in that city," while she was told that "it was impossible for her to obtain quarters in any hotel because of her color."[107] She sued the airline, but got no relief. A California district court decided "in favor of TWA, saying that it was not the airline's fault that the Albuquerque hotels would not accept African American guests."[108]

Colored hotels, when available, were not always a good alternative. When their flight to the Bahamas was grounded in Norfolk, Virginia, in 1957, five Black New Yorkers were taken to a "colored hotel" that was so "shabby and unsanitary" that "they returned to the airport and slept on benches rather than remaining there."[109] Writer Ellen Tarry had somewhat better luck, but also found colored lodgings problematic. In 1946 she endured a torturously roundabout trip from New York City to Birmingham, Alabama, with her eighteen-month-old daughter Elisabeth. Elisabeth was recovering from strep throat, and Tarry was worried about taking her anywhere, but Tarry's grandmother lay dying in Birmingham and Tarry wanted "her to see my baby and have her bestow her blessing upon this first great granddaughter before it was too late." So she booked a flight out of LaGuardia thinking it would be the fastest way to get to her family home in Birmingham. Unfortunately, the flight ran into heavy rain and had to make an emergency landing in Knoxville, Tennessee, where airline officials were hard pressed to find any accommodations for Tarry and her daughter. Finally, after a call to "one of the Negro bellboys at a hotel," they located a room, which turned out to be a sleeping porch of a "Negro Tourist home" located thirteen miles from the airport. But Tarry still had to get there, an ordeal that took until 3 p.m. because "whites and Negroes were not allowed to ride in the same taxi cabs."[110] The next day she had an even harder time returning to the airport. The cab that the airline sent to pick her up had already picked up several white passengers, and when the driver realized that Tarry and her daughter were not white, he refused to take them anywhere. Only after she threatened to launch a civil suit did her airline finally find transportation for her, sending her back in the car that was used to carry airmail to the airport.

Tarry found her journey all the more stressful because she was not accustomed to traveling Jim Crow. Born into Birmingham's middle-class elite, she was very fair-skinned and had always been able to pass for white. But her "caramel colored baby changed everything," as she realized during this trip. The baby made her race visible, or at least suspect, putting her last in line to be "assigned a room" and all but unable to get a cab. Exhausted when she finally arrived in Birmingham, and desperate not to be Jim Crowed out of the seat on the airport limousine that she had booked to take her into town, she kept her place in the car by ignoring the limousine driver's whispered question "Is that a nigger baby that white woman is holding?" But as the limousine carried her into town, she was bitterly aware her that daughter Elisabeth would not have the same luxury and "kept thinking, 'He called my child a *nigger* baby.' He called my child a *nigger* baby.' I wondered if it was fair for Negro mothers to bring them into a world that would scorn them because of their color. I felt guilty and ashamed that I had brought Elisabeth to Alabama to be called a 'nigger baby.'"[111]

Airport segregation only grew more unpredictable over time. Carl Rowan, who flew from Minneapolis to Nashville in 1951, reported that he encountered segregation signs but courteous service in Nashville, Tennessee; while the Louisville, Kentucky, airport where he changed planes had no Jim Crow signs or facilities. Even there, however, counter attendants still practiced the "old racial protocol system" Rowan had known since childhood. He was "served only after all whites had been waited on."[112] By the mid-1950s, an editorial in the *Pittsburgh Courier* noted, Black flyers encountered "a veritable crazy quilt of contradictory policies from one end of the South to the other . . . as to waiting rooms, toilets, and ground transportation," but "almost no exception to the rule that Negroes cannot eat in lunchrooms and dining rooms."[113] During these years some airports voluntarily desegregated; others, like Dannelly Field Airport in Montgomery, Alabama, built new terminals with segregated floor plans. Originally constructed for military use, Dannelly did not open for commercial service until 1956, and completed construction on its passenger terminals in 1958. Funded by the federal-aid airport program, its sleek modern buildings included segregated waiting rooms and restrooms, as well as a "whites only restaurant." As scholar Anke Ortlepp writes, "The 'Airgate to Dixie,' as the airport liked to call itself, also served as the gateway to the status quo."[114]

White waiting room in the Dannelly Field airport in Montgomery, Alabama, 1961.

As this book's remaining chapters will show, the complete desegregation of American airports would not be accomplished until 1963, after a long series of public protests and Department of Justice lawsuits. Likewise, months of freedom rides, federal pressure, and an order from the US Supreme Court were required to bring about the 1961 desegregation of interstate buses and bus stations in the South, while segregation remained in effect in many roadside restaurants and hotels until well after the passage of the Civil Rights Act of 1964. Despite Black travelers' sustained opposition to the segregation of public accommodations, the shaky legal ground on which segregated interstate travel facilities stood, and the complications they imposed on businesses, travel segregation proved difficult to overturn.

6

Traveling for Civil Rights

The Long Fight to Outlaw Transportation Segregation

IRENE MORGAN HAD NO PLANS TO CHALLENGE SEGREGATION WHEN she boarded a Baltimore-bound bus in Gloucester County, Virginia, on the morning of July 16, 1944. A defense worker and twenty-seven-year-old mother of two, she had more personal problems on her mind. Morgan had suffered a miscarriage earlier that summer, and had been visiting with her mother in Virginia while she recuperated. That morning she was returning home to see her doctor. Still "not feeling well," she was eager to secure a seat, and dismayed to find none available. The bus was packed with passengers, both Black and white, and "there were a lot of people standing." Morgan joined them, but she must have looked unsteady on her feet because one fellow passenger—a Black woman sitting at the rear of the bus—told her that she could sit on her lap. Too tired to say no, Morgan accepted this offer, but was pleased to see another seat nearby open up a few minutes later when the bus let off passengers in Saluda, Virginia. She took it, settling into an aisle seat, three rows from the back of the bus and well within "the section designated under Virginia's segregation laws for black passengers."[1]

Shortly after she sat down, the bus driver came and told Morgan and her seatmate, who was a young Black woman traveling with an infant, that they would have to give up their seats to a young white couple who had just boarded the bus. Morgan refused. She offered to change seats with some white people who had taken a seat behind her, but when the driver insisted that she "get up and stand," she said no.[2] "I didn't do anything wrong," she later explained: "I'd paid for my seat. I was sitting where I was supposed to."

Irene Morgan.

Determined to make her move, the bus driver got off the bus, walked across the street to the Saluda Jail, and came back with two sheriff's deputies, who boarded the bus and issued a warrant for her arrest. Morgan, who would later remember being "too enraged to be afraid," tore up the warrant and threw it out the window. Her rage only mounted when one of the deputies grabbed her arm and tried to drag him off the bus. "He touched me," she later remembered. "That's when I kicked him in a very bad place. He hobbled off, and another one came on. He was trying to put his hands on me to get me off. I was going to bite him, but he was dirty, so I clawed him instead. I ripped his shirt. We were both pulling at each other. He said he'd use his nightstick. I said, 'We'll whip each other.'"[3]

In the end the two deputies succeeded in dragging Morgan off the bus, at which point she was charged with resisting arrest and violating Virginia's segregation laws. Morgan pleaded guilty to the former and paid a $100 fine. But she refused to plead guilty to violating Virginia's segregation law—which carried a lesser fine of $10.[4] Instead, she reached out to the Virginia NAACP, which helped her appeal the case. Her appeal was unsuccessful in Virginia's state courts, and the NAACP took the case to the US Supreme Court. In 1946 the Supreme Court sided with Morgan. "No state law can reach beyond its

own border nor bar transportation of passengers across its boundaries," wrote
Justice Stanley Reed, in a verdict that held that Virginia's motor vehicle
segregation imposed an "undue burden" on interstate commerce. "It seems
clear to us," he wrote, "that seating arrangements for the different races in
interstate motor travel require a single, uniform rule to promote and protect
national travel."[5]

"JC Bus Travel Outlawed," the *Washington Afro-American* announced in
red-letter headlines after the verdict was announced.[6] Yet the desegregation
of the South's buses and other common carriers would not be achieved by
any single legal victory or heroic act of resistance. It would require a long
series of lawsuits challenging segregation on buses, trains, and even airplanes,
as well as discrimination in dining cars, bus terminals, railroad station waiting
rooms, railway dining cars, airports, hotels, roadside restaurants, and other
travel accommodations. Although the 1940s and 1950s saw Black activists finally beginning to win such suits, their legal victories were often ignored.
Southern officials found ways to work around or ignore federal court rulings,
and in many areas segregation signs remained in place. Desegregation would
require more than just changes in the law. It would require direct action and
federal intervention.

Although largely fruitless in the short term, the Morgan case and other
Black challenges to Jim Crow laid the groundwork for the desegregation of
southern transportation by exposing blatant injustices that the South's many
segregation statutes imposed on African American travelers, and seeking federal support for their abolition. Over time African American litigants and
lawyers slowly expanded the federal protections to which Black passengers
could lay claim. They inspired continued direct action against travel segregation, and eventually forced the federal government to play an active role
in securing the rights of Black travelers. Such intervention would not come
until the Freedom Riders who traveled the Deep South in 1961 were met with
a level of violence that precipitated a national civil rights crisis. But the
Freedom Riders were not the first to attempt to integrate the nation's southbound buses. In 1947, in the wake of the *Morgan* decision, the Congress of
Racial Equality organized the Journey of Reconciliation, in which an integrated group of riders traversed the Upper South by bus; this was the model
for the far better known rides that took place in 1961. In this chapter I chart
these first journeys, as well as the complex history of organized and individual acts of resistance that set the stage for the civil rights breakthroughs
of the 1960s.

THE MITCHELL CASE

Irene Morgan is sometimes hailed as the "first Freedom Rider," but she was not the first African American plaintiff to win a transportation discrimination case in the US Supreme Court. Her victory came on the heels of *Mitchell v. United States* (1941), an even more deeply forgotten case won by Arthur Wergs Mitchell. Described by *Time* magazine as "big, grey-haired" and "taffy-colored," Mitchell served as the representative for Illinois's first congressional district from 1934 to 1943. During his years there, he was the only African American in Congress.[7] His lawsuit took on the southern practice of barring Blacks from railroad Pullman accommodations, which, as we saw in Chapter 2, posed difficulties for even the most powerful and wealthy African Americans.

Mitchell's case is now barely a footnote in the history of civil rights movements, perhaps not without reason. His suit was not a direct attack on segregation, and in ruling on the case, the Supreme Court did not take up that issue. Instead his case ultimately turned on the question of whether Mitchell could be justly denied Pullman car accommodations that he had purchased—or whether such discrimination violated the Interstate Commerce Act of 1887. The Court ruled in Mitchell's favor, concluding that because this act barred carriers from subjecting "any particular person to any undue or unreasonable prejudice or disadvantage," Blacks could not be excluded from an entire class of transportation that was available to whites.[8]

The case first took shape in the spring of 1937, when Mitchell took a break from his congressional responsibilities to vacation in Hot Springs, Arkansas, a "favorite rest haven of Chicago politicians."[9] He planned to make the long journey from his home in Chicago to Hot Springs by Pullman car and purchased a first-class ticket for his journey from the Central Illinois Railroad, paying a one-cent-per-mile surcharge to secure premium accommodations. However, Blacks could not count on being permitted to travel by Pullman south of the Mason-Dixon Line, and Representative Mitchell was no exception.

He made it through Tennessee, where he transferred to the Chicago, Rock Island and Pacific Railroad. But once his train left Memphis and crossed the Mississippi River into Arkansas, the train conductor told him he could not ride in the Pullman car. Mitchell protested that he had a ticket and identified himself as "Mr. Mitchell, serving in the Congress of the United States." "It don't make a difference who you are so long as you are a nigger you can't ride

Arthur Wergs Mitchell.

in this car," the conductor shot back, and threatened to arrest him if he did not move. Mitchell retired to the Jim Crow car, which was, as usual, "an old car up next to the engine, in front of all the other cars."[10] When he got back to Chicago he sued, filing both a personal damage suit against the railroad and a complaint with the Interstate Commerce Commission. In many respects Mitchell was an unlikely litigant. Born and raised in Alabama, he had studied at the Tuskegee Institute, where he became a lifelong "adherent of Booker T. Washington's formulas for racial progress." A man who maintained that "color does not hold a man back," Mitchell detested "troublemakers" and activists of all kinds.[11] The first Black person to serve in Congress as a member of the Democratic Party, Mitchell was elected as a supporter of Roosevelt's New Deal and prided himself on "placing party and politics above race."[12] Accordingly, he maintained friendly relationships with white southern Democrats, who appreciated both his party loyalty and his advocacy of a conservative doctrine of Black self-help, which held that "what becomes of the Negro and his future is largely a question for the Negro himself to settle."[13]

Mitchell was less popular with Black leaders, who questioned his loyalty to his race. He won his congressional seat by defeating the Black Republican incumbent, Oscar DePriest, a man with a far better civil rights record, who was voted out largely because he opposed Roosevelt's economic relief programs. Although he was an ardent supporter of the New Deal, Mitchell had few other qualifications that appealed to African American voters. Never a member of the NAACP (or any other Black civil rights organization), he took office vowing that he "was not going to Congress as a Negro with a chip on my shoulder," but rather as "a representative of all the people in my District."[14]

Once in office, Mitchell developed an acrimonious relationship with the NAACP's leaders, who found him an undependable ally. In 1935, not long after he was first elected, he derailed their attempt to get Congress to consider a strong anti-lynching bill by introducing a far weaker bill of his own. Neither bill received serious consideration, at least in part because debates over the two competing bills helped prevent the subject of anti-lynching legislation from ever reaching the floor. Mitchell won a reputation as an obstructionist, who might even be in cahoots with the southern Democrats. He was not, but Mitchell did not break ranks with his southern colleagues until 1937, when he finally lent his support to another NAACP-sponsored anti-lynching bill. Still, Mitchell's relationship with the NAACP was never close, and he launched his 1937 lawsuits without first consulting the organization's legal department.

It is not clear that the NAACP would have taken his case, as the organization was still largely avoiding travel segregation cases for lack of funds. NAACP lawyers were also leery of litigating cases that did not clearly undermine segregation, and avoided Pullman car cases for that reason. In 1940 Thurgood Marshall, the newly appointed director-counsel of the NAACP's Legal Defense Fund, which he founded, refused to even review the details of a Pullman car accommodations case against the Gulf, Mobile and Ohio Railroad, even though it was proposed by John LeFlore, the executive secretary of the Mobile, Alabama, branch of the NAACP. "Here is our difficulty with these railroad cases," he told LeFlore. "We are not at all willing to accept as a matter of law the fact that segregation laws in the South are legal or valid. We are therefore placed in a difficult position in requesting the railroads to make their jim-crow accommodations equal to the others."[15]

Mitchell did not share Marshall's concerns. Mitchell had been a young lawyer in Washington, D.C., in 1919 when the bill was passed to return the railroads to private ownership, and he had been a member of the small delegation of Black men who lobbied Congress to add an equal rights clause to the bill—which would have abolished Jim Crow outright. But his 1937

suit, as he initially presented it, was more in keeping with the accommodationist politics that had helped him curry favor with southern Democrats.
The goal of his suit, he explained to the *New York Times,* was not equal
rights, but equal accommodations. He was going to "clean up the Jim Crow
cars of the South and make equipment available for people of my race, which
is equal to that furnished for any other race."[16]

In taking on the exclusion of Blacks from first-class railroad accommodations, Mitchell addressed an issue that had become a pressing personal
problem for him once he was elected to Congress. Like most Blacks, he had
trouble securing Pullman accommodations—and he was frustrated to find
that his congressional status did not improve matters. In the years leading
up to his case, he had even used his status as a member of Congress to seek
"special identification" allowing him Pullman car privileges on a couple of
railroads he used regularly. This request had yielded a letter to stationmas-
ters ordering that he receive "every courtesy and consideration" from the
Atlantic Coast Line, and a far less positive response from the Southern
Railway System, which told him it "could not well afford to establish a precedent of this kind."[17] His trip to Arkansas highlighted the limits of any attempt to get special treatment. He had no special arrangements of any kind
with Rock Island Railroad, and was treated discourteously despite his
status as an elected official. NAACP president Roy Wilkins was largely con-
temptuous of Mitchell's suit for this reason. He saw Mitchell's legal action
as little more than a breach-of-contract suit motivated by his outrage that a
"Negro [who] got as high as Congressman . . . could not get decent accommodations on a train."[18]

Whatever Mitchell's motives, his lawsuit, which he argued himself with
the help of Chicago attorney Richard Westbrooks, was widely misunderstood
as an all-out assault on Jim Crow. Headlines about the case proclaimed,
"Mitchell Battles Jim Crow" and "Segregation is target of Ill. Solon
[Statesman]."[19] For all that Mitchell maintained that his suit was based on "a
violation of contract and not the color question," its proceedings quickly became a referendum on Jim Crow.[20] Mitchell and Westbrooks's central legal
argument was that in refusing to allow Mitchell access to Pullman accommodations, the railroad had violated the nondiscrimination clause in the
Interstate Commerce Act, which prohibits businesses engaged in interstate
commerce from subjecting the citizens of any state to "any undue or unreasonable prejudice or disadvantage."[21]

Accordingly, Mitchell's testimony and legal briefs drew a stark contrast between the "poorly ventilated, filthy" Jim Crow car in which he had been forced to ride, and the first-class accommodations that the Rock Island offered to whites who paid exactly the same fare. For three cents a mile, Mitchell and Westbrooks emphasized, whites rode in well-appointed Pullman coaches equipped with drawing rooms, lounges, and smoking rooms that had bathrooms with running water, soap, and towels, and were staffed by porters and offered meal service, whereas Blacks had access to no such amenities. Instead, Blacks occupied a single dilapidated coach, which also housed the train's baggage compartment and provided seating for the train's crew. While Mitchell disavowed accusations that he was "fighting for the social equality of my people in the South," his demand that "the members of the Race get what they pay for" threatened to abolish Jim Crow cars altogether.[22]

Mitchell relished being lauded as a freedom fighter in the Black press, so his claims for his case grew more radical over time. "I am unqualifiedly opposed to all form[s] of racial segregation by public carriers, and otherwise," he announced after *Time* magazine correctly reported that he was crusading for "equal accommodations" rather than the "elimination of Jim Crowism."[23] And he backed up his tough talk with a tenacious court fight. The Rock Island fought his suit tooth and nail, even to the point of replacing "the old battered Jim Crow cars" on its line from Hot Springs to Memphis with "modern streamlined coaches equipped with running water, air conditioning, flush toilets and comfortable seats," in an attempt to eliminate the unequal accommodations cited in Mitchell's complaint.[24] Thanks to these changes, the railroad won concessions that would have discouraged a less determined plaintiff. The Interstate Commerce Commission (ICC), which rarely ruled against the railroads, readily accepted Rock Island's upgrades to its Jim Crow car as evidence that Blacks no longer encountered "undue prejudice" or "unjust discrimination" on the railroad, and dismissed Mitchell's complaint. It then went on to deny his request for a rehearing. Dining service and other parlor car amenities remained unavailable in the railroad's new and improved Jim Crow cars. But the ICC maintained that, given the fact that the railroad had "comparatively little colored traffic," there was not enough demand for such services "to warrant the running of any extra cars or the construction of partitions."[25]

Mitchell was outraged by the ICC's ruling, which did not even pay lip service to securing equal facilities for Blacks. It ignored specific dictates on this issue laid down by the US Supreme Court in *McCabe v. Atchison, Topeka & Santa Fe Railway Company* (1914). The suit was a challenge to the constitutionality of Oklahoma's separate car laws, and *McCabe* was rejected by the Court on procedural grounds. But in ruling on *McCabe,* the Justices acknowledged that Oklahoma law discriminated against "persons of the African race" insofar as it permitted carriers "to provide sleeping cars, dining cars, and chair cars to be used exclusively by persons of the white race." "If facilities are provided," the Court instructed, "substantial equality of treatment of persons traveling under like conditions cannot be refused. . . . The essence of the constitutional right to equal protection of the law is that it is a personal one, and does not depend upon the number of persons affected."[26]

Convinced that the ICC's decision violated federal law, Mitchell sued the ICC for dismissing the case, first in the Northern District of Illinois federal court, and then in the US Supreme Court when the district court ruled against him. There, the "complex internally divided political system that allowed Arthur Mitchell to hold federal office but not to ride in a first-class car in Arkansas or receive relief from a federal regulatory agency" finally worked in his favor.[27] Mitchell's case attracted the support of Roosevelt's solicitor general, Francis Biddle. A liberal with a commitment to safeguarding the liberties of all Americans, Biddle submitted an influential amicus curiae brief criticizing the ICC's ruling.[28]

On April 28, 1941, the Supreme Court sided with Biddle, and even cited several of his points. Like Biddle, the Justices rejected the ICC commissioners' claims that the comparatively modest demand for first-class accommodations by people of color could "justify the denial of a fundamental right of equality of treatment . . . safeguarded by the provisions of the Interstate Commerce Act" to those who sought out such accommodations. "It is the individual," the Court maintained, restating its dictum from *McCabe,* "who is entitled to the equal protection of the laws—not merely a group of individuals, or a body of persons according to their numbers."[29]

Narrowly worded, the *Mitchell* decision posed no direct threat to the railroad's use of Jim Crow cars for coach-class travel. It held only that Blacks who purchased first-class tickets had a right to "accommodations equal in comforts and conveniences to those afforded to first-class white passengers." Still, it was widely hailed by Black newspapers (and some white ones) as a decisive victory in the battle against travel segregation. "Jim Crow Car Gets a Death Knell" was the headline in the *Detroit Plaindealer;* the *Pittsburgh Cou-*

rier ran the headline "High Court Upholds Mitchell: Present Type of Jim-Crow Coaches Doomed."[30] Such interpretations of the case were encouraged by Mitchell, who had been promising "the dawn of a new day in Negro travel accommodations" ever since the Supreme Court agreed to hear his appeal. A decision in his favor would "upset a whole caste system in the South," he had maintained in a widely cited interview with the Associated Negro Press. "The railroads have said they could not comply and stay in business."[31]

Such predictions help explain the widespread jubilation unleashed by the Supreme Court's ruling in *Mitchell*. Although *Pittsburgh Courier* editor P. L. Prattis would later concede to Roy Wilkins that his paper's headlines exaggerated "the fundamental value of the Mitchell decision," he insisted that he did not overstate the importance of the decision to both Blacks and whites in the South. "Both regard it as highly important," he explained. "I was in Columbia, S.C., when the decision was made known. You would have thought Joe Louis had just won the heavyweight championship of the world."[32]

The response within the NAACP was decidedly more mixed. Roy Wilkins was annoyed to see Mitchell feted as a civil rights pioneer for winning what he saw as little more than a "breach-of-contract action."[33] Wilkins's irritation was no doubt heightened by that fact that as he celebrated his victory, Mitchell went out of his way to let reporters know that the NAACP had played no part in his victory and that he had even rejected the organization's offer to file an amicus curiae brief. Although less bitter than Wilkins, other NAACP leaders, such as Walter Francis White and Thurgood Marshall, also downplayed the significance of Mitchell's victory.[34]

As the nation's premier civil rights organization, the NAACP was flooded with questions about the case—and even received some congratulations for winning it. But the organization's leaders could not provide support to members who asked them to confirm that it "*completely invalidates* the Jim Crow car for any passenger crossing state lines." Instead, given the fact that some newspapers were reporting that Blacks now had "equal train rights," the organization's leaders felt compelled to dampen public expectations about what kind of changes the case might bring.[35]

To that end, Walter White issued a press release on *Mitchell v. United States* on April 29, 1941—one day after the case was decided. "The decision goes no further than the one handed down . . . in the 1914 case of *McCabe v. Atchison, Topeka & Santa Fe Railway*," it maintained. "Both decisions ignore the fundamental issue of segregation and provide merely for substantial equality. . . . The time for real jubilation and belief that democracy is being attained will come when the courts unequivocally strike down all methods and modes of segregation."[36]

White's quelling analysis of the impact of the Mitchell case was not wrong: in fact, it was echoed by southern state officials, who were relieved that the Court's ruling did not challenge the constitutionality of Arkansas's Jim Crow laws. "It is travel as usual," they maintained. "The present state of segregation as practiced in the South is unaffected by the opinion."[37] Yet coming as it did on the cusp of the United States' entry into World War II, the Mitchell case had a far greater impact than these commentators anticipated. Promoted by Mitchell as promising an end to Jim Crow, the case became a mandate for protests against segregated transportation.

Mitchell's court fight had inspired similar battles while it was still wending its way through the lower courts, and became still more inspirational after his victory, especially once the nation entered World War II.[38] During the war, the mobilization of Black and white soldiers, along with the boom in the nation's defense industries, put unprecedented demands on the nation's transportation system at a time when Blacks had lost all patience with traveling Jim Crow. Challenges to segregated transportation proliferated—so much so that by 1944 even Roy Wilkins would have to admit that Mitchell's victory had had an impact. That year he described the "frequent flare-ups over . . . [Jim Crow travel] facilities" that marked the war years as being, at least in part, a product of the *Mitchell* ruling. Blacks were taking "spontaneous advantage of the court decision in the case," he explained. "Countless instances have been reported of Negroes in the Southern hinterland boarding trains and quoting this decision to conductors and others."[39]

TRANSPORTATION AND RACIAL CONFLICT DURING WORLD WAR II

Transportation emerged as a major site of racial conflict early in the war. As railroads and buses throughout the country filled up with the countless soldiers and civilians put into motion by the war, transportation of any kind was increasingly difficult to secure. In November 1942, Roosevelt's Office of Price Administration further compounded this transportation crunch by ordering mandatory gas rationing. The nation was not short of fuel, but it was desperately short of the rubber supply needed to keep its military vehicles moving, as most of the world's rubber came from the rubber tree plantations of Southeast Asia, which had fallen under Japanese control. Tire rationing began as early as 1941, and was subsequently reinforced by gas rationing. Designed to eliminate all nonessential civilian driving, these measures put unprecedented demands on the nation's railroads and buses. In the South, especially, the overcrowding fostered greater contact than usual between the races, and resulted in daily altercations between Black and white travelers.

As we have seen, race relations on buses were particularly volatile. By regional custom, southern whites boarded buses first, leaving Blacks to take whatever seats remained in the rear of the bus once all white passengers had secured seats. As wartime bus usage soared, Black riders who abided by this unwritten racial etiquette often found themselves waiting for hours, or even days, as white passengers filled one bus after another. Those who insisted on claiming some of the space traditionally allotted to them in the rear of the bus had to force their way onto crowded vehicles, and push through white passengers to get to the back of the bus.

Not surprisingly, given these conditions, the war years saw almost daily fights between Black and white passengers, as well as numerous clashes between bus drivers and African American passengers. These conflicts sometimes escalated into serious violence. "Scores of Negroes have been beaten and arrested in Memphis, Tennessee; Beaumont, Texas; Columbus, Georgia; and Jackson, Mississippi, for insisting on transportation on buses overcrowded because of war conditions," Black correspondent Bayard Rustin reported in the summer of 1942.[40] Rustin would go on to be a pivotal leader in the 1963 March on Washington two decades later.

Conditions on the railroads were not much better. The railroads almost doubled their riders during the war years, but did not add additional Jim Crow cars, so Black travelers were often forced to wait many hours for trains that would take them. In the fall of 1943, one Black New Yorker reported having spent twenty-four hours in the railroad station of Rocky Mount, North Carolina, waiting to catch a train home. During that time she witnessed nine or ten northbound trains arrive and depart, all of which "received white passengers but refused to receive any colored passengers."[41]

Accommodations on Jim Crow cars, which had always been bad, became even worse during the war years. Faced with a shortage of passenger

Waiting for a bus at the Memphis station, September 1943.

accommodations of all kinds, some southern railroads turned over all of their Jim Crow car seats to white travelers and started to carry Black passengers in their baggage coaches—alongside "corpses, dogs, trunks and what-have-you."[42] African American travelers were sometimes assigned to prison cars. Specially built coaches with steel bars lining their windows and doors, these cars were built to transport federal prisoners and were used to carry POWs during the war. But according to the *Chicago Defender*, such trains also "occasionally [provided] compulsory methods of travel for Negroes between Atlanta and New Orleans."[43]

The fact that Blacks had to ride in separate cars made race relations less explosive on southern trains than on buses. But violence could flare up even on the trains, especially when Black passengers challenged segregation in any way. On a trip through Mississippi on September 2, 1942, a Morehouse College professor, Hugh Gloster, was "beaten, fined and imprisoned" for approaching the train's conductor to request "that Negroes standing in the Jim Crow car be permitted to move to [an] empty white car adjoining."[44]

Indeed, even leaving their Jim Crow cars could expose Black travelers to violence. A few weeks after Gloster's beating, two African American ministers, who were traveling to a meeting of the National Baptist Convention in Memphis in a Pullman coach chartered by the Baptist Church, were assaulted when they left their coach to speak to some fellow Baptists who were traveling in the Jim Crow car. To get there, they had to pass through two coaches occupied by whites. Reverend S. A. Young took a punch that broke his eyeglasses from a white man who ordered him to "go back" to his own car. After they had turned and were headed back to their car, the other minister, John C. Jackson, the seventy-six-year-old head of the New England Negro Baptist Convention, was punched by another passenger, who broke his glasses and left him with cuts and bruises.[45]

Wartime travel conditions were particularly hard on Black soldiers. The War Department's official policy on transportation "imposed no distinction based on race, color or creed" on members of the armed forces when traveling on commercial carriers, but soldiers were also bound to "all existing laws to the same extent as the general public."[46] In practice, this meant that white soldiers, sailors, and other military personnel who traveled in uniform could generally expect priority seating on buses and trains, whereas Black soldiers who traveled in and out of the South had more limited options.

"It has been my frequent experience to see trains on which Negro soldiers and civilians [are] packed in inadequate coaches and on the platform[s] of these coach[es] while in the next coach and a number of coaches following, there have been vacant seats available for white soldiers and civilians which were unused," wrote Colonel Campbell C. Johnson in 1943 in a "Memorandum on Transportation Facilities for Negroes" that he submitted to General Hersey in the spring of 1943. The crowding was sometimes exacerbated by the fact that "it was the practice of white MP's to bring intoxicated white soldiers back into the Negro coach for detention because their vile language and general actions were revolting to white passengers." Even Black soldiers who traveled on army-issued Pullman sleeping car tickets had to endure these conditions. "Although they have orders, and are told they have reservations for such accommodations, very often [they are] unable to secure them."[47]

Buses were often off-limits to soldiers stationed in the South as well, noted Johnson, who had visited army bases in Virginia, North Carolina, South Carolina, Georgia, Florida, Alabama, Mississippi, Louisiana, Texas, and Arkansas. Throughout the region, it was "the common practice of bus companies serving army camps to not permit any Negro soldiers on the buses until all the white soldiers had been taken care of." This "intensification of the normal practice of permitting Negroes to occupy the rear seats in buses" could keep soldiers leaving on furlough trapped in camp—or force them to try their luck hitchhiking. "No one thing is doing so much to sabotage the morale of Negro soldiers and civilians," Johnson concluded, "as the system of separate accommodations known popularly as jim-crow, as it is practiced against Negro men in uniform in the South."[48]

These concerns were shared by William H. Hastie, who served as the civilian aide to Secretary of War Henry Stimson from 1940 to 1942, as well as by his assistant and successor, Truman K. Gibson, who held the position between 1943 and 1946. Civilian aide was a new position created by Roosevelt in response to pressure from civil rights activists. The civilian aide was charged with representing the interests of Black servicemen. In accepting the appointment, Hastie, a former federal court judge who had been dean of the Howard University School of Law before returning to federal service, had hoped to press for the desegregation of the military from within. But he and Gibson would spend much of their time fielding complaints about racial discrimination and anti-Black violence on buses and trains filed by Black service personnel. Most of these complaints involved Black soldiers who had been stranded without transportation, ejected from Pullman cars, or beaten or shot by bus drivers, but they also included well-publicized reports of African American soldiers having to travel across the country without food because they were "refused service" in railroad dining cars.[49]

Hastie opposed segregation in the military and worried that the mistreatment of Black servicemen could "lead to rioting at any time."[50] He tried to tackle these problems by helping the NAACP press for reform. With Hastie's covert support, NAACP executive secretary Walter White took up the issue of transportation segregation with Joseph B. Eastman, director of the Office of Defense Transportation, who initially seemed willing to find a way "to suspend the application of Jim Crow law for Negroes in uniform," if the negative effect of these laws on Negro soldiers could be documented.[51] But even when the NAACP submitted the information Eastman requested, Eastman refused to act. Walter White had proposed that the Office of Emergency Management use the powers granted to it by Executive Order 8989, which had established the Office of Defense Transportation, to require that all carriers engaged in interstate commerce "cease and desist from . . . segregating members of the United States armed forces and defense workers on account of race or color, all or any laws, customs and usages to the contrary." While Eastman professed to deplore the lack of respect shown to Black servicemen on Jim Crow buses and trains, he replied that White's proposal went too far. "If I were to attempt to set aside the Jim Crow laws by order . . . or recommend to Congress that they be set aside," he explained, "the general opinion, certainly in the South and probably in other parts of the country, would be that I was taking advantage of the war to accomplish a social reform having only a slight relation to efficient transportation."[52]

Truman Gibson took over Hastie's post as civilian aide when Hastie resigned to protest the Army Air Command's commitment to "Jim Crow Air Training." Gibson faced similar problems. He spent much of the war trying to convince the Office of Defense Transportation that "the problem of Negro Transportation in the South is becoming increasingly serious," but none of the cases he documented, or memos on the problem he circulated, ever had much of an effect. Commanders at army bases across the South generally turned a blind eye to segregation, even on vehicles owned by the army.[53] Gibson later glumly concluded that neither he nor Hastie had ever been able to do more than "put out the fires—and the riots in the South." They had no opportunity to develop any "real change in basic Army policy." White southerners were determined "to keep these people in their places, and to not get any ideas, in particular these boys from the North." Instead of challenging white southern prejudices, the Army went along with them. "The Army was not a sociological laboratory," Army chief of staff General George Marshall "constantly reiterated," ignoring the ways that its own policies engineered the experiences of Black soldiers. "You cannot change the attitudes of the community."[54]

Among Blacks, however, attitudes toward Jim Crow were changing in ways that help explain why wartime conflicts over segregated transportation were frequent and often explosive. The overcrowding, inconvenience, and substandard service that African Americans experienced while traveling in the South was only one cause for the growing frustration that Black soldiers and civilians expressed during the war years. Resentment over being relegated to Jim Crow cars ran high even before the war, and it soared when the United States mobilized to go to war in "defense of freedom." "Throughout the war years," historian Bryant Simon has noted, "in thousands of subtle and dramatic ways, black people stopped playing their part in the public theater of segregation. They refused to tip their hats for whites, make room for pedestrians on jammed sidewalks, or give up their seats on crowded buses." These "seemingly uncoordinated assaults on Jim Crow" were especially common in the realm of transportation, where wartime conditions made the "public theater of segregation" increasingly difficult to maintain.[55]

Black enlisted men from both the North and the South often proved unwilling "to take the insults they [might have] swallowed as civilians."[56] They felt that their uniform and status as citizens working in the service of their country should command respect and were unwilling to be rudely ordered around by southern bus drivers and railroad conductors. The flare-ups over segregated travel and transit were "not . . . confined to Northern Negro Soldiers training in the South," reported Roy Wilkins in 1944. "Truth be told *all* Negroes except the hat in hand variety deeply resent this separation."[57] Likewise, the writer Sterling Brown, who traveled the South during the early 1940s, observed a "new militancy in Negroes who were Southern born and bred," regardless of whether they had ever left the South. The protests he heard ranged from "the quietly spoken aside, through twisted humor and sarcasm to stridency." In anecdotes that spread like folktales, Black southerners had begun to lionize "a new sort of hero—the Negro soldier who, having taken all he could stand, shed his coat, faced his persecutors and said: if I've got to die for democracy, I might as well die for some it of right here and now."[58]

Civilian militancy was also common, especially among women employed in the defense industries or by the military. Irene Morgan worked at a defense plant that manufactured B-26 Marauders. Other women who defied Jim Crow during the war years included navy employees Caroline K. Johnson and Mildred Turpin, who were arrested after refusing to move to the back of the Arlington-Fairfax bus they used to travel back and forth from their homes to the Navy Annex building in Arlington, Virginia. In refusing to

move, Johnson and Turpin told the bus driver that "it was their right . . . as
Government employees . . . to sit anywhere on the bus."[59] Even after spending
a night in the Arlington County Jail, they remained defiant. Charged with
violating Virginia's Jim Crow laws, Johnson and Turpin pleaded not guilty.
And when they lost, they appealed their conviction, even though the judge
had suspended the sentence they received—which consisted of a fine and
court costs.

THE WARTIME LAWSUITS

As more and more wartime travelers battled Jim Crow, the NAACP could no
longer put the transportation issue on the back burner. As complaints about
discrimination on trains and buses poured in, the NAACP's legal department
began taking more travel cases, while also working to strategize an effective
legal assault on Jim Crow. Whereas the organization's national office had once
discouraged travel segregation cases, by 1945 it had one hundred transportation cases in federal and state courts and was still taking on more.[60] Flush
from a ninefold increase in membership during the war years, the NAACP
had been able to hire additional staff for its legal office and make a commitment to litigating "a steady stream of cases seeking the breakdown" of segregated transportation.[61]

Many of these cases came in through its regional offices in the South, where
leaders such as Alabama's John LeFlore had long pressed the national office to
do more to address conditions on southern railroads and buses. In 1943 Thurgood Marshall finally agreed to support LeFlore in his struggle to secure
Pullman accommodations in the South. In the wake of the *Mitchell* decision,
many railroads were still refusing to make first-class facilities freely available to Blacks—who were often told that Pullman car seats were sold out,
and were typically permitted to eat in railroad dining cars only after all the
train's white passengers had been served. On the Louisville and Nashville
Railroad, as Thurgood Marshall noted in a letter summarizing some of the
"numerous complaints" his organization had received, "Negroes are not permitted to eat . . . until it is time for the crew to eat and then are required to
eat behind very heavy curtains . . . as if they were convicts or lepers, or alien
enemies, rather than full American citizens." Worse still, while white passengers could "eat in the body of the dining car at any time they see fit,"

Blacks often had to "wait six to eight hours" for seats behind the curtain.[62] Similar conditions prevailed on the Gulf, Mobile and Ohio Railroad, where John LeFlore and Alfred S. Crishon—another leading member of the Mobile, Alabama, NAACP—were denied Pullman and dining car seats in June 1943.

Filed with the ICC later that year, *LeFlore and Crishon v. the Gulf, Mobile and Ohio Railroad* went nowhere. The facts of the case were clear enough. The two men were told that there was no space in their train's Pullman cars on a trip from Meridian, Mississippi, to Mobile, Alabama, only to later observe "unused space" in these cars and be told by the train's Pullman porter that they were instructed to "sell only enclosed space to Negroes." LeFlore and Crishon were also unable to eat dinner or lunch because each time they presented themselves "the steward expressed regret that he was under orders not to serve colored people at the same time white people were in the diner."[63]

Despite the abundant evidence of illegal discrimination, the ICC examiner who reviewed the facts of the case sided with the railroad, which had maintained that it was bound by the state laws of Mississippi and Alabama to supply "separate accommodations for white and colored passengers," and was therefore unable to seat LeFlore and Crishon in the "open area" of a Pullman being used by whites. The examiner also accepted the railroad steward's claim that he had offered to bring food to LeFlore and Crishon at their seats and been refused. The railroad was not at fault, the ICC examiner concluded. State laws did not permit the railroads to "serve both classes of passengers concurrently in the dining car." If the "complainants went without food," it was "because they were unwilling to eat . . . anywhere except in the dining car."[64] On May 8, 1945, the ICC ruled unanimously that LeFlore and Crishon had not been subject to "undue prejudice."[65]

LeFlore, who found the ICC's decision "grossly unfair," wanted to take the case on to the US Supreme Court, which he hoped would once again rule in favor of "equal travel rights for all citizens"—as it had in Mitchell's case.[66] But although Thurgood Marshall agreed that the ICC's decision was deeply flawed, the NAACP was unwilling to take the case any further. The case "was not the type of case which should be taken to the Supreme Court," Marshall told LeFlore. The issue was partly that in his ongoing battle with the railroads, LeFlore had been arguing for better segregated accommodations, and at one point before the case, had even sent a letter to the Gulf, Mobile and Ohio Railroad suggesting improvements that could be made in the segregated services offered to its colored patrons. "The NAACP under no circumstances ever makes suggestions for methods of segregation which we will accept because we are opposed to segregation in all forms," thundered Marshall, who had just learned of this letter.[67] LeFlore's letter could be a liability were the case to go forward.

More to the point, the NAACP had better cases in the pipeline. The organization's litigation strategy, another NAACP lawyer explained to LeFlore, was to abandon all but its strongest cases "if we are unsuccessful up to a certain stage."[68] By the spring of 1945 it had several promising cases in Virginia, where the state conference of the NAACP branches had developed an especially strong interest in fighting Jim Crow transportation.[69] A gateway to the South, Virginia was a perennial hotspot for racial incidents on trains and buses. Its border with the District of Columbia was a point where many southbound Black travelers shifted from integrated to segregated seating, and it lay within commuting distance of both Washington, D.C., and parts of Maryland. Oliver Hill, Martin A. Martin, and Spottswood Robinson—the Richmond law partners who handled most of the Virginia NAACP's litigation—spent the war years fielding transportation cases.

One of the cases they took was that of Irene Morgan, who had made her impromptu stand against segregation in Virginia and proved an ideal litigant for an attack on Jim Crow statutes. Whereas most of the travel complaints flooding the NAACP's various offices came from people who were charged with "disorderly conduct after refusing to move when ordered to comply with Jim Crow statutes," Morgan had been charged with violating Virginia's segregation statute.[70] The NAACP's national office and its Virginia conference collaborated on *Morgan v. Virginia* and won largely on the strength of the argument developed by Spottswood Robinson, a young Howard Law School graduate who was emerging as one of the NAACP's transportation specialists. Robinson had commuted between Richmond and Washington, D.C., on crowded trains during the war years and had seen Jim Crow cars at their worst. He developed an outline for an attack on Jim Crow based on the proposition that "segregation on interstate facilities violated a constitutional rule that states cannot enact laws that interfere with the flow of interstate commerce."[71]

The NAACP thus appealed Morgan's segregation violation by challenging the constitutionality of Virginia's statute requiring the separation of Black and white bus passengers. This separation imposed an undue burden on commerce, argued Thurgood Marshall and William Hastie, who led Morgan's legal team. Because segregation was required in some states and banned in others, an interstate passenger might have to shift seats repeatedly over the course of the same trip. Moreover, Jim Crow laws varied from state to state—as did definitions of who was Negro and who was not. "Unless the Supreme Court makes clear that conflicting local statutes cannot be imposed on interstate travel," they concluded, "serious and burdensome confusion must result."[72]

Virginia's supreme court rejected their argument, but the nation's high court did not. On June 3, 1946, the US Supreme Court struck down a Virginia law requiring racial segregation on commercial interstate buses as a violation of the commerce clause of the US Constitution. Seating arrangements for the different races in interstate motor travel, the Justices concluded in a 7–1 ruling, "require a single uniform rule to promote and protect national travel."[73]

Morgan v. Virginia was the NAACP's first transportation case before the US Supreme Court, and it was a momentous victory. Although the ruling was limited to *interstate* travel, its target was a Virginia *state* law requiring segregated intrastate travel. For the first time in its history, the Court overturned a state statute requiring segregation on public carriers.

But for all the excitement surrounding the decision, it had remarkably little practical effect. In its aftermath, Greyhound's Richmond office announced that it would no longer require its bus operators to separate passengers, regardless of whether they were traveling interstate or intrastate. However, its new policy did not last long. As southern officials across the region were quick to underscore, intrastate transportation segregation was required by law. By contrast, the requirements laid down by the *Morgan* decision were open to interpretation. While the Court's decision held that state segregation statutes put an undue burden on interstate commerce and were therefore unconstitutional, it did not prohibit the carriers themselves from regulating the movements of their interstate passengers.

Accordingly, shortly after the *Morgan* decision, southern bus lines began enacting company regulations designed to segregate passengers. Richmond's Greyhound Bus Company, for example, abandoned its open seating policy in favor of a new "system of numbering tickets for seating on its buses," which effectively seated passengers in "the traditional Jim Crow pattern. . . . Tickets sold to colored people called for seats in the rear only."[74] Other companies were more direct and reinstituted segregation by simply posting signs stating that "white passengers should occupy the space nearest the front and colored

James H. Thomas, twenty-three, of Washington, D.C., boards an Arnold Bus at 12th & Pennsylvania Avenue NW for a trip to Virginia on June 4, 1946, the day after the Supreme Court ruling that outlawed Jim Crow seating on interstate buses. The case, *Morgan v. Virginia*, originated in Essex County, Virginia.

passengers nearest the rear" in terminals and on buses.[75] The state of Virginia moved to make sure that local officials could enforce these regulations now that its segregation law no longer applied to interstate passengers. It did so by passing a new disorderly conduct statute that made it a crime for any person "to create an unnecessary disturbance on a bus—by failing to move to the rear when lawfully requested to do [so] by the driver."[76]

Morgan had a similarly limited impact on railway Jim Crow. Initial doubts about whether it applied to trains were resolved when the editor of the *Baltimore Afro-American*, Ralph Matthews, and two other men won a lawsuit against Southern Railway System after refusing to move into its Jim Crow car in Washington, D.C. But even after the District of Columbia federal circuit court ruled that there was "no valid distinction between segregation in buses and in railroads cars" in *Matthews v. Southern Railway System* (1946), southern railway companies continued to segregate their passengers on the grounds that the circuit court's jurisdiction was limited to Washington, D.C.[77]

These developments were enormously discouraging to the NAACP's legal team. By presenting no explicit ruling against segregation, *Morgan* left decisions about segregation on interstate carriers to the carriers themselves, making them still harder to challenge in court. The Fourteenth Amendment held that no state could deny any person within its jurisdiction "the equal protection of the laws," but it did not prohibit private discrimination. Indeed, in striking down the Civil Rights Law of 1875, the Court had maintained that Congress had no power to regulate private discrimination. Private owners of inns and other public accommodations were not engaged in state action, and were therefore simply exercising ordinary property rights when they picked and chose their clientele.

In 1946 Thurgood Marshall charged his legal team with finding some basis for "attacking the carrier which continues to enforce segregation on its own," but the meeting did not "give birth to any sure fire legal techniques."[78] The organization kept taking cases, but by 1947 Marshall was convinced that segregated transportation might be best addressed outside the courts. He began to urge the NAACP to throw its support behind a bill banning discrimination in interstate transportation proposed by New York congressman Adam Clayton Powell, rather than making further attempts to address this issue in court. "The more we dig in the question of Jim-Crow Transportation," he wrote in a memorandum to Walter White, "the more it becomes apparent that we should double our efforts for passage by Congress of the bill to prohibit segregation in interstate commerce. Our chances of upsetting the present system of segrega-tion by rule of the carrier . . . are slim from a legal standpoint."[79]

Powell's bill never received serious consideration, and Black challenges to segregation continued. Like the *Mitchell* decision, *Morgan v. Virginia* embold-ened African American challenges to Jim Crow. The company regulations that railroads and bus companies now invoked to maintain segregation were not well publicized. Many were genuinely confused about the legal status of segregation—including not just passengers but also the bus drivers and railroad employees charged with enforcing the new regulations. As a result, clashes over Jim Crow seating became ever more numerous, and the NAACP was flooded with complaints and legal work.

As of early December 1946, just six months after the *Morgan* decision, the Virginia branch of the NAACP was handling nineteen new transporta-tion discrimination complaints just involving buses, and hearing reports of many more.[80] And by the fall of 1947 the NAACP's national office was so "swamped with this kind of case" that its lawyers were unable to take on any more. The best they could do was to advise their branch offices to make "some arrangement with private attorneys" to help potential litigants.[81]

THE JOURNEY OF RECONCILIATION

The persistent and highly contested state of interstate transportation after the *Morgan* decision was well documented in the NAACP's files, and was also evi-dent during the 1947 Journey of Reconciliation. Designed to assess and chal-lenge the decision's impact on Jim Crow transportation, this pioneering ex-periment in nonviolent direct action was organized by two closely interrelated organizations, the Congress of Racial Equality (CORE) and the Fellowship of Reconciliation (FOR)—a Pacifist organization that originated during World War I. Founded by members of the Chicago chapter of FOR in 1942, CORE embraced a program of nonviolent resistance to segregation. Its earliest ac-tivities included sit-ins at Chicago restaurants, theaters, and other public facilities.

Guided by the same philosophy of nonviolent direct action, the Journey of Reconciliation involved sending a group of interracial travelers—eight Black men and eight white men—to test whether southern carriers were complying with the Supreme Court's decision in *Morgan*. They aimed "to discover the reaction of bus drivers, passengers, and police to those who nonviolently and persistently challenge Jim Crow in interstate travel."[82]

The "guiding spirit" behind this expedition was Bayard Rustin, a thirty-five-year-old Black Quaker. Like most members of CORE and FOR, Rustin was an admirer of the nonviolent civil disobedience campaign that Indian leader Mohandas Gandhi had used to overturn British rule in India. A fierce and fearless social critic, Rustin incorporated the principles of nonviolent resistance to unjust laws into his daily life. He functioned, his biographer Jervis Anderson writes, "as a one-man civil disobedience movement in his travels across the United States. He occupied 'white only' railroad cars; sat in at 'white only hotels' and refused to budge unless he was forcibly ejected."[83] Such behavior was unquestionably dangerous. It exposed Rustin to a roadside beating by the Nashville police in 1941, as well as many minor misadventures further north.[84] But Rustin's model of civil disobedience also provided Rustin and George Houser, the white war resister and CORE co-founder who planned the Journey of Reconciliation along with Rustin, with an answer to the question of how to make sure the *Morgan* decision was actually honored.

In planning the trip, Houser and Rustin consulted with civil rights leaders across the country, most of whom took a dim view of their plan. Thurgood Marshall, Houser later recalled, was "not a direct actionist, he believed in legal action."[85] Given that his job as special counsel to the NAACP had required him to investigate "every instance of white-on-black race riots since 1940," Marshall trusted neither the police nor America's white public. Any "disobedience movement on the part of Negroes and their white allies," he warned, "if employed in the South, would result in the wholesale slaughter with no good achieved."[86] Likewise, other leaders told Rustin the plan was "absolutely insane"—with the exception of Roy Wilkins, who thought that the journey might "invigorate NAACP branches in the South that found ways to participate."[87] Wilkins's help gave Houser and Rustin access to the NAACP's network of lawyers and local branches, and allowed them to proceed with their planning despite the many warnings about the dangers they would face. They did take the precaution of limiting the trip's route to the Upper South, where the risk of violence was not as high as it would have been in the Deep South. They also decided to limit the trip's participants to men, for fear that "mixing both the races and the sexes would exacerbate an already volatile situation."[88]

The Journey of Reconciliation began on April 9, 1947, and proceeded relatively smoothly—at least in comparison to the 1961 Freedom Ride that it

The Journey of Reconciliation—the first Freedom Ride, 1947. Standing outside the office of attorney S. W. Robinson, Richmond, Virginia, are (left to right): Worth Handle, Wally Nelson, Ernest Bromley, Jim Peck, Igal Rodenko, Bayard Rustin, Joe Felmet, George Houser, and Andy Johnson.

would ultimately inspire. The interracial group of participants started their trip in Washington, D.C., where they spent two days in civil disobedience training and discussion prior to their departure. From there they split into two groups to test both the Trailways and Greyhound bus lines, and traveled through much of Virginia without incident—largely because state officials had "passed the word down that it does not want any application involving the Irene Morgan decision brought to trial."[89] The first of the twelve arrests to take place over the course of the trip came as the bus riders were leaving St. Petersburg, Virginia, for Raleigh, North Carolina. Conrad Lynn, a Black lawyer traveling on the Trailways bus, was arrested for violating the bus company's rules by sitting up front. The arrests multiplied in North Carolina, as did the threat of violence. Three more members of the group were arrested in Durham, North Carolina.

The trip's most chilling moments came in Chapel Hill, where four members of the group were arrested, while the rest were left to face a hostile crowd of taxicab drivers outside the bus station. They assaulted James Peck, one of the white riders, who received "a hard blow to the head" for "coming down here to stir up the niggers." A near riot ensued, forcing the travelers to flee to the house of a local minister and arrange a caravan of cars to take them to Greensboro.[90] From there they resumed their trip, which was largely uneventful thereafter, despite additional arrests in Asheville, North Carolina, and Charlottesville, Virginia.

The Journey of Reconciliation went well enough that it left Rustin and Houser cautiously optimistic about the possibility of using nonviolent direct action to desegregate the South's interstate buses. One of the Journey's missions was educational. With this end in mind, the group had made a point of engaging the many bus drivers and passengers they encountered along their route in dialogue about Jim Crow. In doing so, they found bus passengers, policemen, and bus drivers alike to be confused about the status of Jim Crow on buses in the South. Many "either did not know of the Morgan decision, or if they did, possessed no clear understanding of it." As a result, the bus drivers and police were often unsure about what to do with travelers who insisted on defying segregation by sitting in the wrong section of the bus. Some left them alone, and few were up to date on the newly central status of bus regulations in the enforcement of Jim Crow. "When they took a stand," Houser and Rustin wrote in their report on the trip, "they tended to act on the basis of what they knew—the state Jim Crow law."[91]

White passengers, they found, were largely "apathetic" in the face of challenges to Jim Crow. Except in Chapel Hill, all of the negative reactions were verbal and relatively mild. One South Carolinian said of Conrad Lynn, who had again seated himself in the front of the bus for the group's trip from Greensboro to Winston Salem, North Carolina, "In my state he would either move or be killed." But "he was not particularly angry as he said this," Rustin and Houser noted in their report on the Journey. He remained "calm" as Ernest Bromley "talked to him about the Morgan decision."[92]

The Journey of Reconciliation participants encountered passengers of both races who supported their mission. When two Black members of the group were arrested for sitting in the front of the bus in Chapel Hill, one white passenger refused to serve as a witness for the bus company, saying, "I'm a damn Yankee and I think this is an outrage." The group received quieter forms of support from several southern white women, who "not only defended those who broke with Jim Crow, but gave their names and addresses offering to act as witnesses." The Black passengers they traveled with gave the Journey's participants still more cause for hope. Many were initially alarmed to see them defy Jim Crow regulations, but they were quick to take inspiration from it. "Where cautious Negroes saw resistant Negroes sitting unmolested near the front," Rustin and Houser reported, "they tended to move from the rear to the front too."

The trip left both men convinced that the "great majority of the people in the upper South are prepared to accept the Irene Morgan decision and to ride on buses and trains with Negroes." Even the apathy that many whites had displayed was a promising sign, they maintained, explaining that they had witnessed "one white woman," who after "reluctantly taking a seat beside a Negro man, said to her sister who was about to protest that she should take care: 'I'm tired. Anything for a seat.'"[93]

Rustin and Houser's report closed with a few suggestions on how nonviolent direct action could be used to challenge transportation segregation. But the Journey of Reconciliation did not inspire a mass movement—or not, at least, in the short term. CORE was a small organization with a largely midwestern membership, and as scholar John Emilo notes, it did not have the manpower or the "infrastructure of organizations and activist relationships across the South" needed to "launch a sustained region wide assault of Jim Crow."[94] Instead that assault would continue to be led by individual Black travelers and the lawyers who represented them.

LEGAL VICTORIES

The next decade brought a series of successful court cases against transportation segregation that eviscerated the legal foundations of Jim Crow travel but had little impact on actual practices on carriers. At issue in many of these cases was the questions of the carriers' compliance with the US Supreme Court's decisions in *Morgan* and *Mitchell*, which they continued to "ignore and frustrate."[95]

Launched in 1942, but not decided until 1950, *Henderson v. United States* is a case in point. The case was initiated by Elmer W. Henderson, a Black lawyer who worked as a field representative for President Franklin D. Roosevelt's

Fair Employment Practices Committee (FEPC), and focused on the humiliations of the dining car. Largely off-limits to Blacks prior to the Mitchell case,
the dining car was an amenity to which Blacks continued to have only
limited access even after the Supreme Court ruled that all railroad services
and accommodations had to be available to both races. Still prohibited by regional laws and custom from serving Blacks and whites together, southern
railroads began to "effect compliance" with the Court's decision by installing
curtains in front of the two dining car tables closest to the kitchen. "If Negroes are eating, the curtains are drawn, thus providing 'separate but equal
accommodations,'" explained Black lawyer Marjorie Mackenzie, describing
the new system in a 1942 newspaper column.[96]

This new approach was far from foolproof. If the dining car filled up before any African American passengers arrived, the curtains were pushed back
and white people were seated at the "two theoretically reserved tables,"
leaving no space available for Black diners. Such were the conditions that prevailed when Elmer Henderson tried to secure a meal on a Southern Railway
train on a business trip from Washington to Birmingham on May 17, 1942.
Henderson headed for the dining car at 5:30 p.m., immediately after the first
call for dinner was announced, fully expecting to enjoy a quiet meal behind
the curtain. But when he reached his train's dining car, the curtain was open
and both of the Negro tables were partially occupied by whites. He asked
to be seated in one of the seats that remained available, but was refused. The
dining car's steward told him to return to his seat and wait to be notified
when he could be served. Henderson complied, but never heard back. Eventually he returned to the dining car, only to find the tables reserved for
colored passengers still partially occupied by white passengers. He demanded
to be seated and served, only to be turned down again. He was refused one
more time when he returned half an hour later—at which point "white people
were being served in all parts of the car and interspersed were empty
tables and empty seats."[97] Henderson was still waiting for a meal at 9 p.m.
when the train reached Greensboro, North Carolina, where the dining car
was taken off.

Furious, Henderson filed a complaint with the Interstate Commerce Commission alleging that Southern Railway had "unjustly discriminated against
him . . . by failing to furnish him with dining car service equal to that furnished White passengers." His lawsuit was handled by Belford V. Lawson,
an African American lawyer who managed to persuade his Alpha Phi Alpha

fraternity brothers to provide support for what would turn out to be an eight-year-long battle for justice. With the help of this Black fraternity, Lawson took Henderson's complaint to the ICC, to federal district court, and back to the ICC again, before finally securing a hearing in the US Supreme Court.

The ICC dismissed the case twice, largely because Southern Railway changed its dining rules to make any repetition of Henderson's experience unlikely. The railway reconfigured its cars to reserve "one four-seat table at the kitchen end of the diner exclusively for blacks" (while setting aside all others exclusively for whites). No longer behind a curtain, this table was now fenced off from the rest of the car by a wooden partition. Pro-industry and pro-southern in their biases, the commissioners were willing to accept these new arrangements as a sufficient remedy for the discrimination experienced by Henderson. After all, one table amounted to 8 percent of the seating space in the railroad's dining cars, whereas Black patrons typically accounted for fewer than 5 percent of the passengers served in these cars.

But Lawson would have none of it. So long as Blacks could sit at only one of the dining car's tables, while whites could occupy any of several different tables, he maintained, the dining cars were still discriminating against Blacks. Should any more than four Black passengers ever wish to eat in the dining car at the same time, one would have to wait for a vacant seat at the Jim Crow table, even if seats were available at other tables. Moreover, the solitary kitchen-end table allotted to African American passengers exposed them to the heat, odor, noise, and traffic from the kitchen. Lawson was also unimpressed by the wooden barriers the railroad had installed to replace the Jim Crow curtain, and objected to Blacks having to "sit behind partitions, like cattle."[98]

After the ICC dismissed Henderson's case for the second time, Lawson took it to the Supreme Court, where, as one of the hearing's observers noted, he "took on Jim Crow in the field of transportation using every weapon available to a lawyer at that time."[99] He argued that Southern Railway's dining car policies ran contrary to the ICC's language barring carriers from subjecting anyone who made use of their services to "undue and unreasonable prejudice." He further argued that the railroad's policies violated the commerce clause of the US Constitution by subjecting Black passengers to the kind of ever-changing segregation regulations that the Supreme Court, in *Morgan,* had barred the states from imposing on interstate travelers. If the states could not impose Jim Crow laws on such travelers, he contended, then "why should the carriers be any different?"[100] And finally, he topped it all off with a bold argument that took on *Plessy v. Ferguson* by contending that Southern Railway had denied Elmer Henderson his Fourteenth Amendment rights to due process and equal protection.

Lawson's argument was "a brazen position for a private attorney to take in 1950," recalléd Dovey Johnson Roundtree, who attended the Supreme Court hearing as a Howard University law student.[101] But it was far from inappropriate, given the remarkable circumstances under which Henderson finally received his Supreme Court hearing. As luck would have it, Henderson's case came before the Court during the same week as two of the NAACP's most crucial education cases, *Sweatt v. Painter* (1950) and *McLaurin v. Oklahoma State Regents* (1950), both of which questioned whether graduate programs that segregated students by race could really be considered separate but equal. Taken together, the three cases were an all-out assault on *Plessy*.

Lawson's attack on *Plessy* had the influential support of US attorney general J. Howard McGrath and the nation's solicitor general, Philip B. Perlman. These men spoke on behalf of the Truman administration at a time when the nation's executive was beginning to show some support for desegregation. Although born and raised in a segregated town in Missouri, Harry S. Truman, who became president upon Roosevelt's death in 1945, overcame his southern upbringing to display a cautious commitment to civil rights that may have been shaped by strategic concerns such as securing the support of northern Black voters and addressing Soviet critiques of Jim Crow.[102] Anxious to avoid alienating southern Democrats, his administration made use of the Justice Department to achieve "social policy objectives not readily obtainable in Congress."[103] Accordingly, McGrath, who represented the federal government in the case, conceded that the ICC had "erred in sanctioning segregation on the railway." He described the Supreme Court's "separate but equal" ruling in *Plessy* as "an anachronism which a half-century of history has shown to be a departure from the basic constitutional principle that all Americans, regardless of their race, color, religion or national origin, stand equal and alike in the light of the law."[104] Perlman spoke still more forcefully on Henderson's behalf, presenting an amicus brief that made Dovey Johnson Roundtree want "to shout out halleluiahs from the Howard Bell Tower."[105]

The "segregation of Negroes, as practiced in this country, is universally understood as imposing on them a badge of inferiority," Perlman told the Court, using Henderson's experience on Southern Railway to illustrate his point. "The curtain which fences Negroes off from all other diners exposes, naked and unadorned, the caste system which segregation manifests and fosters. A Negro can obtain service only by accepting or appearing to accept, under the very eyes of his fellow passengers, white and colored, the caste system which the segregation signifies." He closed by urging the Supreme Court to find that the segregated dining car violated the Interstate Commerce Act. And in doing so, he further noted that if the Court needed to reconsider the "separate but equal" doctrine so long marshaled in segregation's defense, it should reject it as a "constitutional anachronism" that subjected Blacks to "humiliation on the pretense that they are being treated as equals."[106]

Perlman also supported the NAACP's drive to overturn *Plessy* in two more amici curiae briefs he drafted in support of *Sweatt* and *McLaurin,* which urged the "court to repudiate the 'separate but equal doctrine' as an unwarranted deviation from the principles of equality before the law." In the end, the Supreme Court stopped short of taking on *Plessy* in all three cases. But the Justices inched in that direction with a set of unanimous decisions rejecting segregation in all three cases. Issued on June 5, 1950, the Court's ruling held that the segregated educational programs challenged in *Sweatt* and *McLaurin* could not guarantee Blacks an equal education, and that Southern Railway's dining car segregation regulations violated the Interstate Commerce Act. Although *Plessy* remained in place, Blacks across the country celebrated what the *Chicago Defender* termed "the mightiest blow for freedom and full citizenship of Negro Americans since the Civil War."[107] Segregation might still exist, but it was no longer fully legal.

"The complete destruction of all enforced segregation is in sight," Thurgood Marshall told the forty-second annual NAACP convention at the end of 1950, and he was right—at least with regard to segregation's legal moorings, which crumbled during the next half decade.[108] In 1954 the Supreme Court finally repudiated *Plessy v. Ferguson* in its famous *Brown v. Board of Education* decision, which held that "in the field of public education, the doctrine of 'separate but equal' has no place." Just as *Sweatt v. Painter* and *McLaurin v. Oklahoma* helped pave the way for the NAACP's legal victory in *Brown v. Board of Education, Henderson v. United States* laid a path for further inroads against segregated transportation. Just a year after *Henderson,* a federal district court decision on the Virginia case *Chance v. Lambeth* (4th Cir., 1951), invalidated the railroad carrier regulations that forced Blacks to change seats on north-to-south trips. (Similar regulations on buses had already been struck in *Whiteside v. Southern Bus Lines* in 1949.)

Elmer Henderson orders a meal on a train after his victory in *Henderson v. United States*, 1950.

But all of these decisions had a limited impact on segregation as practiced by the carriers, which continued to find ways to circumvent the relatively narrow rulings laid out by the courts. Some railroads that offered through tickets from Chicago to Florida maintained segregation while honoring *Chance* by segregating their Black passengers in Chicago, rather than requiring them to move when the train entered the South. Other lines simply avoided offering through services to Black passengers, who had to instead "change to new cars and trains at transfer points."

Such arrangements required the railroads to divide the train reservations by race, an improbably complex process that they achieved in a variety of subtle and not so subtle ways. "In Southern cities, and occasionally in northern and border points," a 1952 Fisk University study reported, passengers were often simply asked, "'Are you colored or are you white?' or 'do you want space in the Negro car or the white car?' or 'in what car do you want space?'" Meanwhile, in northern cities such as Chicago, railroad reservations agents used addresses, telephone prefixes, and conversational "clues" to divine the race of passengers who sought reservations by phone. If they guessed wrong, the railroad ticket agents would find ways to "make a correction" when the passenger came to pick up his or her ticket—usually either by changing the reservation or "pretending a conflict exists with the original assignment."[109]

In the face of such practices, African Americans turned again to courts seeking ever more sweeping rulings against Jim Crow. In 1955 these efforts would finally score a pair of landmark decisions from the ICC that outlawed Jim Crow on interstate transportation. One of these cases was *Sarah Keys v. Carolina Coach Company* (1955), which was brought by Dovey Johnson Roundtree, who by then had graduated from Howard University and started a small law firm in Washington, D.C., with one other partner, Julius Winfield Robinson. Although "dirt-poor rookie lawyers," Roundtree and Robinson were willing to file a complaint for Sarah Keys, a member of the Women's Army Corps (WAC), at a time when most of the city's lawyers who were affiliated with the NAACP had their hands full helping Thurgood Marshall prepare for *Brown*. The case took shape in 1952, when Keys, who was then twenty-two, was traveling from Washington, D.C., to her home in Washington, North Carolina, to enjoy a brief furlough. She was thrown off her Carolina Trailways bus and arrested in Roanoke Rapids, North Carolina, after refusing to yield her seat at the front of the bus to a white Marine. Keys's arrest was deeply troubling to Roundtree, who had had similar experiences as a WAC during World War II. It underscored, as Roundtree later recalled, "how little had changed in nine years' time . . . despite the Supreme Court's decision in *Morgan*." The "carriers simply circumvented that ruling" and continued to "impose their own regulations on black passengers."[110]

Roundtree and Robinson sought to put an end to these practices, first by suing Carolina Coach Company, and then, when that suit foundered on issues of jurisdiction, taking her complaint to the ICC. Known for its "unyielding position on segregation," the ICC seemed like a long shot. But with *Brown* before the Supreme Court, they hoped the ICC would be forced to regard Keys's complaint with the "utmost seriousness."

Launched in 1953, their complaint "marched in step with *Brown*," and remained under investigation long enough to give the young and overstretched lawyers an opportunity to incorporate the Supreme Court's *Brown* verdict into the brief they submitted to the ICC. In its wake, they argued, "it could no longer be doubted that any regulation requiring segregation of passengers in interstate commerce on the basis of race is not only unreasonable but unlawful."[111] Their case acquired additional potential impact in 1954 when the ICC chose to hear it in tandem with a railroad discrimination case, *NAACP v. St. Louis-San Francisco Railway Co.* A compendium of complaints against twelve railroads by seventeen individual passengers, this case challenged the "lawfulness, under the Interstate Commerce Act, of racial segregation of interstate passengers" and asked the ICC to issue a "cease and desist order."[112]

Initially it seemed as if these cases would be no more successful than most previous travel segregation complaints filed before the ICC. *Brown* applied only to public education, the ICC's examiner maintained in his report: it had no bearing on the conduct of private businesses, such as carriers.

But the seismic social and political shifts that had made *Brown* possible finally caught up with the ICC. Federal support for desegregation had been made plain in the deliberations that preceded the *Brown* decision, and the Supreme Court was unlikely to retreat from the position it had taken in that case. In the week after *Brown*, the Justices declined to review lower court orders desegregating municipal golf courses in Houston and a public housing project in San Francisco—decisions suggesting that they believed that their decision in *Brown* overthrew more than just school segregation. The Eisenhower administration also favored outlawing Jim Crow on interstate transportation and submitted a brief to that effect to the ICC. And finally, the ICC itself had changed. Once known as "the Court of the Confederacy" for its strong southern representation, by 1955 its members included many recent Eisenhower appointees with "no strong personal stake in past rulings supporting Jim Crow customs."[113] On November 1, 1955, in a set of decisions with only one dissenting vote—cast by J. Monroe Johnson, a seventy-seven-year-old South Carolina Democrat—the nine-member ICC ruled in favor of Sarah Keys and the NAACP.

With these decisions, the ICC "rejected the separate but equal doctrine for the first time in its history."[114] In doing so, the commissioners conceded that the *Brown* ruling had a "direct bearing" on the *Keys* and *NAACP* complaints, and at long last admitted that the "assignment of [segregated] seating" on trains and buses "was designated as to imply the inherent inferiority of a traveler solely because of race or color, [and] must be regarded as subjecting the traveler to unjust discrimination, and undue and unreasonable prejudice and disadvantage."[115] Whereas *Morgan* had challenged the power of states to segregate interstate travelers, the ICC's ruling addressed the carriers. It ordered the Carolina Coach Company and the St. Louis–San Francisco Railway Company to stop segregating interstate passengers both on their carriers and in their waiting rooms and other terminal facilities as of January 10, 1955.

Newspapers around the country once again announced the end of Jim Crow transportation. "ICC Orders End Segregation on Trains, Buses—Deadline, January 10," announced the *New York Times;* the *Pittsburgh Courier* ran the headline "The ICC Ruling: End of an Era."[116] But again Jim Crow travel arrangements outlived these predictions. It soon became clear that the ICC's ruling had some important limitations. First, its "cease and desist orders" named only the defendants in the *Keys* and *NAACP* suits, leaving other carriers at least theoretically free to continue to segregate interstate passengers. Some took advantage of this loophole. The Richmond-Greyhound Bus Company, for example, chose to retain notices dividing its "colored" and "white" passengers, while making "no effort to enforce recognition of these signs." The ICC order was directed against "certain carriers named in a lawsuit," in which the "Richmond-Greyhound was not a defendant," explained the company's president, L. C. Major. Although he was fully aware that "principles involved in these proceedings will be equally applicable to us," Major further explained that his company had "to comply . . . [with] the laws of the state of Virginia."[117]

The dilemma facing the Greyhound Company in reconciling state law with the ICC's new ruling underscored the second and most critical check on the ICC's power to desegregate the carriers: the Commission had no power over intrastate passengers. The Commission's ruling left the segregation laws of the southern states untouched, which meant that the railroads and bus companies that complied with the ICC's ruling could not simply remove their "white" and "colored" signs. Instead, they had to replace or amend them with signs that read "Colored Waiting Room Intrastate Passengers" and "White Waiting Room Intrastate Passengers."

Deliberately or otherwise, the new signs discouraged desegregation of any kind. Many travelers found the legal distinction between intrastate and interstate passengers confusing, and both custom and law made African Americans wary of disobeying segregation signs, regardless of where they happened to be traveling. Thus, segregation persisted on many buses and trains as well as in bus stations and railway terminals, making it seem like little had changed. Bus companies could no longer legally require such passengers to move to the back, but most instructed their drivers "to ask . . . interstate Negro

A Black airman from New York City reads the "Colored Waiting Room" sign in the segregated Terminal Station in Atlanta, Georgia, 1956.

passengers to move to the rear." Not surprisingly, given the racial hierarchies of the region, such carriers reported that "most interstate passengers comply with this request."[118]

In the Deep South, compliance with such requests was often mandatory. There, local officials were often not content with merely dodging the ICC's desegregation order; they openly defied it. In Jackson, Mississippi, the local police replaced the Illinois Central Railroad's segregation signs immediately after the railroad took them down, and stationed patrolmen in the city's railroad depot and bus station to make sure that the ICC's "nonsegregation order" did not cause "any disturbance."[119] "Signs dividing the races" remained up in the Delta towns of Gulfport and Greenwood and in Atlanta's Southern Railway terminal, where NAACP staffer Clarence Mitchell was discouraged to see a twenty-year-old "blue electric sign" still pointing "a tired finger to a grimy waiting room" when he passed through that city in 1957.[120] In Louisiana this open defiance of the ICC's desegregation ruling had the support of state governor Robert F. Kennon, who maintained that the ICC order was unlawful and ordered "all officials to continue rigid enforcement of state laws requiring the separation of races within its borders."[121]

Instead of desegregation, the ICC's ruling created "a checkerboard pattern of compliance and defiance" that made travel segregation even more difficult to navigate.[122] Visiting Georgia two years after it went into effect, Clarence Mitchell found the South's "crazy quilt pattern of segregation affecting the traveler . . . increasingly bewildering in an age of rapid transit." Segregation still persisted in the airport restrooms at the Atlanta airport, but the "white" and "colored" signs were smaller, so much so that an incoming traveler who was "in a hurry or had poor eye sight" might miss them altogether. But should the "hapless individual" who ignored these notices catch the attention of an aggressive policeman or a disgruntled white traveler, he could easily wind up "in a fist fight or jail cell when all he wanted to do was wash his face."[123]

In the Deep South the *Brown* decision and the ICC ruling both helped foster a "massive resistance" to integration that made any prospect of voluntary desegregation ever more unlikely. Meanwhile, the ICC would do little to enforce its own ruling. The Commission had no law-enforcement arm, and shortly after the *Keys-NAACP* ruling, J. Monroe Johnson—the sole dissenter on the ruling—advanced to the chairmanship of the ICC. He would then use this position, as Dovey Johnson Roundtree notes with some bitterness in her autobiography, to "do everything in his power to prolong its segregationist tradition."[124]

Looking back on Johnson's ascent, Roundtree could only rue the optimism that had made her so convinced that the *Keys* ruling would allow "white and black alike . . . to ride together across the state lines of 48 states." The change she sought, she later realized, was held back by "forces and individuals none of us could have imagined when we celebrated the triumph of *Keys v. Carolina Coach Company*"—including "the intentions of J. Monroe Johnson," whose appointment to the top job on the ICC she had not anticipated, and worse, the fact that there were "thousands of J. Monroe Johnsons across the South, then, more than I had been willing to acknowledge."[125] Changing the law, it seemed, would only take desegregation so far.

7

Traveling for Freedom

The Desegregation of American Transportation

THE SOUTH'S CRAZY-QUILT PATCHWORK PATTERN OF TRAVEL SEGRE-gation was still holding strong when CORE dispatched another interracial group of travelers on another trip south on May 4, 1961. Segregation on trains and buses remained entrenched throughout much of the Deep South even during the tumultuous first years of the civil rights movement. It survived even the highly publicized yearlong boycott that finally won African Americans in Montgomery, Alabama, the right to sit where they wanted to on their city's buses. The historic protest, which marked the beginning both of the modern civil rights movement and of Martin Luther King Jr.'s career as its leader, gave African Americans new reasons to believe that transportation segregation had finally been vanquished. In the aftermath of *Browder v. Gayle* (1956), the Supreme Court case in which Montgomery Blacks successfully challenged the state statutes and city ordinances requiring segregation on Montgomery's buses, newspapers across the nation once again proclaimed "Bus Segregation Is Knocked Out."[1] But *Browder* had little immediate impact outside Montgomery and a few other cities. In most southern communities, it was ignored by officials, who insisted that *Browder* applied only to Mont-gomery.[2] These obstructionist tactics were especially common in Alabama, Mississippi, Georgia, and Louisiana, where, as of 1960, "Jim Crow transit still prevailed in all but three communities."[3]

The desegregation of southern transportation remained at an impasse, de-spite almost two decades of court rulings that had all but eliminated any legal basis for Jim Crow carriers and travel facilities. And in December 1960, Jim Crow travel seemed poised to survive yet another legal rebuke.

On that date the NAACP scored yet another legal victory in the field of interstate transportation in the case of *Boynton v. Virginia*, which overturned a judgment against Bruce Boynton, a Howard University Law School student from Selma. Boynton had been convicted of trespassing in December 1958 after attempting to order a sandwich and a cup of tea in the whites-only restaurant during a layover at the Richmond bus station as he traveled home for Christmas in 1958. Although the racial segregation of interstate bus stations and railway terminals had been outlawed in *Keys* and *NAACP*, these rulings had not banned segregation in terminal restaurants: most remained segregated, even in depots otherwise free of Jim Crow.[4] With *Boynton* the NAACP successfully challenged such segregation, winning a judgment in which the Court conceded that where restaurants "operate[d] as an integral part of the bus carrier's transportation service for interstate passengers," they must serve interstate passengers "without discrimination."[5] In the short run, however, *Boynton* proved to be another pyrrhic victory. A couple of bus lines took down their signs, but Jim Crow persisted in eating establishments at most southern bus stations.[6]

Bruce Boynton's one-man protest against segregation gained new significance in the spring of 1961, when it inspired the leaders of CORE to revisit their organization's 1947 Journey of Reconciliation. They decided to send another group of integrated travelers south on a two-week bus trip. This one would test compliance with the *Boynton* decision. Although still a primarily northern organization, CORE was increasingly active in the South in the aftermath of *Brown*. Energized both by the decision and by the protests it inspired, CORE had provided nonviolence training to protesters who participated in the Montgomery Bus Boycott and the 1960 student sit-in movement. By 1961 the organization was ready for a "bold initiative in the Jim Crow South."[7] James Farmer, who became the director of CORE in February 1961, took reports that the *Boynton* decision was not being enforced as a mandate for action. A founding member of CORE, Farmer had not participated in the Journey of Reconciliation, but he remembered it well and saw it as an ideal model for a new protest designed to pressure the federal government to enforce the *Boynton* decision. This time the bus riders included both men and women, and they traveled in two groups to test the persistence of segregation in the Trailways and Greyhound Bus systems. They also planned to brave the Deep South. They left Washington on a bus route that would take them through Virginia and North Carolina, and on to South Carolina, Georgia, Alabama, and Mississippi, before finally terminating in New Orleans.

Like the Journey of Reconciliation, the "Freedom Ride" of 1961 was small. It began with only thirteen people. The riders' hopes of making "bus desegregation a reality instead of merely an approved legal doctrine" must have seemed wildly improbable.[8] James Farmer's press releases and letters outlining the Freedom Riders' plans attracted virtually no notice, and only a couple of newspapers mentioned the riders' departure from Washington, D.C.[9] The letters Farmer sent out to notify various travel officials and federal authorities about the trip elicited even less attention. When asked many years later whether the Justice Department had made any attempt to discourage the Freedom Ride, Farmer could only laugh and explain that none of his letters to the Justice Department, or any other authority, had received any response. "We got no from reply from Justice. Bobby Kennedy, no reply. We got no reply from the FBI. We got no reply from the White House, from President Kennedy. We got no reply from Greyhound or Trailways. *We got no replies.*"[10]

However, by the time CORE's small band of Freedom Riders reached the Deep South, their journey had exploded into a national news story that put the injustice and ugliness of Jim Crow travel on display for all the world to see. Unlike the Journey of Reconciliation, this Freedom Ride would not be a little-noticed protest that later became a largely forgotten footnote in the history of travel desegregation. It would become *the* news story of 1961, and the event is still credited today with ushering in the end of segregated transportation. The Ride was transformative. It played a crucial role in mobilizing the Justice Department to help secure the civil rights of Black travelers, spurring other successful travel desegregation initiatives—including the "Freedom Highways" campaign dedicated to desegregating roadside accommodations, and the "freedom fly-ins" protesting segregation in southern airports—and helped build momentum for the Title II Civil Rights Act of 1964, which banned racial discrimination in public accommodations. In this chapter I chronicle these interconnected developments.

THE FREEDOM RIDERS

Largely ignored as they traveled through Virginia and North Carolina, the riders did not encounter any serious opposition until they reached the Deep South. On May 4, John Lewis, who was to become one of the nation's most prominent African American congressmen but was then a nineteen-year-old veteran of the Nashville student sit-in movement, was beaten up by two "tough-looking white youths" when he attempted to use a white waiting room in Rockhill, South Carolina.[11] White freedom rider Albert Bigelow suffered a similar fate when he tried to intervene. And two more riders were arrested for integrating a lunch counter in Winnsboro, South Carolina, the following day. The riders would then get through Georgia without incident, only to have all hell break loose in Alabama.

Home to some of the South's most fervent segregationists, Alabama had been mobilizing "massive resistance" to desegregation since *Brown v. Board of Education.* The fierce opposition to federal civil rights legislation among the state's leaders only intensified in the wake of the Montgomery Bus Boycott and the federal court-ordered admission of Autherine Lucy to the University of Alabama; Lucy was the university's first Black student, and her appearance on campus triggered a week-long riot. The man elected governor of Alabama in 1958, John Malcolm Patterson, came into office with the endorsement of the Ku Klux Klan and was committed to using his position and power to resist desegregation. Patterson made no effort to protect the Freedom Riders as they traveled through his state, and law enforcement authorities throughout the state followed his lead.

Warned to expect trouble in Birmingham, the riders found it before then in Anniston, an army town and KKK stronghold less than an hour from the state's eastern border. There, the Greyhound bus carrying one of the two groups of Freedom Riders was attacked by white men carrying knives, clubs, and lead pipes. The mob managed to smash the bus's windows and slash its tires before the Anniston police finally arrived. The police held back the white vigilantes long enough to allow the bus driver to try to steer his passengers to safety by setting out for the highway. But "a line of cars" followed the bus as it lurched out of town, catching it easily six miles west of Anniston, where it was brought to a halt by a flat tire. Once the bus stopped, the mob attacked again. The mob was breaking out the bus's windows and "reaching for passengers" when one of its members lobbed a firebomb into the bus. "In a matter of seconds, the bus was enveloped in a fog of thick, black, choking, smoke" and then rocked by an explosion that scattered the mob and sent the passengers scrambling out of the now-smoldering bus.[12] Amazingly, all of them managed to escape with no more than minor injuries before the bus went up in flames.

The second busload of Freedom Riders fared little better. When their Trailways bus pulled up in Anniston about an hour after the first bus left, eight

Freedom Riders outside their burning bus at Anniston, Alabama, May 14, 1961.

white men got on and forced the Black Freedom Riders to move to the back of the bus. When their white companions objected to this, they too were "pushed, punched and kicked."[13] One of them, Walter Bergman, received a blow to the head that resulted in brain damage—although the seriousness of his injury did not become apparent for some time. The group then traveled on to Birmingham, escorted by their white assailants, who rode in front. A segregationist mob armed with blackjacks and lengths of pipe greeted them at the Birmingham Trailways station. When the Freedom Riders entered the station, the mob rioted. White assailants beat up Freedom Riders James Peck, Charles Person, Ike Reynolds, and Walter Bergman, and assaulted several local newsmen who were on hand to cover the conflict. Unlike the mob and the newsmen, local police were nowhere to be found. It was later discovered that the Birmingham commissioner of public safety, a committed segregationist named Eugene "Bull" Connor, had promised the Ku Klux Klan members fifteen minutes in which they could attack the Freedom Riders without police intervention.[14]

After the police finally dispersed the mob, the Freedom Riders eventually managed to regroup with the help of Birmingham's Black community. Local civil rights activist Reverend Fred Shuttlesworth opened his home to those who had reached Birmingham, and personally led a convoy of armed Black drivers to Anniston, where they picked up the Freedom Riders from the first bus, who had been taken to Anniston's hospital for treatment and were stranded there. The next day both groups of riders returned to the Birmingham bus station, having voted to continue with the ride despite their injuries. Even James Peck, who was covered with bandages and had fifty-three stitches in his head as a result of the beating he received in the Birmingham bus station, insisted on going. "For [even] the most seriously beaten rider to quit," he told his fellow riders when some of them urged him to fly home to recuperate, "could be interpreted as meaning that violence had triumphed over nonviolence. It might convince the ultra segregationists that by violence they could also stop the Freedom Riders."[15]

Peck and other CORE activists were also anxious to capitalize on the fact that the bus burning and beatings had made their protest journey front-page news across the country and beyond. Reporters had captured photographs of their Greyhound bus burning and of Peck's battered face. They had put the violence that sustained the South's system of Jim Crow transportation on display for all the world to see, at a time when the still relatively new medium of television had begun to beam these images directly into the living rooms of Americans across the country, creating a highly public national crisis over the integration of interstate transportation that the federal government could not ignore.

The events in Anniston and Birmingham horrified the Kennedy administration and left the newly inaugurated president anxious to see the Freedom Riders get out of Alabama with no additional casualties. He had his brother Robert F. Kennedy—the nation's attorney general—and the Justice Department push local and state authorities to provide protection for the Riders, but to no avail. Governor John Patterson refused Robert Kennedy's direct request that he secure the group's safe passage through Alabama. "The citizens of this state are so enraged," Patterson replied, "that I cannot guarantee protection for this bunch of rabble rousers."[16]

Patterson's obstructionism was effective in the short term and made it impossible for Peck and his fellow Freedom Riders to continue by bus. With no state protection forthcoming, drivers for Trailways and Greyhound were not willing to drive them to Montgomery. After being stranded at the Birmingham bus station for hours, the Freedom Riders decided to fly to their destination,

New Orleans, rather than continue on by bus. But they had initiated a show-down between the Kennedy administration and Alabama authorities that would continue.

John Lewis, who had left the ride to interview for a fellowship in Nash-ville shortly before the other riders crossed into Alabama, was at a picnic with friends and fellow activists from the Nashville Student Movement when news of the violence broke. As the reports came in on the radio, the students be-came increasingly worried about the survival both of the Freedom Riders and of the Freedom Ride itself. They began talking about "mobilizing reinforce-ments" a full day before the CORE group decided to fly to New Orleans.[17] Once they got word of that decision, the students swung into action and quickly organized a new cadre of "fresh nonviolent troops" to complete the ride.[18] Dispatched with the reluctant approval of CORE leader James Farmer, who warned them "it may be suicide," a new group of ten Freedom Riders arrived in Birmingham on May 17, 1961—just two days after the first group left.

With the arrival of these fresh young activists, the Freedom Rides began to transform into the mass movement so long envisioned by CORE members. Everyone in the small initial group of riders dispatched from Nashville was a participant in the Nashville Student Movement—a coalition of student activ-ists that operated under the "semiofficial" sponsorship of the Nashville Chris-tian Leadership Council. The activists in the Nashville Student Movement also had ties to the Student Nonviolent Coordinating Committee (SNCC)—a national organization with members in colleges across the country.[19] In re-starting the Ride, the Nashville activists envisioned a national movement that would recruit and organize successive waves of Freedom Riders to sustain the movement until it met its goals. They appointed Chicago native Diane Nash, a Nashville Student Movement leader and former Fisk University student who had quit school to work full-time for SNCC, to coordinate the planned waves of riders. Nash also acted as the movement's media liaison. Without ever leaving Nashville, she would be the point person who negotiated with the Kennedy administration to secure buses and federal protection for the riders.

The Kennedy administration was understandably horrified to see the Freedom Ride resume. President Kennedy had been anxious to avoid embar-rassing headlines at a time when he was preparing for a June summit meeting in Vienna with Soviet premier Nikita Khrushchev. He was enraged when he heard news of the violence in Birmingham. "Can't you get your goddamned friends off those buses?" he had asked Harris Wofford, a Justice Department official with close ties to the movement. "Stop them," he demanded. Now the problem was even more urgent. Burke Marshall, the president's special deputy for civil rights, reached out to Justice Department official staffer John Seigenthaler, who was from Nashville, telling him, "You come from that Goddam town. . . . If you can do anything to turn them around, I'd appreciate it."[20] But although Seigenthaler managed to get Diane Nash on the phone, he could not get her to consider postponing the Nashville Freedom Riders' departure. "You are going to get your people killed," he warned her. If that happened, she replied without missing a beat, "then others would follow."[21]

A similar spirit sustained the first wave of new riders. Alabama's leaders remained unrepentant. On hearing that a new group of Freedom Riders were on their way to Birmingham, Governor John Patterson denounced them as "rabble rousing agitators" and refused to protect them.[22] When they arrived in Birmingham, they were arrested and jailed overnight by law enforcement officials who subsequently drove them to the Tennessee border and left them there, after telling them, "You can take a bus back to Nashville."[23] Three days later, when they finally made it to Montgomery, the riders were mobbed by white men carrying pipes and baseball bats. In the melee that followed, the mob beat up the student activists and also several reporters and bystanders, including Kennedy aide John Seigenthaler—who was beaten unconscious and left in the street for nearly half an hour after he tried to help two of the Freedom Riders.

When news of the attacks reached Washington, Robert Kennedy was appalled. He dispatched four hundred federal marshals to Montgomery to protect the Freedom Riders. However, racial violence erupted again the following night when the riders regrouped at Reverend Ralph Abernathy's First Baptist Church, where more than fifteen hundred people had gathered to honor them. Among the speakers at the church that night were Martin Luther King Jr., James Farmer, and Fred Shuttlesworth. Still, the focus of the event soon shifted to the steps of the church, where a mob of several thousand whites had gathered. "Rocks, bricks and Molotov cocktails rained down on the church grounds," reported the *Cleveland Call and Post*, while a line of about a dozen federal marshals armed with nightsticks and tear gas struggled to keep the mob from storming the church itself.[24] Short-staffed because most of the men mobilized by Kennedy were still on their way to Montgomery, the marshals could not control the rioters. The white mob shattered several of the church's windows, and was on the verge of breaking into the church itself when Governor

Patterson finally decided to take action. Aware that Kennedy was closely following events in the church and was about to call in the National Guard, Patterson moved to block further federal action by deploying local police as
well as a force of more than one hundred Alabama National Guardsmen to
disperse the rioters.

In the aftermath of the church attack, the Freedom Riders again resumed
their trip, over the objections of Robert F. Kennedy, who had suggested that
they create a "cooling-off period" by postponing any further action.[25] "To
stop now would be a disaster," John Lewis and other students maintained:
"There was too much commitment, too much momentum. The Freedom Ride
had taken on a life its own."[26] Although some of the student riders from Tennessee State University had to drop out because they were being threatened
with expulsion by Tennessee governor Buford Ellington, Diane Nash had new
volunteers coming in from across the country. Meanwhile, the Justice Department was working behind the scenes to ensure the safety of the riders.
Jackson, Mississippi, was their next stop, and it promised to be even more
dangerous than Alabama. Segregationists there, Justice Department officials
feared, "were even more prone to vigilantism and violence than their Alabama cousins."[27] Fortunately, Mississippi politicians were anxious to avoid
federal interference with law enforcement in their state. This allowed Attorney
General Kennedy to secure Senator James Eastland's promise that the Freedom
Riders would not be beaten up in Mississippi. Eastland, however, refused
to guarantee that the riders would be able to travel through Mississippi
without being detained. And so, with Kennedy's tacit assent, he had them
all arrested.[28]

None of the Freedom Riders ever made it to New Orleans. They were arrested as soon as they entered the Jackson bus terminal's whites-only
waiting room. Convicted of "breach of the peace" and sentenced to sixty days
in the state penitentiary, most would go to jail rather than make bail. Their
"Jail, no Bail" commitment was dictated by the Gandhian philosophy of nonviolent disobedience they embraced, which held that paying bail or fines was
tantamount to accepting the immoral system that imposed these punish-
ments. But even the prospect of spending much of the summer in Mississippi's
Parchman State Prison Farm did not stop the movement. Instead, throughout
the summer of 1961, a Freedom Riders Coordinating Committee, organized
by SNCC, CORE, and the Southern Christian Leadership Council (SCLC),
kept a steady stream of students, ministers, and other volunteers rolling

into Jackson, Mississippi. Faced with a problem that would not go away, the Justice Department began looking for long-term solutions. On May 29, Bobby Kennedy reached out to the ICC and asked it to issue regulations banning segregation in interstate bus terminals. Despite the fact that the Supreme Court had clearly outlawed segregation in bus terminals, Kennedy's request triggered months of deliberations among the Commissioners. Well over three hundred Freedom Riders would travel to Jackson, and virtually all of them would end up in jail before the Commissioners acted.[29] On September 22, 1961, the ICC finally issued an order banning segregation in interstate terminal facilities.[30] With that order, the desegregation of interstate transportation would finally begin.

'It was in the end not simply the bloodshed or mass protest or fear that brought [the] promise of *Keys*," wrote *Keys* lawyer Dovey Johnson Roundtree in her autobiography. "It was shame. The whole world looked, and was horrified, at the image of the freedom bus bursting into flames on a highway outside a little Alabama town called Anniston on May 14, 1961. And the whole world—at least the world that was reached by television—saw the young men and women, Black and white, stepping out to bus platforms in Birmingham and being met by mobs of cursing Klansmen armed with clubs and chains, being beaten and bloodied long before they even reached restaurants and soda fountains they were bent on integrating." The shame was inescapable. "There wasn't a politician in the North who didn't raise an outcry," she recalled, "or a preacher anywhere, who didn't join Martin Luther King, in condemning the violence."[31]

Roundtree's analysis of what finally brought the segregation of interstate transportation to a halt might seem simple, but it provides a good point of departure for understanding how desegregation was finally achieved. Common carriers, which were the first form of public accommodation to be segregated by law, were desegregated earlier than any other major public accommodation—largely because, as James Farmer claimed, the Freedom Riders managed to move "the struggle for dignity on the nation's highways from the courts to the conscience of America."[32] In doing so, they built on the accomplishments of Black lawyers and litigants who had challenged travel segregation in the courts for decades, making it virtually impossible to defend on legal grounds. They were also able to capitalize on the fact that travel segregation was becoming an embarrassment to the United States. Once a regional peculiarity that attracted little attention outside the country, by the beginning of the

1960s the South's Jim Crow buses, trains, and public accommodations had become a highly public symbol of the nation's failure to live up to its own democratic ideals.

For this reason, shame—or concern about segregation's potential for embarrassing America in the eyes of the world—played a crucial role in mobilizing the Justice Department to help secure the civil rights of Black travelers, both during the Freedom Rides of 1961 and long after. In the wake of the Anniston bus burning, Robert F. Kennedy publicly implored "travelers, whatever their mission, to stay out of Mississippi and Alabama until the racial tensions in the two states subsides." He was worried that "innocent people may be injured," but he also emphasized that questions of national interest were at stake. "The President was about to embark on a mission of great importance," he explained. On May 31, John F. Kennedy would be meeting with French president Charles de Gaulle in Paris, and would travel from there to meet with Soviet premier Nikita S. Khrushchev in Vienna. "Whatever we do in the United States at this time, which brings or causes discredit on our country, can be harmful to his mission."[33]

His message was reinforced by Edward R. Murrow, the head of the United States Information Agency, who was still blunter in addressing the Cold War concerns that made the Kennedy administration so eager to avoid any more embarrassing racial incidents in the United States. His agency spent $100 billion a year "to combat Red Propaganda abroad," he told an audience at the National Club on May 24, 1961, but "racial violence blunts our efforts." "To some of us," he said, "the picture of a burning bus in Alabama may merely represent the speed and competence of a photographer, but to those of us in the United States Information Agency, it means that picture will be front-paged tomorrow from Manila to Rabat."[34]

Clearly composed with such photos in mind, the petition requesting the "elimination of racial discrimination in interstate bus transportation" that the Justice Department submitted to the ICC in the spring of 1961 emphasized segregation's negative effect on America's image abroad. Although largely dedicated to documenting that there was abundant evidence of such discrimination, the petition also included a three-page letter from Dean Rusk, the nation's secretary of state, explaining that "the efforts of the United States government in international affairs to build the kind of world we want to live in—with peace, prosperity, and justice for all—cannot be divorced from our ability to achieve the same purposes for all the people in our own country." Segregation ran counter to both goals. An example of America's "failures and shortcomings at home," it created "difficulties and embarrassment in foreign relations."[35]

"WITHOUT REGARD TO RACE, COLOR, CREED, OR NATIONAL ORIGIN"

Effective as of November 1, 1961, the ICC's ruling barring racial segregation in interstate transportation took care of some of these difficulties. Applied to both trains and buses, it decreed that interstate transportation vehicles must comply with desegregation orders. It also required carriers to post notices bearing the message "Seating aboard this vehicle is without regard to race, color, creed, or national origin, by the order of the Interstate Commerce Commission" on tickets for interstate travel and in all buses and trains that served interstate travelers.[36] The order also prohibited carriers serving such passengers from using segregated terminals, restaurants, or other travel facilities. Some of these regulations were new, but some were not. As we have seen, segregation survived the ICC's 1955 ruling that banned segregation on trains and buses, which left many observers wondering whether the new ruling would have much of an impact.

Initial reports were not entirely positive. "A number of negroes" who went to bus stations to "test compliance with the ban were arrested when they entered white waiting rooms or sought service in white restaurants," the *New York Times* reported a day after the new ruling was supposed to take effect. Meanwhile, in Jackson, Mississippi, the police posted new segregation signs on the sidewalk outside stations where "the signs inside terminals had been removed."[37]

The Justice Department was prepared for defiance and moved quickly to make sure that the new rules were enforced by launching court cases against states and municipalities that refused to honor the new regulations. In the first few months immediately following the ruling, the Justice Department secured a series of "fast and favorable" federal court decisions that upheld the legality of the ICC's rules, rejected Mississippi's and Louisiana's Jim Crow station statutes, struck down state court injunctions barring desegregation, and required the removal of Jim Crow signs in various cities.[38] In February 1962 these decisions were strongly reinforced by the Supreme Court's ruling in *Bailey v. Patterson*, an NAACP case challenging the persistence of segregation on municipal transit in Jackson, Mississippi. In this case the Court issued a unanimous and unambiguous opinion: "We have settled beyond question that no state may require racial segregation of interstate or intrastate transportation facilities," it stated forcibly. "The question is no longer open; it is foreclosed as a litigable issue."[39]

While the Justice Department defended the ICC's new rules in court, the Commission took the lead on handling violations of its new nondiscrimination rules by railroads, bus companies, and travel facilities used by their passengers. Once it became clear to the carriers that the federal government was committed to upholding the law even in the face of local resistance to integration, the carriers desegregated readily. Not having to divide passengers by race was, Catherine Barnes notes, "simpler and cheaper" than maintaining segregated seats and facilities, and few passengers protested the change.[40] By contrast, owners of independent depots, restaurants, gas stations, and other stores that served bus lines in rural areas of the Deep South were more likely to resist integration. But when they did so, the ICC's Bureau of Inquiry and Compliance worked with the Justice Department and the carriers to force them into submission.

William G. Roberts, the owner of the Snack Bar Cafe in the Southern Railway's terminal in Decatur, Alabama, had little choice but to desegregate after a Black passenger filed a successful discrimination complaint against him with the ICC. The complaint triggered an FBI investigation, which confirmed that his café did indeed segregate Black diners. The Justice Department then negotiated an agreement with the railroad in which the latter promised to cancel the cafe's lease if the discrimination continued.[41] Not all segregationists succumbed to such pressures, however. Lyman Goolsby, the owner of the Rebel Café in the bus station in Winfield, Alabama, closed his business after the ICC "forced" him to serve both Black and white passengers.[42] But compliance was more common. Even in the Deep South, most independent bus station restaurants and other facilities were desegregated by the end of 1962.[43]

In the early 1960s the Kennedy administration was forced to take action on other forms of travel segregation as well. Airport segregation became an issue the administration had to address after the Freedom Rides inspired "freedom fly-ins" challenging segregation at the Jackson Municipal Airport in Mississippi and the Tallahassee Municipal Airport in Florida. The first of these protests was launched by three Black activists who flew in from St. Louis to test the facilities in the Jackson airport on June 7, 1961. A small airport built in the 1930s, the Jackson Municipal Airport had used city funding to add Jim Crow waiting rooms, restrooms, and dining facilities to its terminal when it renovated in the mid-1950s.[44] The Freedom Flyers were arrested when two of them tried to use the white restrooms and a third entered the airport's whites-only restaurant and refused to leave. They were joined the next day by New York State assemblyman Mark Lane and New York NAACP branch president Percy Sutton, who were arrested in the Jackson airport as they began a journey "in to the Deep South . . . to get a first-hand look at the situation there." On landing, Lane, who was white, and Sutton, who was Black, entered the airport's "white" waiting room together and ended up getting "a full view" of the region "from a Jackson city jail cell"—as one news report put it.[45]

Ten days later an interracial group of eighteen ministers and rabbis known as the Interfaith Freedom Riders had a similar experience in Florida. Organized by CORE, the group's members hailed largely from New York and New Jersey and were flying home after a largely uneventful test of bus segregation between Washington, D.C., and Tallahassee when they came face-to-face with the evil they had come south to confront. The brand-new Tallahassee Municipal Airport, which had opened on April 23, 1961, had segregated waiting rooms and restrooms and a "whites only" restaurant—the Savarin Airport Restaurant—which shut down rather than serve the interracial group. When the riders tried to have a meal before their flight, they were confronted by a handwritten sign saying "closed" on the restaurant's plate glass front door. Inside, they could see patrons still finishing their meals. This inspired ten of them to hold a sit-in at the airport rather than fly home as planned. They were arrested the next day on charges of "unlawful assembly."[46]

Neither the Jackson Freedom Flyers nor the "Tallahassee Ten"—as the group that sat in at Tallahassee's airport came to be known—succeeded in desegregating the airports where they staged their protests, but their actions put pressure on the Justice Department to find a way to desegregate the nation's airports. In early June 1961, Assistant Attorney General Burke Marshall was still maintaining that there was virtually nothing the federal government could do to desegregate airports because "the Interstate Commerce Commission had no jurisdiction over the airports and . . . the Federal Aviation Agency was not a regulatory agency in the sense that I.C.C. was." The government had funded the construction of the South's airports, he acknowledged, but it had no jurisdiction over their segregated terminals because the

Freedom Riders being arrested at the Tallahassee Municipal Airport, June 16, 1961.

federal money had been "used for runways, hangars and other parts of the airport while municipal funds were used for racially sensitive waiting rooms and restaurants."[47] By the end of the month, however, the Department of Justice had changed its position. Under increasing pressure from both civil rights activists and the Federal Aviation Administration to take action on airport segregation, on June 26, 1961, the Justice Department launched a series of federal lawsuits challenging airport segregation. Within a very short time, Robert F. Kennedy, who spearheaded this initiative, promised a meeting of the Black press's National Newspaper Publishers Association in 1962 that "it will be possible to fly to any airport in the country without seeing white and colored signs."[48]

One of the first airports the government took on was Moisant International Airport in New Orleans, which was an especially good target for legal action because it had been built with federal funds that the city had agreed were to be reserved for the "use of airline operations, airline employees and general public on a nonsegregated basis." But as historian Anke Ortlepp notes, the Justice Department also challenged segregation at airports that had not "essentially duped federal regulators."[49] Launched in tandem with its case against Moisant, *United States v. the City of Montgomery* targeted segregation at the Dannelly Field airport in Montgomery.[50] Located near the Tuskegee Institute in a town that housed Martin Luther King Jr.'s Dexter Avenue Baptist Church, Dannelly was a priority to the Justice Department, the *Baltimore Afro-American* newspaper told its readers, because it was subject to "more complaints about segregation . . . than any other airport."[51]

In its suit the Justice Department contended that Dannelly Field's segregated waiting rooms, restrooms, and dining facilities put an undue burden on interstate commerce and violated the nondiscrimination provision of the Federal Aviation Act of 1958, which required air carriers to treat their customers equally. Both Blacks and whites were barred from freely using all of Dannelly Field's facilities, the government pointed out, and "Negro and foreign interstate passengers whose flights are delayed," and "who received food checks or vouchers from the airlines entitling them to obtain dinner service at the expense of the airlines," were not able to eat in the airport's Sky Ranch restaurant.[52] The government won its case against the City of Montgomery in the beginning of 1962, which enabled the Justice Department to pressure most of the southern airports that still maintained Jim Crow facilities to eliminate them within a matter of months. Another lawsuit was required to desegregate the Dobbs House Restaurant in Birmingham's airport later that year, and the Justice Department did not succeed in desegregating the "waiting rooms, eating places and other facilities" in Louisiana's Greater Shreveport Municipal Airport until the spring of 1963.[53] With that victory, Kennedy made good on his promise.

An era of transformative change, the early 1960s also saw the federal government work to end segregation on the nation's roads and highways. The Kennedy administration's interest in this issue, much like its other desegregation initiatives, was shaped by a complex mix of strategic and political concerns. Its remarkable campaign to end segregation along Route 40—a road that was once the major thoroughfare between Washington, D.C., and New York City—helps dramatize the many ways in which travel segregation was becoming increasingly incompatible with the nation's diplomatic and domestic goals—and how civil rights activists capitalized on this development.

THE ROUTE 40 CAMPAIGN

As we have seen in previous chapters, the occasional Jim Crowing of dark-skinned foreign dignitaries in airport restaurants and travel accommodations had long been a source of embarrassment to the State Department. But that embarrassment would become acute during Kennedy's first years in office. Previous administrations had been able to brush off the unflattering headlines created by incidents such as the 1955 Jim Crowing of Indian ambassador Gaganvihari Lallubhai Mehta, who was forced to dine in a windowless room in the Houston airport because he was "mistaken for a Negro."[54]

However unfortunate, such incidents remained relatively rare, so long as Haiti, Liberia, Ethiopia, and a few other Black-majority nations stationed their Black diplomats in the Washington, D.C., area—and sent people who could be counted on to avoid any trouble. Starting in the 1940s, Haiti reportedly replaced its "dark-complexioned diplomats" with "mulattoes 'who can pass' or with white Americans"; diplomats from the other countries simply learned to keep out of trouble.[55] Although dark-skinned, "the Ethiopians and the Liberians, who lived here as representatives of their countries for many years . . . knew exactly how to accommodate themselves in the dismal situation," recalled one State Department official. "They never protested, never got into any trouble."

But the same could not be said of the African diplomats who began taking up residence in the United States as a result of the African decolonization movements of the late 1950s and early 1960s. "The Ghanaians and the Guineans and all these new people" were unfamiliar with American customs and "didn't quite believe in a passive policy. They went wherever they pleased."[56]

The United States, rife with racial discrimination that its leadership generally chose to ignore, was totally unprepared for this new cohort of diplomats. In 1960, the year Kennedy was elected, independence movements came to fruition in seventeen sub-Saharan African nations. Kennedy was delighted by this development: he had long been interested in African affairs, and saw the emergence of all these newly independent African nations as an opportunity to enhance American influence in the United Nations. "The sweep of

[African] nationalism," he had maintained as early as 1957, "is the most po-
tent factor in foreign affairs today. We can resist it or ignore it but for only a
little while; we can see it exploited by the Soviets with grave consequences;
or we in this country can give it hope and leadership, and thus improve im-
measurably our standing and our security."[57] However, despite Kennedy's
eagerness to welcome Africa's envoys, he had not given much thought to the
social conditions they would face in the United States. He himself came from
a privileged background and had spent most of his life in Massachusetts. "He
knew few African Americans," notes historian Thomas Borstelmann, "and
had little sense of the impact of the color bar on their lives."[58]

Both Kennedy and the African diplomats who came to Washington during
his administration received a crash course in American racial relations. A
southern town with a long history of segregation, the District of Columbia
had Jim Crow restaurants, hotels, and other public accommodations until
1953. That year, the venerable activist Mary Church Terrell (introduced in
Chapter 1 confronting Reconstruction-era Jim Crow as a little girl) led a successful campaign to reinstate Reconstruction-era legislation banning racial
discrimination in public accommodations in the District.[59] But the city's
housing remained strictly segregated even after that, which made it very difficult for African diplomats to secure suitable lodgings. Like other members
of the city's diplomatic corps, they needed "quarters where, as representatives of their nations," they could receive "United States officials and representatives of other embassies." But they often found it impossible to rent suitable apartments or houses because, as one reporter for the *Washington Post*
noted in 1960, "neighborhoods which are flattered by the presence of a European or Latin Ambassador are hostile to Negroes."[60]

Meanwhile, travel outside of Washington posed an even greater problem.
Created in early 1961 to deal with the issues faced by diplomats of color, the
State Department's Special Protocol Service Section could and did vouch for
visiting African dignitaries with local landlords and housing agents. But once
diplomats left Washington, the visitors often had to navigate segregated territory on their own. "Warned, mostly by one another, not to travel South,"
many tried to steer clear of discrimination, but segregation surrounded them
in virtually all directions. "More than one newly arrived African on a sight-
seeing tour of this region," noted a reporter for the *Washington Post* in 1960,
"has been ejected . . . from a restaurant in Baltimore, or Annapolis." Others
experienced "their first taste of discrimination" before they even reached

Washington for the first time, "when . . . refused service on [a] highway road stand in Maryland or Delaware."[61]

Indeed, roadside incidents on the highway between Washington, D.C., and New York City were so common that in 1961, segregation on Route 40 began to be a major source of embarrassment to the Kennedy administration. During the spring and summer of that year—the same months when they were trying to contain international fallout created by the Freedom Rides—the State Department and the president were also dealing with a mounting diplomatic crisis caused by the treatment of envoys from newly independent African nations on Route 40.

On April 27 John F. Kennedy had to issue a personal apology to William Fitzjohn, the chargé d'affaires for Sierra Leone, who had been denied service by a "hostile and unfriendly waitress" at a Route 40 Howard Johnson's in Hagerstown, Maryland.[62] Fitzjohn, a Columbia University PhD who was not new to the United States, was all the more humiliated by the incident because he had chosen to stop at a Howard Johnson's because the chain had gained a reputation for serving Black customers in the wake of a similar incident on Route 40 in 1957. Back then the staff of another Howard Johnson's in Dover, Delaware, had refused to serve a glass of orange juice to Komla Agbeli Gbedemah—Ghana's minister of finance.[63] That incident had been followed by a round of widely publicized apologies from the State Department, President Dwight Eisenhower, and "various officials at the Howard Johnson chain"—who maintained that discrimination ran contrary to company regulations while admitting that the company did not "dictate policy" to the approximately 220 privately owned restaurants franchised under its name.[64] Other restaurants along the road also continued to turn away African diplomats after Kennedy's public apology to Fitzjohn.

In the two months after Kennedy met with Fitzjohn, there were four more incidents on Route 40, the most egregious of which involved an insult to Adam Malick Sow, the African Republic of Chad's newly appointed ambassador to the United States. On his way to Washington to take up his appointment, Sow stopped for a coffee at the Bonnie Brae Diner in Maryland, only to be told to get his "'ass' out . . . because he wasn't allowed in there."[65] "He looked like an ordinary run of the mill nigger to me," the diner's female owner later explained to a reporter from *Life* magazine. "I couldn't tell he was [an] ambassador."[66] For Sow there was nothing ordinary about their encounter. "Deeply hurt by this affront," he reported it to the State Department the next

President John F. Kennedy meets with William H. Fitzjohn, chargé d'affaires of Sierra Leone, April 27, 1961.

day, and later to the president. "He did not wish to involve his country in any scandal," he explained, but he did want US officials to know that "situations like this made it very difficult for African diplomats to leave New York and Washington and that they make normal relationships between the United States and African countries very strained."[67]

Compelled to apologize once more, Kennedy now wanted the problem to go away. Reluctant to take any executive action that might alienate his white southern supporters, Kennedy was not eager to take a stand on any civil rights issue, even if it was limited to the rights of African diplomats. "Can't you tell those African ambassadors not to drive on Route 40?" he had asked Angier Biddle Duke, chief of protocol for the State Department, when first apprised of the problems along that route. "It's a hell of a road—I used to drive it years ago, but why would anyone want to drive it today when you can fly? Tell these ambassadors I wouldn't think of driving from New York to Washington. Tell them to fly!"[68] But after speaking to Sow, he realized he had to do something.

Kennedy reached out to Pedro Sanjuan, head of the State Department's new Special Protocol Service Section, and asked him to go see Maryland governor Millard J. Tawes and "end all this business."[69] What Kennedy intended was not clear to Sanjuan and may not have been entirely clear to Kennedy himself. Kennedy's civil rights decisions, according to his aide Harris Wofford, were sometime made "hurriedly . . . without careful consideration of an overall strategy." "You don't solve things by just seeing Governor Tawes," Sanjuan reflected at the time. His doubts would prove accurate: Sanjuan was never even able to secure a meeting with the governor. Unwilling to take a public stand on racial discrimination on Route 40, Tawes dodged the issue by always being "out" when Sanjuan called.[70] In the face of these evasions, Sanjuan, Harris Wofford, and Frederick Dutton, Kennedy's special assistant for interdepartmental and intergovernmental affairs, ended up taking matters into their own hands.

Fortunately, all three men had stronger civil rights commitments than Kennedy. A thirty-one-year-old Cuban émigré who had organized and registered Puerto Rican voters for Kennedy's campaign prior to joining the State Department, Sanjuan was a self-described "rebel," with no patience for bigotry. When, shortly after starting his State Department job, he came across reports about the discrimination African diplomats faced in Washington, he became "really fired up." He found it absurd that at a time when everyone in the Kennedy administration was talking about winning "Africa for democracy," the continent's ambassadors were getting a "picture of America that was appalling."[71] Wofford and Dutton were also unabashedly liberal. Born and raised in New York City, Wofford had embraced egalitarian racial politics as a teenager. The first white man to enroll in Howard University Law School, he was an early supporter of the civil rights movement and a friend of Martin Luther King Jr. He first began working with Kennedy in 1960, when Kennedy sought his help in securing the Negro vote. Dutton, a westerner who grew up in Colorado and California, was a lawyer and Democratic Party power broker who shared Wofford's progressive outlook. He first rose to national prominence as campaign manager for Adlai Stevenson's second presidential bid in 1956, and throughout his political career he supported the idea of a racially inclusive Democratic Party.

Operating largely without direct presidential oversight, the three men organized a campaign "to correct segregation to the maximum extent possible in the places of public accommodation along the highways in [Maryland and

Delaware]."[72] Designed both to encourage voluntary desegregation on Route 40 and to drum up public support for a bill banning segregation in Maryland's public accommodations, their campaign involved encouraging civil rights groups and state lawmakers to pass the legislation they proposed, and pressuring Route 40 restaurant owners to welcome Black customers.

An exercise in public relations as well as politics, this initiative was motivated at least in part by a desire to get ahead of the bad press created by incidents on Route 40. Its goal, as outlined by Dutton, "was to make a hell of a lot of noise and talk about what this government is going to do and how this government is interested in changing this and so on." If nothing else, all the noise might help change the narrative. "Maybe we won't produce this terrible effect that we get every time there's an incident involving one of the Africans."[73]

Although less than noble in its conception, the government's Route 40 campaign was a boon to civil rights activists. Designed to appeal to Cold War conservatives as well as racial liberals, it issued telegrams, press releases, and letters presenting arguments tailored to appeal to both. As Nicholas Murray Vachon notes, some of its promotional materials "addressed the Cold War argument that segregation was driving African nations toward the Communist Bloc," with personal pleas for help from Kennedy, whose signature figured prominently in the campaign. "I want them [the diplomats]," stated one such signed appeal, "to see that this country fully lives in the principles of freedom and equality of opportunity for which we are striving in the world."[74] At the same time, the campaign also "addressed the civil rights argument that discrimination against any individual was immoral irrespective of his or her nationality."[75] "It is most important," wrote Kennedy in a letter calling for the voluntary desegregation of restaurants and other public accommodations along Route 40, "that there be no discrimination of any kind based on race, creed or color against any American citizen or visitor from abroad. That is basic to our moral strength at home and the Nation's leadership in the world.'"[76]

The campaign's civil rights argument was expansive enough to appeal to Black Americans, many of whom had resented the State Department's previous attempts to secure "special privileges [for] foreign Negros."[77] The Kennedy administration's effort to desegregate public accommodations in Maryland even attracted direct support from CORE. In October 1961 the activist organization rallied behind what one of its members dryly described as the State Department's "interference in the internal affairs of the State of

Maryland" by announcing plans to stage sit-ins in Route 40 restaurants on November 11 unless Governor Tawes called a special session of the Maryland legislature to consider a public accommodations law. Just over a month later, CORE canceled its planned Freedom Ride up Route 40 on the news that thirty-five Maryland and twelve Delaware restaurants had pledged to desegregate by December 15.[78] But the Freedom movement continued, as hundreds of CORE volunteers made test visits to restaurants that had not supported the pledge, and visited newly desegregated establishments to make sure that restaurant owners who had pledged to desegregate actually did so,

Segregation persisted briefly even at some of these restaurants, and statewide legislation was not enacted until 1963, when the Maryland General Assembly passed a watered-down public accommodations law that covered only eleven of the state's twenty-three counties, and excluded bars and taverns. But the desegregation of restaurants along Route 40 was a success. The counties covered by the new law were all along Route 40, and many restaurants along that road desegregated even before the state legislature took action.

More importantly, the movement spread. In the spring of 1962, CORE announced a nationwide "Freedom Highways" project targeting segregation at chain restaurants between Washington, D.C., and Florida. "We knocked Jim Crow out of the bus terminal facilities," explained CORE program director Gordon R. Carey. "Now we are trying to expand the right of free travel."[79] Like the Route 40 campaign, the Freedom Highways initiative involved test visits in which CORE members presented themselves as "ordinary customers," followed by negotiations with restaurants that discriminated, which led to sit-ins only when these negotiations failed.[80]

More successful in some places than others, Freedom Highways efforts desegregated forty-three Howard Johnson's restaurants in Florida during its first months of operation.[81] The campaign had more trouble making headway in North Carolina, where, during the summer of 1962, more than eighty CORE members were arrested on charges of trespassing after "making segregation tests" or picketing at chain restaurants.[82] CORE's behind-the-scenes negotiations for voluntary desegregation with North Carolina's governor, Terry Sanford, and other white leaders went nowhere. In time, however, the negative publicity generated by the pickets and arrests forced the issue. In the fall of 1962, picketing of the Howard Johnson's chain—which continued to be one of CORE's major targets—spread to New York City, Rochester, Boston,

Houston, Chicago, Philadelphia, and Cincinnati.[83] By December of that year, all but 18 of the nation's 297 company-operated Howard Johnson's had desegregated, and the chain's complete desegregation seemed imminent.[84]

Even before then the *New York Times* reported that the campaign was triggering "quiet progress" in the desegregation of other highway hotel, motels, and restaurants throughout North Carolina. "Motel and restaurant managers," the article maintained, "were trying to ease away from traditional patterns"— although some were so anxious to avoid any fanfare that they denied that they were making a change. "Some say they will accept only African diplomats, when in fact they accept American Negroes, as well; while others say they are 'desegregated but will accept only diplomats or government officials.'"[85]

THE CIVIL RIGHTS ACT OF 1964

Such distinctions—and indeed, all overt travel discrimination—would be outlawed with the passage of the Civil Rights Act of 1964. This sweeping new law first took shape in 1963 in the aftermath of the SCLC's Birmingham Campaign. Led by the ministers Martin Luther King Jr., Fred Shuttlesworth, and James Bevel, this campaign took on segregation in one of the nation's most racially divided cities in hopes of breaking it down everywhere, with lasting results.

"If you win in Birmingham, as Birmingham goes, so goes the nation," local activist Fred Shuttlesworth told King when he invited King and the SCLC to his city.[86] Birmingham was also known as "Bombingham," because it was the site of fifty racially motivated bombings between 1945 and 1962, and it would be fiendishly difficult to desegregate. Still under control of the arch segregationist Eugene "Bull" Connor, the city arrested 150 of the demonstrators who started sitting in at local stores and municipal facilities in early April 1963, and these arrests only continued after Connor secured a court injunction barring further protests. On April 12, Good Friday, King, Shuttlesworth, and more than sixty others were arrested when they defied the order by staging a protest march.[87] King's arrest attracted international attention and inspired his famous *Letter from a Birmingham Jail*, which he wrote while spending the Easter week in solitary confinement.[88]

But the crescendo of the campaign to desegregate Birmingham came later, in the first week of May, when SCLC staff member James Bevel organized the

Firemen turn their hoses on civil rights protesters, Birmingham, Alabama, 1963.

"Children's Crusade." Designed to reinvigorate a protest that had begun to wane because many of the city's adult residents were reluctant to participate in demonstrations for fear of losing their jobs, the campaign reached out to their children, with explosive results. On May 2, more than one thousand children—ages six to sixteen—skipped school and gathered at the Sixteenth Street Baptist Church and marched toward the city hall, where more than seven hundred of them were arrested and jailed. Things only got worse the next day, when hundreds more returned. Faced with a second day of massive protests, Bull Connor abandoned all restraint and used high-power fire hoses and police dogs to scatter the young demonstrators. Captured by newsmen and camera crews who were on hand to cover the demonstrations, the images of children knocked off their feet by high-pressure streams of water and mauled by police dogs shocked the nation, producing demands for immediate action from the Kennedy administration.

Confronted with these "disastrous picture[s]," Kennedy sent Burke Marshall, his civil rights specialist, to Birmingham to negotiate a truce between the city's business leaders and the Black protesters, and began conferring with Marshall and other advisors on a civil rights bill.

A fresh wave of violence in Birmingham a few days later further underscored the urgent need for federal legislation. On the night of May 11, one
day after Marshall had brokered a "tentative agreement on the gradual desegregation of Birmingham's public facilities," two more bombs went off in
Birmingham, shattering any peace Marshall's negotiations had achieved.[89]
One of the bombs blew a hole through the front of the house of Reverend A. D.
King, Martin Luther King Jr.'s brother; the other bomb demolished much of the
first floor of the A. G. Gaston Hotel—where Martin Luther King and other
SCLC members had stayed during their campaign. In the wake of the explo-
sions, Black protesters once again flooded the streets of Birmingham, and more
than twenty-five hundred Klansmen gathered in a nearby suburb to listen to
leaders denounce the integration agreement by the "flickering light of two
20 foot burning crosses."[90] With a crisis once again looming in Alabama, Kennedy had to put local army units on alert and prepare to federalize the National Guard—if necessary. But he also realized, as the writer Todd S. Purdum
points out, that chaos in the South could no longer be contained by "scrambling to defuse demonstrations or . . . enforce court orders." Something more
was called for. "It was becoming clear to both John and Robert Kennedy that
the only way to end demonstrations was to end the discrimination that
prompted them. And the only way to do that, they reluctantly realized, was
a broad new law."[91]

Just what would be in that bill was a matter of debate, as there was "continuing uncertainty in the White House about the Constitutional grounds on
which the Federal Government could order desegregation." As we saw in
Chapter 1, the Civil Rights Act of 1875, which was Congress's only previous
attempt to ban discrimination in hotels, restaurants, theaters, and other privately owned establishments, had not survived the scrutiny of the Supreme
Court. In the *Civil Rights Cases* (1883), the Court had held that Congress's civil
rights law exceeded its constitutional authority. The Fourteenth Amendment
empowered Congress to intervene when the states denied any of their residents "the equal protection of the laws," but the Court maintained that racial discrimination in places of public accommodation amounted to private
discrimination, not state-sponsored discrimination. "Individual invasion of
individual rights is not the subject matter of the Amendment," it concluded.[92]

With this case very much in mind, Attorney General Robert F. Kennedy
worried about "not having any solution under law" that could desegregate
public accommodations.[93] In an early meeting on the new civil rights law, he

even floated the idea of crafting a bill that simply dodged the issue of desegregating public accommodations. "They can stand at lunch counters," he said.
"They don't have to eat there. They can pee before they come into a store or
supermarket." But Burke Marshall, whose job as the president's special deputy
for civil rights had put him on the ground in the middle of most of the civil
rights crises the administration had faced, would have none of it: "This business of going in and eating at a lunch counter," he told the president, is "one
thing that makes Negroes, regardless of age, maddest."[94] Neither of the Kennedy brothers required much persuasion on this point, according to Marshall,
who would later recall that "the President was acutely aware of the intensity
of feeling about public accommodations and being denied access to these lunch
counters. Sit-ins had been going on since 1960." "After Birmingham," Marshall further noted, the president and Robert Kennedy quickly came to view
the public accommodations problem much "the same way, which was that . . .
[there] was already a terrible problem with the sit-ins and everything and it
was going to get worse and worse and worse and had to be dealt with."[95]

In writing the bill's section on public accommodations, Marshall ultimately
got around the limitations that *Civil Rights Cases* had imposed on Congress's
ability to prohibit private discrimination by making the interstate commerce
clause, rather than the Fourteenth Amendment, the primary source of Congress's authority to prohibit discrimination in public accommodations. "The
Fourteenth Amendment," he later explained, "had an obvious problem—the
Civil Rights Cases. It seemed silly, even recognizing that times and courts
change, to base a statute on an erroneous statute when you didn't have to."
Moreover, such an approach was unnecessary, given that the interstate commerce clause gave Congress "broad and plenary power" over both interstate
commerce and all activities affecting interstate commerce.[96] Given "capacious
readings" by the post-New-Deal-era Supreme Court, the interstate commerce
clause authorized Congress to regulate any business that served out-of-state
customers, or even bought or sold goods from another state.[97]

Marshall's solution was controversial. It gave the Justice Department the
legal backing it needed to craft a statute mandating the desegregation of all
hotels, motels, restaurants, lunch counters, cafes, soda fountains, cinemas, and
theaters, but many supporters of the civil rights bill were disappointed to see
a legislative measure, designed to make America a better country, take its
"principal authority from a seemingly trivial clause of the constitution, when
it could be founded on the solid rock of the Fourteenth Amendment."[98] Sen-

Heart of Atlanta Motel.

ator John Pastore of Rhode Island was one of the disappointed supporters: "I believe in this bill because I believe in the dignity of man, not because discrimination impedes our commerce. I like the feeling that what we are dealing with is morality and that morality comes under the Fourteenth Amendment."[99] However, Marshall remained steadfastly committed to designing a civil rights bill that would "pass Congress and be upheld by the Supreme Court, no matter on what section of the Constitution it may be grounded."[100]

In the end, Marshall prevailed. The legislation that ultimately came out of the Birmingham crisis would take months to debate and revise, and still longer to pass: It did not become law until July 2, 1964—more than six months after the assassination of John F. Kennedy. But when it did pass, the public accommodations section of the Civil Rights Act of 1964 went forward as written, and it withstood the all but inevitable legal challenges that came after it took effect. Designed to guarantee "all persons . . . the full and equal enjoyment of the goods, services, facilities, privileges, advantages, and accommodations

Lyndon B. Johnson signs the Civil Rights Act into law, July 2, 1964.

of any place of public accommodation," it drew on the interstate commerce clause to prohibit discrimination in all establishments that catered to interstate travelers or even served or sold food, gasoline, or other products that had "moved in [interstate] commerce."[101]

Filed just hours after President Lyndon B. Johnson signed the new legislation, *Heart of Atlanta Motel, Inc. v. the United States* (1964) challenged the constitutionality of the public accommodations provisions in the 1964 Civil Rights Act. It was launched by Moreton Rolleston, the owner of a large and lavish whites-only motel and a staunch segregationist who maintained that Congress had no right to force him to serve all customers regardless of race. However, neither the federal district court to which Rolleston first applied for injunctive relief, nor the Supreme Court, where he took his appeal, agreed.

On December 14, 1964, the Supreme Court upheld the constitutionality of the Civil Rights Act of 1964 in terms that underscored the central role that a belated acknowledgment of the discrimination so long experienced by Black travelers played in both securing the passage of this legislation, and providing its rationale in the Constitution. Moreover, the Court came to the same conclusion as *Katzenbach v. McClung* (1964), a similar case decided on the same day.[102]

Katzenbach v. McClung was a case against Ollie McClung, the owner of Ollie's Barbeque Restaurant in Birmingham, who continued to refuse to offer sit-down service to Black customers. It was less obviously linked to travel than the *Heart of Atlanta Motel* case. But both cases were decided with reference to the issue of interstate commerce. Even though Ollie's clientele might be primarily local, the Court ruled in a decision that addressed both cases, 46 percent of the meat it served came from out of state. Moreover, its "discriminatory practices" could "prevent Negroes from buying prepared food served on the premises while on a trip," thereby discouraging travel and obstructing interstate commerce as surely as did the racial restrictions maintained by *Heart of Atlanta Motel*—which had a clientele of primarily interstate travelers.[103]

In its *Heart of Atlanta Motel* decision, the Court rejected Rolleston's argument that Congress had no right to regulate his businesses, and instead embraced an even more direct defense of the rights of Black travelers. Whereas Rolleston, who represented himself, attempted to argue that Title II of the new legislation violated his Fifth Amendment rights to liberty and property and his Thirteenth Amendment right to liberty, the government's case rested entirely on the commerce clause. "The unavailability to Negroes of adequate accommodations interferes significantly with interstate travel," the government's lawyers had maintained, and Congress, "under the Commerce Clause, has power to remove such obstructions and restraints."[104] The Supreme Court concurred, finding Rolleston's claims on the Thirteenth Amendment "entirely frivolous." No serious argument could be made for the idea that "an amendment directed to the abolition of human bondage and the removal of widespread disabilities associated with slavery places discrimination in public accommodations beyond the reach of both federal and state law."

The Court's decision in *Civil Rights Cases* was not "'conceived' in terms of the commerce power" and expressly (as *Civil Rights Cases* noted) did "not apply to those cases in which Congress is clothed with direct and plenary powers of legislation over the whole subject, accompanied with an express or implied denial of such power to the States, as in the regulation of commerce." Had they been, the Warren Court even went on to muse, *Civil Rights Cases* might have turned out differently. "Our populace had not reached its present mobility, nor were facilities, goods and services circulating as readily in interstate commerce as they are today . . . [when] the sheer increase in volume of interstate traffic alone would give discriminatory practices which inhibit travel a far larger impact upon the Nation's commerce than such practices had on the economy of another day." In any case, the Civil Rights Act of 1964 did not require the court to revisit its predecessor's ruling in this case. Both constitutional and necessary, the nation's new law drew directly on the regulatory powers granted to Congress by the Constitution's interstate commerce clause to eliminate "obstructions" to "interstate commerce caused by racial discrimination."[105]

The Court's conclusion was buttressed by a reading of the congressional hearings that preceded the passage of the Civil Rights Act, which, as its decision noted, are "replete with evidence of the burdens that discrimination by race or color places upon interstate commerce." These hearings provide a fitting coda for this book, as they included a remarkable public referendum on the difficulties of traveling Black.[106]

The Senate's twenty-eight-day discussion of the highly controversial "civil rights–public accommodations" issues involved in the proposed bill began with a series of findings that stressed the cost of the discrimination faced by "travelers who are members of minority racial and religious groups . . . particularly Negroes." Such travelers were "frequently unable to obtain adequate overnight accommodations, with the result that they may be compelled to stay at hotels of poor or inferior quality, travel great distances from their normal routes to find adequate accommodations, or make detailed arrangements for lodging far in advance of scheduled interstate travel." They were likewise "frequently unable to obtain adequate food service at convenient places along their routes, with the result that many are dissuaded from traveling interstate, while others must travel considerable distances from their intended routes to obtain adequate food service." Discrimination had a similarly negative effect on businesses, and "fraternal, religious, scientific, and other organizations." They could not always hold "conventions in cities which they would otherwise select because the public facilities in such cities are not open to all members of racial or religious minority groups or are available only on a segregated basis."[107]

The bill's proponents backed up these dry findings by inviting legislators to contemplate the many harms that travel discrimination imposed on those who were subject to it. "Consider the physical and financial inconveniences suffered by Negroes through such discrimination," Robert F. Kennedy asked the Senate. Whereas white travelers were free to find food and lodgings anywhere they felt like stopping, "For the Negro, it is not so simple":

If he makes reservations without first determining whether or not the establishment will accept people of his race, he may well find on arrival that the reservations will not be honored—or that it will have somehow been mislaid. His alternative is to subject himself and his family to the humiliation of rejection at one establishment after another—until, as likely as not, he is forced to accept accommodation of inferior quality, far removed from his route of travel.

And all the while, "white people of whatever kind—prostitutes, narcotics pushers, Communists, or bank robbers—are welcome at establishments which will not admit certain Federal judges, ambassadors, and countless members of our forces."[108]

Invited to discuss the "foreign policy implications" of the proposed legislation, Secretary of State Dean Rusk emphasized that the United States was widely regarded as the "home of democracy," and therefore should serve as a role model for other countries where people were struggling for freedom, human rights, and recognition of human dignity. The nation's stature as a model republic was faltering in the face of the independence movements that had decolonized some fifty countries in Asia, Africa, and the Middle East since World War II. Most of the "newly independent peoples" were nonwhite and "determined to eradicate every vestige of the notion that the white race is superior or entitled to special privileges because of their race. Were we as a nation 'in their shoes' we would do the same."[109] Far from welcoming their emissaries with open arms, Americans often denied them admission to hotels, refused them service in restaurants, and drove them away from public beaches and swimming pools. Other "high level state visitors" were subject to similar slights. "The head of the civil aeronautics board of a West African country, brought here under the sponsorship of the U.S. Government, was denied service in a restaurant. He terminated his trip right then and there." Many foreign students who traveled to the United States both to gain an education and to learn about the American way of life returned home "disappointed and even embittered."[110]

American race relations were a liability that sometimes even alienated white visitors to the United States. "Not too long ago a German student was jailed for having eaten a meal in the colored side of a bus terminal counter," he noted. That student was not a civil rights activist of any kind; rather, he had "chosen to sit there because the white side was completely filled." The provisions of the civil rights bill would eradicate the nation's "most obvious and embarrassing forms of discrimination," he argued, and thereby enable "foreign visitors in our country to travel with much less fear of hindrance and insult." While he focused primarily on the problems encountered by diplomats and other foreign nationals in the United States, Rusk was careful to clarify that he was not attempting to secure such visitors "rights and decencies which are in practice denied to colored American citizens." He insisted that "one should not need a diplomatic passport in order to enjoy ordinary civil and human rights," and that nothing short of "the decent treatment of all human beings, including American citizens," was likely to restore the nation's reputation among its nonwhite visitors.[111]

Just how far the nation still had to go when it came to offering decent treatment to all its citizens was dramatically illustrated in the testimony of NAACP leader Roy Wilkins, who addressed the Senate on July 22. Wilkins opened his prepared statement by reminding the senators that it was "vacation time" for millions of Americans, at which point he was interrupted by Senator John Pastore, who asked him to describe how Black families managed to travel across the country, given the discrimination they faced. "Suppose a colored family starts out from Providence, R.I., or Boston, Mass., and wanted a journey on vacation, to go to the Republican convention in San Francisco, or to go to the Democratic convention in Atlantic City, as I did several years ago with my own family. What do you do?" asked Pastore.[112]

Wilkins responded by outlining some of the time-honored strategies used by Black travelers to survive long car trips. Those who wished to drive across the country, he explained, had to "pick a route; a route sometimes a little out of the way. I have known many colored people who drove from the East to California, but they always drove through Omaha, Cheyenne, and Salt Lake City, and Reno. They didn't take the southern route. And if they were going to Texas, they stayed north as long as they could. They didn't go down the east coast and across the South. They went across the Middle West and down the South." Meanwhile, Blacks who could not avoid driving through the South had to plan their route in advance and travel with great care. "Where you travel through what we might call hostile territory you take your chances," he noted. "You drive and you drive and you drive. You don't stop where there is a vacancy sign out at a motel at 4 o'clock in the afternoon and rest yourself; you keep on driving until the next city or the next town where you know somebody or they know somebody who knows somebody who can take care of you. This is the way you plan it."[113]

But all the careful planning in the world could not guarantee Black travelers trouble-free vacations, Wilkins further emphasized. Discrimination could be found almost anywhere, even in "areas which are thought to be free of it." An African American traveler "in the middle of Iowa, for example, in a small town" might have "almost as much of a problem as . . . in a small town in, say, Alabama." Worse still, Black travelers could never be quite certain when and where they would have problems. Some border cities were problematic, but others welcomed Blacks; and even in the South itself, the segregation of public accommodations was inconsistent and subject to confusing regional variations. "When I go to Louisville, Ky. I can stay at a hotel. If I go to Meridian, Miss., I can't stay at a hotel. But if I go to Miami Beach I can stay at a hotel. If I go to Ocala, perhaps not." No one could really plan around such conditions, he concluded: "You don't figure them out. You just live uncomfortably, from day to day."[114]

Wilkins was followed by Senator Franklin D. Roosevelt Jr., of New York, who backed up his statement with statistics prepared by Marion Jackson, the publisher of a Black travel guide called *Go: Guide to Pleasant Motoring*. The very existence of the guide provided "dramatic testimony to the difficulties for which we are seeking a remedy," said Roosevelt, who presented a chart created by Jackson to illustrate just how scarce accommodations for African American travelers were between Washington, D.C., and various points in the South. "Reasonable sleeping accommodations" for Black travelers were an average of 141 miles apart between Washington and Miami, the chart showed, and a whopping 174 miles apart between Washington and New Orleans. Moreover, most of the establishments that admitted Black travelers were small, and therefore could not be counted on to have vacant rooms. Traveling Black was not just inconvenient, it was dangerous. Often forced to drive for many miles before they could find a place to sleep, African American travelers could not always abide by the National Safety Council's admonition that "the nonprofessional driver should stop after 6 to 8 hours driving and get a night's sleep."[115]

None of these points were new. African Americans had for decades been making similar observations about the ridiculous inequities imposed on them by Jim Crow travel arrangements. But in the hearings, Congress finally addressed issues that whites had been willfully ignoring all these many years

President Lyndon B. Johnson, who would take over the task of getting the bill through Congress after John F. Kennedy was assassinated on November 22, 1963, often framed his support for the bill with a folksy story that made just that point.

Looking back to the early 1950s, when he was in the Senate, he recalled that he and his wife had always "had an extra car to take back to Texas at the close of each Congressional session." So he would usually have his three Black employees—his cook, Zephyr Wright, his maid, Helen Williams, and Helen's husband, Gene Williams—drive the other car back to Texas for him. Once he asked Gene Williams to take the family's beagle dog with him and was surprised by his response. "I didn't think they would mind. Little Beagle was a friendly, gentle dog," but Williams was hesitant and said, "Senator, do we have to take Beagle?" He continued to hesitate, even after Johnson told him that he had no other way to get the dog to Texas and added: "He shouldn't give you any trouble, Gene. You know Beagle loves you." At this point Johnson finally looked directly at him and asked: "Tell me what's the matter. Why don't you want to take Beagle? What aren't you telling me?" Gene's reply laid out some basic facts about traveling Black that had not previously occurred to Johnson. "Well, Senator," he explained. "It's tough enough to get all the way from Washington to Texas":

> We drive for hours and hours. We get hungry. But there's no place on the
> road we can stop and go in and eat. We drive some more. It gets pretty hot.
> We want to wash up. But the only bathroom we're allowed in is usually miles
> off the main highway. We keep going till night comes—till we get so tired
> we can't stay awake any more. We're ready to pull in. But it takes us an-
> other hour or so to find a place to sleep. You see, what I'm saying is that a
> colored man's got enough trouble getting across the South on his own,
> without having a dog along.[116]

Johnson first began to tell this story around the time of the hearing on the civil rights bill, and he told several different versions—so it was, at least in part, political theater. But if all the hard work and backroom politicking he did to shepherd the Civil Rights Act of 1964 through Congress is anything to go by, the lesson he learned from it was real—and one that he hoped to pass on to others. Gene Williams's reluctance to have a dog in the car as he drove to Texas came as an awakening to Johnson, as he later wrote in his memoirs, because it made him realize that while he had "of course" always known "that such discrimination existed throughout the South," he had not thought through what it meant in the daily lives of Black people. Instead, he, along with other southerners, had "somehow . . . deluded ourselves into believing that black people around us were happy and satisfied; into thinking that the bad and ugly things were going on somewhere else, happening to other people."[117]

That delusion faded, at least for a little while, under the pressure of the Freedom Rides, fly-ins, sit-ins, and highway protests staged by participants in the modern American civil rights movement. The product of a brave new post–World War II era in which the United States held itself up as a model of the democratic values to which other nations should aspire, these protests helped make civil rights reforms a Cold War imperative.

"GONE ARE THE OVERT, ASSERTIVE BANNERS OF JIM CROW PIGMENTOCRACY"

With the passage of the Civil Rights Act on July 2, 1964, African Americans across the country ventured out to restaurants, hotels, barbershops, swimming pools, bowling halls, and countless other facilities to test its impact.[118] In doing so, they made history while engaged in otherwise everyday activities. As the *Philadelphia Tribune* recorded, "Negroes ate steak side by side with whites in a Danville, Virginia, restaurant for the first time. A Negro got a haircut at a previously all white barbershop in Kansas, Mo. And Negroes went swimming at a previously segregated swimming pool in Savannah, Ga." Not all these tests were successful. The Robert E. Lee Hotel shut down rather than succumb to integration. Its owners felt that they could not continue to operate an establishment named in honor of this "renowned Confederate Veteran" and "true gentleman of the Old South" if they were not allowed to cater to a "select clientele."[119] Other opponents of the legislation simply refused to abide by it. In Atlanta, Lester Maddox, a restaurant owner and notorious segregationist who would become Georgia's governor in 1967, drove off his first Black customers at gunpoint.

But grudging compliance was far more common than outright defiance, as Black lawyer Solomon Seay discovered when he celebrated the passage of the Civil Rights Act in Alabama. He began his celebration the very day Johnson signed the act by taking his family to the Elite Café in Montgomery, a favorite "lunch spot and evening watering hole for the white establishment in legal, business, and government circles." Although Seay lived in Montgomery, and often walked right past the Elite on the way from his office to the city's US district court, he had never been inside and had wondered whether he would ever "have a chance to see the interior." Eager to do so, on July 2, 1964, he took his wife and two young daughters to dinner at the Elite. They entered the restaurant around 5:30 p.m. and were readily seated, but they eventually realized that while waiters were serving white patrons all around them, no one was coming to their table. When Seay finally managed to flag down a waiter, who then found the manager, he was told that because the president was not scheduled to sign the new law "until 6:20 p.m. Alabama time," Seay and his family "would be served at 6:20 p.m. Alabama time and not one minute sooner."[120]

Still, such slights did not sustain Jim Crow. Compliance with Title II of the Civil Rights Act was, as political scientist James W. Button and other scholars have shown, "relatively prompt and extensive"—even if "acceptance, in Old South, rural areas tended to be 'minimal and grudging.'"[121] Businesses accepted desegregation, happily or otherwise, because they "perceived that they *had* to comply," and that other businesses "would do likewise, and that they could condemn Washington for forcing such compliance."[122]

Business owners who refused to comply with the new legislation faced real penalties. Lester Maddox was elected to Georgia's statehouse on the strength of his support for segregation, but he did not manage to maintain a segregated restaurant. Sued in federal court shortly after the passage of the Civil Rights Act, Maddox was ordered to desegregate within twenty days, at which point he shuttered his Pickrick Restaurant rather than accept Black customers.[123] The Lester Maddox Cafeteria, a new restaurant for whites only that he opened in the same location the following month, also failed to survive. Although Maddox maintained that his new establishment was a "'local,' noninterstate eating place," the court did not accept this subterfuge.[124] On February 5, 1965, federal court judge Frank A. Hooper ordered Maddox to desegregate or pay fines of $200 a day, effectively forcing him out of the restaurant business.[125]

Enforced by the Department of Justice and supported in the courts, Title II of the 1964 Civil Rights Act worked in tandem with the ICC's 1961 ruling barring racial segregation in interstate transportation and put a decisive end to many of the most galling indignities that Blacks had long suffered. While racism is far from dead, the desegregation of public accommodations was, and still is, one of the civil rights movement's most important achievements. Its impact in the field of transportation was nothing short of transformative.

"A trip by car between Washington, D.C., and Columbia, S.C., is radically different today than it was thirty-five years ago," explains law professor Randall Kennedy, whose parents used to drive straight from Washington, D.C., to South Carolina without ever taking a rest stop, in the hope of avoiding all the "filling stations, restaurants. motels, and other public accommodations along the way, where their children might be snarled at by white cashiers and attendants."[126] But with the passage of the Civil Rights Act of 1964, travel lost many of its difficulties:

> Gone is the fear that one might feel the need to use a toilet outside those few areas in which gas station attendants permitted "colored" to use facilities. Gone are signs distinguishing between restrooms for "Negro Women" and "White Ladies." Gone is the sense that the southbound highways out of the District of Columbia constituted a vast no-man's-land to be traveled only after careful planning and still at one's peril. Gone are the overt, assertive banners of Jim Crow pigmentocracy.[127]

Gone too are the colored cars, segregated buses, and Jim Crow railroad stations, airport terminals, and bus depots that made traveling Black on the South's trains, planes, and buses even more difficult than navigating its highways. Indeed, all these problems are forgotten in ways that mark the eradication of Jim Crow travel as one of the twentieth-century Black freedom struggle's most remarkable achievements. At a time when so many of the other goals of the civil rights movement remain unfulfilled, the hard-fought victories of the generations of men and women who challenged Jim Crow transportation in the courts and on the nation's rails and roads changed the world in ways that have come to seem natural.

Epilogue

#BlackTravelMatters

JOHN LEFLORE, WHO SPENT MUCH OF HIS LIFE BATTLING JIM CROW on the South's railroads and buses, lived long enough to see a world in which people took for granted many of the freedoms he had fought so hard to secure. Born in Mobile, Alabama, in 1903, he grew up in a two-room apartment in a dilapidated building less than a quarter of a mile from the railroad tracks. His days were punctuated by the sound of the "all Pullman train" that rattled by his family's building every evening at 11 p.m. His mother called it "the rich people's train," and he never forgot the days when Blacks could not ride in Pullman cars.

Looking back on his life in 1974, he wondered whether these memories meant anything to younger Blacks. The struggle for change had extended "across different eras" in ways that "young blacks who have just come on the scene do not fully appreciate" because they didn't "know anything about . . . being denied. They took their access to ordinary everyday travel amenities for granted. They never worried about 'toilet service.' Or food. They don't know anything about having to go around in the back door to get a hamburger if you got one at all." And they certainly knew "nothing about riding up in a Jim Crow coach where cinders would pour in on you because . . . there were no screens to your windows. . . . They don't know anything about sitting over the hot motor of an inter-city bus. That was the only seat you could occupy. There are so many things they don't know anything about."[1]

This book has understood the collective amnesia that so troubled John Le-Flore as less of a failure of memory than a failure of history. With a dedication to recovering and preserving that history, I have sought in these chapters to capture and preserve the experiences of African American travelers on the nation's highways, and in trains, planes, and buses. A chronicle of a people in motion, over a century of transformative social and technological change, this book tells a story that underscores the importance to American citizenship of the right to travel freely, and it details how hard African Americans have fought for that right.

But it is a right that has yet to be fully realized. The civil rights movement's legal victories ended many of the Jim Crow humiliations forced on Black travelers by law, and opened roadside accommodations to Blacks to a greater degree than ever before. But travel discrimination and transportation inequities persist to this day. As we have seen, the segregation of travel accommodations was never purely a matter of law. Many of the forms of racial discrimination encountered by African American travelers were informal rather than required by law, and many of them have not been eradicated. Today, as in the past, civil rights laws are not always successful in protecting Black travelers. So while John LeFlore's descendants might not know what it was like to travel Jim Crow, African American travelers still have their own distinctive travel woes. Highlighted in contemporary hashtags that compile complaints about #drivingwhileblack and #travelingwhileblack, the inequalities faced by Black travelers today are both similar to and very different from those faced by their forebears. Although perpetuated by familiar forms of racism, and tied to long-standing economic inequities, they are rooted in the social, economic, and technological realities of a new millennium. Obvious in some ways, and invisible in others, they underscore that travel remains a civil rights issue.

In Montgomery, Alabama, where Rosa Parks launched the Montgomery Bus Boycott more than half a century ago, city buses have long been free of segregation. But service on Montgomery's public transit system, which is popularly known as "the M," is far from ideal. Crowded and often overheated, the M's buses pick up passengers along their routes only once every hour or ninety minutes. Even more elusive on the weekends, the M operates on reduced hours on Saturdays and does not run at all on Sundays. While many of Montgomery's African American residents revere Rosa Parks, no one thinks she would be celebrating Montgomery's present-day bus system. "We got the right to sit anywhere we want on the bus," notes Callie Greer of the Mont-gomery Transportation Coalition. But that freedom does not mean much when you have to ask: "OK, now where's the bus?"[2] One of the five states in the nation that spends no money on public transportation, Alabama has a con-stitutional amendment that sets aside the money it collects from state oil and gas taxes for the exclusive support of its roads and bridges—leaving its bus system to rely on woefully inadequate federal and local support.

While some maintain that "Alabama's contentious civil rights history led to policy decisions that undermine public transportation," Alabama is far from the only US state with a minimal commitment to public transit. In fact, its transportation failures highlight a national trend.[3] The civil rights move-ment's desegregation of buses and trains came at a time when all forms of travel by bus and rail were declining. By the 1960s the United States had become a "republic of drivers" as both public and private commitments to transporta-tion increasingly centered on the automobile.[4] On the rise since the 1920s, the growth of automobility was slowed by the Great Depression, and brought to a standstill during World War II, when gas rationing, rubber shortages, and other wartime exigencies spurred a short-lived escalation in the use of mass transportation of all kinds. But America's use of cars soared after that. A product of pent-up demand, the automobile-buying frenzy of the postwar era was partly stimulated by the G.I. Bill. Officially known as the Servicemen's Readjustment Act of 1944, the G.I. Bill introduced a new package of veterans' benefits designed to help servicemen and servicewomen readjust to civilian life. One of those benefits was a massive home loan program, which extended low-cost mortgages to the nation's sixteen million veterans on terms that fa-vored new construction and spurred the proliferation of automobile-dependent suburbs. Beyond the reach of streetcars, buses, and other mass transit, these postwar suburbs transformed the nation's geography in ways that helped ce-ment America's identity as a "car country."[5]

A product of federal policy, the new suburbs were also facilitated by a commitment to road building that first took shape during the Roosevelt ad-ministration and culminated with the passage of the Federal-Aid Highway Act of 1956. The Highway Act authorized and funded a 41,000-mile "national system of interstate and defense highways" dedicated both to facilitating "speedy, safe transcontinental travel" and to securing the nation in case of atomic attack—at which point "the road network [would] permit quick evac-uation of target areas." The most expensive public works project in American history, the interstate highway system both accelerated and subsidized suburban development.[6] Whereas Roosevelt's Federal Highway Act of 1944 had covered only 50 percent of road construction costs, the 1956 measure upped that figure to 90 percent.

The triumph of car culture reshaped both local transportation and long-distance travel. The rise of the automobile decimated passenger service on the railroads, forcing dozens of lines out of business. Today the only commercial railroad lines still in business carry freight. Passenger rail survives only in the form of Amtrak, a quasi-public corporation set up in 1971 to keep passenger trains from disappearing altogether. Of the 366 train routes in operation when it was first established, Amtrak kept only 184. Over the years that number has been whittled down to 30. The Jim Crow cars of the segregation era are long gone; but so are most trains.

The same can be said of the nation's intercity buses, which have greatly declined in number since World War II. Once great rivals, the Greyhound Lines and Trailways Corporation both nearly went out of business in the 1980s, and survive today only by virtue of a 1987 merger that allowed them to "pare operating costs" and eliminate duplicate routes.[7] Only travel by air, which has become both cheaper and more popular during the last half century, poses any competition to the car in this automotive age. As of 2001, Americans used their personal vehicles—cars, pickup trucks, sport utility vehicles—for nine out of ten long-distance trips.[8] At that time air travel was touted as "the second most utilized transportation mode for long-distance travel," but flights accounted for scarcely 7 percent of long-distance trips. Airline ticket sales have mostly been robust since then (except since the beginning of the pandemic in 2020), but the vast majority of Americans still do most of their traveling by car.[9]

The emergence of automobiles as the predominant form of transportation in the United States has been at best a mixed blessing for African Americans, offering a complex coda to the events described in this book. On the one hand, as we have seen, the nation's move toward automobility offered a number of significant benefits to African Americans as a group. Black travelers despised Jim Crow cars, and learned to feel equally negative about buses. Many saw cars as potentially liberating. The automotive industry was one of the first industrial sectors to open up to Black workers, some of whom were able to secure employment as chauffeurs, mechanics, service station attendants, and the like. From Jack Johnson onward, Blacks who could afford to buy their own cars generally celebrated car ownership as a boon, taking pride and pleasure in owning and operating their cars. As an alternative to public transportation, cars often had a special meaning for Black car owners, who relished having command of the wheel and being able to avoid Jim Crow cars and segregated buses. At several key points in American history, automotive technology offered Black travelers (at least briefly) the autonomy they needed to resist other forms of segregated or demeaning forms of transportation. Some of the earliest African American car owners operated Jim Crow jitney services, designed to free Blacks from segregated streetcars, and the leaders of the Montgomery Bus Boycott organized a carpooling system that allowed them to stay off the city's buses for more than a year. But the advances offered by automotive technology were not limitless. The jitney movement produced few successful Black bus companies, and the Montgomery Bus Boycott may have helped create a city that is increasingly difficult to navigate without a car.

Segregation signs no longer divide the South's trains, buses, and travel amenities, but the cars that have replaced so many of the region's trains and buses provide no guarantee of racial justice. Instead, America's increasing dependence on automobiles for transportation has fostered new forms of transportation inequality—and new forms of segregation. Unwelcome in many of the suburban Autopias that took shape after World War II, African Americans were also largely left out of the mass migration to the suburbs that started at that time. Many of these "white flight" suburbs adopted racially restrictive covenants barring Black home buyers, and the federal officials who helped build and fund these developments pursued similar policies. In addition to subsidizing builders who were producing entire subdivisions that were off-limits to Blacks, the Federal Housing Authority (FHA) routinely refused to extend mortgages to Blacks who attempted to buy suburban homes. Convinced that the arrival of Black homeowners might jeopardize the property values of the suburban neighborhoods in which it had insured so much capital, the FHA declined Black loan applicants as a matter of policy. Neighborhoods occupied by "incompatible racial or social groups" were not a good risk, its underwriting manuals maintained.[10]

Stranded in cities as a result of these policies, African Americans did not enter the automotive age on equal terms. Many Black urban areas declined as a result of the construction of the interstate system. Often run-down, and rarely politically powerful, Black and Latino neighborhoods quickly became popular sites for the construction of the urban sections of the interstates. Highways cut through and sometimes even obliterated vital Black business districts, such as Detroit's Black Bottom, Miami's Overtown, Milwaukee's Bronzeville, Durham, North Carolina's Hayti, Dallas's Freedman's Town, California's West Oakland, and Baltimore's Harlem Park—which was razed to make room for a highway that was never built.[11] Although frequently targeted for displacement in the name of urban renewal, slum clearance, or economic development, few of these neighborhoods saw meaningful economic or structural benefits of any kind from the arrival of the interstates. Instead these vibrant African American communities were typically decimated by the construction of what residents began to see as "white roads through black bedrooms."[12]

The new highways not only displaced residents and destroyed Black businesses, they sometimes walled off Black neighborhoods from the cities in which they were located. One case in point is I-278, the Staten Island Expressway, which divides the borough's Black-majority North Shore from its lower two-thirds, cutting a color line so obvious that the expressway is popularly known as Staten Island's "Mason-Dixon Line."[13] And another notable example of the interstate's architecture of exclusion is in Chicago, where city mayor Richard Daley used the construction of the Dan Ryan Expressway in the 1960s as an opportunity to create a durable barrier between the traditionally Irish white neighborhoods on the western side of the city's South Side and the Black neighborhoods to the east.[14]

Another, less well documented, but perhaps equally formidable barrier to car ownership for Black urbanites is the lack of affordable parking. Suburban developments from New York to New Orleans were designed with car ownership (and white flight) in mind, but the older apartment buildings that predominate in urban areas do not include garages or space for parking. As tourism and business travel increasingly displaces other forms of commerce in historically significant cities, even less parking is available to residents—making car ownership ever more expensive and difficult in inner-city neighborhoods.[15]

The structural impediments that cars and highways have imposed on Black mobility extend well beyond Black neighborhoods. Although Black car ownership rates have risen over time, African Americans are still significantly less likely than whites to have access to a car. As of 2015, almost 20 percent of Blacks, as compared to only 6.5 percent of whites, live in households with no car.[16] And car ownership in low-income households is often "ephemeral" at best, as many families that can barely afford a car tend to transition in and out of car ownership.[17] Disproportionately concentrated in urban areas, Blacks who do not own cars are dependent on public transportation and can be immobilized when it fails, as was most dramatically seen during Hurricane Katrina. Of the 270,000 people stranded in New Orleans when the hurricane hit, 93 percent were Black, and 55 percent had no car or other way to evacuate.[18] In this respect, Hurricane Katrina's victims were not unique to New Orleans. During the coronavirus pandemic in 2020, the shutdown of transit services to curb the spread of COVID-19 was especially hard on Blacks and other people of color, many of whom hold essential jobs and rely on public transportation to get to work.[19] Although no longer legally prohibited from traveling freely on the nation's "public highways," as their segregation-era counterparts had been, many contemporary African Americans who do not own cars experience similar restrictions on their mobility.[20]

For many African Americans, the economic challenges posed by car ownership and American car culture are compounded by the expensive and exclusionary forms of discrimination that attend virtually every economic transaction required to acquire and maintain a car. It begins at the point of sale: African Americans routinely pay more than whites for cars of similar value. Though no research group has yet produced a national study of this trend, a 1996 class action suit against an Atlanta-area car dealership revealed that the dealership routinely made between two and seven times as much profit on cars sold to African Americans as it did on cars sold to whites.[21] Broader evidence from a study performed by economists Ian Ayres and Peter Siegelman suggests that such practices are not unusual. Audits of the car prices offered to more than three hundred pairs of trained testers dispatched to negotiate with Chicago-area car dealerships revealed that Black men were asked to pay $1,100 more than white men for identical vehicles. The prices offered to Black and white women exceeded those offered to white men by $410 and $92, respectively.[22] Meanwhile, a 2003 study by Fiona Scott Morton, Florian Zettelmeyer, and Jorge Silva-Risso suggests that the internet has begun to erode this "race premium" by offering "online minority buyers" opportunities to purchase vehicles at "nearly the same prices" as whites. But their analysis of approximately seven hundred thousand purchases found that overall, Black and Hispanic buyers still pay an average 2.1 percent more (or $500 on the average car) than do whites.[23]

Similar surcharges pile on thereafter. Once they do buy a car, Blacks and members of other minority groups often pay significantly more than whites to finance and insure their cars. A recent study of auto loan price quotes offered to a racially diverse group of testers found that nonwhites were assigned higher loan-pricing options 62.5 percent of the time, and that the loans they were offered would cost them $2,662.56 more over the life of the loan than those offered to less-qualified white testers.[24]

Likewise, insurance, although no longer off-limits to African Americans, is far more expensive for Blacks and Latinos. At issue are matters of race and residence. Insurance rates are calibrated by zip code, and insurers have long insisted that a high risk of accidents in the predominantly minority neighborhoods where most Blacks and Latinos live justifies charging their residents higher rates. Imposed on drivers regardless of their driving record, these neighborhood surcharges can exceed 30 percent and appear to be more exploitative than actuarial. A 2017 study of auto insurance pricing in California, Illinois, Texas, and Missouri conducted by *ProPublica* and *Consumer Reports* found no economic rationale that could fully account for the racial disparities in automobile insurance rates charged by major insurers in all these states. The data these organizations collected showed that the differential between auto insurance prices in predominantly minority and predominantly white neighborhoods tended to greatly exceed any verifiable differences in risk. Insurers such as Allstate, Geico, and Liberty Mutual were charging car owners with zip codes in minority-group neighborhoods premiums that could average up to 30 percent higher than the premiums paid "in whiter neighborhoods with similar accident costs."[25]

DRIVING WHILE BLACK

The American dependence on automobiles also imposes burdens that can make driving more dangerous for African Americans in the twenty-first century than it was during the segregation era. Black drivers today have better access to roadside accommodations and other travel amenities, but they face new dangers on the road. Although Black drivers have always attracted special scrutiny from law enforcement, racial profiling on American highways has escalated sharply since the 1970s. These years saw the nation's roads become one of the major sites of the nation's "war on drugs." Introduced by President Richard Nixon in 1971 and greatly enlarged by Ronald Reagan in the 1980s, this initiative designated drug abuse as the nation's "problem number one," greatly expanding federal support for drug control agencies and significantly increasing the policing and punishment of Americans suspected of using or distributing drugs.[26] One of its major innovations has been a massive increase in racial profiling on America's highways.

Legal scholar Michelle Alexander has pointed out that with Ronald Reagan's election, "budgets of federal law enforcement agencies soared. Between 1980 and 1984, FBI antidrug funding increased from $8 million to $95 million. Department of Defense antidrug allocations increased from $33 million in 1981 to $1,042 million in 1991. During that same period, DEA antidrug spending grew from $86 to $1,026 million, and FBI antidrug allocations grew from $38 to $181 million."[27] This money made new forms of drug interdiction both possible and necessary—after all, it had to be spent on something. One of the most consequential of the new programs it funded was a nationwide highway interdiction system known as Operation Pipeline, which focused on searching drivers and vehicles.

Designed and financed by the Drug Enforcement Agency (DEA), Operation Pipeline, which debuted in 1984, has trained more than twenty-seven thousand state and local police officers to use legal traffic stops to screen for drug-related activity. Pipeline's investigative techniques were modeled on the work of maverick crime fighters such as Bob Vogel, a Florida state trooper who claimed to have a "sixth sense" for motorists "likely to be smuggling drugs."[28] Vogel "discovered his unusual talent in the mid-1980s, while working as a Florida state trooper, cruising I-95 outside Daytona Beach and Port Orange, looking for traffic miscreants. Certain drivers, he noticed, just gave him a bad feeling inside. When he searched their cars, he would frequently find drugs or weapons." And when he was deterred by the courts from making traffic stops on the basis of his intuition alone, he found other more constitutional way of justifying his stops.[29] He dug deep in the Florida state legal codes and began using "rarely enforced laws against driving with burned-out license-plate lights, out-of-kilter headlights, obscured tags, and windshield cracks" to justify detaining drivers he found suspicious.[30] By the late 1980s this innovation transformed Vogel from a little-known highway patrolman to a drug war hero. Awarded several law enforcement prizes, he was featured on *Sixty Minutes* and elected sheriff of Volusia County, where he formed a drug squad dedicated to making drug arrests on I-95. At this time, Vogel also became an influential figure in Washington, where his drug interdiction system formed the basis of the DEA's Operation Pipeline.

Race-based from the outset, both Vogel's system and Operation Pipeline targeted drivers by using highly subjective criteria that usually involved race or ethnicity. Some Pipeline trainees were told that "Latinos and West Indians dominated the drug trade and therefore warranted extra scrutiny," or were warned to be on the lookout for "people with dreadlocks and cars with two Latino males traveling together."[31] The full impact of the systematic use of these techniques on busy roads is difficult to gauge. When Operation Pipeline first began, virtually no police departments kept detailed statistics on the race or ethnicity of the people they stopped, searched, questioned, and/or arrested. Indeed, such statistics remain rare today, and even when available, they are difficult to read. Meaningless without context, they would have to be supplemented with additional information on the race and ethnicity of the drivers who were not stopped, as well as information about how many of them committed violations, to give a full picture of the degree to which the police targeted some groups and not others.[32]

Such numbers as scholars have been able to collect and analyze provide strong evidence of racial profiling. Data collected by the Maryland State Police, who were under court order to collect such information between 1995 and 2000, show that Black motorists who committed traffic violations on the stretch of I-95 just north of Baltimore were almost twice as likely to be stopped as white drivers who did the same, and that once stopped, Black drivers were approximately three times more likely to be searched. They were also less likely than white motorists to be carrying drugs, so much so that among all drivers not carrying illegal drugs, African Americans were "eight times more likely to be stopped and searched than whites."[33] Evidence released by New Jersey as a result of a lawsuit filed against the state revealed still more damning patterns of racial profiling. An investigation conducted in 2000 found that "at least 8 of every 10 automobile searches carried out by state troopers on the New Jersey Turnpike over most of the last decade were conducted on vehicles driven by blacks and Hispanics."[34]

Operation Pipeline has had a profound impact on the experiences of minority drivers. By the 1990s, as journalist Gary Webb noted at that time, racial profiling on American roads was so pervasive that it had given "rise to a new catchphrase in the minority community: DWB, Driving While Black, or Driving While Brown."[35] As that phrase suggests, for Black drivers as a group, traffic stops have become a central part of the travel experience. "I have been pulled over more than I care to imagine by police officers," one Black man in

his forties told researchers in 2014. "I've had my car searched for drugs countless times and I have never once tried or experimented with illegal sub-
stances. It has happened everywhere I've ever lived: Delaware, Northern
Virginia, North Carolina. I've had my car searched for drugs. I've never owned
a car that I would identify as a drug dealer's car. Yet, I have had dogs go
through my car a couple of times."[36] His report is echoed by near-identical
complaints from numerous Black drivers.[37]

In recent years African Americans and members of other minority groups
have pushed back against racial profiling, securing anti-profiling laws in
thirty states. But these state laws are relatively toothless. Few include "a definition of profiling that is inclusive of all significantly impacted groups,"
notes a recent NAACP report on the persistence of racial profiling. Anti-
profiling laws offer little protection to Black drivers—or walkers—because
they do not ban what are known as "pretextual stops" of motorists and pedestrians, in which officers "use minor violations such as not using a seat belt
or jay walking as a pretext to search for illegal contraband."[38] Such stops are
central to Operation Pipeline, which still exists today, and they are central
to the criminalization of Black drivers, a stubbornly persistent problem.

Traffic stops are a problem for African American drivers on local roads as
well as highways, and a number of recent studies have suggested that Black
drivers are more likely than white drivers to be ticketed for "relatively minor
traffic infractions, such as equipment violations."[39] To give one example,
Blacks in Kansas City receive far more traffic tickets than whites. A 2017 investigation revealed that 60 percent of all traffic tickets issued to Kansas City
residents went to African Americans, who make up 30 percent of the population. Whites, who make up 59 percent of the city's residents, received only
37 percent. Generally poorer than the city's white drivers, Blacks were most
often ticketed for infractions that are closely related to poverty, such as driving
with expired plates or without insurance—whereas the city's whites were
more likely to be ticketed for speeding. But the discrepancies in the percentage
of tickets received by members of the two groups may be more decisively
shaped by race and residence than they are by the character or frequency of
either group's driving violations. Ticketing levels in Kansas City vary dramatically by neighborhood, with the predominantly Black zip code 64130
being the most common residential zip code of drivers receiving tickets. Not
coincidentally, 64130 is also the most heavily policed neighborhood in the city.
It is a matter of "averages and opportunity," says Ken Novak, a professor of

criminal justice and criminology at the University of Missouri–Kansas City. "The more officers deployed, the greater the likelihood people driving there will be stopped."[40]

Whether caused by race, place of residence, or a combination of the two, the impact of these frequent traffic stops on African American life is far from trivial. For one thing, traffic tickets are not free, and emerging evidence suggests that many communities use them as a source of revenue. Most notorious in this regard is the St. Louis suburb of Ferguson, where a 2014 Justice Department study triggered by the police shooting of Michael Brown, an unarmed African American teenager, found patterns of traffic ticketing far more dedicated to generating revenue than to securing public safety. The city's finance director used highway traffic enforcement as a "revenue pipeline," and had the police working overtime to issue as many tickets as possible.[41] Ferguson is now under a Department of Justice consent decree prohibiting its employees from recommending, developing, or implementing "any law enforcement program, strategy, tactic, or action in order to generate revenue."[42] But researchers have since found that similar practices are common in other "financially strapped jurisdictions with narrow tax bases," and that African Americans, Hispanics, and other low-income groups are especially likely, as a *Washington Post* reporter put it, "to bear the brunt of policing for profit."[43]

Beyond the expensive tickets, traffic stops are psychologically stressful, especially for members of a group with a long and troubled history with the police. When asked about the experience of "Driving While Black" in 2002, some African American informants told researchers that they were terrified of traffic stops for reasons that dated back to the segregation era. A forty-year-old man named Rabbian testified that he could not escape "the ghost of slavery" in a car trip through southern Indiana. As he drove through Indiana's majority-white, largely rural landscape, he found himself praying: "Please God don't let anything happen to me or my car, because if something happens and I get pulled over, I'm going to be missing or hanging from a tree." In no direct danger at any point, he still had "the[se] kinds of things implanted in my head. I still think like that because of the past. It's a part of history."[44] Among less historically minded African American drivers, fears triggered by modern-day conditions predominate. More likely to be stopped than whites, African American drivers are also more likely to be treated disrespectfully by police and are often "left feeling violated, angry, and wary of police and their motives."[45] High-profile incidents of police brutality toward Black drivers—and toward Blacks in general—are common enough to make traffic stops seem dangerous to virtually all African American drivers.

Black Lives Matter, like many of the earlier civil rights initiatives chronicled in this book, has taken shape at least in part around the dangers of traveling Black. A series of linked protests sparked by outrage over police violence against Black people, Black Lives Matter first achieved international recognition in 2014, when the residents of Ferguson, Missouri, took to the streets to protest the police shooting of Michael Brown. Even though Brown was on foot when he clashed with police officer Darren Wilson, years of predatory and oppressive traffic policing contributed to the rage that inspired the city's African American residents to riot in the days immediately following his death. At that time the details of the conflict that led to his death were still unclear, but the city's residents were already furious.

"People in Ferguson did not know whether Brown was attempting to surrender or attempting to attack Wilson when the officer shot him," observed journalist Wesley Lowry, who traveled to Ferguson that summer to cover protests for the *Washington Post*. But they knew something was very wrong with the city's policing. In particular, they resented the fact that "the police in Ferguson looked nothing like them: an almost all-white force charged with serving and protecting a majority Black city. They knew all too well about the near-constant traffic tickets they were being given, and how often those tickets turned into warrants."[46]

Traffic and policing have remained central in subsequent Black Lives Matter protests, many of which were triggered by events that took place during traffic stops. Some of the movement's most prominent martyrs lost their lives either during, or as a result of, roadside altercations with the police. Among them were Samuel DuBose, a Cincinnati man who was shot dead by police during a 2015 traffic stop for a missing front license plate and a suspended license; Sandra Bland, an Illinois woman who traveled to Texas to take a new job, only to end up an apparent suicide in police custody in 2015 after being arrested for being "argumentative and uncooperative" when she was pulled over for a routine traffic violation; Walter Scott, a South Carolina driver who was shot in the back by police in 2016 after being stopped for a nonfunctioning tail light; Terence Crutcher, a Tulsa motorist who was shot while standing outside his car; and Philandro Castile, who was shot seven times during a 2017 traffic stop in Minnesota.

In 2017 the dangers faced by African American drivers were highlighted by the NAACP, which took the unprecedented step of issuing a travel advisory urging African Americans to steer clear of Missouri. Precipitated by a number of incidents of violence against Black people, as well as death threats against students at the University of Missouri in the wake of Black Lives Matter protests there in 2015, the advisory was perhaps above all inspired by reports showing that Blacks were 75 percent more likely than whites to be pulled over for traffic violations.[47] The advisory remains in effect today, and with good reason: a 2019 report issued by the office of Missouri's attorney general revealed no improvement in Missouri's rate of racial disparities in traffic stops. Instead, things have gotten worse: African American drivers there now have a 91 percent greater chance of being pulled over than white drivers.[48]

Missouri may reform itself—eventually—but conditions there underscore that as much as transportation inequalities have changed over time, they remain with us. Indeed, the long history of travel discrimination recounted in this book suggests that while American modes of living and traveling are likely to continue to change, traveling will remain more difficult for members of some groups than for others.[49] As more African Americans have turned to air travel, "flying while Black" complaints have increased. Black flyers have reported being singled out for invasive scrutiny by customs agents, as well as experiencing racial discrimination from other passengers and airline personnel.[50]

How common such incidents are is impossible to say: flying while Black complaints are scattered, and largely anecdotal. A federal report in 2000 did find that among female citizens of the United States, Black women were far more likely than white women to be subject to intrusive customs searches—and far less likely to be carrying contraband. And in 2006, eighty-seven African American women were awarded $1.9 million in compensation for illegal pat-downs and strip searches at Chicago's O'Hare International Airport. The US Department of Homeland Security, which has replaced the Customs Department, admitted to no wrongdoing, but it did pledge to do "a better job of documenting its reasons for doing the appropriate searches that are done."[51] The airlines have also been subject to formal complaints. In October 2017 the NAACP issued a national travel advisory that warned African Americans of "disrespectful, discriminatory or unsafe conditions" on American Airlines, the world's largest airline. The warning was inspired by a series of "disturbing incidents" on American Airlines flights, most of which involved Black passengers who were summarily ejected from flights in the wake of minor disputes with other passengers and/or airline personnel.[52] "All travelers must be guaranteed the right to travel without fear of threat, violence or harm," NAACP president Derrick Johnson noted in announcing the measure. "The growing list of incidents suggesting racial bias reflects an unacceptable corporate culture and involves behavior that cannot be dismissed as normal or random."[53]

The NAACP rescinded its travel warning against American Airlines in July 2018 after finding that the airline had made substantial progress in addressing the mistreatment of Black passengers. As reported to the *Washington Post,* the improvements included introducing a "company-wide training on implicit bias, conducting an independent analysis of where the company falls short on diversity and inclusion measures, overhauling how it investigates customer complaints of discrimination, and making it easier for its own employees to report concerns."[54] But travel discrimination remains an ever-moving target. Even as the airlines seem open to reform, early research on new travel amenities, such as ride-sharing services and Airbnb accommodations, indicates that racism is a problem on these new app-based services. A 2015 Harvard Business School study "found that Airbnb hosts were 16% less likely to accept fictional guests with African American–sounding names than guests with white-sounding names—even though the guests had otherwise identical profiles."[55] Likewise, a 2016 analysis of Uber and Lyft services in Seattle and Boston found that African Americans who sought rides in these cities experienced more frequent cancellations and longer wait times than did whites seeking rides.[56]

These developments are not surprising. Even though the civil rights movement succeeded in abolishing the South's Jim Crow laws, the nation's divided and divisive racial geography remains very much intact. There's no need to travel back in time to travel Black.

NOTES

ACKNOWLEDGMENTS

ILLUSTRATION CREDITS

INDEX

NOTES

INTRODUCTION

1. "'Jim Crow Kit' Latest Fad for Journey South: Minister Equips Himself to Overcome Hardships of Southern Travel," *Chicago Defender*, August 26, 1922.

2. Ray Stannard Baker, *Following the Color Line: An Account of Negro Citizenship in the American Democracy* (New York: Doubleday, 1908), 31.

3. Gunnar Myrdal, *An American Dilemma*, vol. 2: *The Negro Problem and Modern Democracy* (New York: Harper and Brothers, 1944; New Brunswick, NJ: Transaction, 1996), 635.

4. William Pickens, "Re-Visiting the South," *Crisis*, 37, no. 4, April 1930.

5. "Riding a Jim-Crow Bus: Ignorant, Belligerent Bus Drivers Insult Passengers and Get Off with It," *Baltimore Afro-American*, November 20, 1943, 1.

6. Jeannye Thornton, "The Black Traveler Today: His Map, Wallet Stretches Further," *Chicago Tribune*, June 11, 1971, 4.

7. James Clifford, *Routes: Travel and Translation in the Late Twentieth Century* (Cambridge, MA: Harvard University Press, 1997). On the prevalence of "'sedentarist' approaches to social science," see also Kevin Hannam, Mimi Sheller, and Johns Urry, "Editorial: Mobilities, Immobilities and Moorings," *Mobilities* 1, no. 1 (March 2006), 5.

8. Ira Berlin, *The Making of African America: The Four Great Migrations* (New York: Viking, 2010).

9. "Jim Crow Trains Leave 'Pennsy' Station Daily," *Pittsburgh Courier*, June 12, 1943, 14; "Pennsylvania R. R. Explains Jim Crow Rule," *New York Amsterdam News*, December 9, 1944, 1; Albert G Barnett, "Pledge Illinois Ban on Jim Crow Cars on Penn. R. R.," *Chicago Defender*, January 23, 1943, 22.

10. On the experience of traveling Jim Crow from Los Angeles, see Langston Hughes, "How a Poem Was Born in a Jim Crow Car Rattling from Los Angeles to New Orleans," *Chicago Defender*, January 9, 1954, 11.

11. "Dan Burley's Back Door Stuff: Looking through the Window of a Jim Crow Train," *New York Amsterdam News*, November 13, 1943, 1.

12. "Bus Line Segregates to 'Prevent Embarrassment,'" *Baltimore Afro-American*, October 7, 1939, 3.

13. George Schuyler, "Vacation Daze," *Common Ground* 3, no. 3 (1943), 42.

14. Schuyler, "Vacation Daze," 42, 43.

15. Chin Jou, "Neither Welcomed, nor Refused: Race and Restaurants in Postwar New York City," *Journal of Urban History* 40, no. 2 (2014): 235; Thomas Sugrue, *Sweet Land of Liberty: The Forgotten Struggle for Civil Rights in the North* (New York: Random House, 2008).

16. Langston Hughes, "Here to Yonder," *Chicago Defender*, March 30, 1946, 14.

17. C. D. Halliburton, "South of Mason-Dixon," *Philadelphia Tribune*, June 29, 1948, 9.

18. P. L. Prattis, "The Horizon: Information on How to Duck Jim Crow in the North Usually Offered by Negroes in Know," *Pittsburgh Courier*, June 12, 1948, 7.

19. Albon Lewis Holsey, "Zig-Zagging through Dixie," *Opportunity*, November 1925, 325, 326.

20. Carl Rowan, *South of Freedom* (New York: Knopf, 1952), 16, 39.

21. United States Congress, House Committee on Interstate and Foreign Commerce, *Hearings before the Committee on Interstate and Foreign Commerce of the House of Representatives on the Bills to Amend the Interstate Commerce Law (H. R. 146, 273, 2040, 5775, 8337, and 10930), April 8, 1902* (Washington, DC: US Government Printing Office, 1902), 443.

22. "'Caste' in Brooklyn," *New York Times*, October 2, 1894, 4.

23. G. C. S., "Work of the Senate," *Charleston Weekly News and Courier*, February 23, 1898, 12.

24. Leadbelly, "Jim Crow Blues" (ca. 1946), in Guido van Rijn, *The Truman and Eisenhower Blues: African-American Blues and Gospel Songs, 1945–1960* (New York: Continuum, 2004), 46.

25. "Idlewild," *Crisis*, August 1917, 168–169. Recent tourism research suggests that "the highly discriminatory history of mobility and hospitality in the United States" remains an ongoing constraint on Black tourism even today. Less likely to travel for pleasure than other Americans (for economic reasons), African Americans remain "apprehensive travelers," who are more hesitant to visit "unfamiliar places, engage in unplanned situations, or travel alone" than white Americans. "Study: Afro-American Tourists Mostly Visit Families and Sight-See," *New Pittsburgh Courier*, July 24, 1993, 6; Derek H. Alderman, "Introduction to the Special Issue: African Americans and Tourism," *Tourism Geographies* 15, no. 3 (2013): 376.

26. Ron Reaves, "Better Not Bitter," in "Surviving Jim Crow," American Public Media, http://americanradioworks.publicradio.org/features/remembering/surviving.html.

27. "Declaration of the Rights of the Negro Peoples of the World," Universal Negro Improvement Association (UNIA), August 13, 1920, http://historymatters.gmu.edu/d/5122/.

28. Booker T. Washington, "Is the Negro Having a Fair Chance?," *Century Illustrated Magazine*, 85, no. 1 (1912), 51.

29. Charles Houston, "Along This Way," *Baltimore Afro-American*, October 30, 1948, 4.

30. Ramsey also wrote and produced a play on the *Green Book* in 2004. Calvin Alexander Ramsey, *Ruth and the Green Book* (Minneapolis: Lerner Publishing Group, 2010). Just out as this book goes to press are two new books that add to our knowledge of the *Green Book:* Gretchen Sorin, *Driving while Black: African American Travel and the Road to Civil Rights* (New York: Liveright, 2020); and Candacy Taylor, *Overground Railroad: The Green Book and the Roots of Black Travel in America* (New York: Abrams Press, 2020).

31. Sorin, *Driving while Black,* is a notable exception. A broad-ranging history of African Americans and cars, it discusses a wide variety of Black travel guides. See Sorin, chapter 6.

32. "Traveller's Directory," *The Liberator*, April 8, 1842. This list first appeared in *The Liberator* on April 8, 1842, and ran in every issue for over a year. For more information on this list, see Richard Archer, *Jim Crow North: The Struggle for Equal Rights in Antebellum New England* (New York: Oxford University Press, 2017), 106.

33. On early passenger travel, see Patricia Cline Cohen, "Women at Large: Travel in Antebellum America," *History Today* 44, no. 12 (December 1994): 44–51.

34. Samuel Breck, *Recollections of Samuel Breck: With Passages from His Notebooks, 1771–1862* (Philadelphia: Porter and Coates, 1877), 276.

35. Quoted in Amy G. Richter, *Home on the Rails: Women, the Railroad, and the Rise of Public Domesticity* (Chapel Hill: University of North Carolina Press, 2005), 66, 60.

36. Richter, *Home on the Rails*, 60.

37. "What characterized southern transportation as a whole was a lack of a uniform system." Charles A. Lofgren, *The Plessy Case: A Legal-Historical Interpretation* (New York: Oxford University Press, 2014), 17.

38. For a discussion of the civil rights movement as a movement that originated well before the famous protests of the 1950s and 1960s, see Jacquelyn Dowd Hall, who advances this argument in an influential article entitled "The Long Civil Rights Movement and the Political Uses of the Past," *Journal of American History* 91, no. 4 (March 2005): 1233–1263. Hall's article popularized the idea of a "long civil rights movement" and has inspired extensive reflection and debate. See, for example, Sundiata Keita Cha-Jua and Clarence Lang, "The 'Long Movement' as Vampire: Temporal and Spatial Fallacies in Recent Black Freedom Studies," *Journal of African American History* 92, no. 2 (2007): 265–288; Eric Arnesen, "Reconsidering the 'Long Civil Rights Movement,'" *Historically Speaking* 10, no. 2 (April 2009): 31–34; Steven F. Lawson, "Long Origins of the Short Civil Rights Movement, 1954–1968," in *Freedom Rights: New Perspectives on the Civil Rights Movement*, ed. Danielle L. McGuire and John Dittmer (Lexington: University Press of Kentucky, 2011), 9–37; Jeffrey Helgeson, "Essay Review II: Beyond a Long Civil Rights Movement" *Journal of African American History* 99, no. 4 (2014): 442–445; and Christopher W. Schmidt, "Legal History and the Problem of the Long Civil Rights Movement," *Law and Social Inquiry* 41, no.4 (Fall 2016): 1081–1107.

1. THE ROAD TO *PLESSY*

1. Mary Church Terrell, "Being a Colored Woman in the United States," in *Unpublished Papers of Mary Church Terrell* (Alexandria, VA: Alexander Street Press, 2004), 26.

2. Mary Church Terrell, *A Colored Woman in a White World* (Washington, DC: Ransdell, 1940), 15.

3. Terrell, *Colored Woman in a White World*, 15, 16.

4. Terrell, *Colored Woman in a White World*, 16.

5. Alexis de Tocqueville, *Democracy in America*, trans. Henry Reeve, with preface and notes by John C. Spencer (New York: Walker, 1847), 390.

6. "The Railway Carriage System in England," *Scientific American* 8, no. 3, October 5, 1851, 17.

7. James Buffum, "Colorphobia," *The Liberator*, July 19, 1839; Mr. Bradburn in *Proceedings of the General Anti-Slavery Convention* (London: British and Foreign Anti-Slavery Society, 1841), 328. For more on responses to early Black travelers, see Elizabeth Stordeur Pryor, *Colored Travelers: Mobility and the Fight for Citizenship before the Civil War* (Chapel Hill: University of North Carolina Press, 2016), chap. 2.

8. Thurlow Weed, *A Chapter from the Autobiography of Mr. Thurlow Weed: Stagecoach Traveling Forty-Six Years Ago* (Albany, NY: Printing House of Charles Van Resthuysen and Sons, 1870), 8–9.

9. "Disgraceful," *The Liberator*, August 3, 1833, 123; David Ruggles, "For the Emancipator," *Emancipator and Free American* (New York) 2, no. 3, January 28, 1834, 1.

10. "Scene on Board of a Steam-Boat," *The Liberator*, May 24, 1839.

11. Alexander Crummell, "Eulogium on Henry Highland Garnet, D.D." (1882), reprinted in *Destiny and Race: Selected Writings, 1840–1898,* ed. Wilson Jeremiah Moses (Amherst: University of Massachusetts Press, 1992), 58–59. See also Joel Schor, *Henry Highland Garnet: A Voice of Black Radicalism in the Nineteenth Century* (Westport, CT: Greenwood Press, 1977), 12–13.

12. See, for example, *The Liberator,* December 10, 1831; Henry Drayton and Henry Johnson to Garrison, June 28, 1832, published in *The Liberator,* July 7, 1832, and August 3, 1833; *The Liberator,* February 1, 1834; "Disabilities of Colored People," *Colored American,* September 30, 1837; "Persecuted Everywhere," *Colored American,* April 12, 1838; "Stage Coach Meanness in Rochester," *North Star* (Rochester, NY), October 3, 1850, 41, col. A.

13. "Go by Foot, Brethren," *Colored American,* June 30, 1838.

14. On the railroads' "annihilation of space and time," see Wolfgang Schivelbusch, "Railroad Space and Railroad Time," *New German Critique* 14 (1978): 31–40.

15. "Dear Brother Cornish," *Colored American* (New York), September 16, 1837.

16. "Editorial Correspondence," *Colored American* (New York), July 20, 1839.

17. Henry Scott, "To the Public," letter to the *Massachusetts Spy* (Worcester), December 4, 1838, reprinted in *The Liberator,* December 14, 1838.

18. From a letter that was excerpted in a Garrison editorial, *The Liberator,* September 20, 1839.

19. December 1, 1841, Eastern Railroad regulation cited in the *Tenth Annual Report of the Board of Managers of the Massachusetts Anti-Slavery Society* (Boston: Dow and Jackson's Press, 1842), 76.

20. Joseph Grinnell, quoted in David Ruggles, "Lynching in New Bedford," *The Liberator,* August 6, 1841, 127.

21. "Rail Road Abuse," *Colored American,* June 19, 1841.

22. Frederick Douglass, *My Bondage and My Freedom* (New York: Miller, Orton and Mulligan, 1855), 399, 400.

23. For additional information and background on these cases, see Richard Archer, *Jim Crow North: The Struggle for Equal Rights in Antebellum New England* (New York: Oxford University Press, 2017), 97–98; and Pryor, *Colored Travelers,* 95–97.

24. "The Case of Mr. Downing," *Colored American* 1, no. 53, February 20, 1941.

25. See Richard Archer, *Jim Crow North,* chap. 7.

26. Louis Ruchames, "Jim Crow Railroads in Massachusetts," *American Quarterly* 8, no. 1 (1956): 74.

27. Douglass, *My Bondage and My Freedom,* 455.

28. Harriet Ann Jacobs, *Incidents in the Life of a Slave Girl* (Boston: Published by the author, 1861), 248.

29. Jacobs, *Incidents in the Life of a Slave Girl,* 248.

30. William Lloyd Garrison, "Condition of the Colored People," *The Liberator,* March 15, 1861, 4.

31. "Our Visit to Gouldtown," *Christian Recorder* (Philadelphia), February 2, 1861.

32. For more on the development of southern railroads, see William G. Thomas, *The Iron Way: Railroads, the Civil War, and the Making of Modern America* (New Haven, CT: Yale University Press, 2011); and Aaron W. Marrs, *Railroads in the Old South: Pursuing Progress in a Slave Society* (Baltimore: Johns Hopkins University Press, 2009).

33. Lyman Abbott, *Reminiscences* (Boston: Houghton Mifflin, 1915), 104.

34. Frederick Law Olmsted, *A Journey in the Seaboard Slave States in the Years, 1853–1854,* 2 vols. (New York: G. P. Putnam's Sons, 1904), 1:19–20.

35. Dernoral Davis, "A Contested Presence: Free Blacks in Antebellum Mississippi, 1820–1860," *Mississippi History Today*, Mississippi Historical Society. n.d., http://mshistorynow.mdah .state.ms.us/articles/45/a-contested-presence-free-blacks-in-antebellum-mississippi-18201860.

36. James Redpath, *The Roving Editor, or Talks with Slaves in the Southern States*, ed. John R. McKivigan (1859; University Park: Pennsylvania State University Press, 1996), 94.

37. Quoted in Barbara Young Welke, *Recasting American Liberty: Gender, Race, Law, and the Railroad Revolution, 1865–1920* (New York: Cambridge University Press, 2001), 256.

38. Hugh Davis, *"We Will Be Satisfied with Nothing Less": The African American Struggle for Equal Rights in the North during Reconstruction* (Ithaca. NY: Cornell University Press, 2011), 147.

39. Frank J. Webb Jr., "Our Civil Rights," *African Methodist Episcopal Church Review* 8, no. 4 (1892): 406.

40. Eliza Frances Andrews, *The Wartime Diary of a Georgia Girl* (New York: D. Appleton, 1908), 251. On postwar conflicts over space on the sidewalk, see James West Davidson, *"They Say": Ida B. Wells and the Reconstruction of Race* (New York: Oxford University Press, 2008), 19.

41. On Black mobility during this period, see William Cohen, *At Freedom's Edge: Black Mobility and the Southern White Quest for Racial Control, 1861–1915* (Baton Rouge: Louisiana State University Press, 1991).

42. "The Negro, Interesting Facts about the Liberated Slaves. Their Horrible Condition. Extravagant Idea about What Freedom Means," *New York World*. June 8, 1865, reprinted in *Mt. Vernon Democratic Banner* (Mount Vernon, OH), June 24, 1865, 1.

43. Quoted in Gilbert Thomas Stephenson, "The Separation of the Races in Public Conveyances," *American Political Science Review* 3, no. 2 (May 1, 1909): 181.

44. Congressman Richard Harvey Cain of South Carolina, speaking of the Civil Rights Act of 1875 on January 10, 1874, *Congressional Record*, vol 2, part 1, 43rd Congress, 1st Session (Washington, DC: US Government Printing Office, 1874), 565–567.

45. "Negro Equality in Arkansas," *Hancock Democrat* (Greenfield, IN). August 27, 1868.

46. Whitelaw Reid, *After the War: A Southern Tour: May 1, 1865, to May 1, 1866* (Cincinnati: Moore, Wilstach and Baldwin, 1866), 420–421.

47. *Journal of the House of Representatives of the State of Georgia, at the Annual Session of the General Assembly Convened at Atlanta, January 10, 1870* (Atlanta, 1870), part 1, 309; *Journal of the Senate of the State of Georgia, at the Annual Session of the General Assembly, Atlanta, January 10, 1870* (Atlanta, 1870), part 2, 261; part 3, 508.

48. "Dr. Fuller on the Civil Rights Bill," *Christian Recorder*, August 27, 1874. This observation was confirmed by many subsequent observers, including South Carolina senator Robert Smalls, who told Congress in 1884 that on crossing into Georgia, Black travelers were invariably "compelled to go into the 'Jim Crow Car,' which is next to the locomotive." United States Congress, *Interstate Commerce: Debate in Forty-Eighth Congress, Second Session [Fiftieth Congress], on the Bill (H.R. 5461) to Establish a Board of Commissioners of Interstate Commerce and to Regulate Such Commerce &c., &c*, 1884, 320.

49. James M. McPherson, *The Abolitionist Legacy: From Reconstruction to the NAACP* (Princeton, NJ: Princeton University Press, 1995), 14.

50. Belton O'Neall Townsend writing under the pseudonym "A South Carolinian," "South Carolina Society," *Atlantic Monthly* 39, June 1877, 676. Similar claims about segregation in South Carolina can be seen in the work of George W. Cable, who cited news reports noting that in South Carolina "respectable colored people who buy first class tickets on any railroad

ride in the first class as their right, and their presence excites no comment." George W. Cable, *The Silent South* (New York: C. Scribner's Sons, 1885), 85–86.

51. T. McCants Stewart, "Rambles in the South," *New York Freeman,* April 25, 1885.

52. "Negro Equality in Arkansas."

53. *DeCuir v. Benson,* an 1875 challenge to segregation aboard a steamboat operating between New Orleans and Mississippi, contains testimony suggesting that segregation was then still "the universal custom" of steamboats operating on the Mississippi River. *DeCuir v. Benson,* 27 La. Ann. 1, 1–13 (1875). The historian Howard Rabinowitz likewise notes that throughout both Reconstruction and Redemption, "steamboats remained the most segregated form of transportation." Howard Rabinowitz, "From Exclusion to Segregation: Southern Race Relations, 1865–1890," *Journal of American History* 63, no. 2 (September 1976): 341.

54. John William Graves, "Jim Crow in Arkansas: A Reconsideration of Urban Race Relations in the Post-Reconstruction South," *Journal of Southern History* 55, no. 3 (August 1, 1989): 425.

55. James MacPherson, *The Abolitionist Legacy,* 14.

56. Charles Sumner, "Rights and Duties of Our Colored Fellow Citizens: Letter to the National Convention of Colored Citizens, Columbia, South Carolina, October 12, 1871," in *The Works of Charles Sumner* (Boston: Lee and Shepard, 1883), 14:317.

57. Civil Rights Act of 1875, 18 Stat 335–337.

58. "The Civil-Rights Bill," *Chicago Tribune,* November 3, 1874, 4.

59. John Hope Franklin, "The Enforcement of the Civil Rights Act of 1875," in *Race and History: Selected Essays, 1938–1968* (Baton Rouge: Louisiana State University Press, 1989).

60. "The Civil Rights Bill: Southern Press Opinions upon the Measure," *Cincinnati Enquirer,* February 11, 1875, 2; "Can the Civil Rights Bill Be Enforced?," *New York Times,* March 6, 1875, 4.

61. "The Civil Rights Bill in Practice," *Sun* (New York), March 8, 1875, 2.

62. "The Civil Rights Bill: Southern Press Opinions upon the Measure."

63. Franklin, "Enforcement of the Civil Rights Act of 1875."

64. "Equal Rights in Trade and Travel," *New York Times,* November 29, 1979, 4.

65. Marilyn Hall Mitchell, "From Slavery to Shelley: Michigan's Ambivalent Response to Civil Rights," *Wayne Law Review* 26, no. 1 (1979): 19.

66. "Status of the Negro in Free States," *Civilian and Gazette Weekly* (Galveston, TX), November 23, 1858, quoted in Kyle G. Volk, *Moral Minorities and the Making of American Democracy* (New York: Oxford University Press, 2014), 162.

67. *West Chester & Philadelphia Railroad v. Miles,* 55 Pa. 209, Pa. Supreme Court (1867).

68. *West Chester & Philadelphia Railroad v. Miles,* 55 Pa. 209, Pa. Supreme Court (1867).

69. *DeCuir v. Benson* 27 La. Ann. 1 (1875).

70. *Hall v. DeCuir* 95 U.S. 485 (1877).

71. *Hall v. DeCuir* 95 U.S. 485 (1877).

72. Welke, *Recasting American Liberty,* 339n54.

73. *Hall v. DeCuir* 95 U.S. 485 (1877).

74. *The Chicago & Northwestern Railway Company v. Anna Williams,* 55 Ill. 185 (1870), in *The American Corporation Cases: Embracing the Decisions of the Supreme Court of the United States, the Circuit Courts of the United States, and the Courts of Last Resort in the Several States, Since January 1, 1868, of Questions Peculiar to the Law of Corporations.* III: *Private Corporations,* Thomas F. Withrow and Henry Binmore, eds. (Chicago: E. B. Myers, 1880), 271.

75. Barbara Y. Welke, "When All the Women Were White, and All the Blacks Were Men: Gender, Class, Race, and the Road to *Plessy,* 1855–1914," *Law and History Review* 13, no. 2 (1995): 266.

76. A Yankee, "Railway Travelling in America," *Spectator* 37, September 3, 1864, 1018.

77. From the *Weekly News and Courier* (Charleston, SC), *"Our Women in the War": The Lives They Lived; the Deaths They Died* (Charleston, SC: News and Courier Book Presses, 1885), 163.

78. A Yankee, "Railway Travelling in America."

79. Terrell, *Colored Woman in a White World*, 297.

80. According to historian Barbara Welke, Black female litigants outnumbered Black male litigants in railway segregation cases until 1887. Welke, *Recasting American Liberty*, 297, 300.

81. *United States v. Dodge*, et al., 1. Texas Law J 47, District Court W. D. Texas, October 3, 1877

82. *Brown v. Memphis & C. R. Co.*, Circuit Court, W. D. Tennessee, 7 F. 51, April 5, 1881.

83. On this point, see also Kenneth W. Mack, "Law, Society. Identity, and the Making of the Jim Crow South: Travel and Segregation on Tennessee Railroads, 1875–1905," *Law and Social Inquiry* 24, no. 2 (1999): 377.

84. "Invited Out. A Colored New Orleans Politician In Trouble. Civil Rights Not Such a Blessing," *Augusta Chronicle*, May 27, 1876, 4.

85. "Invited Out. A Colored New Orleans Politician In Trouble. Civil Rights Not Such a Blessing."

86. William Jenkins, "Outrage in Alabama: A Party of Colored Ladies and Gentlemen Assaulted on a Railroad—What Is the Proper Redress?," *New York Freeman*, April 21, 1877.

87. "*Civil Rights Cases* 109 U.S. 3 (1883)." *Justia Law*, U.S. Supreme Court, https://supreme.justia.com/cases/federal/us/109/3/case.html

88. "*Civil Rights Cases* 109 U.S. 3 (1883)."

89. "Civil Rights: The Supreme Court Declares the Bill to Be Unconstitutional," *Atlanta Constitution*, October 16, 1883.

90. "The Civil Rights Act," *New-York Tribune*, October 17, 1883, 4.

91. Frederick Douglass, "Speech of Hon. Frederick Douglass," in *Proceedings of the Civil Rights Mass-Meeting Held at Lincoln Hall, October 22, 1883* (Washington, DC: C. P. Farrell, 1883), available through University of Delaware Library, https://udspace.udel.edu/handle/19716/21266.

92. "*Civil Rights Cases* 109 U.S. 3 (1883)."

93. "*Civil Rights Cases* 109 U.S. 3 (1883)."

94. Douglass, speech at Civil Rights Mass-Meeting.

95. T. Thomas Fortune, "The Civil Rights Decision," *New York Globe*, October 20, 1883, 2; "Turner on the Civil Rights," *Arkansas Mansion*, October 27, 1883, 1.

96. Indignation meetings were held in Washington, New York, Philadelphia, Pittsburgh, Cleveland, St. Louis, Chicago, Columbus, Louisville, Springfield, MO, Birmingham, Norwich, CT, and Texas. For more on this subject, see Marianne L Lado, "A Question of Justice: African-American Legal Perspectives on the 1883 Civil Rights Cases," *Chicago-Kent Law Review* 70, no. 3 (1995): 1123–1195, at 1130.

97. Quoted in Lado, 1149.

98. Douglass, speech at Civil Rights Mass-Meeting.

99. "The Civil Rights Decision," *People's Advocate* (Washington, DC), October 10, 1883.

100. On its repeal, see George Brown Tindall, *South Carolina Negroes, 1877–1900* (Columbia: University of South Carolina Press, 1952), 291–293.

101. "Civil Rights Law: An Extract from Hon. John Mercer Langston's Great Lecture (October 19, 1883)," *Cleveland Gazette*, November 3, 1883.

102. A cluster of counties located in central and eastern North Carolina. O'Hara's district was known as "The Black Second" because the communities included in the district were mostly majority-Black in population and still managed to elect Black local and state officials even after the Democrats regained control of North Carolina in the 1870s.

103. Philip Dray, *Capitol Men: The Epic Story of Reconstruction through the Lives of the First Black Congressmen* (New York: Mariner Books, 2010), 345.

104. *Congressional Record: Proceedings and Debates,* vol. 15, 48th Congress, 1st Session, (Washington, DC: Government Printing Office, 1884), 282.

105. *Interstate Commerce Debate in 48th Congress, Second Session, on Bill (H.R. 5481) to Establish a Board of Commissioners of Interstate Commerce* (Washington, DC: Government Printing Office, 1884), 309, 312.

106. *Interstate Commerce Debate in 48th Congress, Second Session,* 312, 313.

107. *Interstate Commerce Debate in 48th Congress, Second Session,* 314.

108. *Interstate Commerce Debate in 48th Congress, Second Session,* 319.

109. Interstate Commerce Act (1887), 49th Congress, 2nd Session, December 6, 1886, http://www .ourdocuments.gov/doc.php?flash=true&doc=49&page=transcript.

110. Catherine Barnes, *Journey from Jim Crow: The Desegregation of Southern Transit* (New York: Columbia University Press, 1983), 7.

111. Mack, "Law, Society, Identity," 384.

112. *Corporation Laws of Tennessee: Including Counties and Municipalities, also Federal Corporation Income Tax Law* (Nashville, TN: Marshall and Bruce Co., 1910), 401.

113. See also Kenneth Mack, "Law, Society, Identity." Mack notes that "by the mid-1880s, railroad conductors [in Tennessee] grew more intent on confining first class black passengers to smoking cars than they had been before passage of the 1881/82 laws," 386.

114. Reverend H. C. Calhoun, "Dastardly Treatment," *Christian Recorder,* November 1883. On the lack of first-class service for Blacks on Tennessee trains, see also "Civil Rights: With the Railroad Companies in the Role of Defendant," *Cincinnati Inquirer,* October 3, 1881, 6.

115. *The Chesapeake, Ohio & Southern Railroad v. Ida Wells,* Declaration (January 23, 1884), Tennessee State Library and Archives.

116. Robert T. Shannon, *Report of Cases Argued and Determined in the Supreme Court of Tennessee,* vol. 85 (Louisville: Fetter Law Book Co., 1902), 616.

117. Ida B. Wells, *The Memphis Diary of Ida B. Wells,* Miriam DeCosta-Willis, ed. (New York: Beacon Press, 1995), 141.

118. *General Acts and Resolutions Adopted by the Legislature of Florida,* Office of the Floridian and Journal. 1887, 116.

119. *General Laws of the State of Texas,* Secretary of State, 1891, 45.

120. "An Act to Promote the Comfort of Passengers on Railroads by Requiring Separate Accommodations for the White and Colored Races," *Acts Passed at the . . . General Assembly of the State of Tennessee* (Nashville, TN: A. A. Hall & F. S. Heiskell, 1891), 135.

121. Howard N. Rabinowitz, *Race, Ethnicity, and Urbanization: Selected Essays* (Columbia: University of Missouri Press, 1994), 155.

122. David M. Key, "Speech by David M. Key: The Legal and Political Status of the Negro [delivered July 2, 1885]," *Journal of Negro History* 54, no. 3 (1969): 291.

123. "The Shooting of Miss MacEwan: An Argument for Separate Cars for the Races," *Courier Journal* (Louisville, KY), October 8, 1891, 8. For a Black perspective on this development, see S. E. Smith, ed., *History of the Anti-Separate Coach Movement in Kentucky* (Evansville, IN: National Afro-American Journal and Directory Publishing Co., 1895).

124. Charles Postel, *The Populist Vision* (New York: Oxford University Press, 2007), 177.

125. Stephen Kantrowitz, *Ben Tillman and the Reconstruction of White Supremacy* (Chapel Hill: University of North Carolina Press, 2000), 143.

126. Quoted in Nina Mjagkij, *Organizing Black America: An Encyclopedia of African American Associations* (New York: Routledge, 2001), 76.

127. Anne E. Marshall, "Kentucky's Separate Coach Law and African American Response, 1892–1900," *Register of the Kentucky Historical Society* 98, no. 3 (2000): 241–259.

128. The US Supreme Court had already ruled that Mississippi's 1888 separate-car law "requiring all railroads carrying passengers in that state (other than street railroads) to provide equal but separate accommodations for the white and colored races" was constitutional in *Louisville, New Orleans & Texas Ry. Co. v. Mississippi*, 133 U.S. 587 (1890).

129. *Plessy v. Ferguson*, 163 U.S. 537 (1896).

130. Terrell, *Colored Woman in a White World*, 15.

131. Terrell, "Being a Colored Woman in the United States," 26.

2. TRAVELING BY TRAIN

1. W. E. B. Du Bois, "On Being Black," *New Republic*, 21, no. 272, February 18, 1920.

2. Du Bois, "On Being Black," 339.

3. Du Bois, "On Being Black," 340.

4. Donald M. Itzkoff, *Off the Track: The Decline of the Intercity Passenger Train in the United States* (Westport, CT: Greenwood Press, 1985), 8; and United States Congress Senate Committee on Interstate and Foreign Commerce, *Study of Domestic Land and Water Transportation: Hearings before the Subcommittee on Domestic Land and Water Transportation of the Committee on Interstate and Foreign Commerce, United States Senate* (Washington, DC: US Government Printing Office, 1950), 1407.

5. "Move against New Trains' Segregation: NAACP Warns Railroads Some Action Must Be Taken," *Chicago Defender* (national edition), August 2, 1941, 6.

6. *Georgia Edwards v. Nashville, Chattanooga & St. Louis Railway Company operating The Western & Atlantic Railroad*, 12 I.C.C. Rep., 247, as summarized in the *Twenty First Annual Report of the Interstate Commerce Commission* (Washington, DC: Government Printing Office, 1907), 67.

7. "The First Rough Experience of Travelling South," *Christian Recorder*, October 10, 1889.

8. "Statement of Rev. Walter Brooks," *Hearings before the Committee on Interstate and Foreign Commerce of the House of Representatives on the Bills to Amend the Interstate Commerce Law (H. R. 146, 273, 2040, 5775, 8337, and 10930), April 8, 1902* (Washington, DC: US Government Printing Office, 1902), 446.

9. "Statement of Rev. Walter Brooks," 446.

10. "Jim Crow Matters," *Crisis*, 4, no. 4, August 1912, 174.

11. Quoted in Neil R. McMillen, *Dark Journey: Black Mississippians in the Age of Jim Crow* (Champaign: University of Illinois Press, 1990), 293.

12. "Jim Crow Matters."

13. A contemporary, quoted in Helen G. Edmonds, *The Negro and Fusion Politics in North Carolina, 1894–1901* (Chapel Hill: University of North Carolina Press, 2013), 190.

14. A contemporary, quoted in Edmonds, *The Negro and Fusion Politics*, 190.

15. John H. White, *The American Railroad Passenger Car* (Baltimore: Johns Hopkins University Press, 1978), 394.

16. Complaints that air conditioning is lacking in Jim Crow cars (on trains where it is available in other cars) become increasingly common starting in the 1930s. See, for example, the

following report of a complaint filed by Christine O. Crable, who was "forcibly carried" into the Jim Crow car on the Atlantic Coast Line Railroad after she refused to leave an air-conditioned coach: "Va. State Coed Files $25,000 Jim Crow Rail Suit," *Jet*, 5, no. 10, January 14, 1954, 5.

17. United States Congress House Committee on Interstate and Foreign Commerce, *Safety on Railroads: Hearings before a Subcommittee of the Committee on Interstate and Foreign Commerce, House of Representatives, Sixty-Third Congress, Second Session, on Bills Relative to Safety on Railroads. Dec. 6, 1913–Jan. 31, 1914* (Washington, DC: US Government Printing Office, 1913), 90.

18. White, *American Railroad Passenger Car*, 144–145.

19. W. O. Scroggs, "Desirable Civic Reforms in the Treatment of the Negro," in *The Human Way: Addresses on Race Problems at the Southern Sociological Congress, Atlanta, 1913*, ed. James Edward McCulloch (Nashville, TN: Southern Sociological Congress, 1913), 19.

20. "Eight Negro Excursionists Killed in a Head-On Collision at Hamlet," *Charlotte Daily Observer* (Charlotte, NC), July 28, 1911.

21. "29 Die in Wreck, 23 Injured, Head-On Collision Near Hamlet, the Dead Mostly Negroes," *Columbus Enquirer-Sun* (Columbus, GA), July 24, 1906.

22. This petition from October 29, 1914, is reprinted in "Negroes Ask for Relief from Wooden Coach," *Greensboro Daily News*, October 30, 1914, 3.

23. For more on this wreck, see Betsy Thorpe, *The Day the Whistles Cried: The Great Cornfield Meet at Dutchman's Curve* (Kingston Springs, TN: Ideas into Books, Westview, 2014).

24. "Only Seven of Dead Are White Persons, as Majority Were Killed in Negro Compartment," *Daily Oklahoman*, September 29, 1917, 1.

25. "100 Killed, 100 Hurt in Train Wreck: Fast Express and an Accommodation Train in Head-On Collision Near Nashville. Most of Victims Negroes," *New York Times*, July 10, 1918.

26. "Jim Crow Car Escapes in Ga. Wreck," *Baltimore Afro-American*, January 1, 1927.

27. Untitled editorial, *Cleveland Gazette*, August 10, 1907, 2.

28. Quoted in Charles A. Simmons, *The African American Press: A History of News Coverage during National Crises, with Special Reference to Four Black Newspapers, 1827–1965* (Jefferson, NC: McFarland, 1998), 57.

29. "'Jim-Crow' Coach Wrecked, Many Killed: Bodies of 13 Victims Recovered," *Pittsburgh Courier*, March 28, 1925, 1, 2.

30. "9 Die in Jim Crow Car Wreck," *Baltimore Afro-American*, March 28, 1925, 1.

31. J. A. Rogers, "What Are We, Negroes or Americans?," *The Messenger*, 8, no. 8 (August 1926), 238.

32. "13 Persons Killed in Train Wreck," *Plattsburgh Sentinel* (Plattsburgh, NY), August 20, 1929. In the aftermath of the Henryetta crash, Nick Chiles, editor of the African American newspaper the *Plaindealer*, appealed to Chicago congressman Oscar De Priest to take up the issue of Jim Crow car casualties with the ICC. Chiles, "Open Letter to Congressman, by Editor, *Plaindealer*," August 30, 1929. Any effort that De Priest might have made does not seem to have been fruitful.

33. On the usage of the phrase "Jim Crow wreck," see, for example, "9 Die in Jim Crow Car Wreck," *Baltimore Afro-American*, March 28, 1925; and Dutton Ferguson, "Criminal Action Looms in Jim-Crow Wreck: Seek to Get Testimony of Gov't Probes," *Pittsburgh Courier*, June 2, 1934. The last widely reported Jim Crow wreck took place in Alabama in 1951. This head-on collision, which killed 18 people, 15 of whom were Black, inspired the NAACP and

other civil rights organizations to put renewed pressure on the Interstate Commerce Commission to ban segregation on interstate trains, which it finally did in 1952—although its order had little immediate impact. For a discussion of that crash, see "JC Cars Must Go," *Baltimore Afro-American*, December 8, 1951, 4.

34. J. A. Rogers, "What Are We, Negroes or Americans?"

35. "'TICKETS!': Big Meeting of the Railroad Commission Yesterday. The Colored People Asking for Equal Accommodations for Equal Money on the Railroads—Other Business." *Atlanta Constitution*, April 4, 1888, 7.

36. *Annual Report of the Rail Road Commissioners of Alabama, for the Year Ending June 30, 1882*, Office of Rail Road Commission of Alabama (Montgomery: Allred and Beers, State Book and Job Printers, 1882), 166.

37. Booker T. Washington, "Letter to the Editor, *Montgomery Advertiser*, April 30, 1885," in *African American Political Thought, 1890–1930: Washington, Du Bois, Garvey, and Randolph*, ed. Cary D. Wintz (Armonk, NY: M. E. Sharpe, 1995), 23.

38. Michael Perman, *Struggle for Mastery: Disfranchisement in the South, 1888–1908* (Chapel Hill: University of North Carolina Press, 2001), 260.

39. The *Chattanooga Observer*, quoted in untitled article in the *Plaindealer* (Detroit), July 3, 1891, 4.

40. On the early history of Virginia's railroad regulation, see A. Caperton Braxton, "The Virginia State Corporation Commission," *Virginia Law Register* 10, no. 1 (1904): 1–18.

41. Special Dispatch to the *Baltimore Sun*, "The 'Jim Crow' Law: Why It Was Introduced—The Practice at Hagerstown," *Sun*, January 16, 1902.

42. "The Evil Effects of the Jim Crow Car Law in the South," *Broad Axe* (Chicago), January 2, 1904, 8.

43. "Declaration of the Rights of the Negro Peoples of the World," Universal Negro Improvement Association (UNIA), August 13, 1920, http://historymatters.gmu.edu/d/5122/.

44. "Race Problem on Railroads: The Plan in North Carolina for Running Separate Coaches," *New York Times*, December 18, 1898. South Carolina fares quoted in "News and Other Gleanings," *Friends' Intelligencer and Journal* (Philadelphia) 57, no. 8, Second Month [February] 24, 1900, 159.

45. "Reaching Alabama before Six O'Clock on Saturday, the 27th," *Christian Recorder* (Philadelphia), June 8, 1899.

46. "A Step Backward," *Frank Leslie's Illustrated Newspaper*, September 19, 1891, 98.

47. Charles W. Chesnutt, "The White and the Black," *Boston Evening Transcript*, March 20, 1901, 13.

48. Founded in 1900 and headquartered in Norfolk, Virginia, the Sea Board Air Line Railway ran along the South's eastern coast, terminating in Florida. Despite its name, it owned no airplanes. Before the days of air travel, "air line" (as in a straight line drawn in the air) was a term widely used to describe the shortest distance between two points, and it became part of the name of a number of nineteenth-century railroads whose proprietors wished to emphasize that their routes were more direct than those of competing roads.

49. "E. A. Johnson, John C. Dancy, R. H. W. Leak et al. vs. Seaboard Airline and Southern Railroad," in *Eighth Annual Report of the Board of Railroad Commissioners of North Carolina* (Raleigh: Guy V. Barnes, Printer to the State, 1898), 110.

50. "E. A. Johnson, John C. Dancy, R. H. W. Leak et al. vs. Seaboard Airline and Southern Railroad."

51. Chesnutt, "The White and the Black," 13.

52. Ray Stannard Baker, *Following the Color Line: An Account of Negro Citizenship in the American Democracy* (New York: Doubleday, 1908), 223.

53. "Atlanta Terminal of the Southern Railway," *International Railway Journal* 8, no. 5 (August 1905): 17.

54. Benjamin Mays, *Born to Rebel: An Autobiography* (New York: Scribner, 1971; Athens, GA: University of Georgia Press, 2003), 78.

55. Mays, *Born to Rebel*, 79.

56. A Florida statute passed in 1907 required "Separate Waiting Rooms and Ticket Windows," *The Compiled Laws, 1914, of the State of Florida* (St. Paul, FL: West, 1915), 2960e.

57. Joan Steinau Lester, *Eleanor Holmes Norton: Fire in My Soul* (New York: Simon and Schuster, 2003), 24.

58. Du Bois, "On Being Black."

59. Anna Julia Cooper, *A Voice from the South* (Xenia, OH: Alpine Printing House, 1892), 90.

60. Du Bois, "On Being Black."

61. "Tells of Jim Crow by Railroad," *Chicago Defender*, October 5, 1946, 14. Complaints about being Jim Crowed in Cairo, Illinois, go as far back as the World War I era. See, for example, "Jim Crow in Illinois," *Chicago Defender*, July 18, 1914, 8; "Ill. Central Mistreats Colored Passengers," *Chicago Defender*, September 5, 1914, 1.

62. "Dan Burley's Back Door Stuff: Looking through the Window of a Jim Crow Train," *New York Amsterdam News*, November 13, 1943, 8B.

63. Du Bois, "On Being Black."

64. Langston Hughes, "From Rampart Street to Harlem, I Follow the Trail of the Blues," (December 6, 1952), in *The Collected Writings of Langston Hughes*, vol. 10: *Fight for Freedom and Other Writings on Civil Rights* (Columbia: University of Missouri Press, 2001), 245.

65. *The Code of Alabama: Adopted by Act of the General Assembly . . . Approved February 16, 1897*, prepared by William Logan Martin (Atlanta, GA: Foote and Davies, 1887), chap. 95, art. 2, 3455, p. 975.

66. *The General Code of the City of Birmingham, Alabama, of 1930: (Includes All Ordinances of a General and Permanent Nature except as Specified in Sec. 6113)*. (Birmingham Printing Company, 1930), 215.

67. T. Montgomery Gregory, "The Jim-Crow Car: An N.A.A.C.P. Investigation, Part III," *Crisis*, February 1916, 196.

68. William Pickens, "Jim-Crowed," *Socialist Review* 9, no. 2 (1920): 126.

69. *The Autobiography of Martin Luther King, Jr.*, ed. Clayborne Carson, chap. 1, https://kinginstitute.stanford.edu/king-papers/publications/autobiography-martin-luther-king-jr-contents/chapter-1-early-years.

70. "Dr. Proctor and His Bacon," *Appeal* (St. Paul, MN), 37, no. 32, August 6, 1921.

71. Lucius Morris Beebe, *Mr. Pullman's Elegant Palace Car: The Railway Carriage That Established a New Dimension of Luxury and Entered the National Lexicon as a Symbol of Splendor* (Garden City, NY: Doubleday, 1961), 144.

72. "Sleeping Cars and Civil Rights," *Atlanta Constitution*, May 16, 1875, 2.

73. "The Negro in the Palace Car," *Atlanta Constitution*, April 13, 1875, 2; "Sleeping Cars and Civil Rights."

74. "The Civil Rights Act and the Pullman Sleeping Cars," *Atlanta Constitution*, March 31, 1875, 2.

75. Larry Tye, *Rising from the Rails: Pullman Porters and the Making of the Black Middle Class*, (New York: Owl Books, 2004), 23.

76. "The Civil Rights Act and the Pullman Sleeping Cars," *Atlanta Constitution*, April 6, 1875, 7.

77. Booker T. Washington to T. McCants Stewart, February 23, 1892, in *The Booker T. Washington Papers,* vol. 4: *1895–98,* ed. Louis R. Harlan (Urbana: University of Illinois Press, 1972–), 555.

78. "A Chance for Trouble," *New York Times,* April 12, 1887, 3.

79. *Acts and Resolutions of the General Assembly of the State of Georgia, 1899* (Atlanta: Franklin Printing and Publishing Co., 1899), 67; *Acts and Resolutions of the General Assembly of Arkansas* (Little Rock: A. M. Woodruff, State Printer, 1893), 200; *General Laws of the State of Texas Passed by the Thirteenth Legislature* (Austin: Von Boerkmann Co. Printers, 1907), 59.

80. The act did not apply to servants traveling with their employers. *Acts and Resolutions of the General Assembly of the State of Georgia, 1899,* 67.

81. "No Car Berths for Negroes," *Boston Evening Transcript,* December 22, 1899; "Bishop Barred from Sleeper; Color Line Drawn in Case of the Rev. H. W. Turner of Georgia," *New York Times,* December 22, 1899.

82. "Denies Negro Bishop a Berth," *Chicago Tribune,* December 22, 1899, 1.

83. Wilford H. Smith, "The Negro and the Law," in *The Negro Problem: A Series of Articles by Representative American Negroes of Today* (New York: James Pott, 1903), 183.

84. Wilford H. Smith to W. E. B. Du Bois, December 15, 1902, W. E. B. Du Bois Papers Series 1A, General Correspondence, Special Collections and University Archives, University of Massachusetts Amherst Libraries.

85. W. E. B. Du Bois, "The Georgia Negro Again," ms. ca. 1900, p. 6, W. E. B. Du Bois Papers Series 3, Articles, Special Collections and University Archives, University of Massachusetts Amherst Libraries.

86. W. E. B. Du Bois, *The Correspondence of W. E. B. Du Bois: Selections. 1877–1934,* ed. Herbert Aptheker (Amherst: University of Massachusetts Press, 1973), 45.

87. *Palace Car Company v. Cain,* 40 S.W. 220 (Tex. App. 1897).

88. *McCabe v. Atchison, Topeka & Santa Fe Railway Company* was filed by the Constitutional League of Oklahoma in 1908 and rejected because, at the time the case was launched, Oklahoma's 1907 Separate Car law had yet to take effect. The five Black men who filed the case had yet to have "personally been refused accommodations equal to those afforded to others," the Court concluded, and "the allegations of the bill were too vague and uncertain to entitle the complainants to a decree." *McCabe v. Atchison, T. & S. F. Ry. Co.,* 235 U.S. 151 (1914).

89. Cleland B. MacAfee, "Some South Problems," *Park College Historical Club Papers,* ser. 1, vol. 2, June 1898, 18.

90. "The Troubles of a Sleeping Car Agent," *Railway Gazette,* July 24, 1891, 518.

91. Hannibal Gerald Duncan, *The Changing Race Relationship in the Border and Northern States* (Philadelphia: University of Pennsylvania Press, 1922), 61.

92. Emmett J. Scott and Lyman Beecher, *Booker T. Washington, Builder of a Civilization* (Garden City, NY: Doubleday, Page and Co., 1916), 100.

93. "Avoids Jim Crow," *New York Times,* September 11, 1911. Accused of avoiding his race, Washington later claimed that he traveled with "two dozen other colored people, most of whom lived in Texas, who accompanied me." "Denies He Avoided Race," *Washington Post,* October 13, 1911, 10.

94. Mays, *Born to Rebel,* 195.

95. Gregory, "The Jim-Crow Car."

96. Albon Holsey, "Most Influential Colored Man in Dixie Town Is One Who Can Get Whites to Straighten Things Out," *Baltimore Afro-American,* March 23, 1929, 6.

97. Robert Penn Warren, interview with Clarie Collins Harvey, February 9, 1964, tape 2, transcript, in Robert Penn Warren, *Who Speaks for the Negro?*, Archival Collection, Jean and Alexander Heard Library, Vanderbilt University, https://whospeaks.library.vanderbilt.edu /interview/clarie-collins-harvey.

98. William Pickens, "What It Costs a Negro to Get a Pullman Berth from Louisville, KY., to Birmingham, ALA.," *Crisis*, 8, no. 5, September 1914, 248–249.

99. See, for example, Du Bois's account of securing a Pullman berth for himself in Ohio by avoiding the ticket office, and boarding the train and staying put even after the conductor told him he had to get off and buy a ticket at the ticket office. As Du Bois seems to have hoped, once the train started moving the conductor sold him a ticket. "The Spanish Fandango," *Crisis*, 23, no. 6, April 1922, 250–251.

100. *Reports and Resolutions of South Carolina to the General Assembly*, January 12, 1915 (Columbia, SC: Gonzales and Bryn State Printer, 1915), 615.

101. Catherine Cocks, *Doing the Town: The Rise of Urban Tourism in the United States, 1859–1915* (Berkeley: University of California Press, 2001), 66.

102. Stetson Kennedy, *Jim Crow Guide to the U.S.A.: The Laws, Customs and Etiquette Governing the Conduct of Nonwhites and Other Minorities as Second-Class Citizens* (Tuscaloosa: University of Alabama Press, 2011), 186.

103. Hughes, "From Rampart Street to Harlem."

104. Kenneth Robert Janken, *Rayford W. Logan and the Dilemma of the African American Intellectual* (Amherst: University of Massachusetts Press, 1993), 179.

105. "Stenographer's Minutes before the Interstate Commerce Commission, No. 29210, in the matter of John LeFlore and Alfred S. Crishom v. Gulf, Mobile and Ohio Railroad Company, September 1, 1944, 8," and "Pullman and Dining Car Discrimination Complaint against the Gulf, Mobile and Ohio Railroad Company on the Lines between Mobile, Alabama and St. Louis, June 27, 1943," John LeFlore and Alfred S. Crishom, Complainants, 6, both in Papers of the NAACP, Library of Congress, Part 15, Segregation and Discrimination, Complaints and Responses, 1940–1955, Series A, Legal Department Files, ProQuest History Vault, folder 001444-016-0305.

106. Mrs. Suzie Givens to Mrs. Carrie Clifford, *Crisis*, 2, no. 6, October 1911, 255.

107. Mrs. Suzie Givens to Mrs. Carrie Clifford.

108. Mrs. Suzie Givens to Mrs. Carrie Clifford.

109. In 1902, for example, he pledged to underwrite a "portion" of the expense involved in W. E. B. Du Bois's (ultimately unsuccessful) challenge to Georgia's sleeping-car segregation law, "provided I can hand it to you personally and not have any connection with your committee." Booker T. Washington to W. E. B. Du Bois, November 28, 1902, in Jacqueline M. Moore, *Booker T. Washington, W. E. B. Du Bois, and the Struggle for Racial Uplift* (Lanham, MD: Rowman and Littlefield, 2003), 141.

110. "June 7 and 8 as Railroad Days," *New York Age*, April 16, 1914, 1.

111. R. H. Boyd, *The Separate or "Jim Crow" Car Laws or Legislative Actions of the Fourteen Southern States* (Nashville, TN: National Baptist Publishing Board, 1908), 5.

112. Boyd cites the ICC's ruling in *Edwards* in his introduction to Boyd, *Separate or "Jim Crow,"* 6.

113. *Georgia Edwards v. Nashville, Chattanooga & St. Louis Railway Company, operating The Western & Atlantic Railroad*, 12 I.C.C. Rep., 247, in *Interstate Commerce Commission Reports: Reports and Decisions of the Interstate Commerce Commission of the United States* (Washington, DC: L. K. Strouse, 1908), 250.

114. "The Traveling Rights of Negroes," *The Public: A National Magazine of Fundamental Democracy* (Chicago) 10, no. 484, July 13, 1907, 346. For other similar interpretations of the case, see, for example, "Better Cars for Them: Railways to Be Forced to Provide for Negroes," *Baltimore Sun*, April 9, 1908, 2. "Interstate Commerce Ruling: Decision Given Upholding Jim Crow Cars. Accommodation for Whites and Negroes Must Be Equal in Personal Comfort," *Wall Street Journal*, July 9, 1907, 7.

115. "President Theodore Roosevelt to the Department of Justice Regarding Train Segregation," April 1, 1908, General Records of the Department of Justice, National Archives, Record Group 60, identifier 7455571, https://catalog.archives.gov/id/7455571.

116. "May Discontinue 'Jim Crow' Cars: I.C.C. Finds Southern Roads Do Not Give the Races Equal Accommodations," *Detroit Free Press*, January 22, 1911.

117. Alexander Walters, quoted in Shawn Leigh Alexander, *An Army of Lions: The Civil Rights Struggle before the NAACP* (Philadelphia: University of Pennsylvania Press, 2013).

118. Susan D. Carle, *Defining the Struggle: National Racial Justice Organizing, 1880–1915* (New York: Oxford University Press, 2013), 118.

119. Paul D. Nelson, *Fredrick L. McGhee: A Life on the Color Line, 1861–1912* (St. Paul: Minnesota Historical Society Press, 2002), 160.

120. W. E. B. Du Bois, Niagara Movement, General Secretary. Membership letter no. 4, Atlanta, Ga., April 10, 1907, Niagara Movement Papers, W. E. B. Du Bois Library, Special Collections and University Archives, University of Massachusetts Amherst Libraries.

121. Carle, *Defining the Struggle*, 219.

122. NAACP, *Fourth Annual Report* (New York: NAACP, 1914), 9.

123. *Chiles v. Chesapeake and Ohio Railway*, 218 U.S. 71 (1910). In deciding this case, the court drew on *Hall v. DeCuir*, 95 U.S. 485 (1877) to conclude that "the interstate commerce clause of the Constitution does not constrain the action of carriers, but on the contrary leaves them to adopt rules and regulations for the government of their business, free from any interference except by Congress."

124. For more on the history of the National African American Council and other early civil rights organizations, see Benjamin R. Justesen, *Broken Brotherhood: The Rise and Fall of the National Afro-American Council* (Carbondale: Southern Illinois University Press, 2008); Angela Jones, *African American Civil Rights: Early Activism and the Niagara Movement* (Santa Barbara, CA: Praeger, 2011); Carle, *Defining the Struggle;* and Shawn Leigh Alexander, *An Army of Lions.*

125. *How to Solve the Race Problem: The Proceedings of the Washington Conference on the Race Problem in the United States* (Washington, DC: Beresford, 1904), 267.

126. *Hearings before the Committee on Interstate and Foreign Commerce of the House of Representatives on the Bills to Amend the Interstate Commerce Law (H. R. 146, 273, 2040, 5775, 8337, and 10930), April 8, 1902* (Washington, DC: US Government Printing Office, 1902), 439.

127. Carle, *Defining the Struggle*, 148.

128. Quoted in Benjamin R. Justesen, *George Henry White: An Even Chance in the Race of Life* (Baton Rouge: Louisiana State University Press, 2001), 394.

129. Michael Perman, *Struggle for Mastery: Disfranchisement in the South, 1888–1908* (Chapel Hill: University of North Carolina Press, 2003), 263; George Henry White, quoted in Justesen, *George Henry White*, 394. The controversy over this legislation is also discussed in Daniel W. Crofts, "The Warner-Foraker Amendment to the Hepburn Bill: Friend or Foe of Jim Crow?," *Journal of Southern History* 39, no. 3 (1973): 341–353.

130. Walter Hines, "Memorandum for the Director General," May 26, 1918, U.S Railroad Administration Records, 1918–1920, (RG 14)—Records of the Director General, File No. P19-3, National Archives, College Park, Maryland, ProQuest History Vault, folder 001337-006-0405.

131. "Return of the Railroads to Private Ownership, Extension of Remarks of Hon. Martin B. Madden," *Congressional Record: Proceedings and Debates of the First Session of the Sixty-Sixth Congress* (Washington, DC: US Government Printing Office, 1919), 9055.

132. "Threatens House with Riots," *Baltimore Afro-American*, November 21, 1919, 1; *Return of the Railroads to Private Ownership, Hearings before the Committee on Interstate and Foreign Commerce of the House of Representatives*, Sixty-Sixth Congress, first session, on H.R. 4378, vol. 2, 2006.

133. *Return of the Railroads to Private Ownership*, 2022.

134. Part of the problem in drumming up support for the abolition of Jim Crow cars, argued William Pickens, was that whites were not forced to ride in them. "The only way to know it is to be compelled to use it. . . . The greatest difficulty in getting the President of the United States, the members of Congress, the members of the state legislature interested in the institution is the fact no president, no legislator rides in the Jim Crow Car. They don't know what it is." William Pickens, "The Jim Crow Car from Within," *Christian Science Monitor*, October 14, 1920, 3.

135. "Texas 'Jim Crow Laws' Are Said to Be Worst in the Country," *Baltimore Afro-American*, August 17, 1923.

3. TRAVELING BY CAR

1. Jack Johnson, *Jack Johnson: In the Ring and Out* (Chicago: National Sports, 1927; Mineola, NY: Dover, 2018), 7.

2. Paul Gilroy, *Darker than Blue: On the Moral Economies of Black Atlantic Culture* (Cambridge, MA: Belknap Press of Harvard University Press, 2011), 99.

3. Geoffrey C. Ward, *Unforgivable Blackness: The Rise and Fall of Jack Johnson* (New York: Vintage, 2006), 182.

4. "Jack Johnson to Drive: To Appear behind Wheel of Racing Car at Indianapolis. Despite Protests of Racing Pilots, Who Threaten to Boycott the Motor Speedway, He Will Be Featured," *Washington Post*, July 24, 1910, 8.

5. Randy Roberts, *Papa Jack: Jack Johnson and the Era of White Hopes* (New York: Free Press, 1985).

6. "He did not win the Oldfield-Johnson race, but he did not crash," wrote one reporter, which left "a lot of white men feeling somehow cheated." "Makes Johnson Look Foolish: Barney Oldfield Wins Match Auto Race with Negro Pugilist in Straight Heats," *Detroit Free Press*, October 26, 1910.

7. Stephen B. Goddard, *Getting There: The Epic Struggle between Road and Rail in the American Century* (Chicago: University of Chicago Press, 1996), 56.

8. Quoted in Blaine A. Brownell, "A Symbol of Modernity: Attitudes toward the Automobile in Southern Cities in the 1920s," *American Quarterly* 24, no. 1 (March 1, 1972): 34.

9. John Urry, "The 'System' of Automobility," *Theory, Culture & Society* 21, no. 4–5 (October 1, 2004): 25–39. For more on American automobility, see Cotten Seiler, *Republic of Drivers: A Cultural History of Automobility in America* (Chicago: University of Chicago Press, 2008).

10. "Auto Cars in Virginia: 3,321 Registered This Year in the Old Dominion," *Washington Post*, October 31, 1909.

11. Reuben R. Arnold, "Georgia Railroad Strike: The Negro as a Citizen," *Locomotive Firemen's Magazine* 47, no. 4, October 1909, 598.

12. South Carolina, *Reports and Resolutions of South Carolina to the General Assembly* (Columbia, SC: Gonzales and Bryan, State Printers, 1912), 959.

13. "The Business of Prejudice," *Crisis*, 11, no. 6 (1916), 300.

14. "The Negro Chauffeur Question Not Settled," *Miami News*, January 4, 1916.

15. "Millionaires Denounce Race Prejudice in Miami," *Chicago Defender*, March 27, 1915.

16. "'Queering' the Negro Driver: The Process Lands Three Men in Jail on Charges of Malicious Mischief—How They Fixed a Car," *Motor World* (New York), 22, no. 8, February 24, 1910, 560a.

17. "Chauffeurs Draw the Color Line," *Motor World* (New York), 20, no. 14, July 1, 1909, 555.

18. "The Reform in Chauffeurs," *Literary Digest* 44, no. 6, February 1912, 273, 274.

19. Betty Glad, *Key Pittman: The Tragedy of a Senate Insider* (New York: Columbia University Press, 1986), 33.

20. William August Crossland, *Industrial Conditions among Negroes in St. Louis* (St. Louis: Mendle Printing Co., 1914), 67.

21. Kevin L. Borg, *Auto Mechanics: Technology and Expertise in Twentieth-Century America* (Baltimore: Johns Hopkins University Press, 2010), 59.

22. "Cosmopolitan Automobile School," advertisement, *Crisis*. 1, no. 1, November 1910, 19.

23. Advertisement, *Pittsburgh Courier*, March 25, 1911, 5.

24. Letter from Topeka, Kansas, May 1, 1917, in Emmett J. Scott, "Letters of Negro Migrants, 1916–1918," *Journal of Negro History* 4, no. 3 (July 1919): 290–340, 297–298.

25. Christopher Nelson, *The C. R. Patterson and Sons Company: Black Pioneers in the Vehicle Building Industry. 1865–1939* [Hurricane, WV: CreateSpace, 2010).

26. Alice Dunbar-Nelson, "Negro Women in War Work," in Emmett Jay Scott, *Scott's Official History of the American Negro in the World War* (Chicago: Homewood Press, 1919), 395.

27. "The Nation's Industrial Progress," *Outlook Magazine*, March 26, 1919, 536.

28. Lerone A. Martin, *Preaching on Wax: The Phonograph and the Shaping of Modern African American Religion* (New York: NYU Press, 2014), 141.

29. Langston Hughes, "Bright Chariots," in *The Collected Works of Langston Hughes*, vol. 9: *Essays on Art, Race, Politics, and World Affairs*, ed. Christopher De Santis (Columbia: University of Missouri Press, 2002), 325.

30. Rudi Volti, *Cars and Culture: The Life Story of a Technology* [Baltimore: Johns Hopkins University Press, 2006), 49.

31. Beth Tompkins Bates, *The Making of Black Detroit in the Age of Henry Ford* (Chapel Hill: University of North Carolina Press, 2012).

32. "Negroes 'Drafted' to Build Roads for Whites in Dixie," *Chicago Tribune*, May 17, 1929, 36.

33. Leon Litwack, *Trouble in Mind: Black Southerners in the Age of Jim Crow* (New York: Alfred A. Knopf, 1998), 335.

34. Andrew Michael Manis, *Macon Black and White: An Unutterable Separation in the American Century* (Macon, GA: Mercer University Press, 2004), 54.

35. Hugh Pearson, *Under the Knife: How a Wealthy Negro Surgeon Wielded Power in the Jim Crow South* (New York: Free Press, 2000), 88.

36. Jason Chambers, "Equal in Every Way: African Americans, Consumption and Materialism from Reconstruction to the Civil Rights Movement," *Advertising and Society Review* 7, no. 1 (2006).

37. Thomas R. Hietala, *The Fight of the Century: Jack Johnson, Joe Louis, and the Struggle for Racial Equality* (Armonk, NY: M. E. Sharpe, 2004), 156.

38. Jerrold M. Packard, *American Nightmare: The History of Jim Crow* (New York: St. Martin's Griffin, 2003), 91.

39. James Weldon Johnson, "The Practice of Lynching," *Century Magazine,* 115 (November 1927): 67.

40. William Styron, *This Quiet Dust and Other Writings* (New York: Vintage, 1993), 23.

41. The Arkansas Traveler, "Autos and Busses Cut Down Travel on Jim Crow Cars," *Baltimore Afro-American,* January 8, 1927, 18.

42. Charles S. Johnson, *Patterns of Negro Segregation* (New York: Harper and Brothers, 1943), 270.

43. "Automobiles and Jim Crow Regulation," *Negro World,* October 11, 1924, 6.

44. Quoted in Kathleen Franz, "'The Open Road': Automobility and Racial Uplift in the Inter-War Years," in *Technology and the African-American Experience: Needs and Opportunities for Study,* ed. Bruce Sinclair (Cambridge, MA: MIT Press, 2004), 140.

45. "Automobiles and Jim Crow Regulation."

46. Quoted in Franz, "'The Open Road': Automobility and Racial Uplift in the Inter-War Years," 141.

47. Gretchen Sullivan Sorin, "Keep Going: African Americans on the Road in the Age of Jim Crow" (PhD diss., SUNY–Albany, 2009), 32.

48. "Sales in the South Are Good," *Automobile,* December 13, 1917, 1065.

49. "Cotton's Magical Rise Enriching the Nation," *Literary Digest,* 53, no. 24, December 9, 1916, 1521.

50. Quoted in Nan Elizabeth Woodruff, *American Congo* (Cambridge, MA: Harvard University Press, 2009), 44.

51. Bradford Knapp, *Safe Farming in the Southern States* (Washington, DC: US Government Printing Office, 1920), 4.

52. Woodruff, *American Congo,* 44.

53. Emmett J. Scott, *Negro Migration during the War* (New York: Oxford University Press, 1920), 84.

54. Quoted in Woodruff, *American Congo,* 44.

55. Theodore Rosengarten, *All God's Dangers: The Life of Nate Shaw* (Chicago: University of Chicago Press, 2000), 251.

56. Edmond Threatt, "Black on Route 66," in *A Route 66 Companion,* ed. David King Dunaway (Austin: University of Texas Press, 2012), 72.

57. John Dollard, *Caste and Class in a Southern Town* (Madison: University of Wisconsin Press, 1949), 102.

58. Arthur Franklin Raper, *Preface to Peasantry: A Tale of Two Black Belt Counties* (Chapel Hill: University of North Carolina Press, 1936; Columbia: University of South Carolina Press, 2005), 87.

59. Charles E. Hall, "The Negro Farmer in the United States," Census of Agriculture, 15th Census of the United States: 1930, United States Bureau of the Census (Washington, DC: US Government Printing Office, 1933), 7.

60. Quoted in Corey T. Lesseig, *Automobility: Social Changes in the American South, 1909–1939* (New York: Routledge, 2001), 113.

61. Howard Kester, "Sharecroppers: America's Refugees," *Crisis,* 43, no. 7, March 1940, 93.

62. *Hearings before the Select Committee to Investigate the Interstate Migration of Destitute Citizens*, House of Representatives, Seventy-Sixth Congress, Third Session (Washington, DC US Government Printing Office, 1940–1941), 773.

63. "30 Cent Cotton Brings Prosperity," *Baltimore Afro-American*, May 10, 1918, 1.

64. Raper, *Preface to Peasantry*, 175.

65. Raper, *Preface to Peasantry*, 174, 175.

66. Charles S. Johnson, *Patterns of Negro Segregation* (New York: Harper and Brothers, 1943), 124, 124–125, 125.

67. Stephan Thernstrom and Abigail Thernstrom, *America in Black and White: One Nation, Indivisible* (New York: Simon and Schuster, 1999), 44.

68. James Weldon Johnson, "The Practice of Lynching.'

69. Jerrold M. Packard, *American Nightmare: The History of Jim Crow* (New York: St. Martin's Griffin, 2003), 167.

70. Stetson Kennedy, *Jim Crow Guide to the U.S.A.: The Laws, Customs and Etiquette Governing the Conduct of Nonwhites and Other Minorities as Second-Class Citizens* (Tuscaloosa: University of Alabama Press, 2011), 221.

71. In 1931, "a football coach at a black college in Alabama was beaten to death in Birmingham for parking in a lot reserved for whites." Laurie F. Leach. *Langston Hughes: A Biography* (Westport, CT: Greenwood Press, 2004), 67.

72. Michael K. Honey, *Black Workers Remember: An Oral History of Segregation, Unionism, and the Freedom Struggle* (Berkeley: University of California Press, 2000), 67. For more on the subject of parking, see Sarah Leavitt, "Inside the Lines: Parking and Social Stratification," National Building Museum, January 7, 2010, https://www.nbm.org/inside-lines-parking-social-stratification/.

73. Johnson, *Patterns of Negro Segregation*, 126.

74. Arthur Raper, "Race and Class Pressures," unpublished manuscript [1940], in the Arthur Franklin Raper Papers #3966, folder 90, p. 9, Southern Historical Collection, Wilson Library, University of North Carolina at Chapel Hill.

75. Johnson, *Patterns of Negro Segregation*, 126.

76. Johnson, *Patterns of Negro Segregation*, 125.

77. Kennedy, *Jim Crow Guide*, 223.

78. Johnson, *Patterns of Negro Segregation*, 125.

79. Packard, *American Nightmare*, 167.

80. Johnson, *Patterns of Negro Segregation*, 125.

81. "Boston Man Denied Auto Insurance," *Baltimore Afro-American*, January 21, 1933, 19.

82. "Auto Drivers Considered Good Risks," *Baltimore Afro-American*, July 15, 1933, 9.

83. "Discriminatory Practices by White Insurance Co. Affect Driver's License," *Plaindealer* (Kansas City), 41, no. 3, January 20, 1939, 2.

84. "Would Ban Jim Crow in Pa. Auto Insurance Law," *Negro Star* (Wichita, KS), 29, no. 33, February 5, 1937, 1.

85. Thurgood Marshall, Special Counsel, to Roger Baldwin, American Civil Liberties Union, April 19, 1940, Papers of the NAACP, Part 15, Segregation and Discrimination, Complaints and Responses, 1940–1955, ProQuest History Vault, folder 001444-006-0067.

86. W. E. B. Du Bois, "Jim Crow Cars Usually Empty," *Baltimore Afro-American*, February 16, 1929, 6.

87. Du Bois, "Jim Crow Cars Usually Empty."

88. Du Bois, "Jim Crow Cars Usually Empty."

89. Quoted in Susan V. Spellman, "All the Comforts of Home: The Domestication of the Service Station Industry, 1920–1940," *Journal of Popular Culture* 37, no. 3 (February 1, 2004): 469.

90. Spellman, "All the Comforts of Home," 471.

91. "Colored? Then You Can't Buy Gasoline Here: Resentment Aroused over Refusal to Sell to Negroes," *New Journal and Guide*, August 18, 1934.

92. See Albert Edgar Smith, "Through the Windshield," *Opportunity*, May 1933, 144; and Algernon Brashear Jackson, *Jim and Mr. Eddy; a Dixie Motorlogue* (Washington, DC: Associated Publishers, 1930).

93. "Force Standard Oil to Drop Cafe Jim Crow," *Chicago Defender*, February 28, 1948.

94. "Shell Gas Is Sorry about Cab's Sister: Refusal of Rest Room Facilities to Her Now Deplored," *New York Amsterdam News*, June 26, 1937, 2.

95. Charles Johnson, *Patterns of Negro Segregation*, 128.

96. W. E. B. Du Bois to George Crawford, November 1, November 6, 1929, W. E. B. Du Bois Papers Special Collections and University Archives, University of Massachusetts Amherst Libraries.

97. Du Bois's letter is reprinted in Sarah Harrison, *The Traveler's Guide* (Philadelphia: Hackley and Harrison's, 1931), 5.

98. For more on these works, see Gretchen Sorin, *Driving while Black: African American Travel and the Road to Civil Rights* (New York: Liveright, 2020), chap. 6.

99. *Hackley & Harrison's Hotel and Apartment Guide for Colored Travelers* (1930), reprinted in Lisa Pertillar Brevard, *Biography of Edwin Henry Hackley (1859–1940): African-American Attorney and Activist* (Lewiston, NY: Edwin Mellen Press, 2002), 87.

100. Smith, "Through the Windshield," 143.

101. Smith, "Through the Windshield," 142, 143.

102. Winifred Hawkridge Dixon, *Westward Hoboes* (New York: C. Scribner's Sons, 1921), 238.

103. Quoted in Marguerite Shaffer, *See America First: Tourism and National Identity, 1880–1940* (Washington, DC: Smithsonian Institution Press, 2001), 164.

104. Smith, "Through the Windshield," 142.

105. Smith, "Through the Windshield," 142.

106. Smith, "Through the Windshield," 143.

107. Smith, "Through the Windshield," 142.

108. "Some Hotel Thoughts: Lack of Adequate Stopping Places for Our Travelers Arouses Caustic Criticism," *Pittsburgh Courier*, September 1, 1923, 11.

109. Jesse Thomas, "Below the Mason-Dixon Line," *Pittsburgh Courier*, January 18, 1930, 18.

110. "Some Hotel Thoughts."

111. William H. Chafe, Raymond Gavins, and Robert Korstad, *Remembering Jim Crow: African Americans Tell about Life in the Segregated South* (New York: New Press, 2014), 146.

112. Smith, "Through the Windshield," 143.

113. Nat Hentoff, *At the Jazz Band Ball: Sixty Years on the Jazz Scene* (Berkeley: University of California Press, 2010), 114.

114. Martha Ackmann, *Curveball: The Remarkable Story of Toni Stone, the First Woman to Play Professional Baseball in the Negro League* (Chicago: Chicago Review Press, 2010), 156.

115. W. E. B. Du Bois, "Segregation in the North," *Crisis*, April 1934, 116.

116. "Survey Reveals Negroes Not Welcome in 94 Percent of Hotels, Motels," *Plaindealer* (Kansas City), 57, no. 6, February 10, 1956, 1.

117. Smith, "Through the Windshield," 142, 143.

118. Smith, "Through the Windshield," 144.

119. "Luck's Appointment Puts Responsibility on Autoists Claimed," *New Journal and Guide*, November 4, 1933, 3.

120. The only announcement of the service I've come across is a brief notice describing Conoco's "Guide for Colored Motorists," *Crisis*, 43, no. 7, July 1936, 221.

121. "D. B. Luck, Conoco Official, Tells of New Travel Bureau: Aggressive Young Representative of Continental Oil Co. Reveals Novel Travel Service for Race Tourists—Visits Pittsburgh," *Pittsburgh Courier*, September 29, 1934, A6.

122. Julian Bond, quoted in *Postal Record*, 16, November 2014, 23.

123. Sorin, *Driving while Black*, 183.

124. Robert Duke is mentioned in "The Green Book: The Forgotten Story of One Carrier's Legacy Helping Others to Navigate Jim Crow's Highway," *Postal Record*, 16, November 2014, 23. I can find little additional information on him, but Black musicians tended to be knowledgeable about travel conditions. Indeed, William H. (Billy) Butler, the publisher of *Travelguide*, was also a musician and first began compiling the material he would later include in his guide while on the road with a vaudeville troupe. "Jimcro Made Ex Musician Go Into Publishing Field," *New Journal and Guide* (Norfolk), August 6, 1955, 18.

125. *The Negro Motorist Green Book, 1937 Edition* (New York: Green and Smith, 1937), 1.

126. *The A.L.A. Green Book: Official Route Book of the Automobile Legal Association* (Boston: Scarborough Guide Co., 1920), vol. 1.

127. Sorin, "Keep Going," 187.

128. Michael Berkowitz, "A 'New Deal' for Leisure," in *Being Elsewhere: Tourism, Consumer Culture, and Identity in Modern Europe and North America*, ed. Shelley Osmun Baranowski and Ellen Furlough (Ann Arbor: University of Michigan Press, 2001), 203–204.

129. Mordecai Lee, *See America: The Politics and Administration of Federal Tourism Promotion, 1937–1973* (Albany: State University of New York Press, 2020), 41–43; Richard K. Popp, *The Holiday Makers: Magazines, Advertising, and Mass Tourism in Postwar America* (Baton Rouge: LUS Press, 2012), 70–81; Berkowitz, "A 'New Deal' for Leisure."

130. "Travel Bureau Is Eliminated," *Atlanta Daily World*, December 1, 1941; "Travel Bureau at N.Y. Is Dissolved," *Chicago Defender*, December 6, 1941.

131. "Grayson's Travel Guide Off the Press," *Atlanta Daily World*, December 25, 1937, announces the 1937 edition and makes reference to an inaugural edition in 1936, and a "new 1946 Post-War Edition" is advertised in the *Chicago Defender*, April 20, 1946, 6. At more than one hundred pages, *Grayson's Guide* was longer and more lavish than the *Green Book*, which was initially ten pages long and never exceeded eighty. It was also more expensive: the *Guide* cost one dollar in 1946, while the 1946 *Green Book* cost 75 cents. But *Grayson's Guide* never seems to have achieved the same circulation. Extremely rare, and all but unknown today, it was also never as widely advertised as the *Green Book*.

132. *Grayson's Guide: A National Directory of Hotels, Cafes, Resort [and] Motels*, n.p., n.d [1941?].

133. Sorin, "Keep Going," 266.

134. John A. Jakle and Keith A. Sculle, *America's Main Street Hotels: Transiency and Community in the Early Auto Age* (Knoxville: University of Tennessee Press, 2009), 111.

135. "Why hotels for colored men? . . . The colored man must not draw the line himself if he doesn't want the white man to do it," journalist Ray Stannard Baker was once told. Ray Stannard Baker, "An Ostracized Race in Ferment," *American Magazine*, 66, May 1908, 6.

136. James A. Jackson, "Big Business Wants Negro Dollars," *Crisis*, 42, no. 2, February 1935, 46.

137. Jackson, "Big Business Wants Negro Dollars," 45.

138. "J. A. Jackson's Work Covered Wide Area: Business Specialist Covered 18,911 Miles and Talked to 29,004 People in Past Fiscal Year," *Baltimore Afro-American,* August 2, 1930, 7; "James A. Jackson, Business Specialist, Doubles Contacts . . . Traveled 44,019 Miles in Gathering Data for U.S. Bureau," *New Journal and Guide,* July 11, 1931, 1; "James Jackson, 83, Ex-Esso Publicist," *New York Times,* November 18, 1960, 31.

139. Jackson, "Big Business Wants Negro Dollars," 36.

140. "Not Only Happy Motoring but Happy Traveling by Any Method Is Obtainable through the Green Book Routing Say ESSO Special Representatives." *The Negro Motorist Green Book* (New York: Victor Green and Co., 1947), 10.

141. W. O. Walker, "Down the Big Road," *Cleveland Call and Post,* August 31, 1939, 6.

142. Earl Hutchinson Sr., *A Colored Man's Journey through 20th Century Segregated America* (Los Angeles: Middle Passage Press, 2000), 87.

143. *Negro Motorist Green Book* (New York: Victor H. Green Publishers, 1948).

144. "Green Book, National Tourist's Guide Lists Principal Hotels, Including Dead Ones, Also Shifts Few Cleveland Businesses Off Center," *Cleveland Call and Post,* November 30, 1946, 12A.

145. Al Smith, "Adventures in Race Relations: Suspense," *Chicago Defender,* August 27, 1949, 7.

146. "Automobiles and Jim Crow Regulations," *Negro World,* October 11, 1924, 6.

147. "Automobiles and Jim Crow Regulations."

148. Price M. Cobbs, *My American Life: From Rage to Entitlement* (New York: Atria Books / Simon and Schuster, 2005), 27.

149. J. Freedom du Lac, "Guidebook That Aided Black Travelers during Segregation Reveals Vastly Different D.C.," *Washington Post,* September 12, 2010, 28.

150. Brent Staples, "John Hope Franklin," *New York Times,* March 26, 2009.

151. On the use of cars and the harassment of Black drivers during the Montgomery Bus Boycott, see Xavier Macy, "Drive toward Freedom: African American: The Story of Black Automobility in the Fight for Civil Rights" (master's thesis, James Madison University, 2015).

4. TRAVELING BY BUS

1.   "Negro Automobile Line: Problem Aroused by Nashville's Proposed Solution of Street Car Differences," *Gazette* (Little Rock), reprinted in *Washington Post,* October 19, 1905, 6.

2.   Boyd founded the Baptist Publishing Board (BPB) in 1898. By 1906 the BPB was the largest African American publisher in the world. He was also one of the founders of the One-Cent Savings and Trust Company Bank, a successful African American–owned bank, which first opened its doors in 1904. Joe Early Jr., "Richard Henry Boyd: Shaper of Black Baptist Identity," *Baptist History and Heritage* 42, no. 3 (2007): 91–104.

3.   Quoted in Kevin L. Borg, *Auto Mechanics: Technology and Expertise in Twentieth-Century America* (Baltimore: Johns Hopkins University Press, 2007), 58.

4.   C. Vann Woodward, *The Strange Career of Jim Crow,* 3rd rev. ed. (1974; repr. New York: Oxford University Press, 2001), 116. On the lack of work on the history of the bus, see Margaret Walsh, "The Bus Industry in the United States," EH.Net Encyclopedia, ed. Robert Whaples, Economic History Association, January 27, 2003, http://eh.net/encyclopedia/the -bus-industry-in-the-united-states/.

5.   Louisiana bus law Section 194, cited in House of Representatives, 83rd Congress, 2nd Session, May 12–14, 1954, *Amending Interstate Commerce Act (Segregation of Passengers),*

Hearings before the Committee on Interstate and Foreign Commerce (Washington, DC: US Government Printing Office, 1954), 112.

6. "Jitney Buses," *Automotive Topics*, January 23, 1915, 913.

7. "Negro 'Jitneys' Prove Popular," *New Berne Weekly Journal*, New Bern, North Carolina, March 18, 1915, 1.

8. "Jim Crow Jitneys Running in Texas: Service Provided Exclusively for Negroes," *Motor Age*, 27, no. 10 (March 11, 1915): 27.

9. Pauli Murray, *States' Laws on Race and Color* (1954; Athens, GA: University Press of Georgia, 1997), 483, 484, 485.

10. "'Jitney' Bus Is Taking Many Cities by Storm," *New York Times*, January 31, 1915, 2.

11. Jennifer Roback, "The Political Economy of Segregation: The Case of Segregated Streetcars," *Journal of Economic History* 46, no. 4 (1986): 893–917, 899–906.

12. *The General Statutes of the State of Florida* (St. Augustine, FL: Record Co., 1906), 1550.

13. *Cleveland Gazette*, July 29, 1905, quoted in August Meier and Elliott Rudwick, "Negro Boycotts of Jim Crow Streetcars in Tennessee," *American Quarterly* 21, no. 4 (1969): 757.

14. Walker, quoted in Blair Murphy Kelley, *Right to Ride: Streetcar Boycotts and African American Citizenship in the Era of Plessy v. Ferguson* (Chapel Hill: University of North Carolina Press, 2010), 129.

15. Murray, *States' Laws*, 194.

16. Murray, *States' Laws*, 484; Ann Field Alexander, *Race Man: The Rise and Fall of the "Fighting Editor," John Mitchell Jr.* (Charlottesville: University of Virginia Press, 2002), 129.

17. Lester C. Lamon, *Black Tennesseans, 1900–1930* (Knoxville: University of Tennessee Press, 1976), 30.

18. Gilbert Thomas Stephenson, *Race Distinctions in American Law* (New York: Association Press, 1910), 230.

19. "Birmingham's Race Problem," *Electric Railway Journal*, 54, no. 22, December 27, 1919, 1064.

20. Jerrold M. Packard, *American Nightmare: A History of Jim Crow* (New York: St. Martin's Press, 2002), 88.

21. "Whites Ride in Jim Crow Section, Then Complain of Presence of Race," *Chicago Defender*, February 25, 1939, 11.

22. "Jitney Buses," *Automobile Dealer and Repairer* (New York), vol. 17–18, February 15, 1915, 78.

23. Robert Cervero, *Paratransit in America: Redefining Mass Transportation* (Westport, CT: Praeger, 1997), 224.

24. Ross D. Eckert and George W. Hilton, "The Jitneys," *Journal of Law and Economics* 15, no. 2 (1972): 293–325.

25. "Jitneys Beat the 'Jim Crow' Laws," *San Francisco Municipal Record*, 8, no. 13, April 1, 1915, 102.

26. "The Latest in Jitney," *Wall Street Journal*, July 3, 1915, 2.

27. "The Jitney Buses Inaugurate Jim Crow," *California Eagle*, 27, no. 43, December 2 [? microfilm illegible], 1914, 1.

28. "Chinese and Negroes Must Be Carried," *Motor World*, 42, no. 10, March 10, 1915, 40.

29. See *James Smith et al. v. Howard Nunelly et al.*, August 19, 1915, in Ellsworth Nichols and Henry Clifford Spurr, *Public Utilities Reports* (Rochester, NY: Lawyers Co-operative Publishing Co., 1915) 177–191.

30. "Jitneys Beat the 'Jim Crow' Laws."

31. "Notes from Southern Cities," *Electric Railway Journal*, 59, no. 17, April 29, 1922, 710.

32. City of Austin, "An Ordinance to Define the Term 'Jitney'; to License and Regulate the Operation of Jitney on the Streets and Public Places of the City of Austin; and Prescribing Penalties for the Violation Thereof," June 17, 1915, Office of the City Clerk, Austin, TX, Ordinance Book, 611, http://www.austintexas.gov/edims/document.cfm?id=111920; "Over the Way from Mexico," *Electric Railway Journal*, 52, no. 13, September 28, 1918, 552.

33. E. S. Koelker, "The Jitney Bus Problem," *Wisconsin Municipality*, 15, no. 2, February 1915, 87; John P. Fox, "The Lessons of the Jitney," *Town Development*, 15, no. 4, August 1915, 106.

34. Quoted in Blaine A. Brownell, "A Symbol of Modernity: Attitudes toward the Automobile in Southern Cities in the 1920s," *American Quarterly* 24, no. 1 (1972): 34, 35.

35. J. Douglas Smith, *Managing White Supremacy: Race, Politics, and Citizenship in Jim Crow Virginia* (Chapel Hill: University of North Carolina Press, 2003), 142.

36. Ronald H. Bayor, *Race and the Shaping of Twentieth-Century Atlanta* (Chapel Hill: University of North Carolina Press, 2000), 188–189.

37. "'Our Company': Safe Bus, Started in 1926, Was Source of Pride in Winston-Salem's Black Community," *Winston-Salem Journal*, June 16, 2013.

38. Ron Grossman "Before Uber, There Was Jitney," *Chicago Tribune*, March 9, 2014. See also "Jitney Cabs Flout City Laws Openly," *Chicago Tribune*, August 14, 1949, 1.

39. "Pittsburgh Jitney Service Illegal, but Thriving," *Pittsburgh Post-Gazette*, September 7, 2013.

40. "Autos and Busses Cut Down Travel on Jim Crow Cars," *Baltimore Afro-American*, January 8, 1927.

41. "John Drew's Jitney Service and the Darby Hilldales," Darby [PA] History, http://www.darbyhistory.com/DarbySigns08-10DRAFT.pdf.

42. "No Jim Crow for Them," *Baltimore Afro-American*, July 22, 1921; the Florida bus line is referenced in "Autos and Busses Cut Down Travel on Jim Crow Cars."

43. "North Carolina and the Bus Problem," *Pittsburgh Courier*, July 20, 1929.

44. "Negroes Being Forced to Choose between Two Evils—Railroads and Buses," Associated Negro Press release, n.d., n.p., Claude A. Barnett Papers, Chicago Historical Society, box 380, folder 99, Travel and Buses—Transit Systems, 1930–1952, ProQuest History Vault, folder 001595-008-0479. The document references the North Carolina Interracial Commission's successful struggle to open up the state's buses to Blacks, which suggested it was written sometime in 1930.

45. "Can't Ride Busses in Portsmouth," *Baltimore Afro-American*, August 15, 1931; Richard Bowling, "The Guide Post: Reality vs. Theory," *New Journal and Guide*, June 8, 1929.

46. "United's Jim Crow Bus Line Sued: Fight against United's J. C. Busses Begun," *Baltimore Afro-American*, August 1, 1924.

47. "Street Railway Company Ducks Jim-Crow Issue: Assistant President Promises, Then Declines to Make Written Statement. Only Whites Ride Afro to Ask Show-Down from P. S. Commission," *Baltimore Afro-American*, July 6, 1929.

48. Charles S. Johnson, *Patterns of Negro Segregation* (New York: Harper and Brothers, 1943), 48.

49. "Reporters Find Persistence Is All Needed to Ride Busses," *Baltimore Afro-American*, July 20, 1929.

50. Monroe Nathan Work and Jessie Parkhurst Guzman, eds., *Negro Year Book: An Annual Encyclopedia of the Negro, 1931–1932* (Tuskegee Institute, AL: Negro Year Book Publishing Co., 1931), 54.

51. "N. C. Buses Must Carry Colored, Court Decides: Two-Year Fight Won by Interracial Commission Common Carriers Separate but Equal Accommodations Ordered," *New Journal and Guide*, February 22, 1930.

52. *News and Observer*, quoted in "Carolina Case Brings Bus as Common Carrier and Jim Crow Law to Front," *New Journal and Guide*, May 16, 1925.

53. "Citizens Fight Bus Boycott: N. Carolina High Court Gets Dispute, State Says Busses Not Common Carriers," *Chicago Defender*, June 29, 1929, A1.

54. "Citizens Fight Bus Boycott."

55. "Ask for an Interpretation of Jim Crow Law," *Brownsville Herald*, January 14, 1929, 13.

56. "Attempts to Ride 'Jim Crow' Bus, Arrested," *Pittsburgh Courier*, February 28, 1925.

57. "Can't Ride Busses in Portsmouth."

58. "Action of Bus Driver Causes Suit," *Indiana Recorder*, December 17, 1927.

59. "Seeks $500 Damages for Bus Discrimination," *Chicago Defender*, December 31, 1927.

60. "Discrimination Charge Blacks Bus Stand Please," *Springfield Union* (Springfield, MA), December 30, 1930.

61. Murray, *States' Laws*, 345, 372–373, 47.

62. Lyman Johnson, *The Rest of the Dream: The Black Odyssey of Lyman Johnson* (Knoxville: University Press of Kentucky, 1988), 125.

63. "Citizens Open War on Jim Crow Motor Busses," *Chicago Defender*, national ed., June 18, 1927, 1.

64. Andrew Judson Smith, "Victory: Cartoon Corrects Vicious Practice," *Chicago Defender*, April 30, 1932, 2.

65. "Texas Lawmakers Overlook Jim Crow: Forgot to Bar Negroes from Buses in State," *New Journal and Guide*, April 16, 1932.

66. "Jim Crow Law: Measure Segregating Negroes on Trains, Interurbans and Streetcars Does Not Apply to Buses, Court Rules," *Lubbock Morning Avalanche*, March 24, 1932; see also *Patillo v. State*, 47 S. W. 2d 847, No. 145848, Court of Criminal Appeals of Texas, March 23, 1932.

67. Leonard B. Murphy, "A History of Negro Segregation Practices in Texas, 1865–1958" (master's thesis, Southern Methodist University, 1958), 215–216; *Texas Annotated Penal Code* (Kansas City, 1957), 111: 703–705.

68. Albert A. Libby, "Exposes Bus Segregation in Chicago," *Chicago Defender*, November 19, 1927, 1.

69. Libby, "Exposes Bus Segregation in Chicago."

70. Libby, "Exposes Bus Segregation in Chicago."

71. "Defender Wins Stand for Rights on Busses," *Chicago Defender*, July 7, 1928.

72. "Chicago N.A.A.C.P. to Fight Jim Crow Bus," *Chicago Defender*, September 28, 1929.

73. "Nevin to the Coast," *Time*, January 2, 1933.

74. "Riders Insist Nevin Bus Line Jim Crows Race," *Baltimore Afro-American*, August 10, 1929. See also "No Segregation on Inter-City Bus Line: Nevin Company Explains Policy of New York, Philadelphia, Balto, D.C. Route," *Baltimore Afro-American*, August 3, 1929, 2.

75. "Where Is the N.A.A.C.P., Asks Burlington Physician as Jim Crow on Busses Becomes Apparent," *Baltimore Afro-American*, August 17, 1929.

76. "No Segregation on Inter-City Bus Line."

77. Beatrice Washington to the NAACP, July 8, 1931, Papers of the NAACP, Part 11: Special Subject Files, 1912–1939, ProQuest History Vault, folder 001421-028-0265.

78. "Nevin Driver Is Fired: No Back Seats on Nevin Bus Lines Now," *Baltimore Afro-American*, May 7, 1932, 1.

79. "Nevin Driver Is Fired."

80. J. O. Phillips complains about experiencing discrimination on Short Line buses to Mr. Phillip Cameron in a letter written on January 12, 1932, which is in the Claude A. Barnett Papers, Series I: Race Relations, 1923–1965, Segregation and Desegregation: Travel—Buses and Transit Systems, Correspondence, 1930–1952, box 380, folder 9, Chicago Historical Society, ProQuest History Vault, folder 001595-008-0479. For another complaint about Short Line buses, see Ethelyn Patrick to the NAACP, September 1, 1936, Papers of the NAACP, Part 11: Special Subject Files, 1912–1939, ProQuest History Vault, folder 001421-029-0500. Discrimination on Great Eastern System buses is discussed in Thurgood Marshall to Great Eastern System, Inc., January 27, 1937, Papers of the NAACP, Part 11: Special Subject Files, 1912–1939, Series A, ProQuest History Vault, folder 001421-028-0431, which also contains complaints about Union Bus Company in Oklahoma.

81. "Urban League Official Scores Bus Jim Crow: Jesse O. Thomas Sent Letter to Passenger Agents," *New Journal and Guide*, August 8, 1931, 5.

82. Philip A. Cameron, "Passenger Exposes Alleged Jim Crow Tactics of Bus Co.," *Chicago Defender*, January 9, 1932, 1.

83. "Buses Lose Business because of Policy: Jim-Crow by Greyhound Line Alleged," *New Journal and Guide*, May 14, 1932, 7.

84. On Greyhound's history, see Carlton Jackson, *Hounds of the Road: History of the Greyhound Bus Company* (Bowling Green, OH: Bowling Green State University Popular Press, 1984).

85. "Memorandum for the Joint Committee of the NAACP and the American Fund for Public Service, Inc. from Charles H. Houston, October 26, 1934," Papers of the NAACP, Part 03: The Campaign for Educational Equality, Series A, Legal Department and Central Office Records, 1913–1940, ProQuest History Vault, folder 001509-001-0811.

86. Quoted in Leland B. Ware, "Setting the Stage for *Brown:* The Development and Implementation of the NAACP's School Desegregation Campaign, 1930–1950," *Mercer Law Review* 52, no. 2 (2001): 642.

87. Roy Wilkins to Mrs. H. N. Clark, September 17, 1932, New York, Papers of the NAACP, Part 11: Special Subject Files, 1912–1939, ProQuest History Vault, folder 001421-028-0265.

88. Roy Wilkins to Mr. Ernest O. Boone, January 18, 1933, New York, NAACP Papers Administrative Subject Files Discrimination Transportation, 1933.

89. Thurgood Marshall to Maude A. Tollefson, September 23, 1938, Papers of the NAACP, Part 11: Special Subject Files, 1912–1939, ProQuest History Vault, folder 001421-029-0162.

90. Roy Wilkins to Mr. W. P. Mims, April 18, 1932, Papers of the NAACP, Part 11: Special Subject Files, 1912–1939, ProQuest History Vault, folder 001421-029-0001.

91. "N.A.A.C.P. Takes Bus Jim Crow to Court," Baltimore *Afro-American*, April 9, 1932, 11.

92. J. B. Walker, Vice President, Greyhound Company, to Roy Wilkins, Assistant Secretary, NAACP, April 29, 1932, 1, Papers of the NAACP, Part 11: Special Subject Files, 1912–1939, ProQuest History Vault, folder 001421-029-0001.

93. Roy Wilkins, Assistant Secretary, NAACP, to J. B. Walker, Vice President, Greyhound Company, May 5, 1932, 2, Papers of the NAACP, Part 11: Special Subject Files, 1912–1939, ProQuest History Vault, folder 001421-029-0001.

94. "Firm Stand against Bus 'Jim-Crow' Urged: Bias of Certain Employees Blamed," *Pittsburgh Courier*, July 9, 1932, 3.

95. "Principal of the School Was Jim Crowed," *Call*, January 20, 1933.

96. "Pa. Woman Sues Greyhound Bus Line for Jim Crow," *Baltimore Afro-American*, October 6, 1934, 1.

97. "Court of Appeals Condones Bus Lines' Jim Crow Tactics: No Cause to Test Constitutionality of Virginia Statutes, It Rules," *Chicago Defender*, January 2, 1937.

98. "Court of Appeals Condones Bus Lines' Jim Crow Tactics."

99. "Trenton Woman Pressing 5-Year Battle on Jim Crow Bus Arrest," *Baltimore Afro-American*, November 6, 1937, 4; "Sues Bus Line for $10,000 Damages," *New York Age*, 50, no. 28, March 14, 1926, 1.

100. "Trenton Woman Pressing 5-Year Battle"; "Cases of Bus Jim Crow Show the Barbarity of the Policy," *Baltimore Afro-American*, June 15, 1946, 11. United States Court of Appeals, District of Columbia Circuit, *Kinchlow v. Peoples Rapid Transit*, CO88 F.2d 764 (D.C. Cir. 1936), decided December 21, 1936.

101. "Greyhound Bus Office Admits J. C. Over-the-Wheels Policy," *Baltimore Afro-American*, October 5, 1935, 15.

102. "Woman Sues Bus Line; Wins Damages for Jim Crow," *Chicago Defender*, April 6, 1935, 13.

103. "Best Judgement Need for Negroes to Ride Greyhound Bus Line," *Plaindealer* (Kansas City), 37, no. 33, August 13, 1935, 1.

104. Thurgood Marshall to Ethelyn Patrick, December 8, 1936, New York, Papers of the NAACP, Part 11: Special Subject Files, 1912–1939, ProQuest History Vault, folder 001421-029-0500.

105. See, for example, "N.A.A.C.P. Will Not Use Bus Transportation: Roy Wilkins in Letter to Greyhound Lines Hits Jim Crow," *New Journal and Guide*, April 18, 1936; "NAACP Refuses Greyhound Bus Service," *Kansas American* (Topeka, KS) 9, no. 53, April 17, 1938, 3.

106. "N.A.A.C.P. Will Not Use Bus Transportation."

107. "Bus Lines' Jim-Crow Racket Resented by Advanced White Workers," *The Liberator*, 3, no. 2, March 14, 1931, 5.

108. "Best Judgement Need for Negroes to Ride Greyhound Bus Line."

109. Libby, "Exposes Bus Segregation in Chicago."

110. "'Ma' Rainey Co. Tours Country in Auto Bus," *Pittsburgh Courier*, June 11, 1927, A3; Steve Goodson, "Gertrude Ma Rainey (1886–1939): 'Hear Me Talkin' to You,'" in *Georgia Women: Their Lives and Times*, vol. 2, ed. Kathleen Ann Clark and Ann Short Chirhart (Athens, GA: University of Georgia Press, 2014), 162. "Harry 'Sweets' Edison: Musical Travels & Travails: Archival Interview from Bob Watt with the Late Great Trumpeter," *JazzTimes*, April 26, 2019, http://jazztimes.com/articles/30311-harry-sweets-edison-musical-travels -travails.

111. "Harry 'Sweets' Edison."

112. Billie Holiday, *Lady Sings the Blues* (New York: Double Day, 1956), 73.

113. Greyhound Post House Menu, Tacoma, Washington n.d., Photo Collection 617, M59-3, Special Collections, University of Washington Libraries, https://digitalcollections.lib .washington.edu/digital/collection/menus/id/288/rec/20.

114. James W. Martin to Walter White, Oakland, California, March 26, 1932, and Walter White to James W. Martin, April, 1932, both in Papers of the NAACP, Part 11: Special Subject Files, 1912–1939, Series A, ProQuest History Vault, folder 001421-028-0751.

115. Dr. Joice Christine Bailey Lewis, *My Ancestral Voices: Stories of Five Generations of the Blackburn Family from Slavery to the Present Day* (Bloomington, IN: Xlibris, 2013), 245.

116. United States Department of the Interior, National Park Service, National Register of Historic Places, Registration Form for Montgomery Greyhound Bus Station, April 13, 2011, https:// www.nps.gov/nr/feature/weekly_features/2011/MontgomeryGreyhoundBusStation.pdf.

117. Cassie Lewis to Walter White, Clinton College, Rock Hill, South Carolina, May 22, 1939, 1, 2. Papers of the NAACP, Part 11: Special Subject Files, 1912–1939, Series A, ProQuest History Vault, folder 001421-028-0505.

118. W. D. Williams, Tampa NAACP, to Dr. D. G. Howe, President, Florida Motor Lines, Jacksonville, Florida, n.d. [1939], Papers of the NAACP, Part 11: Special Subject Files, 1912–1939, ProQuest History Vault, folder 001421-028-0505.

119. Roy Wilkins to the Great Eastern Bus System, New York City, January 9, 1936, Papers of the NAACP, Part 11: Special Subject Files, 1912–1939, Series A, ProQuest History Vault, folder 001421-028-0348.

120. Pauli Murray to General Manager, National Trailways System, New York, April 17, 1939, Papers of the NAACP, Part 11: Special Subject Files, 1912–1939, folder 001421-028-0505.

121. Lewis, *My Ancestral Voices*, 245.

122. "Bus Co. Sued," *Cleveland Call and Post*, January 26, 1935.

123. Ida Montgomery to Walter White, Pittsburgh, Pennsylvania, July 8, 1935, Papers of the NAACP, Part 11: Special Subject Files, 1912–1939, Segregation of Bus Station, ProQuest History Vault, folder 001421-029-0097.

124. Charles Hamilton Houston to T. G. Nutter, July 12, 1935, and Charles Hamilton Houston to Homer S. Brown, July 13, 1935, both in Papers of the NAACP, Part 11: Special Subject Files, 1912–1939, ProQuest History Vault, folder 001421-029-0097.

125. J. Rupert Jefferson to Charles Hamilton Houston, July 24, 1935, Papers of the NAACP, Part 11: Special Subject Files, 1912–1939, ProQuest History Vault, folder 001421-029-0097.

126. Homer S. Brown to Charles H. Houston, August 17, 1935, and Homer S. Brown to Charles H. Houston, September 30, 1935, both in Papers of the NAACP, Part 11: Special Subject Files, 1912–1939, ProQuest History Vault, folder 001421-029-0097.

127. Homer S. Brown to Charles H. Houston, September 30, 1935; Homer S. Brown to Charles H. Houston, August 30, 1935, Papers of the NAACP, Part 11: Special Subject Files, 1912–1939, Segregation of Greyhound Bus Station, ProQuest History Vault, folder 001421-029-0097.

128. Richard S. Jones, Brown and Jones Attorneys at Law, to Charles H. Houston, March 2, 1936, Papers of the NAACP, Part 11: Special Subject Files, 1912–1939, Series A, January 1, 1936–December 31, 1936, Segregation on Greyhound Buses and Bus Stations, ProQuest History Vault, folder 001421-029-0127.

129. A. Bliss McCrum, General Counsel for Atlantic Greyhound, to Brown and Jones, Attorneys, July 27, 1936, in Papers of the NAACP, Part 11: Special Subject Files, 1912–1939, Series A, January 1, 1936–December 31, 1936, Segregation on Greyhound buses and Bus Stations, ProQuest History Vault, folder 001421-029-0127.

130. Charles Houston to Homer S. Brown, July 12, 1935, Papers of the NAACP, Part 11: Special Subject Files, 1912–1939, Segregation of Greyhound Bus Station, ProQuest History Vault, folder 001421-029-0097.

131. William Pickens, "More Miss. Jim Crow," *Plaindealer* (Kansas City) 42, no. 16, April 26, 1940, 3.

132. Ralph Ellison, *Going to the Territory* (New York: Vintage Books, 1986), 154, 156.

133. Ellison, *Going to the Territory*, 154, 155.

134. Ellison, *Going to the Territory*, 155.

135. Bernard D. Watts, "Fight for Social and Economic Equality," *Plaindealer* (Kansas City) 43, no. 40, September 26, 1941, 7.

136. William Henry Chafe, Raymond Gavins, and Robert Korstad, eds., *Remembering Jim Crow: African Americans Tell about Life in the Segregated South* (New York: New Press, 2001), 313.

137. Advertisement, no title, *New York Times*, October 24, 1933, 43; advertisement, no title, *Washington Post*, September 12, 1935, 5.

138. Walsh, "The Bus Industry in the United States."

139. Catherine A. Barnes, *Journey from Jim Crow: The Desegregation of Southern Transit* (New York: Columbia University Press, 1983), 150. See also Charles S. Johnson, "The Present Status of Race Relations in the South," *Social Forces* 23, no 1 (1944): 27–32, which presents evidence from a 1943 study that ranked racial incidents involving transportation as a source of racial tension second only to conflicts over employment.

140. "Ga. Legislature Would Increase Bus Jim Crow," *Chicago Defender*, February 3, 1945, 9.

141. John W. Childs, Corporal, "Protests Discrimination on Greyhound Bus," *Chicago Defender*, July 15, 1944, 12.

142. "Soldiers in Louisiana Told to Obey J. C. Laws," *Baltimore Afro-American*, May 8, 1943, 3; for a memo outlining the army's policy on this issue. see "Army Tells Va. Soldiers to Take Jim Crow and Like It: War Department Camp Lee, Va. Camp Headquarters," *Baltimore Afro-American*, October 10, 1942, 9.

143. James G. Thompson, letter to the editor, *Pittsburgh Courier*, originally printed January 31, 1942, reprinted April 11, 1942, 5.

144. Adam Fairclough, *Better Day Coming: Blacks and Equality, 1890–2000* (2001; repr. New York: Penguin Books, 2002), 192.

145. "Preferred Death to Jim Crow," *Baltimore Afro-American*, March 14, 1942, 18. See also Carl Dubar Lawrence, "Greyhound Cop Kills Passenger," *Chicago Defender*, March 7, 1942, 1.

146. Barnes, *Journey from Jim Crow*, 40; "Soldier Near Death in Texas for Riding in White Section of Bus," *Chicago Defender*, August 8, 1942, 1.

5. TRAVELING BY PLANE

1. Josh White "Uncle Sam Says," *Southern Exposure: An Album of Jim Crow Blues*, September 1941.

2. C. Vann Woodward, *The Strange Career of Jim Crow*, 3rd rev. ed. (1974; repr. New York: Oxford University Press, 2002), 117.

3. For an important new book that begins to fill in some of this story, see Anke Ortlepp, *Jim Crow Terminals: The Desegregation of American Airports* (Athens, GA: University of Georgia Press, 2017).

4. "One Way to Avoid Jim Crow Cars," *Baltimore Afro-American*, October 10, 1936, 1.

5. Charles A. Lindbergh, *The Spirit of St. Louis* (1953; New York: Simon and Schuster, 2003), 288.

6. Quoted in Kevin M. McCarthy and William L. Trotter, *Aviation in Florida* (Sarasota, FL: Pineapple Press, 2003), 3.

7. "Twenty-Fifth Anniversary of the First Airplane Flight: Proceedings of the Exercises Held at Kitty Hawk, N.C." (Washington, DC: United States Government Printing Office, 1929), 70th Congress, 2d Session, House, Doc. 520.

8. Jennifer Van Vleck, *Empire of the Air: Aviation and the American Ascendancy* (Cambridge, MA: Harvard University Press, 2013). 46.

9. Major Robert J. Jakeman, "America's Black Air Pioneers, 1900–1939," Student Report 88-1355, Air Command and Staff College, April 1988, 7, http://www.dtic.mil/dtic/tr/fulltext/u2/a210437.pdf.

10. Charles A. Lindbergh, "Aviation, Geography, and Race," *Reader's Digest*, November 1939, 64–67.

11. Kenneth Brown Collings, "America Will Never Fly," *American Mercury*, July 1936, 292, 290.
12. Quoted in Ulysses Lee, *The Employment of Negro Troops* (Washington, DC: Office of the Chief of Military History, US Army, 1966), 56.
13. Quoted in Lee, *Employment of Negro Troops*, 56.
14. "Race Discrimination Fight at Ohio Airport: Action for Damages Filed Refused Ride in Airplane after Paying the Required Fee," *Pittsburgh Courier*, May 25, 1929, 3; "Doctor Has Airplane Now Needs Air Port," *Baltimore Afro-American*, October 20, 1928, 1.
15. Judy L. Hasday, *The Tuskegee Airmen* (New York: Chelsea House, 2003), 20.
16. Connie Plantz, *The Life of Bessie Coleman: First African-American Woman Pilot* (Berkeley Heights, NJ: Enslow Publishers, Inc., 2014), 72, 44.
17. "Aviatrix Must Sign Away Life to Learn Trade," *Chicago Defender*, October 8, 1921, 2.
18. "Doctor Has Airplane."
19. Joseph J. Corn, *The Winged Gospel: America's Romance with Aviation* (New York: Oxford University Press, 1983; Baltimore: Johns Hopkins University Press, 2002), 12.
20. "What Will the Negro Contribute to Aviation? His Accomplishment in Other Fields of Adventure Presage Worthy Contributions for His Pioneering Spirits," *New York Amsterdam News*, June 22, 1927.
21. "Youths Must Prepare for Aviation Age: Proposes School in Honor of Aviatrix," *Chicago Defender*, October 29, 1927.
22. Harry Levette, "Call of the Wings," *Pittsburgh Courier*, May 16, 1931, 10. Levette's poem was also published as "Poem a Week: Call of the Wings!" in *New Journal and Guide*, May 23, 1931.
23. "Daring Aviators Near Goal," *Pittsburgh Courier*, October 8, 1932, 1.
24. "Some Facts concerning Transcontinental Flight," *Chicago Defender*, August 5, 1933, 2.
25. M. J. Washington, "U.S. Approves Flight of Goodwill Aviators: Pan-American Tour Ready to Begin, Report Pan-American Flyers Ready," *Chicago Defender*, November 3, 1934, 3.
26. Phillip Thomas Tucker, *Father of the Tuskegee Airmen, John C. Robinson* (Washington, DC: Potomac Books, 2012), 39.
27. Tucker, *Father of the Tuskegee Airmen*, 71.
28. Jakeman, "America's Black Air Pioneers," 14.
29. Lee, *Employment of Negro Troops*, 55.
30. William Powell, "Race Neglects Its Opportunities in Aviation: Engineer Tells Why We Should Become More Air-Minded," *Chicago Defender*, November 17, 1934, 10.
31. "Col. Robinson, Ethiopian Air Hero, Tells Story in Three Eastern Cities: Describes Possibilities of an Air Line in Southern States Manned by Race Pilots," *Pittsburgh Courier*, June 27, 1936.
32. F. Robert van der Linden, *Airlines and Airmail: The Post Office and the Birth of the Commercial Aviation Industry* (Lexington: University Press of Kentucky, 2002).
33. Dominick Pisano, *To Fill the Skies with Pilots: The Civilian Pilot Training Program, 1939–46* (Urbana: University of Illinois Press, 1993).
34. Douglass Hall, "Aviation May Alter Jim-Crow Travel Policies," *Baltimore Afro-American*, October 23, 1943.
35. Neil Scott, "Does Not Believe Negroes Will Fly Skyliners: Bias Will Prevail Says Air Official," *Pittsburgh Courier*, March 27, 1943.
36. The first African American pilot to be hired by the airlines was David Harris, who began flying for American Airlines in 1964; Green began flying for Continental in 1965, after the resolution of his court case.

37. "First Commercial Air Line Launched at Christening," *Baltimore Afro-American,* November 18, 1944, 3. See also "First Negro Airlines Offer Empoyment [*sic*] to Pilots in Postwar World," *Cleveland Call and Post,* November 18, 1944, 11B.

38. The only reference to Union Air Line after 1944 is a 1946 news item from the *New Journal and Guide* (Norfolk, VA) reporting that the Union Air Line was sending "Mary Bethune" on a nationwide tour, which was scheduled to stop in Norfolk that fall. The tour was dedicated to "creating greater interest in aeronautics among Negroes." "Negro Airliner Open to Public Here on June 30," *New Journal and Guide* (Norfolk, VA), June 29, 1946, A20. And although the Universal Skyways airline received a certificate of incorporation from the state of Delaware in the spring of 1944 and filed an application with the Civil Aeronautics Board "to engage in charter air transportation between the terminal points Chicago, Houston and Atlanta," there is no evidence that its backers ever even managed to buy a plane. "Second Airline Charter Sought," *Philadelphia Tribune,* November 24, 1945.

39. "GI's Start Airline. With-Pay 'Pool,'" *Baltimore Afro-American,* July 7, 1945, 11.

40. Kathleen M. Barry, *Femininity in Flight: A History of Flight Attendants* (Durham, NC: Duke University Press, 2007), 17.

41. Ben B. Follett, *Careers in Aviation* (Boston: Waverly House, 1942), 101.

42. Barry, *Femininity in Flight,* 17.

43. Follett, *Careers in Aviation,* 101.

44. Barry, *Femininity in Flight,* 14.

45. PAA, Latin American Division, *Customer Service Manual,* 1954?, 25–27, Pan American Airways Collection, Otto G. Richter Library, University of Miami, Coral Gables, quoted in Liesl Miller Orenic, "Rethinking Workplace Culture: Fleet Service Clerks in the American Airline Industry, 1945–1970," *Journal of Urban History* 30, no. 3 (2004): 455.

46. "Deny Woman Right to Fly in Airplane: Passenger Enters Suit against Concern," *Chicago Defender,* June 1, 1929, 3.

47. "By Changing to a Hindu, Wilton Crawley Makes the Grade Dodges Jim Crow," *Wyandotte Echo* (Kansas City), November 11, 1932, 1.

48. "Jim Crow?," *Time,* 22, no. 17, October 23, 1933, 58

49. "Rhines Sues Air Transport," *Baltimore Afro-American,* October 14, 1933, 3; "Air Transport Line Sued for $100,000," *Philadelphia Tribune,* October 19, 1933, 15.

50. Armistead Mason Dobie, *Handbook on the Law of Bailments and Carriers* (St. Paul: West, 1914), 519.

51. Frank E. Quindry, "Airline Passenger Discrimination," *Journal of Air Law* 3 (1932): 479.

52. Robert G. Dixon Jr., "Civil Rights in Air Transportation and Government Initiative," *Virginia Law Review* 49, no. 2 (March 1963): 207.

53. Charles S. Mangum Jr., *The Legal Status of the Negro* (Chapel Hill: University of North Carolina Press, 1940), 221.

54. Robert J. Serling, *Eagle: The Story of American Airlines* (New York: St. Martin's / Marek, 1985), 288.

55. "Color Bars Woman from Air Trip South," *Pittsburgh Courier,* August 13, 1932, A9.

56. Ralph Matthews, "Afro Man Hits Attempt at Air Jim Crow," *Washington Afro-American,* October 15, 1938.

57. Matthews, "Afro Man Hits Attempt at Air Jim Crow."

58. J. A. Rogers, "J. A. Rogers Has Breakfast in Midwest, Dinner on Coast," *Pittsburgh Courier,* August 1, 1936, 12.

59. Howard B. Woods, "Airlines Admit Jim Crow on Chicago Planes," *Chicago Defender*, March 10, 1945.

60. Donna Akiba Sullivan Harper, *Not So Simple: The "Simple" Stories by Langston Hughes* (Columbia: University of Missouri Press, 1995), 41.

61. Langston Hughes, "Planes versus Trains," *Chicago Defender* (national edition), January 12, 1946, editorial page.

62. Horace R. Cayton, "So Sorry, Please: They Have a Nice Little Jim Crow Formula on the Airplanes, Too," *Pittsburgh Courier*, July 6, 1946, 7.

63. Cayton, "So Sorry, Please."

64. Paul Evans, "Our Readers Say . . . : Is Air Really Free?," *Baltimore Afro-American*, February 18, 1950.

65. Complaint of the Jewish Congress and Gabriel Gladstone against American Airlines, Inc., September 28, 1951, Memorandum of Law, *American Jewish Congress and Gladstone v. American Airlines Inc.*, Queens County: State of New York, September 28, 1951, box 150, folder 23, American Jewish Congress, records, I-77, American Jewish Historical Society, https://archives.cjh.org/repositories/3/archival_objects/1218953.

66. Robert L. Carter to Jacob W. Rosenthal, 1949, Papers of the NAACP; Part 15: Segregation and Discrimination, Complaints and Responses, 1940–1955, ProQuest History Vault, folder 001444-013-0323.

67. Complaint of the Jewish Congress and Gabriel Gladstone against American Airlines, Inc.

68. Dale Wright, "Airlines Back Down on Bias: Queens D.A. Requests that Others Cease," *New York Amsterdam News*, October 6, 1951, 1. See also "Says Airline Uses Code to Discriminate," *Chicago Defender*, October 6, 1951, 1; "Agree to End Jim Crow on American Airlines (2)," *Chicago Defender*, October 13, 1951, 3.

69. Thomas R. Page, "To Have or Have Not?," *Pittsburgh Courier*, January 10, 1953, 6.

70. "Sues Airline, Charges Bias," *Pittsburgh Courier*, August 16, 1947.

71. Chris Lamb, "'I Never Want to Take Another Trip Like This One': Jackie Robinson's Journey to Integrate Baseball," *Journal of Sport History* 24, no. 2 (1997): 177–191.

72. "Ella Wins $7,500 Suit," *Plaindealer* (Kansas City), February 1, 1957, 5, 6; *Ella Fitzgerald, John Lewis, Georgiana Henry, and Norman Granz vs. Pan American World Airways, Inc.*, Civil 97-356, ca. December 23, 1954, Civil Case Files, National Archives, Records of District Courts of the United States, Record Group 21, identifier 2641486.

73. Peter B. Heister, "Discriminatory Bumping," *Journal of Air Law and Commerce* 40 (1974): 534.

74. James L. Hicks, "Powell Hit by Race Bias," *New York Amsterdam News*, October 31, 1959, 1.

75. "Don't Expect Colored People by Air," *Baltimore Afro-American*, April 9, 1932, 2.

76. Robert L. Carter to Jacob W. Rosenfeld, Esq., February 3, 1949, Papers of the NAACP, Part 15: Segregation and Discrimination, Complaints and Responses, 1940–1955, ProQuest History Vault, folder 001444-013-0323.

77. Charles C. Diggs, Member of Congress, to Robert F. Six, President of Continental Airlines, Inc., May 12, 1955, Smithsonian Air and Space Museum, https://airandspace.si.edu /multimedia-gallery/14299hjpg.

78. "Edgar Brown Suing Washington Airport for Discrimination," *Philadelphia Tribune*, August 14, 1941, 3.

79. "Edgar Brown Sues Airplane Company in Airport Jim-Crow," *Cleveland Call and Post*, August 16, 1941, 1.

80. Charles Houston, "Along the Highway," *Baltimore Afro-American*, October 30, 1948, 4.

81. "Jim Crow Southernaires in D.C. Airport Cafeteria," *Chicago Defender*, December 13, 1941, 4; "Airport Jim Crow Hits Radio Stars," *Baltimore Afro-American*, December 13, 1941, 2.

82. "CAA Chief Evades Action on Airport Jim-Crow: Federal Official Refuses to Move against Washington Airport Restaurant That Refused Service to 'Southernaires,'" *Cleveland Call and Post*, January 3, 1942, 2B.

83. Mamie E. Davis to Mr. P. S. Damon, President, American Airlines, August 8, 1946, Papers of the NAACP, Part 15: Segregation and Discrimination, Complaints and Responses, 1940–1955, ProQuest History Vault, folder 001444-019-0747.

84. *To Secure These Rights*, Report of the President's Committee on Civil Rights (Washington, DC: US Government Printing Office, 1947), 171–172.

85. Azza Salama Layton, *International Politics and Civil Rights Policies in the United States, 1941–1960* (New York: Cambridge University Press, 2000), 86.

86. Robert G. Dixon Jr., "Civil Rights in Air Transportation and Government Initiative," *Virginia Law Review* 49, no. 2 (1963): 220.

87. Francis Mitchell, "Racial Separation Ordered in Dining Room of Norfolk Airport: Port Body Authorizes Jim Crow Restaurant Manager Begins Segregation in 'Azalea Room,'" *New Journal and Guide*, January 24, 1953, 2.

88. "Three Fliers Get a Taste of Airport Bias," *Pittsburgh Courier*, March 7, 1953, 19.

89. "Segregation of Indian Brings U.S. Apologies," *Washington Post and Times-Herald*, August 24, 1955.

90. Samuel Hoskins, "'Jim-Crow Incident': Furore Narrowly Avoided," *Baltimore Afro-American*, September 3, 1955, 6.

91. N. D. B. Connolly, "Timely Innovations: Planes, Trains and the 'Whites Only' Economy of a Pan-American City," *Urban History* 36, no. 2 (2009): 257.

92. Alice A. Dunnigan, "Washington Inside Out: The Black and the White of It . . . ," *Pittsburgh Courier*, March 22, 1958.

93. Theodore Kirkland, *Spirit and Soul: Odyssey of a Black Man in America* (Bloomington, IN: Xlibris, 2012), 37.

94. Charles C. Diggs to Robert F. Six, May 12, 1955.

95. Enoc P. Waters, "Adventures in Race Relations: Shoes Shined Inside," *Chicago Defender*, March 7, 1953, 10.

96. "Dixie Travelogue," *Chicago Defender*, April 26, 1952.

97. Carl Murphy, "Vacation Notes," *Baltimore Afro-American*, September 16, 1950, 18.

98. James Baldwin, "They Can't Turn Back," *Mademoiselle*, August 1960, 324–325, 351.

99. Moss H. Kendrix, "Kendrix Komments: If You Fly—You Know," *Atlanta Daily World*, March 25, 1951.

100. B. Phillips, "Yes, Leave the South, Now! Report Is that Only Long War Will Civilize Dixie," *Baltimore Afro-American*, February 26, 1944, 1; "Charges Jim Crow by Dallas Air-Cab," *Pittsburgh Courier*, February 12, 1949, 7.

101. "Singer Forced to Sit in Bus Eight Hours, May Sue Airlines," *Baltimore Afro-American*, January 26, 1946, 11.

102. William H. Gray, President, The Florida Agricultural & Mechanical College, to G. T. Baker, President, National Airlines, Inc., September 4, 1947; G. T. Baker to William H. Gray, September 14, 1947, Papers of the NAACP, Part 15, Series A, Legal Department Files, ProQuest History Vault, folder 001444-004-0844.

103. Stanley de J. Osborn, Vice President, Eastern Airlines, to Willam H. Gray, September 19, 1947, Papers of the NAACP, Part 15, Series A, Legal Department Files, ProQuest History Vault, folder 001444-004-0844.

104. "So Sorry, Thought You Were Negroes," *Pittsburgh Courier*, September 3, 1955, 16.

105. Houston, "Along the Highway."

106. "Singer Forced to Sit in Bus Eight Hours."

107. "Sues Airline, Charges Bias."

108. Records of the District Court of the United States, Central District of California, Civil Case 7435 (1949), *Ruth Wyatt v. Transcontinental & Western Air*, in *Federal Records Relating to Civil Rights in the Post–World War II Era*, compiled by Walter B. Hill Jr. (Washington, DC: National Archives and Records Administration, 2006), 222–223.

109. Al Nall, "Five to Fight Airline Bias," *New York Amsterdam News*, December 7, 1957.

110. Ellen Tarry, *The Third Door: The Autobiography of an American Negro Woman* (New York: David McKay, 1955), 246, 247, 276.

111. Tarry, *The Third Door*, 246, 250–251.

112. Carl Rowan, *South of Freedom* (New York: Knopf, 1952), 15.

113. "Operation Airport," *Pittsburgh Courier*, May 1, 1954.

114. Anke Ortlepp, *Jim Crow Terminals: The Desegregation of American Airports* (Athens, GA: University of Georgia Press, 2017), 35.

6. TRAVELING FOR CIVIL RIGHTS

1. Carol Morello, "The Freedom Rider a Nation Nearly Forgot: Woman Who Defied Segregation Finally Gets Her Due," *Washington Post*, July 30, 2000, A1.

2. Richard Dier, "Morgan vs. State of Virginia: Case to Be Supreme Court Hot Potato," *Baltimore Afro-American*, January 26, 1946.

3. Morello, "Freedom Rider a Nation Nearly Forgot."

4. "State Supreme Court Upholds Jim Crow Travel Law," *New Journal and Guide*, June 16, 1945, 1.

5. *Morgan v. Virginia*, 328 U.S. 373 (1946).

6. "JC Bus Travel Outlawed," *Washington Afro-American*, July 14, 1944, 1.

7. "Jim Crow Suit," *Time*, May 24, 1937, 13.

8. *Mitchell v. United States*, 313 U.S. 80 (1941).

9. "Jim Crow Suit."

10. Before the Interstate Commerce Commission, Initial Brief of Arthur W. Mitchell, August 18, 1938, *Arthur W. Mitchell, Complainant vs. Frank O. Lowden, James E. Gorman, Trustees of the Estate of the Chicago, Rock Island, and Pacific Railroad Company*, Docket No. 27844 (Chicago: Chicago Law Printing Co., 1938), 22, 25; Arthur W. Mitchell Papers, 1898–1968, Papers: April 16–19, 1938, Chicago Historical Society, ProQuest History Vault, folder 252249-038-0002.

11. Dennis Sven Nordin, *The New Deal's Black Congressman: A Life of Arthur Wergs Mitchell* (Columbia: University of Missouri Press, 1997), 180, 179.

12. Nordin, *New Deal's Black Congressman*, 209.

13. Quoted in Nordin, *New Deal's Black Congressman*, 145.

14. Quoted in Nordin, *New Deal's Black Congressman*, 88.

15. Thurgood Marshall to John LeFlore, December 18, 1940, Papers of the NAACP, Library of Congress, Part 15, Segregation and Discrimination, Complaints and Responses, 1940–1955, ProQuest History Vault, folder 001444-016-0033.

16. "Negro Congressman Sues for $50,000, Charging He Was Ejected from Pullman," *New York Times*, May 11, 1937.

17. Nordin, *New Deal's Black Congressman*, 250.

18. Roy Wilkins, "Watchtower," *New York Amsterdam Star-News*, March 29, 1941, 16.

19. "Mitchell Battles Jim Crow," *Chicago Defender*, July 1, 1939, 14; "Segregation Is Target of Ill. Solon," *New Journal and Guide*, May 22, 1937, 1.

20. "Rock Island R.R. Files Reply to Mitchell Suit: Railroad Admits Breach of Contract with Congressman," *Baltimore Afro-American*, July 10, 1937.

21. Interstate Commerce Act (1887), 49th Congress, 2nd Session, December 6, 1886, http://www .ourdocuments.gov/doc.php?flash=true&doc=49&page=transcript.

22. D. W. Kellum, "Quiz Congressman Mitchell in Suit," *Chicago Defender*, March 12, 1938.

23. "Mitchell Rebukes 'Time': Its Statement That He Okeys [sic] J. C. Cars 'Absolutely False,'" *Baltimore Afro-American*, June 12, 1937.

24. Nordin, *New Deal's Black Congressmen*, 257.

25. *Mitchell v. United States*, 313 U.S. 80 (1941).

26. *McCabe v. Atchison*, T. & S. F. Ry. Co., 235 U.S. 151 (1914).

27. Desmond S. King and Rogers M. Smith, *Still a House Divided: Race and Politics in Obama's America* (Princeton: Princeton University Press, 2011), 15.

28. "Memorandum for the United States, *Mitchell v. United States*," reprinted in George Crockett Jr., "Comments on *Mitchell v. United States*," *National Bar Journal* 1, no. 2 (1941): 157–197. For a discussion of Biddle's civil rights commitments, see Risa L. Goluboff, *The Lost Promise of Civil Rights* (Cambridge, MA: Harvard University Press, 2007), 120–169.

29. *Mitchell v. United States*, 313 U.S. 80 (1941).

30. "High Court Upholds Mitchell: Present Type of Jim-Crow Coaches Doomed," *Pittsburgh Courier*, May 3, 1941, 1; "Supreme Court Grants Negroes Equality on Interstate Trains," *New York Herald Tribune*, April 29, 1941, 1.

31. "Mitchell Predicts 'Dawn of New Day' in Negro Travel," *Pittsburgh Courier*, December 28, 1940, 13. See also "Mitchell Sees New Travel Era in South," *Baltimore Afro-American*, December 28, 1940; "Mitchell's Case Seen Changing R.R. Travel: To Probe Segregation by Railroad of Illinois Congressman," *Philadelphia Tribune*, December 26, 1940.

32. P. L. Prattis to Roy Wilkins, May 14, 1941, 1, NAACP discrimination complaint files, Arthur Mitchell decision on transportation case, ProQuest History Vault, folder 001444-017-0491.

33. Roy Wilkins to J. E. Mitchell, Managing Editor, *St. Louis Argus*, April 23, 1941, NAACP discrimination complaint files, Arthur Mitchell decision on transportation case, ProQuest History Vault, folder 001444-017-0491.

34. Albert Anderson, "Mitchell Says He Alone Beat Railroads: Rejects Offer of Help from NAACP Group," *Chicago Defender*, May 3, 1941.

35. George F. Miller, M.D., to Thurgood Marshall, May 14, 1941, NAACP discrimination complaint files, Arthur Mitchell decision on transportation case, folder 001444-017-0491; Gerald Griffin, "Court Grants Negroes Equal Train Rights," *Baltimore Sun*, April 29, 1941, 1.

36. Statement by Walter White, Secretary NAACP, for the *New York Evening Post*, April 29, 1941, Papers of the NAACP, Part 15, Segregation and Discrimination Complaints and Responses, 1940–1965, ProQuest History Vault, folder 001444-017-049.

37. "Southern States Seek to Console Themselves over Railroad Jim-Crow Ruling," *Cleveland Call and Post*, May 10, 1941, 15.

38. "Citizens Take Mitchell's Cue," *Baltimore Afro-American*, January 7, 1939, 18.

39. Roy Wilkins, "The Negro Wants Full Equality," in *What the Negro Wants*, ed. Rayford W. Logan (Chapel Hill: University of North Carolina Press, 1944), 127.

40. Bayard Rustin, "The Negro and Nonviolence" (1942), in *Time on Two Crosses: The Collected Writings of Bayard Rustin*, ed. Devon W. Carbado and Donald Weise (San Francisco: Cleis Press, 2003), 6.

41. "Unequal Rail Facilities Hit in Plea to ICC: Day-Long Wait for Jim Crow Car Cited in NAACP Petition," *Chicago Defender*, national ed., September 18, 1943.

42. John Leflore, "Dixie Trains Jam Negro Passengers in Prison Cars," *Chicago Defender*, April 7, 1945; "Fill Jim Crow Coach with Whites; Put Negroes in Train Baggage Car," *Pittsburgh Courier*, May 6, 1944.

43. Leflore, "Dixie Trains Jam Negro Passengers in Prison Cars."

44. "NAACP Demands Probe of Beatings: Redress Sought through FDR," *Atlanta Daily World*, September 19, 1942.

45. "Dixie Gets Rougher with Negroes," *New York Amsterdam Star-News*, September 19, 1942, 1.

46. Robert P. Patterson, Under Secretary of War, to Walter White, April 17, 1942, Papers of the NAACP, Part 18, Special Subjects, 1940–1955, Series A, ProQuest History Vault, folder 001455-004-0708.

47. Lt. Col. Campbell Johnston, memo to General Hersey, June 2, 1943, Subject: Transportation Facilities in the South, African Americans in the Military, Part 3: subject files of Judge William Hastie, Civilian Aide to the Secretary of War, N–Z, ProQuest History Vault, folder 102613-029-0001.

48. Lt. Col. Campbell Johnston, memo to General Hersey, June 2, 1943.

49. "Bender Tells Congress of Jim-Crowism," *Cleveland Call and Post*, May 23, 1942, 1.

50. Gilbert Ware, *William Hastie: Grace under Pressure* (New York: Oxford University Press, 1984), 116.

51. Thurgood Marshall, "Memorandum from Mr. Marshall to Mr. White," May 27, 1942, Papers of the NAACP, Part 09: Discrimination in the U.S. Armed Forces, Series B, Armed Forces' Legal Files, 1940–1950, ProQuest History Vault, folder 001537-015-0510.

52. Joseph B. Eastman, Office of Defense Transportation, to Walter White, August 15, 1942, 2, Papers of the NAACP, Part 9: Discrimination in the U.S. Armed Forces, Series B, Armed Forces' Legal Files, 1940–1950, ProQuest History Vault, folder 001537-015-0510.

53. The army addressed this practice only once, in a July 8, 1944, circular that noted that restriction of personnel to "certain sections" of buses, trucks, or other army transportation "because of race will not be permitted either on or off post, camp or station, regardless of local civilian custom." The order was included in a general circular restating the War Department's "standing policy on racial discrimination," which was so little known or practiced that its reiteration inspired protests in the South. "Here's the Army's No J. C. Order: It Forbids Segregation in PX, Bus, Theatre," *Baltimore Afro-American*, September 2, 1944, 2. On southern responses to the order, see Alan M. Osur, *Blacks in the Army Air Forces during World War II: The Problems of Race Relations* (Washington, DC: Office of Air Force History, 1977), 77.

54. Truman Gibson, interview with Carol Briley, Harry S. Truman Library, Independence, Missouri, July 27, 2001; transcript available at https://www.trumanlibrary.org/oralhist /gibsont.htm.

55. Bryant Simon, introduction to Howard W. Odum, *Race and Rumors of Race: The American South in the Early Forties* (Chapel Hill: University of North Carolina Press, 1943; Baltimore: Johns Hopkins University Press, 1997), x.

56. Marjorie McKenzie, "Pursuit of Democracy: Southern Jim Crow Cause of Friction between Soldiers," *Pittsburgh Courier*, November 8, 1941.

57. Wilkins, "The Negro Wants Full Equality," 127.

58. Sterling A. Brown, "Count Us In," in Logan, *What the Negro Wants*, 3:5.

59. "Jail Two Girl Employees of Navy Department for Failure to Take Jim Crow Seats on Virginia Bus," *New York Age*, January 16, 1943, 1.

60. Thurgood Marshall to John LeFlore, July 3, 1945, 3, NAACP discrimination complaint files, LeFlore and Crishon v. Gulf, Mobile and Ohio Railroad Co., January 1, 1943–December 31, 1945, Papers of the NAACP, Part 15, Segregation and Discrimination, Complaints and Responses, 1940–1955, Series A, ProQuest History Vault. folder 001444-016-0187.

61. Thurgood Marshall to Larry Eisenberg, September 5, 1945, Papers of the NAACP, Part 15: Segregation and Discrimination, Complaints and Responses, 1940–1955, Series A, Legal Department Files. ProQuest History Vault, folder 001444-011-0465.

62. Thurgood Marshall to Mr. G. U. Yager, General Passenger Agent, Louisville and Nashville Railroad, June 12, 1942, Papers of the NAACP, Part 15, Segregation and Discrimination, Complaints and Responses, 1940–1955, ProQuest History Vault, folder 001444-011-0108.

63. J. L. LeFlore, "Brief of Discrimination Discovered in Traveling on the Gulf, Mobile and Ohio Railroad, between Meridian and Return," 2, Papers of the NAACP, Part 15, Segregation and Discrimination, Complaints and Responses, 1940–1954, ProQuest History Vault, folder 001444-016-0305.

64. Interstate Commerce Commission, No. 29210, John L. Flore and Alfred S. Crishon, Proposed Report by Examiner Claude A. Rice, February 15, 1945, Papers of the NAACP, Part 15, Segregation and Discrimination, Complaints and Responses, 1940–1954, ProQuest History Vault, folder 001444-016-0305.

65. Interstate Commerce Commission, No. 29210, John LeFlore and Alfred S. Crishom v. Gulf, Mobile and Ohio Railroad Company, 5. Papers of the NAACP, Part 15, Segregation and Discrimination, Complaints and Responses, 1940–1954, ProQuest History Vault, folder 001444-016-0305.

66. John LeFlore to Thurgood Marshall, June 8, 1950, 5, Papers of the NAACP, Transportation, John LeFlore, 1940–1950, Part 15, Segregation and Discrimination, Complaints and Responses, 1940–1955, Series A, Legal Department Files, ProQuest History Vault, folder 001444-016-0033.

67. Thurgood Marshall to John LeFlore, July 3, 1945, 2, Papers of the NAACP, Part 15, Segregation and Discrimination, Complaints and Responses, 1940–1955, ProQuest History Vault, folder 001444-016-0187.

68. Edward R. Dudley, NAACP Assistant Special Counsel, to John LeFlore, June 4, 1945, Papers of the NAACP, Part 15, Segregation and Discrimination, Complaints and Responses, 1940–1955, ProQuest History Vault, folder 001444-016-0187.

69. Catherine A. Barnes, *Journey from Jim Crow: The Desegregation of Southern Transit* (New York: Columbia University Press, 1983), 44.

70. Mark V. Tushnet, *Making Civil Rights Law: Thurgood Marshall and the Supreme Court, 1936–1961* (New York: Oxford University Press, 1994), 73.

71. Tushnet, *Making Civil Rights Law*, 72. Because Robinson had not been a lawyer long enough to qualify to argue a court case before the Supreme Court, the case was presented by Thurgood Marshall and William Hastie, with the aid of Robinson, who sat at the counsel table and passed them notes on commerce clause theory. Charles L. Zelden, *Thurgood*

Marshall: Race, Rights, and the Struggle for a More Perfect Union (New York: Routledge, 2013), 50.

72. *Morgan v. Commonwealth of Virginia*, Transcript of Appeal, 10, Papers of the NAACP, Part 15, Segregation and Discrimination, Complaints and Responses, 1940–1955, ProQuest History Vault, folder 001444-018-0238.

73. *Morgan v. Virginia*, 328 U.S. 373 (1946).

74. "Travelers Face New Barriers: Violations Ordered by Companies, Say Operators," *New Journal and Guide* (Norfolk), September 21, 1946, 1.

75. "Virginia Court Uses Old Law to Circumvent Supreme Court Ruling," *Pittsburgh Courier*, November 30, 1946, 1.

76. Va. Code Ann. 4533a (Cum. Supp. 1946). This statute was later overturned by Virginia's supreme court in *Taylor v. Commonwealth*, 187 Va. 214, 46 S.E.2d 384 (1948). For a brief discussion of the latter, see "Criminal Law. Mere Failure to Move to Another Seat in Compliance with Carrier's Regulations Does Not Constitute Disorderly Conduct under Virginia Statute," *Virginia Law Review* 34, no. 5 (1948): 627–629.

77. *Matthews v. Southern Railway System*, 157 F.2d 609, 610–611 (D.C. Cir., 1946).

78. NAACP Assistant Special Counsel, Robert L. Carter to Spottswood W. Robinson, III, Esq., September 16, 1946, Robert L. Carter to Joshua Freeland, Esq., February 4, 1947, in Papers of the NAACP, Part 15: Segregation and Discrimination, Complaints and Responses, 1940–1955, Series A, Legal Department Files, ProQuest History Vault, folders 001444-014-0001 and 001444-019-0573.

79. "Memorandum to Mr. White from Thurgood Marshall," February 3, 1947, Papers of the NAACP, Part 15, Segregation and Discrimination, Complaints and Responses, 1940–1955, Series A, Legal Department Files, ProQuest History Vault, folder 001444-014-0747, January 1. On Powell's bill, see "A Bill to Back," *Pittsburgh Courier*, March 22, 1947, 6.

80. Martin A. Martin, of Hill, Martin and Robinson, to Nelle Morton, General Secretary, The Fellowship of Southern Churchmen, Papers of the NAACP, Part 15, Series A, Legal Department File, ProQuest History Vault, folder 001444-013-0267.

81. Marian Wynn Perry, Assistant Special Counsel, NAACP National Office, to Walter Allyn Hill, Executive Secretary, District of Columbia Branch NAACP, September 30, 1947, Papers of the NAACP, Part 15, Segregation and Discrimination, Complaints and Responses, 1940–1955, ProQuest History Vault, folder 001444-013-0432.

82. "Journey of Reconciliation, A Report Prepared by George M. Houser and Bayard Rustin," Papers of the NAACP, Part 15, Segregation and Discrimination, Complaints and Responses, 1940–1955, Series A, Legal Department Files, ProQuest History Vault, folder 001444-015-0326.

83. Jervis Anderson, *Bayard Rustin: Troubles I've Seen—A Biography* (New York: HarperCollins, 1997), 111.

84. Raymond Arsenault, *Freedom Riders: 1961 and the Struggle for Racial Justice* (New York: Oxford University Press, 2006), 27. See, for example, "N.Y. Guest Spends Night in Minn. Hotel Lobby," *Baltimore Afro-American*, February 8, 1947.

85. Quoted in John D'Emilio, *Lost Prophet: The Life and Times of Bayard Rustin* (Chicago: University of Chicago Press, 2004), 134.

86. Arsenault, *Freedom Riders*, 36.

87. D'Emilio, *Lost Prophet*, 134.

88. Derek Charles Catsam, *Freedom's Main Line: The Journey of Reconciliation and the Freedom Rides* (Lexington: University Press of Kentucky, 2009), 21.

89. D'Emilio, *Lost Prophet*, 136.

90. George M. Houser and Bayard Rustin, "Journey of Reconciliation: A Report," 4, Fellowship of Reconciliation, Congress of Racial Equality, [1947?], Beinecke Rare Book and Manuscript Library, Yale University, https://brbl-dl.library.yale.edu/vufind/Record/3684526.

91. Houser and Rustin, "Journey of Reconciliation," 9.

92. Houser and Rustin, "Journey of Reconciliation," 8.

93. Houser and Rustin, "Journey of Reconciliation," 11.

94. D'Emilio, *Lost Prophet*, 140.

95. Bayard Rustin, "Memo on Bus Travel in the South" (1947), in *I Must Resist: Bayard Rustin's Life in Letters*, ed. Michael G. Long (San Francisco: City Lights Books, 2012), 93.

96. Marjorie McKenzie, "Pursuit of Democracy: In Which a Columnist Writes of an Incident Which Happened in Dixie," *Pittsburgh Courier*, September 12, 1942 7

97. "Files Suit for Equal Dining Car Service: Southern Railway Made Defendant in I.C.C. Action," *New Journal and Guide* (Norfolk, VA), October 17, 1942.

98. Lawson, quoted in Barnes, *Journey from Jim Crow*, 70.

99. Katie McCabe and Dovey Johnson Roundtree, *Justice Older than the Law: The Life of Dovey Johnson Roundtree* (Jackson: University Press of Mississippi, 2009), 111.

100. McCabe and Roundtree, *Justice Older than the Law*, 111.

101. McCabe and Roundtree, *Justice Older than the Law*, 111.

102. For an overview of Truman's civil rights agenda that includes discussion of historians' very different assessments of his civil rights commitments, see Jon E. Taylor, *Freedom to Serve: Truman, Civil Rights, and Executive Order 9981* (New York: Routledge, 2013).

103. Cornell W. Clayton, *The Politics of Justice: The Attorney General and the Making of Legal Policy* (Armonk, NY: M. E. Sharpe, 1992; New York: Routledge, 2015), 126.

104. McGrath, quoted in Patricia Sullivan, *Lift Every Voice: The NAACP and the Making of the Civil Rights Movement* (New York: New Press, 2009), 380.

105. McCabe and Roundtree, *Justice Older than the Law*, 111.

106. Perlman, quoted in Anthony Lewis, "Abroad at Home: 'Imposing on Them a Badge of Inferiority,'" *New York Times*, January 22, 2000.

107. "Smashes Jim Crow Rule: U.S. Supreme Court K.O.'s Jim Crow Travel, Education," *Chicago Defender*, June 10, 1950.

108. Quoted in Sullivan, *Lift Every Voice*, 384.

109. Herman Hodge Long, "Segregation in Interstate Railway Coach Travel A Field Research Project of the Race Relations Department," American Missionary Association, Board of Home Missions, Congregational Christian Churches, Nashville, TN: Fisk University, 1952, MS, 31–33, 43, 50, 51.

110. McCabe and Roundtree, *Justice Older than the Law*, 126.

111. McCabe and Roundtree, *Justice Older than the Law*, 147.

112. "NAACP v. St. Louis-San Francisco Railway Co., Interstate Commerce Commission, No. 31423, November 7, 1955," *Race Relations Law Reporter* 1, no. 1 (1956), 264, 263; "NAACP Opens Attack on Segregation in Travel," *Pittsburgh Courier*, December 26, 1953.

113. Barnes, *Journey from Jim Crow*, 100.

114. Barnes, *Journey from Jim Crow*, 99.

115. *Sarah Keys v. Carolina Coach Company*, 64 MCC 769 (1955).

116. Luther A. Huston, "I.C.C. Orders End of Segregation on Trains, Buses; Deadline Jan. 10," *New York Times*, November 26; "ICC Ruling: End of an Era," *Pittsburgh Courier*, December 10, 1955.

117. "Greyhound Bus Signs Still Up; Co. Won't Enforce Them," *Baltimore Afro-American,* February 11, 1956.

118. Henry Lesesne, "No Early End in Sight: South Segregates Intrastate Travel," *Christian Science Monitor,* December 7, 1955, 17.

119. "Mississippi Police Defy ICC; Replace Segregation Signs at Depots," *Atlanta Daily World,* January 10, 1956, 1.

120. Clarence Mitchell, "From the Work Bench: Interstate Travel Problem," *Baltimore Afro-American,* November 30, 1957, 4.

121. "South Obeys, Defies Ban on Travel Bias," *Chicago Defender,* January 21, 1956, 1.

122. Robert Denley, "Jan. 10 'D' (Down) Day for Travel Bias Signs," *New Journal and Guide* (Norfolk, VA), January 14, 1956.

123. Clarence Mitchell, "From the Work Bench: Interstate Travel Problem," *Baltimore Afro-American,* November 30, 1957, 4.

124. McCabe and Roundtree, *Justice Older than the Law,* 154.

125. McCabe and Roundtree, *Justice Older than the Law,* 154.

7. TRAVELING FOR FREEDOM

1. "Bus Segregation Is Knocked Out," *Alabama Journal,* November 13, 1956.

2. On Browder's impact, see Randall Kennedy, "Martin Luther King's Constitution: A Legal History of the Montgomery Boycott," *Yale Law Journal* 98, no. 6 (April 1989): 1058.

3. Raymond Arsenault, *Freedom Riders: 1961 and the Struggle for Racial Justice* (New York: Oxford University Press, 2006), 77.

4. Catherine A. Barnes, *Journey from Jim Crow: The Desegregation of Southern Transit* (New York: Columbia University Press, 1983), 150.

5. *Boynton v. Virginia,* 364 U.S. 454 (1960).

6. Barnes, *Journey from Jim Crow,* 150.

7. Arsenault, *Freedom Riders,* 94.

8. Freedom Ride 1961 Press Release, March or April 1961, quoted in Derek Charles Catsam, *Freedom's Main Line: The Journey of Reconciliation and the Freedom Rides* (Lexington: University Press of Kentucky, 2009), 69.

9. The only two predeparture references to the 1961 Freedom Ride that I've been able to find are "Freedom Ride Will Test Bus Service," *New York Amsterdam News,* April 8, 1961, 4; and "CORE to Test Bus Bias in 'Freedom Ride,' 1961," *Philadelphia Tribune,* April 18, 1961, 9.

10. James Farmer, quoted in Howell Raines, *My Soul Is Rested: Movement Days in the Deep South Remembered* (New York: Penguin Books, 1977), 110.

11. James Farmer, *Lay Bare the Heart: An Autobiography of the Civil Rights Movement* (New York: Arbor House, 1985), 199.

12. "Mob Freedom Riders in Ala. Bus Is Set Afire," *Cleveland Call and Post,* May 20, 1961, 2A.

13. James Peck, *Freedom Ride* (New York: Simon and Schuster, 1962), 128.

14. Barnes, *Journey from Jim Crow,* 160.

15. James Peck, quoted in Arsenault, *Freedom Riders,* 167.

16. "More 'Riders' Go to Birmingham; Drivers Balk," *Atlanta Daily World,* May 18, 1961, 1.

17. Arsenault, *Freedom Riders,* 179.

18. Nash, quoted in Farmer, *Lay Bare the Heart,* 203.

19. Arsenault, *Freedom Riders,* 182.

20. Quoted in Arsenault, *Freedom Riders,* 182.

21. Quoted in Arsenault, *Freedom Riders*, 183.

22. "More 'Riders' Go to Birmingham."

23. John Lewis interview, in Raines, *My Soul Is Rested*, 118.

24. "It's No Time to Cool Off," *Cleveland Call and Post*, June 3, 1961, sec. 2.

25. Victor Wilson and Stuart H. Loory, "'Freedom' Ride into a Mississippi Jail: Federal Warning to Any Travelers: Shun Two States, Stay at Home on the Bus," *New York Herald Tribune*, May 25, 1961, 1–4.

26. Catsam, *Freedom's Main Line*, 237.

27. Arseneault, *Freedom Riders*, 252.

28. Robert F. Kennedy, *Robert Kennedy, in His Own Words: The Unpublished Recollections of the Kennedy Years*, ed. Edwin O. Guthman and Jeffrey Shulman (New York: Bantam, 1988), 97.

29. The exact number of people who participated in Freedom Rides is difficult to estimate with great certainty, as is the number jailed in Jackson. But Raymond Arsenault's carefully researched roster of the riders puts the overall total of Freedom Ride participants at 436 and suggests that, of those, approximately 340 traveled to Jackson. Virtually all who reached Jackson were arrested, with a couple of exceptions. On the exceptions see Arsenault, *Freedom Riders*, 384. For the overall numbers, and tallies of those who traveled to Jackson, see Arsenault's appendix, "Roster of the Riders," 587, 533–557.

30. Interstate Commerce Commission No. MC-C-3358, "Discrimination in the Operations of Interstate Motor Carriers of Passengers," decided September 22, 1961, reprinted in *Crisis*, November 1961, 537–551.

31. Katie McCabe and Dovey Johnson Roundtree, *Justice Older than the Law: The Life of Dovey Johnson Roundtree* (Jackson: University Press of Mississippi, 2009), 156.

32. James Farmer, quoted in Arsenault, *Freedom Riders*, 439; on the relatively earlier integration of common carriers versus other accommodations, see Barnes, *Journey from Jim Crow*, 204.

33. Wilson and Loory, "'Freedom' Ride into a Mississippi Jail," 4.

34. Wilson and Loory, "'Freedom' Ride into a Mississippi Jail," 4.

35. "Statement of the Secretary of State," letter from Dean Rusk to Attorney General Robert F. Kennedy, May 29, 1961, Interstate Commerce Commission MC-C-3358, Appendix D., Records of the Interstate Commerce Commission, Record Group 134, National Archives, College Park, Maryland, ProQuest History Vault, folder 104868-009-0001.

36. Part 180a, Regulations in the Operation of Interstate Motor Common Carriers of Passengers, *The Code of Federal Regulations of the United States of America* (Washington, DC: US Government Printing Office, 1961), 9.

37. Claude Sitton, "I.C.C. Travel Rule Is Defied in South," *New York Times*, November 2, 1961, 1.

38. Barnes, *Journey from Jim Crow*, 180.

39. *Bailey v. Patterson*, 369 U.S. 31 (1962).

40. Barnes, *Journey from Jim Crow*, 178. Additional information on interstate transportation antidiscrimination legislation, court cases, and statistics on investigations in southern states can be found in the Records of the Interstate Commerce Commission, Record Group 134, National Archives, College Park, Maryland, ProQuest History Vault, folder 104868-018-0832.

41. Southern Railway Co. and Louisville and Nashville Railroad terminal alleged racial discrimination against Joseph Echols Lowery at Decatur, Alabama, station restaurant, March 30, 1962–May 29, 1962, Federal Government Records: Record Group 134, Records of the Interstate Commerce Commission, National Archives, College Park, Maryland, folder 104868-010-0665.

42. Federal Bureau of Investigation, memo, April 28, 1962. FBI review of Freedom Riders' test of racial desegregation at Winfield, Alabama, bus station and Rebel Café, Records of the Interstate Commerce Commission, Record Group 134, National Archives, College Park, Maryland, ProQuest History Vault, folder 104868-010-0759.

43. Barnes, *Journey from Jim Crow*, 183.

44. Anke Ortlepp, *Jim Crow Terminals: The Desegregation of American Airports* (Athens, GA: University of Georgia Press, 2017), 48.

45. "Learn of Dixie Bigotry First-Hand," *New Journal and Guide*, June 17, 1961, 1.

46. "On Florida 'Freedom Ride': 13 Clerics Arrested," *Baltimore Afro-American*, June 24, 1961, 1.

47. David Halberstam, "Airport Segregation in South Poses a Knotty Problem for U.S.," *New York Times*, June 12, 1961, 16.

48. "Tells of Gain in Integration," *Des Moines Register*, June 23, 1962, 18.

49. Ortlepp, *Jim Crow Terminals*, 116.

50. James E. Clayton, "U.S. to Push Race Curb Fight," *Washington Post and Times-Herald*, July 3, 1961; Ortlepp, *Jim Crow Terminals*, 116.

51. "U.S. Suit Attacks Ala. Airport Bias," *Baltimore Afro-American*, August 5, 1961, 6.

52. Ortlepp, *Jim Crow Terminals*, 123.

53. "Birmingham Sued by U.S. on Airport," *New York Times*, June 20, 1962, 17; *United States v. the City of Birmingham*, no. 10196 (1962); "Appeals Court Upholds Ban on Shreveport Segregation," *New York Times*, May 23, 1963; *United States v. City of New Orleans*, Civil Action no. 11254 (1963).

54. Robert M. Ratcliffe, "Behind the Headlines," *Pittsburgh Courier*, September 10, 1955, 17.

55. "US Ousts Black Envoys!," *Chicago Defender*, January 22, 1944, 1. The *Defender* does not name the "highly confidential and authoritative sources" for its claim that the State Department encouraged Haiti to recall its "dark-complexioned diplomats."

56. Pedro A. Sanjuan, interview by Dennis O'Brien, Washington, DC, August 6, 1969, JFK #1, oral history interview, John F. Kennedy Presidential Library and Museum, Boston, p. 12, transcript available at https://www.jfklibrary.org/sites/default/files/archives/JFKOH /Sanjuan,%20Pedro%20A/JFKOH-PAS-01/JFKOH-PAS-01-TR.pdf.

57. "Algeria, July 8, 1957," in John Fitzgerald Kennedy, *A Compilation of Statements and Speeches Made during His Service in United States Senate and House of Representatives* (Washington, DC: US Government Printing House, 1964), 532.

58. Thomas Borstelmann, *The Cold War and the Color Line: American Race Relations in the Global Arena* (Cambridge, MA: Harvard University Press, 2001), 137.

59. These laws were reinstated by *District of Columbia v. John R. Thompson Co. Inc.* (1953). For more on Terrell's campaign, see Joan Quigley, *Just Another Southern Town: Mary Church Terrell and the Struggle for Justice in the Nation's Capital* (New York: Oxford University Press, 2016).

60. Milton Viorst, "D.C. Is a Hardship Post for Negro Diplomats," *Washington Post*, August 28, 1960, E1.

61. Viorst, "D.C. Is a Hardship Post."

62. "Restaurant Snub of Negro Bared," *Pittsburgh Press*, April 12, 1961, 34.

63. Constance Feeley, "Negro Envoy Snubs Stir U.S. Action: Maryland Incident Brings Apology," *Washington Post and Times-Herald*, April 11, 1961.

64. "Restaurant Bars African Leader," *New York Times*, October 9, 1957, 20; "Snubbed Ghana Official Invited to Eat with Ike," *Daily Boston Globe*, October 10, 1957, 18; Morrey Dunie, "Snubbed Ghana Visitor Gets Bid to Breakfast with President, Nixon," *Washington Post and Times-Herald*, October 10, 1957, 2.

65. Sanjuan interview, 27.

66. "Big Step Ahead on a High Road," *Life* magazine, December 8, 1961, 34.

67. "Report of Incident Involving Ambassador Malick Sow of Chad" (undated file), Papers of John F. Kennedy, Presidential Papers, President's Office Files, Counties, Box 113A Chad: General, 1961–1962, Kennedy Presidential Library and Museum, Boston.

68. James T. Patterson, *Grand Expectations: The United States, 1945–1974* (New York: Oxford University Press, 1996), 475.

69. Sanjuan interview, 28.

70. Sanjuan interview, 28.

71. Sanjuan interview, 26.

72. Sanjuan interview, 29.

73. Sanjuan interview, 29.

74. Nicholas Murray Vachon, "The Junction: The Cold War, Civil Rights, and the African Diplomats of Maryland's Route 40," *Primary Source* [Indiana University Undergraduate Journal of History] 2, no. 2 (Spring 2012): 48, https://psource.sitehost.iu.edu/PDF/Archive%20Articles/Spring2012/2012%20-%20Spring%20-%208%20-%20Murray%20Vachon,%20Nicholas.pdf.

75. Vachon, "The Junction," 49.

76. John F. Kennedy to John Field, September 22, 1961, "Human Rights: 2: ST 16 (Kansas)-ST 23 (Minnesota): Executive" folder, White House Central Staff Files, John F. Kennedy Presidential Library and Museum, Boston.

77. Joe Steinfeld to Gordon Carey, October 9, 1961, Papers of the Congress of Racial Equality, 1941–1967, quoted in Vachon, "The Junction," 49.

78. Joe Steinfeld to Gordon Carey; James S. Keat, "U.S. 'Freedom Ride' Canceled, 47 Places Plan to Desegregate," *Baltimore Sun*, November 9, 1961, 46.

79. Claude Sitton, "New Tactics Replacing Freedom Rides," *New York Times*, June 17, 1962, 146.

80. Sitton, "New Tactics Replacing Freedom Rides."

81. "Howard Johnsons Serving All in 3 Southern States," *New York Amsterdam News*, June 23, 1962, 29.

82. "N.C. 'Freedom Highways' Drive Brings Conferences," *Atlanta Daily World*, September 6, 1962, 5.

83. Ralph Katz, "Pickets Protest Arrests in South," *New York Times*, October 7, 1962, 67.

84. The chain did not have complete control over an additional 339 Howard Johnson's restaurants operated and licensed by local proprietors, so it could not desegregate all the restaurants operating under its name. But the company was "confident that the trend toward moderation and desegregation will continue." To that end, after two months of negotiations with CORE and the NAACP, the chain finally put itself "on record against segregation" by declaring "a national policy of providing service without discrimination." "Howard Johnson Calls for Chain Open Policy," *New York Amsterdam News*, December 15, 1962, 37.

85. Hedrick Smith, "North Carolina Spurs Race Gain: Many Hotels Desegregate . . . ," *New York Times*, October 11, 1962, 29.

86. Fred Shuttlesworth, quoted in Henry Hampton and Steve Fayer, *Voices of Freedom: An Oral History of the Civil Rights Movement from the 1950s through the 1980s* (New York: Bantam, 1990; repr. New York: Random House, 2011), 125.

87. "Dr. King vs. Bull Connor: Eyes of World on Bitter Birmingham Struggle," *Baltimore Afro-American*, April 20, 1963, 1.

88. Martin Luther King Jr., *Letter from the Birmingham Jail* (San Francisco: Harper, 1994).

89. Todd S. Purdum, *An Idea Whose Time Has Come: Two Presidents, Two Parties, and the Battle for the Civil Rights Act of 1964* (New York: Henry Holt, 2014), 31–32.

90. "Klan Denounces Integration Pact," *Philadelphia Inquirer,* May 12, 1963, 8.

91. Purdum, *An Idea Whose Time Has Come,* 33.

92. *Civil Rights Cases,* 109 U.S. 3 (1883).

93. Burke Marshall, interview by Anthony Lewis, Washington, DC, June 20, 1964, JFK #5, oral history interview, John F. Kennedy Presidential Library and Museum, Boston, transcript available at https://www.jfklibrary.org/sites/default/files/archives/JFKOH/Marshall%2C%20Burke/JFKOH-BM-05/JFKOH-BM-05-TR.pdf.

94. This exchange is quoted in Jonathan Rosenberg and Zachary Karabell, *Kennedy, Johnson, and the Quest for Justice: The Civil Rights Tapes* (New York: Norton, 2003), 120.

95. Marshall interview, 103, 104.

96. "Material re: Title II, H.R. 7152," in Civil Rights during the Kennedy Administration, 1961–1963, Part 2, The Papers of Burke Marshall, Assistant Attorney General for Civil Rights, Civil Rights Act of 1964, Title II (public accommodations), 75, Part 2: The Papers of Burke Marshall, Assistant Attorney General for Civil Rights, ProQuest History Vault, folder 001351-022-0387.

97. Randall Kennedy, "The Struggle for Racial Equality in Public Accommodations," in *Legacies of the 1964 Civil Rights Act,* ed. Bernard Grofman (Charlottesville: University of Virginia Press, 2000), 159.

98. Robert Wallace, "Racial Trouble Shooter: An Intimate Report on Burke Marshall, Bobby Kennedy's Man in the Middle," *Life,* August 9, 1963, 78.

99. Statement of Sen. John O. Pastore, senator from Rhode Island, in *Hearings on Civil Rights-Public Accommodations before the Senate Committee on Commerce,* 88th Congress. 1st Session (Washington, DC: US Government Printing House, 1963), 252.

100. Wallace, "Racial Trouble Shooter," 78.

101. Civil Rights Act of 1964, Public Law 88-352, 78 Stat. (1964), 243.

102. *Katzenbach v. McClung,* 379 U.S. 294 (1964). For a detailed discussion of both cases, see Richard C. Cortner, *Civil Rights and Public Accommodations: The Heart of Atlanta Motel and McClung Cases* (Lawrence: University Press of Kansas, 2001).

103. *Katzenbach v. McClung,* 379 U.S. 294 (1964).

104. *Heart of Atlanta Motel, Inc. v. United States,* 379 U.S. 241 (1964).

105. *Heart of Atlanta Motel, Inc. v. United States,* 379 U.S. 241 (1964).

106. The hearings are discussed in detail in a number of works on the legislative history of the, most of which focus largely on the difficulties of its passage. They include Clay Risen, *The Bill of the Century: The Epic Battle for the Civil Rights Act* (New York: Bloomsbury Press, 2014); Purdum, *An Idea Whose Time Has Come;* Charles Whalen and Barbara Whalen, *The Longest Debate: A Legislative History of the 1964 Civil Rights Act* (Washington, DC: Seven Locks Press, 1985). Less common are works that discuss these hearings in reference to what they reveal about the experiences of Black travelers, although valuable discussions on this subject can be found in Susan Sessions Rugh, *Are We There Yet? The Golden Age of American Family Vacations* (Lawrence: University Press of Kansas, 2008), esp. 68–91; and Alberto B. Lopez, "The Road to, and through, Heart of Atlanta Motel," *Savannah Law Review* 2, no. 1 (2015): 59–72.

107. Robert F. Kennedy, in *Hearings on Civil Rights-Public Accommodations,* 407, 408.

108. Kennedy, in *Hearings on Civil Rights-Public Accommodations,* 18.

109. Dean Rusk, in *Hearings on Civil Rights-Public Accommodations before the Senate Committee on Commerce,* 88th Congress. 1st Session (Washington, DC: US Government Printing House, 1963), 282.

110. Rusk, in *Hearings on Civil Rights-Public Accommodations*, 285.

111. Rusk, in *Hearings on Civil Rights-Public Accommodations*, 287.

112. John Pastore, in *Hearings on Civil Rights-Public Accommodations before the Senate Committee on Commerce*, 88th Congress. 1st Session (Washington, DC: US Government Printing House, 1963), 656.

113. *Hearings on Civil Rights-Public Accommodations*, 656–657.

114. *Hearings on Civil Rights-Public Accommodations*, 657.

115. *Hearings on Civil Rights-Public Accommodations*, 695.

116. Robert A. Caro, *The Years of Lyndon Johnson: Master of the Senate* (New York: Knopf, 1982), 888.

117. Caro, *Years of Lyndon Johnson*, 888. Caro also discusses Johnson's use of this story and gives an account on one other variation (888–890).

118. J. C. Tanner, "Civil Rights Test," *Wall Street Journal*, July 2. 1964, 1.

119. "Violence Greets Ga. Rights Tests," *Philadelphia Tribune*, July 7, 1964, 1.

120. Solomon Seay, "Solomon Seay Seeks Public Accommodation," in *Voices of Civil Rights Lawyers: Reflections from the Deep South, 1964–1980*, ed. Kent Spriggs (Gainesville: University Press of Florida, 2017).

121. James W. Button, *Blacks and Social Change: Impact of the Civil Rights Movement in Southern Communities* (Princeton, NJ: Princeton University Press, 1989), 182. See also Gavin Wright, *Sharing the Prize: The Economics of the Civil Rights Revolution in the American South* (Cambridge, MA: Harvard University Press, 2013), and Briar. K. Landsberg, "Public Accommodations and the Civil Rights Act of 1964: A Surprising Success?," *Hamline University's School of Law's Journal of Law and Public Policy* 36, no. 1 (2015): 1–5.

122. Button, *Blacks and Social Change*, 182.

123. *Willis v. Pickrick Restaurant*, 231 F. Supp. 396 (N.D. Ga. 1964); Ralph Matthews, "I Couldn't Help Laughing When Lester Maddox Wept," *Baltimore Afro-American*, August 29, 1964, 5.

124. "Negroes Barred Again by Maddox Cafe in Atlanta," *New York Times*, September 28, 1961.

125. "Ordered to Mix, Maddox to Sell," *Baltimore Afro-American*, February 20, 1965, 14; Bob Short, *Everything Is Pickrick: The Life of Lester Maddox* (Macon, GA: Mercer University Press, 1999), 64.

126. Kennedy, "Struggle for Racial Equality,"161; Randall Kennedy, "The Civil Rights Act's Unsung Victory and How It Changed the South," *Harper's*, June 2014, 35.

127. Kennedy, "Struggle for Racial Equality," 161.

EPILOGUE

1. John L. LeFlore, newly elected Black legislator and veteran leader of Black politics in Mobile, Alabama, interview by Jack Bass and Walter de Vries, July 14, 1974, Southern Oral History Program Interviews, A0013, University of North Carolina Libraries, https://cdr.lib.unc.edu/record/uuid:76d13701-adb5-4060-86f4-057803f28465.

2. Debbie Elliot, "60 Years after the Boycott, Progress Stalls for Montgomery Buses," *All Things Considered*, National Public Radio, November 12, 2015, https://www.npr.org/2015/11/12/455670897/60-years-after-the-boycott-progress-stalls-for-montgomery-buses.

3. Elliot, "60 Years after the Boycott."

4. Cotten Seiler, *Republic of Drivers: A Cultural History of Automobility in America* (Chicago: University of Chicago Press, 2008).

5. Christopher W. Wells, *Car Country: An Environmental History* (Seattle: University of Washington Press, 2012).

6. W. Kaszynski, *The American Highway* (Jefferson, NC: McFarland, 2000); James H. Kunstler, *The Geography of Nowhere* (New York: Simon and Schuster, 1993).

7. Thomas C. Hayes, "Greyhound in Deal for Trailways," *New York Times*, June 21, 1987.

8. "Long-Distance Trips and Trip Miles by Mode, in Millions," US Bureau of Transportation Statistics, May 20, 2017, https://www.bts.gov/archive/publications/highlights_of_the_2001 _national_household_travel_survey/table_a22. Data are drawn from the "2001 National Household Travel Survey," US Department of Transportation. "Long-distance trips" are trips of fifty miles or more from home to farthest destination. Unfortunately, more-recent figures for long-distance travel are unavailable; the bureau stopped compiling data on long-distance travel after 2001. For a notation recording this change in the data compiled by the bureau, see N. McGuckin and A. Fucci, "Summary of Travel Trends: 2017 National Household Travel Survey," Federal Highway Administration, US Department of Transportation, July 2018, 1, https://nhts.ornl.gov/assets/2017_nhts_summary_travel_trends.pdf.

9. On the robust airline ticket sales prior to the pandemic, see "U.S. Travel Agencies Set Air Ticket Sales Record in 2019," *businesswire*, January 15, 2020, https://www.businesswire.com /news/home/20200115005122/en/U.S.-Travel-Agencies-Set-Air-Ticket-Sales-Record-in-2019. On the steep decline in ticket sales in 2020, see Elaine Glusac, "5 Things We Know about Flying Right Now," *New York Times*, August 20, 2020, https://www.nytimes.com/2020/08/20 /travel/airplanes-coronavirus.html. On car travel, see Sherie Rosenbloom, "The Great American Road Trip: Shorter and More Popular than Ever," *New York Times*, February 18, 2018, 3.

10. Federal Housing Administration, *Underwriting Manual: Underwriting and Valuation Procedure under Title II of the National Housing Act*, Washington, DC, 1938, 1474. For more on the FHA's long history of denying loans to Black applicants, see Richard Rothstein, *The Color of Law: A Forgotten History of How Our Government Segregated America* (New York: Liveright, 2017).

11. For a longer list, see "Interstate Injustice: Plowing Highways through Minority Neighborhoods—Updated," *Panethos* blog, April 7, 2018, https://panethos.wordpress.com /2018/04/07/interstate-injustice-plowing-highways-through-minority-neighborhoods/.

12. B. Drummond Ayres Jr., "White Roads through Black Bedrooms," *New York Times*, December 31, 1967. On transportation racism and inequities, see also Robert D. Bullard, Glenn S. Johnson, and Angel O. Torres, eds., *Highway Robbery: Transportation Racism & New Routes to Equity* (Cambridge, MA: South End Press, 2004).

13. Jim O'Grady, "Flipping the Race Card: Accusations of Bias Become a Tactical Weapon," *New York Times*, April 6, 1997, CY15.

14. On the idea of architectural exclusion and the role of roads therein, see Sarah Schindler, "Architectural Exclusion: Discrimination and Segregation through Physical Design of the Built Environment," *Yale Law Journal* 124, no. 6 (April 2015): 1836–2201.

15. Scholarly literature on parking and car ownership is hard to find, but cities such as New York and New Orleans typically have "limited and high cost parking," which in the case of New Orleans is not offset by effective public transportation. Robert I. Dunphy and Kimberly Fisher, "Transportation, Congestion, and Density: New Insights," *Transportation Research Record* 1552, no. 1 (1996): 91.

16. "Car Access," United States, 1990–2017, National Equity Atlas, n.d., https://nationalequityatlas .org/indicators/Car_access.

17. N. J. Klein and M. J. Smart, "Car Today, Gone Tomorrow: The Ephemeral Car in Low-Income, Immigrant and Minority Families," *Transportation* 44, no. 3 (2017): 495–510.

18. Bob Quigley, "Six Months after Katrina: Who Was Left Behind," February 1, 2006, Global Action on Aging, http://globalag.igc.crg/armedconflict/countryreports/americas/sixkatrina.htm. Quigley draws on FEMA statistics.

19. Shelly Tan, Alyssa Fowers, Dan Keating, and Lauren Tierney, "Amid the Pandemic, Public Transit Is Highlighting Inequalities in Cities," *Washington Post*, May 15, 2020, national section.

20. For a more detailed overview of these restrictions, see Mia Bay, "Invisible Tethers: Transportation and Discrimination in the Age of Katrina," in *Katrina's Imprint: Race and Vulnerability in America*, ed. Keith Wailoo, Karen C'Neill, and Roland Anglin (New Brunswick, NJ: Rutgers University Press, 2010).

21. Marjorie Whigham Desir, "Are You Being Taken for a Ride—African-Americans Charged More for Automobiles," *Black Enterprise*, April 1997.

22. Ian Ayres and Peter Siegelman, "Race and Gender Discrimination in Bargaining for a New Car," *American Economic Review* 85, no. 3 (1995): 307.

23. Fiona Scott Morton, Florian Zettelmeyer, and Jorge Silva-Risso, "Consumer Information and Discrimination: Does the Internet Affect the Pricing of New Cars to Women and Minorities?," *Quantitative Marketing and Economics* 1, no. 1 (2003): 66, 89. Not surprisingly, Scott, Zettelmeyer, and Silva-Risso conclude that internet shopping "is particularly beneficial to those whose characteristics disadvantage them in negotiating" (65).

24. Lisa Rice and Erich Schwartz Jr., "Discrimination When Buying a Car: How the Color of Your Skin Can Affect Your Car-Shopping Experience," National Fair Housing Alliance, 2018. Other earlier studies had similar results. See, for example, Delvin Davis, "Non-Negotiable: Negotiation Doesn't Help African Americans and Latinos on Dealer-Financed Car Loans," unpublished manuscript, January 23. 2014, https://ssrn.com/abstract=2386005; and Consumer Federation of America, "African-Americans Pay Higher Auto Loan Rates but Can Take Steps to Reduce This Expense," press release, May 7, 2007, https://consumerfed.org/press_release/african-americans-pay-higher-auto-loan-rates-but-can-take-steps-to-reduce-this-expense/.

25. Julia Angwin, Jeff Larson, Lauren Kirchner, and Surya Mattu, "Minority Neighborhoods Pay Higher Car Insurance Premiums than White Areas with the Same Risk," *ProPublica*, April 5, 2017, https://www.propublica.org/article/minority-neighborhoods-higher-car-insurance-premiums-white-areas-same-risk.

26. Paula Mallea, *The War on Drugs: A Failed Experiment* (Toronto: Dundurn, 2014), 145. See also Michelle Alexander, *The New Jim Crow: Mass Incarceration in the Age of Colorblindness*. 10th anniv. ed. (New York: New Press. 2020); Elizabeth Hinton, *From the War on Poverty to the War on Crime: The Making of Mass Incarceration in America* (Cambridge, MA: Harvard University Press, 2017); Frank R. Baumgartner, *Suspect Citizens* (New York: Cambridge University Press, 2018).

27. Alexander, *The New Jim Crow*, 49.

28. "Court Wisely Rejects 'Sixth Sense,'" *South Florida Sun-Sentinel*, September 21, 1986, https://www.sun-sentinel.com/news/fl-xpm-1986-09-21-8602250771-story.html. On Vogel's role in the creation of Operation Pipeline, see Gary Webb, "DWB," *Esquire*, April 1999, 118–127; Frank R. Baumgartner, Derek A. Epp, and Kelsey Shoub, *Suspect Citizens: What 20 Million Traffic Stops Tell Us about Policing and Race* (New York: Cambridge University Press, 2018), 8. Sarah Seo cites Charles Remberg, a journalist who is an expert in police tactics, as another key proponent of traffic stops: Sarah A. Seo, *Policing the Open Road. How Cars Transformed American Freedom* (Cambridge, MA: Harvard University Press, 2019), 254–255.

29. On the complex legal history and case law relating to traffic stops, see Seo, *Policing the Open Road*.

30. Webb, "DWB," 118.

31. David Kocieniewski, "New Jersey Argues That the U.S. Wrote the Book on Race Profiling," *New York Times*, November 29, 2000.

32. On the difficulties of generating illuminating statistics on racial profiling, see Lori Montgomery, "Racial Profiling in Maryland Defies Definition—or Solution," *Washington Post*, May 16, 2001.

33. Samuel R. Gross and Katherine Y. Barnes, "Road Work: Racial Profiling and Drug Interdiction on the Highway," *Michigan Law Review* 101, no. 3 (2002): 651–754.

34. David Kocieniewski and Robert Hanley, "Racial Profiling Was the Routine, New Jersey Finds," *New York Times*, November 28, 2000.

35. Webb, "DWB."

36. Gina Castle Bell, Mark C. Hopson, Richard Craig, and Nicholas W. Robinson, "Exploring Black and White Accounts of 21st-Century Racial Profiling: Riding and Driving while Black," *Qualitative Research Reports in Communication* 15, no. 1 (2014): 33–42.

37. See, for example, Michael A. Fletcher, "For Black Motorists, a Never-Ending Fear of Being Stopped," *National Geographic*, March 12, 2018, https://www.nationalgeographic.com /magazine/2018/04/the-stop-race-police-traffic/.

38. Niaz Kasravi and Carlton T. Mayers, "Born Suspect: Stop-and-Frisk Abuses and the Continued Fight to End Racial Profiling in America," NAACP Report, September 2014, https://www.naacp.org/wp-content/uploads/2016/04/Born_Suspect_Report_final_web.pdf.

39. See, for example, J. McDevitt, A. Farrell, and M. Yee, "Providence Traffic Stop Statistics Compliance, Final Report," Institute on Race and Justice, Northeastern University, October 31, 2003, https://repository.library.northeastern.edu/files/neu:344642; J. R. Ingram, "The Effect of Neighborhood Characteristics on Traffic Citation Practices of the Police," *Police Quarterly* 10, no. 4 (2007): 371–393.

40. Aaron Randle and Kelsey Ryan, "Black KC Drivers Get More Tickets than Whites: Race Is Only Part of the Problem," *Kansas City Star*, May 20, 2018.

41. US Department of Justice Civil Rights Division, "Investigation of the Ferguson Police Department," March 4, 2014, 13. See also Jamiles Lartey, "'Predatory Police': The High Price of Driving while Black in Missouri," *Guardian*, July 5, 2018, US news section.

42. *United States of America v. The City of Ferguson*, Consent Decree, United States District Court Eastern District of Missouri Eastern Division, Case: 4:16-cv-00180-CDP Doc. #: 12-2, Filed: 03/17/16, 19.

43. Fredrick Kunkle, "Lawsuit Shows How Traffic Tickets and Other Municipal Fines May Skew Justice," *Washington Post*, June 5, 2018.

44. Bell et al., "Exploring Black and White Accounts," 38; S. LaFraniere and A. W. Lehren, "The Disproportionate Risk of Driving while Black," *New York Times*, October 25, 2015.

45. Rob Voigt, Nicholas P. Camp, Vinodkumar Prabhakaran, et al., "Language from Police Body Camera Footage Shows Racial Disparities in Officer Respect," *Proceedings of the National Academy of Sciences* 114, no. 25 (June 20, 2017): 6521–6526; Fletcher, "For Black Motorists."

46. Wesley Lowery, *They Can't Kill Us All: Ferguson, Baltimore, and a New Era in America's Racial Justice Movement* (New York: Little, Brown, 2016).

47. "Travel Advisory for the State of Missouri," August 2, 2017, NAACP, https://www.naacp.org /latest/travel-advisory-state-missouri/.

48. "NAACP Says Travel Advisory to Remain in Effect," KMOX-AM, July 23, 2018, https://kmox
.radio.com/articles/naacp-says-travel-advisory-remain-effect; Eoin Higgins, "'Wake-Up Call'
Report Shows Black Drivers in Missouri 91 Percent More Likely to Be Pulled Over by
Police," *Common Dreams*, June 11, 2019, https://www.commondreams.org/news/2019/06/11
/wake-call-report-shows-black-drivers-missouri-91-percent-more-likely-be-pulled-over; Eric
Schmitt, Missouri Attorney General, "2018 Vehicle Stops, Executive Summary," https://ago
.mo.gov/home/vehicle-stops-report/2018-executive-summary.

49. Rachel Lippmann, "Criminal Justice Reforms Advance in Missouri House, State Rep. Shamed
Dogan Says Provisions Are 'Morally Right and Fiscally Sound,'" *St. Louis American*,
March 29, 2019.

50. On customs issues, see Yvonne D. Newsome, "Border Patrol: The U.S. Customs Service and
the Racial Profiling of African American Women," *Journal of African American Studies* 7,
no. 3 (2003): 31–57. For a roundup of "flying while Black" stories, see https://www.theroot
.com/tag/flying-while-black.

51. Michael Higgins, "O'Hare Strip Search Suit Settled," *Chicago Tribune*, February 5, 2006.

52. Jamiles Lartey, "NAACP Warns Black Passengers of Flying American Airlines after
'Disturbing Incidents,'" *Guardian*, October 25, 2017, US news section.

53. Jonah Engel Bromwich, "N.A.A.C.P. Advisory on American Airlines Warns Black Travelers
to Steer Clear," *New York Times*, January 20, 2018, Travel section.

54. Tracy Jan, "NAACP Lifts Travel Warning against American Airlines," *Washington Post*,
July 17, 2018, Business section.

55. Kara Brandeisky "Airbnb Hosts Are Racist, Study Finds," *Money*, December 10, 2015, http://
money.com/money/4144426/airbnb-racism-racist-harvard/.

56. Yanbo Ge, Christopher R. Knittel, Don MacKenzie, and Stephen Zoepf, "Racial and Gender
Discrimination in Transportation Network Companies," National Bureau of Economic
Research, Working Paper 22776, October 2016.

ACKNOWLEDGMENTS

This book has been so long in coming that I am not sure I can remember all the people who helped me write it.

An incomplete list would have to start with my many friends and colleagues at Rutgers University, which was my institutional home when I first began working on *Traveling Black*. There, I received research support from the history department and spent a generative decade working first as the associate director and later as the director of the Rutgers Center for Race and Ethnicity (CRE), where I previewed most of the chapters in this book.

I will always be grateful to Keith Wailoo for creating the center and for including me in the exciting collaborative work that took place there. At the CRE, I had the privilege of working with Ann Fabian, the best of colleagues and an unfailing champion of this book, and I received invaluable support from the CRE's program director, the late Mia Kissil, whom I sorely miss. I was also able to share portions of this project with an incredibly rich community of postdoctoral fellows, faculty, and graduate students. This project benefited greatly from conversations with Stephen Allen, Mekala Audain, Jesse Bayker, Miya Carey, Brittney Cooper, Kaisa Esty, Virginia Harbin, Christopher Hayes, Grace Howard, Naa Oyo A. Kwate, Tasia Milton, Richard Mizelle, Melanye Price, Melissa Stein, Nafisa Tanjeem, Shatema Threadcraft, Wendy Wright, Hakim Zainiddinov, and many other CRE affiliates.

My work on this book was also sustained by other Rutgers colleagues, both in New Brunswick and beyond. I could not have written it without all the help I got from Beryl Satter, who read every word and helped me get across the finish line. Others who provided crucial support include Paul Clemens, Melissa Cooper, Belinda Davis, Belinda Edmondson, Marisa Fuentes, Zeva Galili, James Goodman, Seth Koven, Bonnie Smith, and Camilla Townsend. I am also indebted to the former and current Rutgers students Ashleigh Lawrence Sanders, Dara Walker, Meagan Weirda, and Joseph Williams for their research assistance.

Another key source of support has been the National Humanities Center, where I was able to use an Alphonse Fletcher Fellowship to complete preliminary research on *Traveling Black* during 2010–2011. I loved working within the white walls of the center, where Geoffrey

Harphan, Kent Mullikan, Sara Payne, Don Solomon, and other members of the community made me feel very much at home. Friends I made there who helped with my research and writing include Joseph Boone, Jared Farmer, Sharon Harley, Bayo Holsey, Michael Kulikowski, Magda Maczynska, Gerry Passannante, Walter Rucker, and Ellen Stroud.

The Department of History at the University of Pennsylvania, where I now teach, has been a wonderful place to finish this book. Warm thanks to Mary Berry, Kathy Brown, Sally Gordon, Sophia Lee, Serena Meyari, Marcy Norton, Daniel Richter, Sophia Rosenfeld, Barbara Savage, Beth Wenger, and the rest of my Penn family for welcoming me and engaging with my work.

I am also indebted to Joy de Menil, whose editing greatly improved this book, Thomas LeBien and Ben Platt, who both gave it very useful readings, and friends who read chapters and supplied citations—you know who you are, and I love you.

ILLUSTRATION CREDITS

7 Library of Congress, Prints and Photographs Division, LC-DIG-fsa-8a17588.

27 Library of Congress, Prints and Photographs Division, LC-DIG-ds-00886.

30 Library of Congress, Prints and Photographs Division, LC-USZ62-45698.

46 Digital image courtesy of the Oberlin College Archives.

54 Digital image courtesy of the Special Collections Research Center, University of Chicago Library.

65 Wikimedia Commons.

69 Digital image courtesy of the Springfield-Greene County Library District, Springfield, Missouri.

72 Digital image courtesy of the Durham Historic Photographic Archives, Durham County Library, Durham, North Carolina.

73 Photo by H. C. Hill. Courtesy of Betsy Thorpe.

83 Library of Congress, Prints and Photographs Division, LC-USF33-001172-M4.

85 Reproduced from *Railway Age*, July 6, 1900.

91 Reproduced from Joseph Husband, *The Story of the Pullman Car* (Chicago: A. C. McClurg and Co., 1917).

96 Boston & Maine Railroad Historical Society.

109 interlochenpublicradio.org/Wikimedia Commons.

122 Library of Congress, Prints and Photographs Division, LC-USF34-052459-D.

123 Library of Congress, Prints and Photographs Division, LC-USF34-040841-D.

129 William D. Workman, Jr., Papers, South Carolina Political Collections, University of South Carolina.

133 Library of Congress, Prints and Photographs Division, LC-USF34-051945-D.

134 Digital image courtesy of the *New Pittsburgh Courier*.

137   Alfred E. Smith Papers, Special Collections, University of Arkansas Libraries, Fayetteville, Arkansas.

145   Claude A. Barnett Papers, Chicago History Museum.

148   Digital image courtesy of the New York Public Library.

155   Library of Congress, Prints and Photographs Division, LC-DIG-ggbain-22847.

164   Courtesy of the AFRO American Newspaper Archive.

168   *Chicago Defender*, December 19, 1931.

182   Digital file courtesy of the University of South Florida Libraries, B29-v-00002604.

183   Library of Congress, Prints and Photographs Division, LC-DIG-ppmsc-00199.

190   Courtesy of the AFRO American Newspaper Archive.

196   Library of Congress, Prints and Photographs Division, LC-USZC2-1058.

200   Smithsonian National Air and Space Museum (NASM 83-98).

203   Smithsonian National Air and Space Museum (NASM 90-7010).

204   Courtesy of the AFRO American Newspaper Archive.

207   Courtesy of the AFRO American Newspaper Archive.

213   Postdlf/Wikimedia Commons/GNU Free Documentation License.

224   Tallahassee Democrat Collection, Florida Memory, State Archives and Library of Florida.

225   © Danny Lyon/Magnum Photos.

229   National Archives at Atlanta.

231   Courtesy of the AFRO American Newspaper Archive.

234   US House of Representatives/Wikimedia Commons.

242   Library of Congress, Prints and Photographs Division, LC-USW3-037973-E.

251   Reprinted with permission of the DC Public Library, Star Collection @ Washington Post.

255   Estate of Bayard Rustin.

262   Bettmann/Getty Images.

266   William J. Smith/AP/Shutterstock.

272   Bettmann/Getty Images.

282   Tallahassee Democrat Collection, Florida Memory, State Archives and Library of Florida.

287   John F. Kennedy Presidential Library and Museum, Boston, Massachusetts.

292   Library of Congress, Prints and Photographs Division, LC-DIG-ppmsca-37819.

295   Lane Brothers Commercial Photographers Photographic Collection, 1920–1976. Photographic Collection, Special Collections and Archives, Georgia State University Library.

296   Lyndon Baines Johnson Library.

INDEX

AAA (American Automobile Association), 107, 146

Abernathy, Ralph, 275

abolitionists, 28, 29, 38–40; Douglass, 28, 50, 51, 52

abolition of slavery, 19, 20. *See also* emancipation; slavery

accommodationist politics, 11, 93, 98, 99, 100, 234, 236. *See also* Mitchell, Arthur Wergs; Washington, Booker T.

accommodations, public. *See* air travel; buses; dining facilities; gas stations; lodgings; railroads; restrooms; roadside accommodations

Adamson Act, 103

affluence. *See* class, socioeconomic; elite African Americans

African American League, 61

African diplomats, 284, 286–287, 288, 289, 291. *See also* image, America's

agency, 150

Agnew, Daniel, 40

agrarian political movements, 60, 76, 77

airlines: African American-owned, 206; African Americans excluded from business, 203–206; American Airlines, 210, 215–216, 220, 319–320; as common carriers, 209; economic inequities and, 12; lack of nondiscrimination policy, 223; lawsuits against, 206, 209, 217; as private carriers, 209. *See also* airports; air travel; aviation; common carriers

airplanes. *See* airlines; airports; air travel; aviation; pilots

airports: Dannelly Field Airport, 228, 283; desegregation of, 229, 280–283 (*see also* desegregation); dining facilities, 193, 216, 218, 219–220, 222, 223; Federal Airport Act of 1946, 221; funding for, 221; ground transportation services, 193, 218, 224–226, 227–228 (*see also* buses; taxis/cabs); inconsistent discrimination in, 8, 223, 228; jurisdiction over, 218–220, 281; protests at, 280–281; resistance to desegregation orders 257; segregated facilities in, 3, 193, 217–229; Washington National Airport, 218–221. *See also* restrooms; waiting rooms

air travel, 192; access to, 193; African American passengers excluded from, 209–211; airport accommodations and, 226–227; avoiding Jim Crow and, 202, 203, 211; customs searches, 319; early African American passengers, 202; by elite African Americans, 219–220; flight attendants, 206, 208; flying while Black, 319–320; Freedom Flyers, 280–281; ground transportation, 193, 218, 224–226, 227–228 (*see also* buses; taxis/cabs); international incidents and, 222; Interstate Commerce Act of 1887 and, 210; lawsuits and, 209, 215–216, 217, 219, 227; segregation in, 2–3, 193, 212–217, 222. *See also* airlines; airports; aviation; pilots

Alabama: airports in, 228, 283; Anniston, 271–272, 273; bus stations in, 181–182; dining facilities in, 86, 280; Freedom Rides in, 271–272, 273, 275, 276; Jim Crow laws in, 158; LeFlore, 235, 247–249, 306, 307; Montgomery Bus Boycott, 12, 268, 271, 307, 310; Patterson, 271, 273, 275, 276; public transportation in, 308; Railroad Commission, 77–78; resistance to desegregation in, 268, 271; restrooms in, 184; train travel

Alabama (*continued*)
in, 68, 77–78; Tuskegee Army Air Field,
202, 205; Tuskegee Institute, 200, 234, 283.
See also Birmingham, Alabama; Montgomery,
Alabama; Washington, Booker T.
Alexander, Michelle, 314
Alpha Phi Alpha, 258–259
amenities. *See* dining facilities; food; gas
stations; lodgings; restrooms; roadside
accommodations; waiting rooms
American Automobile Association (AAA),
107, 146
American Dilemma, The (Myrdal), 2
Anderson, Marian, 83
antebellum era, 21–25. *See also* North (region),
antebellum; South (region), antebellum
anti-lynching bill, 235
Arkansas: bus segregation in, 166–167; restrictions in post-Civil War era, 37; sleeping car
law, 90; streetcar segregation in, 156
armed services. *See* military; servicemen,
African American
Army. *See* military; servicemen, African American
aspirations, African American, 26
Atlanta, Georgia, 161, 223. *See also* Georgia
Automobile Green Book (Automobile Legal
Service), 142
automobiles. *See* car ownership; cars;
chauffeurs; drivers, African American;
roadside accommodations
automobility, system of, 109
aviation: African Americans considered unfit for,
195–197; African Americans hired in, 209;
Army Air Corps, 202; Civil Aeronautics Act of
1938, 210, 217; Civil Aeronautics Authority,
210, 218, 220, 221; Civil Aeronautics Board, 215;
as crucial to future of African Americans,
198–199; Federal Aviation Act of 1958,
283; fleet service work, 208; ground service
workers, 208–209; military's Jim Crow
air training, 245; War Training Service,
202; white racial greatness and, 194–196.
See also airlines; airports; air travel; common
carriers; pilots

bail, 276
Bailey v. Patterson, 279–280
Baker, Ray Stannard, 2, 82
Baldwin, James, 224
Barnes, Catherine, 56
Barry, Kathleen, 208

bathrooms. *See* restrooms
Berlin, Ira, 4
Bethune, Mary McLeod, 206
Bevel, James, 291
Biddle, Francis, 238
Billboard (magazine), 138, 146
Birmingham, Alabama: acquiring Pullman
tickets in, 93; Children's Crusade, 292;
Connor, 272, 291, 292; federal intervention
and, 294; Freedom Rides in, 272–273, 275;
Ollie's Barbeque Restaurant, 297; Shuttles-
worth, 273, 275; streetcar segregation in,
158; violence in, 291–293. *See also* Alabama
Birmingham Campaign, 291–293
Black codes, 35
blackface minstrelsy, 26, 50
Black Lives Matter protests, 318, 319
Black nationalists, 23
Black separatist movement, 11
Blackstone, William, 50
Bland, Sandra, 318
Blease, Cole L., 111
Bond, Julian, 142
boycotts: Montgomery Bus Boycott, 12, 268,
271, 307, 310; streetcar, 151, 157. *See also*
direct action
Boyd, R. H., 98–100, 151, 157
Boynton, Bruce, 269
Boynton v. Virginia, 269
Breck, Samuel, 14
brothels, 139–140
Brotherhood of Liberty, 61
Browder v. Gayle, 268
Brown, Michael, 318
Brown v. Board of Education, 61, 261, 263, 264,
267, 269, 271
Brown v. Memphis, 47
buses, 153; African American, 153, 154, 162;
African Americans allowed on, 164; African
American servicemen on, 189–191, 244;
African Americans excluded from, 162–166;
after *Morgan* decision, 250, 252; airport bus
services, 226; amenities of, 170, 183–186;
avoidance of, 188; back of, 154, 166–169,
178–179; complaints involving, 253; decline
of, 309; during Depression, 173, 186; desegregation of, 229, 232, 253–257 (*see also*
Freedom Rides); Double V campaign, 189–191;
early, 152–153, 161, 162; economic inequities
and, 12; Freedom Rides, 12, 154, 232, 254,
270–279; Greenfield Bus Body Company, 114;

growth of, 186; humiliation of African American passengers, 172; initially welcomed by African Americans, 152; intrastate vs. interstate transportation and, 250, 265 (see also *Irene Morgan v. the Commonwealth of Virginia*); jitneys, 153, 154, 158–161, 162; lawsuits against, 177, 178 (see also *Irene Morgan v. the Commonwealth of Virginia*); modern civil rights movements and, 191; Montgomery Bus Boycott, 12, 268, 271, 307, 310; necessity of, 188; persistence of segregation on, 250, 252, 265–267; race relations on, 189, 241; rear-facing seats, 167–168; restrooms and, 170, 183–186; segregation laws and, 164–165, 172, 173; segregation of, 2, 152, 153–154, 166–169; segregation of, in North, 5, 169–171, 174–179; separate but equal, 164; Union Transportation Company, 151–152, 154; waiting rooms, 181–183; during World War II, 188–191, 241. See also common carriers; Greyhound; *Irene Morgan v. the Commonwealth of Virginia*; Trailways

Button, James W., 304

cabs, 7, 193, 218, 224–226, 227–228
California, 5. See also West (region)
car ownership, 115–123; ability to leave South and, 120, 123; agency and, 150, 188; avoiding Jim Crow and, 309–310; barriers to, 310–313; during Depression, 123; by farmers/rural African Americans, 119–123; freedom struggle and, 150; insurance, 127–129, 313; new forms of discrimination and, 150; violence against owners, 117; white resentment of, 124. See also cars; drivers, African American; roadside accommodations
car rentals, 8
cars, 2, 107; African American mechanics, 113–115; automotive education, 113, 114; avoidance of Jim Crow travel and, 108–109, 129–130, 137, 158; chauffeurs, 110–115; compared to bus travel, 188; cost of, 116, 312; democratic effects of, 124–125; effects of on African American life, 116, 311–312; employment and, 309; empowerment and, 124–125; housing and, 308–309, 310; Lyft, 320; maintenance of, 112; motor sports, 107–108; parking, 110, 111–112, 126; as predominant form of transportation, 308–309; road trips, 136; state regulation

of driving, 110; stereotypes about mechanical incompetence and, 108, 110, 113, 115; suburbs and, 308–309; as symbol, 109, 129; system of automobility, 109–110; Uber, 320; during World War I era, 108. See also car ownership; drivers, African American; roads/highways; roadside accommodations

Carter, Robert, 215, 218
Castile, Philandro, 318
celebrities, African American, 115. See also elite African Americans; *individual celebrities*; musicians, African American
Chambers, Jason, 117
Chance v. Lambeth, 261, 262
chauffeurs, 110–115. See also cars; drivers, African American
Chesnutt, Charles, 81
Chicago, 178, 311
Chicago & Northwestern Railway Company v. Anna Williams, 43–44
Children's Crusade, 292
Chiles v. Chesapeake and Ohio Railway, 101
Church, Robert, 18, 20, 218
Church, Mary, 9, 18–19, 20, 45–46, 62, 285
citizenship, 35, 40, 49–50. See also Fourteenth Amendment
civil disobedience. See direct action
civil rights, 37; enforcement of, 48–49; Interstate Commerce Commission and, 16 (see also Interstate Commerce Commission [ICC]); loss of, 42, 49–56, 62; O'Hara's proposals for, 53–55. See also civil rights struggles; legislation; voting rights
Civil Rights Act of 1866, 35, 52
Civil Rights Act of 1875, 32, 37, 38–40, 42; *Civil Rights Cases* and, 49–56, 60, 293, 294, 297–298; enforcement of, 39–40, 52; lawsuits and, 46–47; nullification of, 32, 49–56, 60, 252, 293; Pullman and, 88–89; rights under, 32
Civil Rights Act of 1964, 5, 270, 291; challenges to, 296–298; commerce clause and, 294–296; congressional hearings for, 298–303; design of, 294–296; effects of, 304–305; foreign policy implications of, 299–300; reactions to, 303–304; roadside accommodations and, 305
Civil Rights Cases (1883), 49–56, 60, 293, 294, 297–298
civil rights leaders. See *individuals*; leaders, African American

civil rights struggles, 3; bus segregation and, 191; car ownership and, 150; dining facilities and, 294; in early twentieth century, 100; in post-emancipation North, 32–33
civil service, resegregation of, 104
Civil War. *See* emancipation; North (region), post-emancipation; Reconstruction; South (region), post-emancipation
class, socioeconomic: ladies' cars and, 45, 47; resistance to travel discrimination and, 11, 67; separate car laws and, 59; social contact and, 14; spaces divided by, 21–25. *See also* elite African Americans; first-class travel; middle-class African Americans
Clifford, James, 3
Clifford, Nathan, 43
Cocks, Catherine, 95
Cold War, 278, 289, 303. *See also* image, America's
Coleman, Bessie, 197–198
colleges, Black, 83–84, 114, 171, 226
color line, moving, 13–14
commerce, interstate, 42–43, 51, 61–62. *See also* Interstate Commerce Commission (ICC)
commerce clause, 294–296, 297. *See also* Interstate Commerce Commission (ICC)
Commerce Department, 220
common carriers: airlines as, 209; in antebellum era, 19, 21–25 (*see also* stagecoaches; steamboats); development of, 14; ICC and, 16, 264–267; laws regulating, 166; right of to segregation, 40–41, 42
complaints about travel discrimination. *See* Interstate Commerce Commission (ICC); lawsuits/legal challenges; NAACP; resistance to travel discrimination
Congress, US: authority of to prohibit private discrimination, 294; hearings for Civil Rights Act of 1964, 298–303; regulation of interstate commerce and, 42–43, 51, 62 (*see also* Interstate Commerce Commission [ICC])
Congress of Racial Equality (CORE), 232, 253, 268; Freedom Highways project, 290–291; Freedom Rides, 12, 154, 232, 254, 270–279; Journey of Reconciliation, 232, 253–257, 269, 270; membership of, 257; Route 40 campaign and, 289–290
Connelly, Donald B., 220
Connor, Eugene "Bull," 272, 291, 292

convicts: forced labor by, 117; in railroad cars, 69–70, 242
Cooper, Anna Julia, 84–85
CORE (Congress of Racial Equality). *See* Congress of Racial Equality (CORE)
coronavirus pandemic, 312
courts: lack of help for African Americans in, 48–49. *See also individual cases*; lawsuits/legal challenges; Supreme Court, US
COVID 19, 312
Crishon, Alfred S., 248
Crisp, Charles R., 55
Crummell, Alexander, 23–24
Crutcher, Terence, 318

Daley, Richard, 311
Day v. Owen, 40
DEA (Drug Enforcement Agency), 314–316
decolonization, 299. *See also* diplomats
DeCuir, Josephine, 41–43
Defense Department, war on drugs and, 314
Defense Transportation, Office of, 245
democracy, 300, 303
Democrats, 53, 56, 235, 288
desegregation: of airports, 229, 280–283; of buses/bus stations, 229, 232, 253–257 (*see also* Freedom Rides); of dining facilities, 290; direct action, need for, 232; federal intervention, need for, 232 (*see also* Civil Rights Act of 1964; legislation); groundwork for, 232; ICC's ruling barring racial segregation in interstate transportation, 263–267, 279, 304; legal victories for, 257 (*see also individual cases*); orders for, effects of, 265–267; resistance to, 104–105, 150, 266–267, 271; of roadside accommodations, 283, 286–291; Truman's support for, 260. *See also* Civil Rights Act of 1964
de Tocqueville, Alexis, 20
Diggs, Charles C., 218, 221, 223
dining facilities: African American servicemen excluded from, 244; in airports, 193, 216, 218, 219–220, 222, 223; bus travel and, 170; civil rights movement and, 294; continued segregation of, 229, 269; desegregation of, 280; diplomats and, 286; in *Green Book*, 143; Howard Johnson's, 286, 290–291; inconsistent segregation in, 8; Ollie's Barbeque Restaurant, 297; roadside, 131; Route 40 campaign and, 290; segregation of in North, 6; separate but equal and, 87; train travel

and, 64, 86–88, 247–248, 258–261. *See also*
food; roadside accommodations
diplomats, 284, 286–287, 299; African, 288,
289, 291; air travel segregation and, 222.
See also image, America's
direct action: Journey of Reconciliation,
253–257; need for, 232; optimism about,
256–257. *See also* boycotts; Freedom Rides;
resistance to travel discrimination
directories, travel. *See* travel guides
"dirt cars." *See* Jim Crow railroad cars
discrimination. *See* Jim Crow; segregation;
travel discrimination/segregation
disenfranchisement, 60, 156. *See also* voting rights
displacement, 3, 4. *See also* migration; mobility,
African American; movement; travel
District of Columbia, segregation in, 285. *See also*
diplomats
Dixon, Winifred Hawkridge, 136
Dollard, John, 121
domesticity, 15, 131
Double V campaign, 189–191
Douglass, Frederick, 28, 50, 51, 52
Dred Scott v. Sanford, 40
Drew, John, 162
drivers, African American: accidents and,
144; automobility experienced by, 149;
chauffeurs, 110–115; criminalization of,
316; dangers faced by, 2, 8, 13, 319; DWB
(Driving While Black/Brown), 13, 315;
empowerment of, 124–125; hostility to, 124;
insurance, 127–129, 313; isolation of, 149–150;
Jim Crow kits, 149–150; Johnson, 107–108;
parking, 110, 111–112, 126; police brutality
and, 317–319; racial profiling of, 17, 313–319;
racial right-of-way and, 125–129; roadside
accommodations and (*see* roadside accommodations); roads used by, 127; Smith's
experiences as, 135–141; traffic stops,
314–319; travel advisories for, 319. *See also*
car ownership; cars; roadside accommodations
driving, state regulation of, 110
Drug Enforcement Agency (DEA), 314–316
drugs, war on, 313–316
Du Bois, W. E. B., 10; *Darkwater,* 63; finding
lodgings and, 133–135; Foraker-Warner
Amendment and, 103; on gas stations, 130;
train travel and, 85–86, 91–92, 129–130; *W. E. B.
Du Bois v. Southern Railway Company,* 91–92
Du Bose, Sam, 318
Dulles, John Foster, 222

Dunn, Oscar J., 38
Dutton, Frederick, 288, 289

Eastland, James, 276
Eastman, Joseph B., 244
economic inequities, 11–12, 75–80
education: automotive schools, 113; *Brown v.
Board of Education,* 61, 261, 263, 264, 267, 269,
271; NAACP and, 260, 261; *Plessy* and, 260
Edwards, Georgia, 99; *Georgia Edwards v.
Nashville. St. Louis and Chattanooga
Railroad Company,* 99–100
Eisenhower, Dwight, 264, 286
elite African Americans: air travel and, 203,
216–217, 219–220, 223, 227–228; in antebellum North, 22–23; car ownership and,
115–116, 119; housing market and, 119; lack
of access to luxuries, 64, 115, 119; Pullman
cars and, 90–97, 236; travel discrimination
faced by, 9; white resentment of, 9, 18–19,
32, 117–118. *See also* class, socioeconomic;
free Blacks; *individuals*; leaders, African
American; middle-class African Americans
Elkins Act, 102
Ellington, Duke, 10, 139
Ellison, Ralph, 186–188
emancipation: African American mobility after
19, 34. *See also* abolition of slavery; North
(region), post-emancipation; Reconstruction;
slavery; South (region), post-emancipation
"emigrant cars," 25, 26, 29. *See also* Jim Crow
railroad cars
employment, African American: auto manufac-
turing and, 116; at Esso, 145–146; need for
cars and, 309; public transit and, 312
enfranchisement. *See* voting rights
equality, social, 38
equality of facilities, 103. *See also* separate but
equal
equal rights struggle. *See* civil rights struggles
Esch-Cummins Act (1920), 104–105
Esso, 145–147
Ethiopia, 201, 284
Evans, Paul, 214

Farmer, James, 269, 270, 274, 275, 277
farmers, 60, 76, 77, 119–123
FBI: Freedom Ride and, 270; war on drugs
and, 314
Federal-Aid Highway Act of 1956, 308–309
Federal Aviation Act of 1958, 283

Federal Aviation Administration (FAA), 281, 282
Federal Housing Authority (FHA), 310
federal intervention, 232, 274–276. *See also*
    Civil Rights Act of 1964; legislation
Federal Possession and Control Act (1917), 103
Federal Road Aid Act, 116
Fellowship of Reconciliation (FOR), 253
Ferguson, Missouri, 317, 318
Fifteenth Amendment, 35. *See also* voting
    rights
Fifth Amendment, 297
filling stations. *See* gas stations; roadside
    accommodations
fines, 276
first-class travel: African American access to,
    20, 48; gendered parameters of, 44 (*see also*
    ladies' cars)
Fitzgerald, Ella, 10, 217
Fitzgerald v. Pan American World Airways,
    Inc., 217
flight attendants, 206, 208
flying. *See* airlines; air travel; aviation; pilots
Following the Color Line (Baker), 2
food: musicians and, 180; while traveling, 1, 138,
    216–217. *See also* dining facilities; roadside
    accommodations
Foraker-Warner Amendment, 103
Fourteenth Amendment, 38, 252, 293, 294, 295;
    equal protection clause, 16 (see also *Plessy*
    v. Ferguson; separate but equal); limits placed
    on, 49–50. *See also* citizenship
France, African American pilots in, 197
Franklin, John Hope, 149–150
fraternities, 258–259
free Blacks: in antebellum North, 22–24; on
    antebellum Southern railroads, 31–32.
    See also elite African Americans; middle-class
    African Americans
free-born African Americans, white resentment
    of, 60
Freedman's Bureau, 34
Freedom Flyers, 280–281
Freedom Highways project, 290–291
Freedom Rides, 12, 154, 232, 254, 270–279.
    See also buses
freedom struggles. *See* civil rights struggles

Gandhi, Mohandas, 276
Garland, Charles, 173
Garnet, Henry Highland, 23–24
Garvey, Marcus, 11, 80

gas stations, 10, 130–132; Conoco, 141; economic
    inequities and, 12; Esso, 145–147; in *Green*
    Book, 143. *See also* roadside accommodations
Gbedemah, Komla Agbeli, 286
gender: first-class travel and, 20, 44 (*see also*
    ladies' cars); social contact and, 14; spaces
    divided by, 21; train segregation and, 15, 19;
    waiting rooms and, 82. *See also* ladies' cars;
    men, African American; women
gender segregation: cited in rulings, 41, 43–44;
    problems posed by, 44–49; separate car
    laws and, 58
Georgia: airports, 267; Atlanta, 161, 223; buses
    in, 160, 167–168, 189; Crisp, 55; Railroad
    Commission, 77; resistance to desegregation
    in, 266, 267, 268; restrictions in post-Civil
    War era, 36; separate car law, 155–156;
    sleeping car law, 90–92; streetcars, 155–156,
    161; train fares in, 77; train stations, 82–84;
    waiting rooms in, 82–84
Georgia Edwards v. Nashville, St. Louis and
    Chattanooga Railroad Company, 99–100
G.I. Bill, 308
Gibson, Truman K., 244, 245
girls, African American, vulnerability of, 45
Granger Movement, 76, 77
Grant, Ulysses S., 39
Grayson, Burt E., 144
Great Depression: buses during, 173, 186; car
    ownership during, 123; migration during,
    123; NAACP during, 174, 178; New Deal,
    234, 235; travel market during, 135, 173.
    See also Roosevelt, Franklin Delano
Great Migration, 4, 66, 116, 120. *See also* migration
Green, Alma, 142
Green, Marlon, 206
Green, Victor H., 141–142, 147
Green, William, 142
Green Book, The (film), 13
Green Book, The (Green), 13, 141–147
Gregory, Thomas Montgomery, 87
Greyhound, 153, 162, 309; during Depression, 173;
    dining facilities, 181, 182; drivers, 175–178;
    effects of desegregation orders on, 265–267;
    lawsuits and, 177 (see also *Irene Morgan v.*
    the Commonwealth of Virginia); management,
    175, 176; NAACP and, 174–179; responses
    to complaints, 186; Robinsons' experience
    on, 217; segregationist practices of, 170–171,
    172–173; treatment of African American
    passengers, 180. *See also* buses

ground transportation services, 193, 218,
224–226, 227–228
guides. *See* travel guides

Hackley, Edwin Henry, 135
Hall v. DeCuir, 41–43
Harlan, John Marshall, 50–51
Harrison, Sarah D., 134–135, 144
Hasday, Judy L., 197
Hastie, William H., 244, 249–250
Heart of Atlanta Motel, Inc. v. United States, 5,
296, 297
Henderson, Elmer W., 257–261
Henderson v. United States, 257–261
Hepburn Act of 1906, 102–103
Highway Act, 308–309
Hill, Oliver, 249
Holliday, Billie, 180–181
Holsey, Albon Lewis, 7–8
Homeland Security, Department of, 319
home loans, 308
hotels. *See* lodgings; roadside accommodations
Houser, George, 254–257
housing: diplomats and, 285; elite African
Americans and, 119; suburbs, 308, 310
Houston, Charles Hamilton, 174, 185, 219
Hughes, Langston, 6; on air travel, 212; on cars,
115–116; on Pullman accommodations, 96

ICC (Interstate Commerce Commission). *See*
Interstate Commerce Commission (ICC)
Illinois, 178, 311
Illinois Supreme Court, 43–44
image, America's, 278–279; Civil Rights Act of
1964 and, 299–300; desegregation and, 284
(*see also* diplomats); Freedom Rides and,
274–275. *See also* Cold War
independence movements, 299. *See also* diplomats
Indiana, 165, 317
inequities in facilities, 11–12, 81, 83. *See also*
separate but equal
insurance, automobile, 127–129, 313
integration. *See* desegregation
international incidents: air travel and, 222. *See*
also diplomats; image, America's
interstate commerce, 42–43, 51, 61–62. *See also*
commerce clause; Interstate Commerce
Commission (ICC)
Interstate Commerce Act of 1887, 53, 261;
air travel and, 210; *Mitchell* and,
233–240

Interstate Commerce Commission (ICC), 16,
53–56; Freedom Rides and, 277; Henderson's
complaint to, 258–259, 260; Jim Crow
railroad cars and, 70, 71; members of, 264, 267;
railroad rate regulation and, 102; regulatory
powers of, 55, 102; rejection of separate but
equal, 264–267; ruling barring racial segregation in interstate transportation, 263–267,
279, 304; on separate cars, 66; sleeping car
laws and, 91–92; support for struggle
against travel segregation, 56; support of
segregation, 56, 99. *See also individual cases*
interstates, 309, 310–311. *See also* roads/highways
Irene Morgan v. the Commonwealth of Virginia, 191,
231–233, 249–250, 259, 264; compliance with,
257; effects of, 250, 252–253; testing, 254, 256

Jackson, James "Billboard," 146, 148
Jakeman, Robert J., 195
Jim Crow: confusion about legal status of, 256;
constitutionality of, 240; emergence of in
post-emancipation South, 33–37; evading,
118, 129–130, 137, 202, 203, 211; first wave
of laws, 60; minstrel character, 26; transferred to new forms of transportation, 152.
See also segregation

Jim Crow kits, 1, 149–150
Jim Crow railroad cars, 63; African Americans
moved to in South, 5, 85, 97; in all regions,
4–5; in antebellum North, 19; avoiding, 83,
93, 129–130 (*see also* air travel; cars; Pullman
sleeping cars); boarding / disembarking,
84–85; challenges to, 97–106; conditions in,
1–2, 25–26, 29, 30–31, 62, 64, 67–71, 79, 80,
187–188, 237, 249; development of, 26; fares
for, 75–80; food access and, 86–88; inconsistent enforcement of, 67–68; *Mitchell* and,
233–240; passengers in, 69–70, 97; records
of experience of, 67; resentment of, 2, 64,
75, 80; resistance to, 66–67; retirement of
wooden cars, 75; seats for African American
passengers, 70; as symbol of loss of rights,
62; as unavoidable, 66; during World War I,
66; during World War II, 66, 241; wrecks
and, 71–75, 115. *See also* railroads; separate
but equal; separate car laws
Jim Crow travel. *See* travel discrimination /
segregation
jitneys, 153, 154, 158–161, 162
Johnson, Andrew, 35
Johnson, Campbell C., 243–244

Johnson, Charles S., 125, 126–127, 163
Johnson, Jack, 10, 107–108, 115, 116
Johnson, James Weldon, 117–118, 125
Johnson, J. Monroe, 264, 267
Johnson, Lyndon B., 296, 302–303
Journey of Reconciliation, 232, 253–257, 269, 270
Justice Department: airports and, 281–283; authority to mandate desegregation, 294; Civil Rights Act of 1964 and, 304; civil rights and, 278; Freedom Rides and, 270, 273, 274, 277; study of Ferguson, 317. *See also* Marshall, Burke

Katrina (hurricane), 312
Katzenbach v. McClung, 296–297
Kemp, A. N., 205
Kennedy, John F.: African diplomats and, 284–287; desegregation of roadside accommodations and, 286; federal intervention and, 293, 294 (*see also* Civil Rights Act of 1964); Freedom Rides and, 270, 273, 274–275; Route 40 campaign and, 286–290
Kennedy, Randall, 305
Kennedy, Robert F., 276; Civil Rights Act and, 293–294, 298–299; on desegregation of airports, 282; Freedom Rides and, 270, 273, 275–276, 277, 278; international image and, 278
Kennedy, Stetson, 96, 126, 127
Kennon, Robert F., 267
Kentucky, separate car laws, 61, 78–79
Keys, Sarah, 263; *Sarah Keys v. Carolina Coach Company*, 263–267, 269, 277
King, Martin Luther, Jr., 10, 88, 268, 275, 283, 291
Knapp, Bradford, 120
Ku Klux Klan, 271, 272, 293

labor, African American: chauffeurs, 110–115; road work, 117
labor disputes, 103
ladies' cars, 18; African American women excluded from, 97; in post-emancipation South, 45; problems posed by, 44–49; segregation and, 58; Wells removed from, 57–58. *See also* gender
L&N Railroad, 78, 97
Langston, John Mercer, 52–53
law enforcement, racial profiling by, 313–319
Lawson, Belford V., 258–261
lawsuits/legal challenges, 16; air travel and, 209, 215–216, 217, 219, 227; in antebellum era, 40;

bus companies and, 177, 178, 191; challenging Civil Rights Act of 1964, 296–297; Civil Rights Act of 1875 and, 39; effects of, 43–44, 262, 268; filed by African American women, 46–47; gender segregation and, 41, 43–49; Jim Crow railroad cars and, 28; in post-Civil War era, 40–43; Pullman segregation and, 91–92, 96–97; reaction to, 268; support for, 258–259; test cases, 61, 91–92; during World War II, 247–253. *See also individual cases*; Interstate Commerce Commission (ICC); resistance to travel discrimination; Supreme Court, US
leaders, African American, 9, 98; legislation and, 103; on treatment of African American travelers in North, 24. *See also* elite African Americans; *individuals*

Lee, Ulysses, 202
LeFlore, John, 235, 247–249, 306, 307. *See also* NAACP
LeFlore and Crishon v. the Gulf, Mobile and Ohio Railroad, 248
legislation: attempts to ban Jim Crow on railroads, 101–106; enforcement of, 39–40; legalizing segregation, 56–59 (*see also* separate but equal; separate car laws); in post-Civil War era, 35–37; Powell's bill, 252–253. *See also* civil rights; *individual laws*; resistance to travel discrimination
Levette, Harry, 198–199
Lewis, John, 270–271, 274, 276
Liberia, 284
limousines. *See* ground transportation services
Lindbergh, Charles, 194–196
lodgings, 2, 132–141; Airbnb hosts, 320; airport accommodations, 226–227; avoidance of commercial establishments, 149; *Billboard's* guide to, 138; continued segregation of, 229; diplomats and, 285; finding, 138, 301; mandated segregation of, 140; private residences, 139, 144–145, 149; segregation of in North, 5–6; solutions to, 139–140; tourist/auto camps, 132–134, 140. *See also* roadside accommodations
Louisiana: airports in, 282–283; bus segregation in, 172; civil rights law, 42; resistance to desegregation orders in, 267, 268; Separate Car Act, 16, 61; streetcar segregation in, 157. See also *Plessy v. Ferguson*
Lower 13, 95–96
Luck, Dudley B., 141
lynching, 177, 235

Mack, Kenneth, 57
MacPherson, James M., 36
Maddox, Lester, 303, 304
mailmen, 142
Mangold, Nathan, 173, 174
Mangum, Charles S., Jr., 210
Marshall, Burke, 275, 281, 292, 293, 295
Marshall, Thurgood, 10, 174, 235, 247, 252–253, 294; car insurance and, 128–129; on end of legal segregation, 261; *Irene Morgan v. the Commonwealth of Virginia* and, 249–250; *Mitchell* and, 239; opposition to separate but equal, 248–249; view of direct action, 254. See also *Brown v. Board of Education*; NAACP
Martin, Lerone A., 115
Martin, Martin A., 249
Maryland, 163, 288, 289–290, 315
Massachusetts, 28, 166
Matthews, Ralph, 211, 252
Matthews v. Southern Railway System, 252
Mays, Benjamin, 83, 93
McCabe v. Atchison, Topeka & Santa Fe Railway Company, 92, 238, 239
McDowell, Charles, 143
McLaurin v. Oklahoma State Regents, 260, 261
McMillan, Neil R., 125
meals. See dining facilities; food
mechanical aptitude, stereotypes about, 108, 110, 113, 115
mechanics, African American, 113–115
Mehta, Gaganvihari Lallubhai, 284
men, African American, 47–49. See also gender
middle-class African Americans: in antebellum North, 22–24; targeted by early travel segregation regulations, 20; in Tennessee, 56; white resentment of, 56–57. See also class, socioeconomic; elite African Americans; free Blacks
migration, 3, 66, 123. See also displacement; Great Migration; mobility, African American; movement; travel
military: aviation training, 196–197, 202, 205, 245; segregation of, 197, 244. See also servicemen, African American
Mississippi: Freedom Rides in, 276; resistance to desegregation orders, 266, 268; separate car law, 58, 68
Missouri, 159, 316–317, 318, 319
Mitchell, Arthur Wergs, 104, 233–240

Mitchell, Clarence, 266–267
Mitchell, Marilyn Hall, 40
Mitchell v. United States, 233–240, 247, 248; compliance with, 257; effects of, 238–240, 253
mobility, African American: after emancipation, 13, 34; enfranchisement and, 36; Freedman's Bureau and, 34; lack of federal protection for, 50; in post-Civil War era, 19, 34–37; relation with African American freedom struggle, 3; white resentment of, 120–121. See also displacement; migration; movement; travel
Montgomery, Ada, 184–185
Montgomery, Alabama: Dannelly Field Airport, 228, 283; Freedom Rides in, 275; public transit system, 307–308 (see also Montgomery Bus Boycott); streetcar boycott, 157. See also Alabama
Montgomery Bus Boycott, 12, 268, 271, 307, 310
Morgan, Irene, 230–233, 246, 249
Morgan v. Virginia, 191, 231–233, 249–250, 253, 259, 264; compliance with, 257; effects of 250, 252–253; testing, 254, 256
Morrell amendment, 102
Morrow, James Glover, 191
Morton, Fiona Scott, 312
motels. See lodgings
motor sports, 107–108
movement: African American struggles for, 3; significance of in African American life, 4. See also migration; mobility, African American; travel
movement and place, narrative of, 4
Murray, Pauli, 10, 183
Murrow, Edward R., 278
musicians, African American, 139, 142; air travel and, 209, 217, 226–227; finding food and, 180; travel guides and, 138, 146
Mutual United Brotherhood of Liberty, 61
Myrdal, Gunnar, 2

NAACP: air travel and, 215, 220; attacks on *Plessy*, 260, 261; bus segregation and, 170–171, 173, 178, 179, 191; bus station bathrooms and, 184–186; car insurance and, 128; during Depression, 174, 178, 186; education cases and, 174, 260, 261; finances, 101, 173, 235, 247; food discrimination and, 181; gas stations and, 131; goals of, 174;

NAACP (*continued*)
information gathering by, 174; Jim Crow
railroad car challenges and, 97–98; legal
counsel, 101, 173–174; Legal Defense Fund,
235; litigation strategy, 249; military segregation and, 244–245; predecessors, 100;
publicizing of transportation discrimination,
179; on racial profiling, 316; transportation
cases and, 101, 174, 235, 247, 253; travel
advisories, 319–320; waiting rooms and,
182–183. *See also individual cases*; LeFlore,
John; Marshall, Thurgood; Pickens,
William; Wilkins, Roy
NAACP v. St. Louis-San Francisco Ry Co.,
264–267, 269
Nash, Diane, 274, 275, 276
National Afro-American Council, 100, 102
National Association for the Advancement of
Colored People (NAACP). *See* NAACP
National Equal Rights League (NERL), 32
Nebraska, 178–179
Negro Baseball leagues, 139
Negro Motorist Green Book, The (Green), 13,
141–147
Nelson, Paul, 101
New Deal, 234, 235
New York City: African American car ownership
in, 115–116; automotive schools in, 113;
buses in, 172, 186–187; chauffeurs in,
111–112
New York State, discrimination in, 6
Niagara Movement, 80, 100–101
Nixon, Richard, 313
nonviolent direct action. *See* direct action;
Freedom Rides
North (region), 5–6; bus segregation in,
5, 169–171, 174–179; restaurants in, 6;
segregation in, 4–6; spaces for African
American travelers in, 21–22; travel
restrictions in, 142
North (region), antebellum: abolition of slavery
in, 19; early segregation and, 20; Jim Crow
railroad cars and, 19; middle-class African
Americans in, 22–24; railroad segregation
in, 26, 28; social order in, 22; travel dis-
crimination in, 26, 28–29. *See also* ante-
bellum era
North (region), post-emancipation, 32–33
North Carolina: buses in, 164–165, 166; Freedom
Highways efforts in, 290; jitneys in, 159, 161;
Journey of Reconciliation in, 255–256;

O'Hara, 53–55; Railroad Commission, 79,
82; railroad fares in, 79, 80; railroad
segregation in, 70; railroad wrecks in,
72–73; streetcar segregation in, 158;
waiting rooms in, 81–82
North Carolina Interracial Commission, 165
Novak, Ken, 316–317

O'Hara, James E., 53–55
O'Kelley, Berry, 164–165
Oklahoma, 90, 92, 166
Oldfield, Barney, 107
Olmstead, Frederick Law, 31
Operation Pipeline, 314–316
opposition to travel segregation. *See* resistance
to travel discrimination
Ortlepp, Anke, 228, 283

Packard, Jerome, 117, 127
parking, 110, 111–112, 126. *See also* cars;
chauffeurs; drivers, African American
passengers, travelers as, 14
Pastore, John, 295, 300
paternalism, legal, 48
Patillo, Sadie, 168–169
Patterson, Frederick Douglass, 114
Patterson, John Malcom, 271, 273, 275, 276.
See also Alabama
"pauper cars." *See* Jim Crow railroad cars
Peck, James, 256, 272, 273
Pennsylvania, 40–41, 162
Pennsylvania Greyhound Company, 174–177
Pennsylvania Public Service Commission,
175
performers, African American, 180. *See also*
musicians, African American
Perlman, Philip B., 260–261
Pickens, William, 87, 94, 105, 186, 187, 217
pilots: African American, 193, 197–202, 204,
205–206; Civilian Pilot Training Program
(CPT), 202; Lindbergh, 194–196. *See also* air
travel; aviation
Pittman, Key, 112–113
planes. *See* air travel; aviation; common carriers;
pilots
Plessy, Homer, 60–61
Plessy v. Ferguson, 12, 16, 21, 41, 60–62, 67,
101, 174; application to travel segregation,
61–62; attacks on, 260, 261; *Henderson* and,
260; Supreme Court's repudiation of, 261.
See also railroads; separate but equal

police brutality, 317–319
poll taxes, 52
Populist movement, 60, 76
postal workers, 142
Powell, Adam Clayton, 252–253
Powell, William J., 198, 204, 205
power, cars and, 124–125
Prattis, P. L., 6, 239
press, African American: African American
  pilots in, 201–202; Associated Negro Press,
  239; reaction to *Civil Rights Cases* in, 52; on
  John Robinson, 201–202; train wrecks in,
  74–75; on treatment of African American
  travelers in North, 24
prison cars, 242
protests: in Birmingham, 291–293; Black Lives
  Matter, 318, 319; Children's Crusade, 232.
public accommodations: Civil Rights Act of 1875
  and, 39; in post-emancipation North, 32–33.
  See also dining facilities; gas stations;
  lodgings; restrooms
public transportation, 307–308; coronavirus pandemic and, 312; decline of, 17, 308; employment and, 312. *See also* buses; railroads
Pullman sleeping cars, 88–97, 233–240; acquiring
  tickets for, 90, 92–95; in advertising, 54;
  African American servicemen excluded
  from, 244; conditions in, 96; desegregation
  of, 233–240; *LeFlore and Crishon v. the Gulf,
  Mobile and Ohio Railroad*, 248; Lower 13,
  95–96; NAACP and, 247; tickets not honored,
  96–97

race leaders. *See individuals*; leaders, African
  American
racial profiling, 17, 313–319. *See also* drivers,
  African American
racial right-of-way, 125–129
Radical Reconstruction, 35
Radical Republicans, 35, 38
radicals, Black, 103. *See also* Du Bois, W. E. B.
Rahn, Muriel, 226–227
railroads: advertising by, 64; African Americans'
  refusal to move to segregated cars, 18–19, 26,
  28; agrarian political movements and, 76, 77;
  amenities of, access to, 64; Amtrak, 309; in
  antebellum North, 26, 28–29; in antebellum
  South, 29–32; attempts to ban Jim Crow on,
  101–106; baggage cars, 31, 78; Big Change
  Terminals, 5; boarding/disembarking, 84–85;
  combination cars, 68–69; decline of, 106, 309;

dining cars, 64, 86–88, 247–248, 258–261;
  division of spaces in, 21; early, 24–25; elimination of second-class fare, 75–81; gender
  and, 15 (*see also* ladies' cars); golden age of,
  64; Great Migration and, 66; guide to, 13;
  half-fare coaches, 25 (*see also* Jim Crow
  railroad cars); improved conditions on,
  70–71; inconsistent segregation on, 7–8, 29,
  31; inequitable conditions on, 1–2; intrastate
  vs. interstate, 16; jurisdiction and, 252; labor
  disputes, 103; *Morgan's* impact on, 252;
  NAACP and, 247; nationalization of, 103;
  necessity of, 66; Pennsylvania Railroad,
  4–5; persistence of segregation on, 265;
  in post-emancipation South, 34; private
  ownership of, 104, 235; public domesticity
  and, 15; rates for, 25, 75–81, 102, 103; restrooms
  and, 64; segregation of, 4–5, 12, 15, 18–19,
  26, 28 (*see also* Jim Crow railroad cars; *Plessy
  v. Ferguson*; separate car laws); Separate Car
  Act, 16 (see also *Plessy v. Ferguson*; separate
  car laws); smoking cars, 45, 78; state railroad
  commissions, 76, 77; ticket booths, 63, 84;
  United States Railroad Administration (USRA),
  104; waiting rooms, 63, 81–84, 98, 105; white
  station personnel, 84–86; during World War II,
  241; wrecks and, 71–75. *See also* common
  carriers; Jim Crow railroad cars; ladies'
  cars; Pullman sleeping cars; separate
  car laws
Rajagopalan, B. A., 222
Ramsey, Calvin, 13
Raper, Arthur, 121, 124, 126
Ray, Charles, 24–25, 28
Reagan, Ronald, 313
Reconstruction, 20, 35–36, 37, 104. *See also* Civil
  Rights Act of 1875; emancipation; South
  (region), post-emancipation
Reed, Stanley 232
"refuse cars." *See* Jim Crow railroad cars
Reid, Whitelaw, 36
Republicans, 50, 53–55, 57
resistance to travel discrimination: as constant
  civil rights movement, 16–17; as cross-class
  issue, 11, 15, 16; inequities in facilities and,
  11–12; in post-Civil War era, 36; proliferation of challenges, 240–252; support for,
  16–17. *See also* direct action; lawsuits/legal
  challenges; legislation
restaurants. *See* dining facilities; roadside
  accommodations

restrooms, 2, 131, 132; access to, 12; in airports, 193; bus travel and, 170, 183–186; inconsistent segregation in, 8; train travel and, 64. *See also* roadside accommodations
Rice, Thomas Dartmouth "Daddy," 26
Richter, Amy, 15
Rickenbacker, E. V. (Eddie), 194, 211
right-of-way, racial, 125–129
roads/highways, 116–117; desegregation of, 283, 286–291 (*see also* desegregation); Highway Act, 308–309; interstates, 310–311; Jim Crow, 124; transcontinental highways, 137; used by African American drivers, 127
roadside accommodations: Civil Rights Act of 1964 and, 305; desegregation of, 283, 286–291; guides to (*see* travel guides). *See also* cars; dining facilities; drivers, African American; food; gas stations; lodgings; restrooms
road trips, 136
Robinson, Jackie, 10, 216–217
Robinson, John C., 198, 200–202, 204, 205
Robinson, Julius Winfield, 263
Robinson, Sallie J., 48–49, 51
Robinson, Spottswood, 249
Robinson and Wife v. Memphis & Charleston Railroad Company, 48–49, 51. See also *Civil Rights Cases* (1883)
Rogers, J. A., 75, 76, 211
Rolleston, Moreton, 296, 297
rooming houses. *See* lodgings
Roosevelt, Franklin Delano, 222; Black Cabinet, 96, 136, 219, 221; civilian aide position, 244; Fair Employment Practices Committee (FEPC), 257; New Deal, 234, 235; Office of Price Administration, 240
Roosevelt, Franklin D., Jr., 301
Rosengarten, Theodore, 121
Roundtree, Dovey Johnson, 260, 263, 267, 277
Route 40 campaign, 286–290
Rowan, Carl, 8, 228
Ruggles, David, 23, 28
rural African Americans, 120–123, 125. *See also* farmers
rural whites, 125. *See also* farmers
Rusk, Dean, 278, 299
Rustin, Bayard, 10, 241, 254–257
Ruth and the Green Book (Ramsey), 13

safety, 2, 8, 13, 319. *See also* violence
Safeway Company, 178
Sanjuan, Pedro, 288

Sarah Keys v. Carolina Coach Company, 263–267, 269, 277
Scarborough, William, 81
Schuyler, George, 5, 10
SCLC (Southern Christian Leadership Council), 276, 291–293
Scott, Walter, 318
Seay, Solomon, 303–304
segregation: America's image abroad and, 278–279; confusion about legal status of, 253, 256; encouraging acceptance of, 9, 93, 98, 99, 100, 234 (*see also* Washington, Booker T.); inconsistency in, 6–8, 16; maintenance of, 262; New South's commitment to maintaining, 156; persistence of, 265–267; servitude and, 59; South's journey to, 19; white supremacy and, 60. *See also* Jim Crow; travel discrimination/segregation
separate but equal, 12, 56; attacks on, 260, 261; buses, 164; dining facilities and, 87; enforcement of, 64, 98–99; first law for, 57; ICC's rejection of, 264–267; inferior accommodations under, 167; interstate travel and, 16; as Mitchell's goal, 236, 237; opposition to, 248–249. See also *Brown v. Board of Education*; inequities in facilities; Jim Crow railroad cars; *Plessy v. Ferguson*; separate car laws
separate car laws, 56–59, 155–156; challenges to, 92; enforcement of, 98; impetus behind, 59–60; inconsistent enforcement of, 67–68; 70; as legalized segregation, 80; *McCabe v. Atchison, Topeka & Santa Fe Railway Company*, 92, 238, 239; message sent by, 64; sleeping car laws, 90–92; white supremacy behind, 59–60. *See also* Jim Crow railroad cars; *Plessy v. Ferguson*; separate but equal
Serling, Roderick, 210
servicemen, African American: civilian aide and, 244; resentment of Jim Crow, 246; segregation of, 192; travel conditions for, 104, 105, 189–191, 214, 243–245. *See also* World War I era; World War II
Servicemen's Readjustment Act of 1944, 308
service stations. *See* gas stations; roadside accommodations
servitude: flight attendants and, 208; separate car laws and, 59
shame, 277, 278
sharecroppers, 121. *See also* farmers
Shuttlesworth, Fred, 273, 275, 291

Sidney, Thomas, 23–24
Silva-Risso, Jorge, 312
Simon, Bryant, 246
slavery, 4. See also abolition of slavery; emancipation
sleeping accommodations. See lodgings; Pullman sleeping cars
sleeping car laws, 90–92
Smalls, Robert, 55
Smith, Alfred Edward, 135–141, 147–148
Smith, Isabella, 176–177
smoking cars, 45, 78. See also Jim Crow railroad cars
snack bars, 131. See also dining facilities; food
SNCC (Student Nonviolent Coordinating Committee), 274, 276
social contact, 14
soldiers. See servicemen, African American
Sorin, Gretchen Sullivan, 119, 142, 144
South (region), antebellum, 29–32
South (region), post-emancipation, 33–37, 41–43, 45. See also Reconstruction
South Carolina: bus segregation in, 167–168; Railroad Commission, 95; repeal of civil rights laws and, 52; restrictions in post-Civil War era, 36–37; separate car law, 79; Smalls, 55; streetcar segregation in, 158; train fares in, 79, 80
South Carolina Motor Vehicle Department, 164
Southernaires, 219–220
Southern Christian Leadership Council (SCLC), 276, 291–293
southerners, Black, 3, 4
southerners, white, 104–105, 150
Sow, Adam Malick, 286–287
space of travel, 14
stagecoaches, 4, 14, 21–24, 26. See also common carriers
State Department, 284, 286–290. See also diplomats
state visitors, 299. See also diplomats
steamboats, 25, 37; division of spaces in, 21–22, 23; gender segregation on, 44; Hall v. DeCuir, 41–43; public domesticity and, 15; segregation of, 4, 41–43; separate but equal regulations for, 59; transition to railroads and, 26. See also common carriers
Stewart v. The Sue, 61
Stimson, Henry, 244
Strange Career of Jim Crow, The (Woodward), 152, 192

streetcars: avoidance of, 158–159; boycott of, 151, 157; conductors, 157; segregated, 2, 151, 153, 155–158, 166, 167
streets. See roads/highways
Student Army Training Corps, 114
Student Nonviolent Coordinating Committee (SNCC), 274, 276
Styron, William, 118
suburbs, 308, 310
suffrage. See civil rights; voting rights
Sumner, Charles, 37, 38–40
Supreme Court, US: airline industry discrimination case, 206; Civil Rights Act of 1875 and, 32, 43, 49–56, 60, 252, 293; Civil Rights Act of 1964 and, 296–298; endorsement of segregation, 21, 43, 92, 101 (see also Plessy v. Ferguson; separate but equal); erosion of federal protection for African American civil rights, 49–56; interstate commerce and, 61–62. See also individual cases; lawsuits/legal challenges
surveillance, white, 125
Sutton, Percy, 281
Sweatt v. Painter, 260, 261

Tarry, Ellen, 227–228
Tawes, Millard J., 288, 290
taxis/cabs, 7, 193, 218, 224–226, 227–228
Tennessee: Freedom Riders and, 276; Nashville Student Movement, 274; separate car law, 56–59, 79; streetcars in, 151–152, 156, 157; train fares in, 79
Terrell, Mary Church, 9, 18–19, 20, 45–46, 62, 285
test cases, 61, 91–92. See also lawsuits/legal challenges
Texas: buses in, 165, 168–169; jitney ordinances in, 160; separate car law, 59; sleeping car law, 90; streetcar segregation in, 157, 159
Thernstrom, Abigail, 125
Thernstrom, Stephen, 125
Thirteenth Amendment, 49–50, 52, 297
Thomas, Jesse O., 138–139, 172
Thornton, Jeannye, 2
Tillman, Ben, 60
toilets. See restrooms; roadside accommodations
Townsend, Belton O'Neall, 37
traffic stops, 314–319
Trailways, 162, 183, 270, 309. See also buses
train travel. See Jim Crow railroad cars; Pullman sleeping cars; railroads

transportation, 3, 319. *See also* common carriers; public transportation; travel; travel discrimination/segregation

travel: as civil rights issue, 307; importance of history of, 3; necessity of, 24–25, 66. *See also* migration; mobility, African American; movement

travel advisories, 319–320

travel amenities. *See* dining facilities; gas stations; lodgings; restrooms; roadside accommodations; waiting rooms; water fountains

travel discrimination/segregation, 3; collective amnesia about, 306; inconsistency in, 22, 25, 29, 218; inequities in facilities and, 11–12; inevitability of encountering, 8–10; obscurity of, 13–14; persistence of, 307; publicizing of, 179; resistance to (*see* resistance to travel discrimination)

travel guides: AAA's, 146; *Billboard's*, 138, 146; Conoco's, 141; *Go: The Guide to Pleasant Motoring*, 301; *Grayson's Guide*, 144; *The Green Book*, 13, 141–147; *Hackley and Harrison's Hotel and Apartment Guide for Colored Travelers*, 135–136; *Jim Crow Guide to the USA*, 96, 126; limitations of, 147–148; need for, 135; *The Separate or "Jim Crow" Car Laws or Legislative Actions of the Fourteen Southern States*, 98–100; Smith's call for, 141; *The Traveler's Guide*, 135; "Travellers' Directory," 13; USTB's *Directory*, 143, 144, 146

travelogues, 136–137

Triple A, 107, 146

Truman, Harry, 221, 260

Turner, Herbert A., 170

Tuskegee Institute, 200, 234, 283

unemployment, 114

unions, for chauffeurs, 112, 113

Union Transportation Company, 151–152, 154

United States Information Agency, 278

United States Railroad Administration (USRA), 104

United States Travel Bureau (USTB), 143, 144, 146

United States v. the City of Montgomery, 283

Universal Negro Improvement Association (UNIA), 11, 80

urbanization, 156

Urban League, 172

Urry, John, 109

USRA (United States Railroad Administration), 104

USTB (United States Travel Bureau), 143, 144, 146

vacations, 10, 131, 300–301

Vachon, Nicholas Murray, 289

Van Vleck, Jennifer, 194

veterans, African American, 8. *See also* servicemen, African American

Vincent, Sténio, 222

violence, 17; African American vote and, 52; in Birmingham, 291–293; buses and, 191, 241 (*see also* Freedom Rides); against car owners, 117; police brutality, 317–319; possibility of, 8; on railroads, 28; on trains, 243; vulnerability of African American girls to, 45

Virginia: African American travel cases and, 249; airports in, 219, 221; buses in, 163, 165, 252; dining facilities in, 219–220; jitneys in, 160–161; railroad commission, 79; Richmond, 157, 159; streetcar segregation in, 156, 158, 160; train fares in, 79; transportation discrimination complaints in, 253. *See also Irene Morgan v. the Commonwealth of Virginia*

visitors, foreign, 299. *See also* diplomats

Vogel, Bob, 314–315

voting rights: African American mobility and, 36; disenfranchisement, 60, 156; during Reconstruction, 35; reduction of, 52. *See also* civil rights; civil rights struggles

Waite, Thomas, 42, 43

waiting rooms, 105, 181–183, 218; after desegregation orders, 265; in airports, 193, 223–224; train travel and, 63, 81–84, 98, 105

War Department, 196, 243, 244. *See also* military; servicemen, African American

war on drugs, 313–316

Washington, Booker T., 9, 11; accommodations philosophy, 93, 98, 99, 100, 234; avoidance of Jim Crow travel, 93, 98; "Is the Negro Having a Fair Chance?," 11–12; "Railroad Days" campaign, 98; on train fares, 78; use of Pullman cars, 90

water fountains, 10, 12, 218

wealth, African American: hostility to, 117–118. *See also* elite African Americans

Webb, Frank Jr., 33

W. E. B. Du Bois v. Southern Railway Company, 91–92

Welke, Barbara, 15, 43, 44
Wells, Ida B., 9, 57–58
West (region): Jim Crow cars in, 4, 5; jitneys
    in, 158, 159; lodging in, 140
West Chester and Philadelphia Railroad v.
    Miles, 40
West Virginia, 159, 184–185
White, George Henry, 9, 102, 103
White, Walter Francis, 181, 182–183, 185, 245;
    air travel and, 196–197; military segrega-
    tion and, 244–245; *Mitchell* and, 239–240.
    See also NAACP
white flight, 310
Whiteside v. Southern Bus Lines, 261
white supremacy: separate car laws and,
    59–60; South's built environment and, 81
Wilkins, Roy, 174; bus segregation and, 175,
    176; congressional testimony of, 300–301;
    on Greyhound, 179; *Mitchell* and, 236, 239;
    on servicemen's resentment of Jim Crow,
    246; view of Journey of Reconciliation,
    254. *See also* NAACP
Williams, George H., 39
Wilson, Woodrow, 103–104, 116
Wofford, Harris, 274, 288
women, 15. *See also* gender; ladies' cars
women, African American: customs searches
    of, 319; excluded from spaces traditionally
    set aside for women, 23; ladies' car and,
    45–49, 97; lawsuits filed by, 46–47; with
    male companions, 47–49; railroad station

personnel and, 84–85; vulnerability of, 45;
    waiting rooms and, 82; during World War I,
    114; during World War II, 246–247. *See also*
    individual women
women, white: gas station design and, 131;
    racial right-of-way and, 127; support for
    Journey of Reconciliation, 257
Woodruff, Nan, 120
Woodward, C. Vann, 152, 192
World War I era: African American car owner-
    ship in, 120; African American pilots in,
    197; cars during, 108; demand for skilled
    labor in, 114; opportunity for federal action
    against racial discrimination during, 103–105;
    train travel during, 66, 104. *See also*
    servicemen, African American
World War II: aviation during, 202; bus segrega-
    tion during, 188–191; challenges to segregated
    transportation and, 240–252; demands on
    transportation system, 240–241; Double V
    campaign, 189–191; lawsuits during, 247–253;
    resentment of Jim Crow and, 245–247;
    segregation of African American servicemen
    during, 192, 243–245; train travel during, 66;
    travel discrimination during, 188–191;
    travel needs of military personnel during,
    212. *See also* servicemen, African American
Wyatt, Ruth, 227
Wyoming, 181

Zettelmeyer, Florian, 312